Women in American History   SERIES EDITORS
Mari Jo Buhle
Nancy A. Hewitt
Anne Firor Scott

A list of books in the series appears at the end of this book.

Mining Cultures

Mining Cultures

*Men, Women, and Leisure
in Butte, 1914–41*

Mary Murphy

University of Illinois Press

URBANA AND CHICAGO

An earlier version of chapter 2 appeared as "Bootlegging Mothers and Drinking Daughters: Gender and Prohibition in Butte, Montana" in *American Quarterly* 46 (June 1994): 174-94; an earlier version of chapter 6 appeared as "Messenger of the New Age: Station KGIR in Butte" in *Montana Magazine of Western History* 39 (Autumn 1989): 52-62.

1   2   3   4   5   C   P   5   4   3   2

This book is printed on acid-free paper.

Library of Congress Cataloging-in-Publication Data
Murphy, Mary.
    Mining cultures : men, women, and leisure in Butte,
1914-41 / Mary Murphy.
        p.   cm. — (Women in American history)
    Includes bibliographical references and index.
        ISBN 0-252-02267-X (alk. paper). — ISBN 0-252-06569-7
(pbk. : alk. paper)
        1. Butte (Mont.)—History. 2. Butte (Mont.)—Social life and
customs. 3. Copper mines and mining—Montana—Butte—
History. 4. Cities and towns—Montana—Growth—Case studies.
I. Title. II. Series.
F739.B8M87   1997
978.6'68—dc20   96-9990
                                                            CIP

For the people of Butte, who took me in

Contents

Illustrations follow pages 70 and 168

Acknowledgments

Although this book is a community study, my thanks go to all corners of the country. Jacquelyn Dowd Hall, Roger Lotchin, Peter Filene, Leon Fink, John Kasson, Nancy Hewitt, Elizabeth Faue, Anastatia Sims, and Dale Martin read the entire manuscript and provided thoughtful, generous criticisms. Jacquelyn Dowd Hall inspired me and supported me since we first met and established my model for what good historical writing should be. Anastatia Sims saw me through this as she has done through previous projects, with great wit and graceful editing. Dale Martin not only read every word—more than once—but he also listened to me sort out ideas, advised me on details of technology and industry, drew wonderful maps, made me innumerable cups of tea, and was simply always there. David Emmons, Marianne Keddington, Bill Lang, Laurie Mercier, and Susan Rhoades Neel read various chapters or portions of them and improved them immensely. For ushering this text through the University of Illinois Press my thanks go to Liz Dulany and Mary Giles. Carrie Johnson, Dale Martin, Sr., Leila Martin, and Maggie, Mark, and Toby Gan offered hospitality and research assistance in my travels, and I thank them for their help and the pleasure of their company.

Archivists and librarians at the Montana Historical Society, the Butte-Silver Bow Public Archives, the Butte-Silver Bow Free Public Library, the libraries at Montana Tech of the University of Montana, the Montana State University-Bozeman, the University of Montana-

Missoula, and at various branches of the National Archives made all sorts of treasures available. I would especially like to thank Dave Walter, Sue Jackson, Bill Summer, Ellen Arguimbau, Jodie Foley, Kathryn Otto, Bob Clark, Brian Shovers, Dorothea Simonson, Lory Morrow, Becca Kohl, Bonnie Morgan, Kirby Lambert, Bill Walker, Sara Boyett, Ellen Crain, Jean Hartman, John Hughes, Mike Anderson, Dale Johnson, and Joyce Justice.

Members of the Butte Historical Society and the Anaconda-Deer Lodge Historical Society helped me locate obscure pieces of information, loaned me materials from their personal collections, copied photographs, shared their research, and kept me on a straight course guided by their memories of living and working in Butte. I owe debts of gratitude to Paul Anderson, Pam Campbell, Janet and Jay Cornish, Pam Garcia, Jerry Hansen, Jim Harrington, Al Hooper, Marilyn Maney, Jim Masker, Fred and Mindy Quivik, Alice Smith, and Gerry Walter. Their friendship has been a boon to my work. Alice Finnegan generously allowed me to use her oral history interviews from her work on Anaconda and shared her genealogical expertise. My warmest thanks to those men and women whom I interviewed and to all who agreed to be interviewed during the many oral history projects that have taken place in Butte.

Several organizations gave me financial support for this work. My thanks to the Montana Historical Society for a James M. Bradley Fellowship, to the State Historical Society of Wisconsin for an Alice E. Smith Fellowship, to the Western Association of Women Historians for their Graduate Fellowship, to the University of North Carolina's History Department for a George Mowry Research Award, to the National Endowment for the Humanities for a travel grant, to the Montana State University College of Letters and Sciences for a Research and Creativity grant, and to the American Council of Learned Societies for a generous fellowship.

Thanks, too, to my colleagues in the Department of History and Philosophy at Montana State University who make work a pleasure. My deepest thanks to my parents, John and Virginia Murphy, who took me to the library every Saturday morning for as long as I can remember.

Introduction

Butte, Montana, was a hard place to call home. An industrial copper mining city set in the Montana wilderness, Butte has been described as an "island entirely surrounded by land." Uncertainty, transience, and fear of injury, death, and the blacklist were ever-present. Yet people formed surprising allegiances to Butte based on a shared sense of place and experience. Everyone, no matter their sex, class, ethnicity, occupation, or religion, was dependent on the copper industry—in particular the Anaconda Copper Mining Company—and the consequent unpredictability of a boom-and-bust economy, a given in a community based on natural resource extraction. Living with a sense of impermanence shaped the decisions of Butte men and women.

Butte bore three monikers in the early twentieth century. To capitalists, it was "the richest hill on earth," a treasure trove of copper ore, control of which made the Anaconda Company one of the most powerful corporations in the country. Workers knew it as the "Gibraltar of Unionism," where nearly every working person from theater usher to hoist engineer belonged to a labor union. And everyone recognized it as a wide-open town for gambling, liquor, and sex. Yet each nickname posed ironies and contradictions and masked contentious meetings of class and gender. Exactly who got rich, and how did they spend that money? How solid was the Gibraltar, and did working-class consciousness extend outside the walls of the union hall or the workplace? For whom was Butte wide open? This book examines Butte during the interwar years, when the labor movement suffered crippling defeats, decline and depression dampened the city's cocky sense of itself, and residents sought to recreate the city's social life in the wake of tremendous economic, political, and demographic upheavals caused by World War I.

Butte serves as a laboratory for examining several phenomena of urban development. It was an "instant city" of the American West, "shaped by rapid change and fickle chance" as Gunther Barth would say. Between 1880 and 1916 its population multiplied thirty times, from approximately three thousand to ninety thousand, making it the largest metropolis in the five-state region of the northern Rockies and plains. Unlike other western communities that began as missions, fur trading posts, or military installations and slowly evolved into urban centers, Butte was conceived in the full flush of the industrial revolution and grew helter-skelter into a major city. Built upon large-scale industrial extraction of metallic ores—at one point called "the Pittsburgh of the West"—Butte shared with other cities dominated by single heavy industries an economy controlled by large corporations, cycles of boom-and-bust, skilled male workers, and women workers relegated almost exclusively to the service sector.

What happened in Butte during the 1920s and 1930s can offer insights into the urban development of many cities in the United States. In 1920 only New York, Chicago, and Philadelphia had more than a million inhabitants. Of the almost three hundred cities with a population of twenty-five thousand or more, more than two-thirds had fewer than seventy-five thousand residents. Although historians have based patterns of urban development upon studies of New York, Chicago, and Philadelphia, most urban dwellers during the early twentieth century lived in cities the size of Butte. A much shrunken Butte now seems a place to stop on the interstate between Minneapolis and Seattle, to eat a Cornish pasty, tour the historic district, and shake one's head over the environmental impact of mining. Yet during the late nineteenth and early twentieth centuries it was an exemplar of the rush into an urban, industrial age.[1]

In 1937 Helen Lynd and Robert Lynd, reassessing their original study *Middletown*, observed, "What a people does with its leisure, like the way it trains its young, affords a sensitive index to its values." Leisure is the lens through which I have viewed Butte in the years between the first and second world wars, aiming to examine the values of a mining city poised in a paradoxical time. Economic depression and population decline, shifting gender roles, and a defeated labor movement created a less exuberant and expansive Butte at the same time that wartime experiences broadened men's and women's vision of work and leisure. As commercial amusements proliferated, access to cash became increasingly important. As the Lynds argued, how men and women chose to spend their "play" money and how they comported themselves in new playgrounds can tell us much about their values and the evolution of urban life.[2]

Beginning in the late nineteenth century, a decrease in the hours of work and small but measurable increases in wages provided working-class people in the United States with a combination of more free time and disposable income. This social and economic configuration, combined with new technologies, contributed to a proliferation of commercial amusements. Movie theaters, dance halls, arcades, department stores, and amusement parks, as well as saloons and their successor speakeasies were integral to the landscape of even small cities in the 1920s. People had more income to spend on ready-to-wear clothing, on beauty aids, and on the new toys of a burgeoning consumer culture: Victrolas, radios, and especially automobiles. Urbanization, industrialization, and the commercialization of leisure went hand in hand. Yet consumerism and commercialization must always be seen in their particular context. Bill Burke, a Butte poet, captured the erratic nature of mass consumption in "The Miner's Wife." One stanza describes boom times:

> Yep, she's one in a billion, tho' she'll dress like a million,
> And give the bill to the miner to pay;
> But that's only human, and when things are boomin',
> She knows he'll have little to say.

Yet when the mines were down, "It's then she sews and she presses, and makes her own dresses, / And cajoles the land-lord away from her door." Butte residents embraced the advent of mass consumerism and the commercialization of leisure, but always within the constraints of working-class life.[3]

Like the workers Roy Rosenzweig studied in Worcester, Massachusetts, who demanded "eight hours for work, eight hours for rest, and eight hours for what we will," Butte miners did not want to "wear a copper collar but for the eight hours" they were "down in the hole." How they, their families, and their friends spent their earnings during their "eight hours for what we will" is the subject of this study. What kinds of public and private entertainment did Butte residents choose? What kinds of amusement received public support? Did residents feel enough sense of commitment to Butte—despite the unpredictability of employment—to shoulder the costs of cultural and recreational institutions or programs that contribute to the quality of life in any community? Butte, as a political entity, tended to favor the "permissive" side of twentieth-century amusements. Between 1914 and 1972, in a series of ballots on the regulation of boxing, drinking, and various forms of gambling, metropolitan Butte always voted for the least restrictive alternative.[4]

A major constraint on workers' choices was the power of the Anaconda Company. By the late 1920s, "the Company" owned almost all of the mines in Butte, the state's major newspapers, the amusement park, the water company, the street railway system, and a good portion of the state's legislators as well as local politicians. Yet Butte was never a company town in the sense of southern cotton mill villages, coal towns across the country, or even the copper towns of Arizona. During the late 1910s and 1920s, when many American corporations embraced welfare capitalism, the Anaconda Company did not. Anaconda did not build company houses, require shopping at a company store, construct churches and recreation centers, and sponsor regular social events or self-improvement classes—although it supported some of these institutions to some degree. Its control of social life was more subtle, and it shaped leisure in Butte more by default than by intervention. Thus there was a great deal of maneuverability in the recreational terrain of the mining city.

Butte was wedded to the rough pleasures of a wide-open town, and the company did little to alter that. Unlike many American cities, Butte lacked an effective progressive movement that worked to eradicate vice and impose middle-class standards of behavior. Campaigns to expunge prostitution and prizefighting, to curb drinking and gambling, and to establish a system of urban parks and wholesome recreation scarcely made a ripple. Butte ignored laws regulating vice and ridiculed or shunned the few reformers who came to town. Middle-class voluntary groups, the troops of the reform movement in other cities, in Butte limited their efforts to less controversial issues such as art and literature classes, summer camps for children, and private charities.

Ironically, the reason for this phenomenon lies both in the power of the Anaconda Company and the strength of the working class. Butte was a working man's city. Miners, carpenters, blacksmiths, pipefitters, teamsters, and thousands of others associated with the mines organized the bulk of Butte's clubs and sports leagues and were the majority of consumers. In neighborhoods, dance halls, brothels, movie theaters, lodges, and on ball fields, men fashioned a social life that dominated Butte's public culture. At the same time, the Anaconda Company adopted a laissez-faire attitude toward commercial recreations. It gave only tacit support to Prohibition and no encouragement to social hygiene campaigns or efforts to expand public parks and recreation. Without the political and monetary support of the company and without access to the newspapers, reformers made little headway in Butte.

That male-contoured social landscape began to change during the years between the wars. Montana women won suffrage in 1914, took on new work and social roles in World War I, and were instrumental in instituting state prohibition in 1919. During the 1920s and 1930s some Butte women and their male allies worked to create a community in which their daily needs for physical and spiritual nourishment were met. The re-creation of Butte was in many ways the result of the struggle of women and men to adjust to new gender roles after World War I. The wrangling that resulted was only one of the many tugs-of-war between a variety of interests in the city: between ethnic groups, between single men and families, between classes, and between the rough and the respectable. As Butte matured, various groups patched together coalitions to work on some particular issue they believed would improve the quality of urban life. A sense of individual self-preservation cued to the vagaries of boom-and-bust times, however, meant that it was difficult to form lasting alliances.

Much has been written about Butte up to 1920, for its early history was filled with dramatic events that compel retelling. Scholars and novelists have chronicled its origins as a typical boom-and-bust mining camp, the discovery of copper that led to its metropolitan growth, its significance as the birthplace of the Anaconda Copper Mining Company and the Western Federation of Miners, and its notoriety as the wide-open town of the northern Rockies. Most of the literature stops in 1920, after the tumultuous years of World War I when the city began to decline. The war was a watershed; Butte's boisterous youth came to a bloody end. Its population eroded steadily, the labor movement went into eclipse, changing roles for women in particular forced residents to redefine public spaces, and new technologies bound Butte more closely to the fads and fashions of national culture. The mining city faced the 1920s and 1930s with an altered sensibility yet never lost its unique character and voice.

Butte became a city where stories counted among the treasures won from the mines. Turning the vicissitudes and triumphs of daily life into stories became a way of coping with the limits of control over the conditions of work and the quality of life. There are many voices telling many stories in this book. Immigrant miners, housewives, flappers, clubwomen, prostitutes, bootleggers, boxers, and newsboys all have their say. I have, of course, overlaid my narrative on those voices. This is a tale full of the ironies and contradictions of life in Butte, of stories that helped people to persevere, flourish, and maintain a remarkable allegiance to a precarious community.

Mining Cultures is a study about choice and the factors circumscribing it. The people of Butte had more options for spending their free time and disposable income than they did for choosing work or political candidates. But even decisions about playing were overdetermined. Class and ethnicity shaped cultural patterns of leisure. Accepted standards of morality and public behavior dictated deportment. The peculiarities of Butte's demography ensured commercial recreation geared to the desires of single men. This book examines social interactions primarily during time away from work, or at least away from paid work, but how work shaped play is an implicit theme.

Underlying every interaction in the city was the relationship between the Anaconda Company and the thousands of workers who wrested ore from the earth—an arduous, dangerous occupation whose constancy was dictated by markets far from Butte. Work and play were twined in the mining city. Hard work shaped hard play. Working underground, men gambled with their lives; aboveground they gambled with their virtue. Men and women, in responding to the consequences of mining life, did the best they could to survive and enjoy Butte.

NOTES

1. Barth, *Instant Cities,* xv; Butte Business Men's Association, *Butte, Montana;* Reynolds, ed., *The New World Atlas and Gazetteer, 1924,* 134.

2. Lynd and Lynd, *Middletown in Transition,* 292.

3. Nasaw, *Going Out,* 3–4; Burke, *Rhymes of the Mines,* 52–53; Horowitz, *The Morality of Spending;* Montgomery, "Class, Capitalism, and Contentment"; Montgomery, "Thinking about American Workers."

4. Rosenzweig, *Eight Hours for What We Will,* 1; Green, *Wobblies, Pile Butts, and Other Heroes,* 191; Waldron and Wilson, *Atlas of Montana Elections, 1889–1976,* 152–53.

Mining Cultures

1

Copper Metropolis

The city wasn't pretty. —DASHIELL HAMMETT

It is safe to say that no one who has ever been there has forgotten it. —BURTON K. WHEELER

One Friday in the early 1920s John Hutchens and Evan Reynolds, each just eighteen and armed with $50 in savings, boarded a train in Missoula and headed to Butte for the weekend. Checking into the venerable Thornton Hotel, John and Evan ventured to the Italian suburb of Meaderville, where they "cautiously drank" the homemade red wine served with dinner. Then, throwing caution to the wind, they returned uptown to the Atlantic. The Atlantic was Butte's biggest and busiest saloon, where gambling made up for any revenue lost to a loosely enforced Prohibition. After witnessing the shooting of a cheating card sharp, the young men tried the craps table, where a run of good luck filled their pockets with silver dollars. A stroll down Galena Street, where "faintly red lights shone through ruby-colored transoms" and the prostitutes tapped on their windows to attract attention, convinced them that Butte was "a good town."[1]

The journalist Joseph Kinsey Howard once described Butte as "a very bully of a city, stridently male, blusteringly profane, boisterous and boastful." As a mining city early Butte was shaped by a largely single male work force. But Howard and other observers agreed that by the late 1930s his description was no longer apt. Butte was a sobered community, the bluster and boastfulness of its men punctured by a series of economic hardships and political defeats. World War I was a watershed for the wide-open "Gibraltar of Unionism." The events of the war years reconfigured the social landscape. The draft, failed strikes, a mine disaster, the blacklist, and murder demolished the once powerful Butte Miners' Union. Prohibition challenged men's primary social retreat, the saloon. The high cost of living taxed the efforts of working-class families to enjoy the fruits of a maturing consumer society. The flu epidemic swept through the mining city, leaving grief in its wake. A postwar depression drove thousands from the city when the mines shut down.[2]

In the 1920s and 1930s Butte's men and women reconstructed Butte's social life along lines not as "stridently male" as before the war. Boisterous Butte went through a trial by fire in World War I and in its aftermath some members of the city sought to fashion a community that catered to the needs and desires of women and children, of families, in addition to those of single men. Butte remained a rough-and-tumble city, but it never regained its prewar population or gusto.

■ ■ ■

Butte grew from a heart of copper. Metallic wealth had lured men to the arid Summit Valley of southwestern Montana, situated more than a mile high in the northern Rocky Mountains. Settlers named a distinctive volcanic cone in the valley's northwest corner "Big Butte" and a granitic, thousand-foot rise to its east "the Hill." The Hill was a treasure trove of billions of dollars worth of gold, silver, zinc, lead, manganese, and, above all, copper. Between 1880 and 1975, when underground mining virtually ceased in Butte, miners wrested from the earth nearly two-and-a-half million tons of zinc, more than twenty-four thousand tons of silver, over one hundred tons of gold, and over ten million tons of copper—enough to form a copper cube 330 feet square. But the land did not relinquish its riches easily. Hundreds of miners died in the shafts and stopes of the mines that honeycombed the Butte Hill. Thousands of others were injured, crippled, or disabled by silicosis, commonly called miner's consumption, a disease caused by breathing the silica dust-laden air generated by hardrock drilling.[3]

While miners challenged the earth for its riches, capitalists battled for control of the wealth their employees brought to the surface. The War of the Copper Kings, a legend in the history of American business, pitted three ruthless men against each other. Marcus Daly, William A. Clark, and F. Augustus Heinze deployed money, mining engineers, lawyers, judges, politicians, journalists, and editors in one of the most vicious struggles for corporate dominance waged during the Gilded Age. The denouement was the triumph of Marcus Daly's Anaconda Copper Mining Company (ACM). By the late 1920s Anaconda had become the eighth largest industrial company in the United States. Its holdings included mines, smelters, foundries, brass mills, coal fields, coke ovens, timberlands, sawmills, newspapers, and the Butte, Anaconda and Pacific Railway, which shuttled ore, supplies, and people between Butte and its companion city, Anaconda. In 1883 Marcus Daly founded the town of Anaconda, twenty-six miles from Butte, at a source of plentiful water, as the site of the Anaconda Company's first copper smelter. Anaconda's empire reached far beyond the borders of Montana and the United States. Mines and smelters in Mexico, Chile, and Poland took direction from corporate headquarters in New York and Butte, where general officers occupied the infamous sixth floor of the Hennessy Building. Despite various reorganizations and renamings in response to antitrust legislation, Anaconda was known—and is still referred to many years after its departure from Butte—as "the company," a term, as Montana Senator Burton K. Wheeler noted, "simple yet awe-inspiring."[4]

Butte began like hundreds of other western mining camps. Prospectors first struck gold in Silver Bow Creek in 1864, and gold seekers hastily erected huts and storefronts that housed the highly transient population of miners, merchants, prostitutes, and traveling performers. When the gold played out, just about everyone left. In 1875, when William L. Farlin began mining and reducing silver ore, another rush to the valley occurred.[5]

Silver turned Butte into one of the half-dozen richest metal mining districts in the United States. Government demand for the white metal to back currency and mint coins guaranteed a booming economy between the mid-1870s and early 1890s. Butte's silver mines rivaled those in Leadville and Aspen, Colorado, the Coeur d'Alene valley in Idaho, and Virginia City, Nevada. With silver came a sense of permanency and the railroad. Residents platted a townsite in 1876 and incorporated their community as Butte City in 1879. In 1881 the Union Pacific completed a line from northern Utah to Butte to cash in on Butte's lucrative freight traffic.[6]

With the repeal of the Sherman Silver Purchase Act in 1893, the nation's silver market collapsed. Butte's fortunes had been wedded to copper since 1882, however, when Marcus Daly discovered "the largest deposit of copper sulphide that the world had ever seen" at the three-hundred-foot level of the Anaconda Mine. The vast, rich reserves of copper in the Hill ultimately distinguished Butte from other western mining camps and turned it into the world's largest producer of the red metal until the late 1920s. Copper, filling a new demand created by the electrical revolution, fueled Butte's rise to a major city of the Rocky Mountain West. Between 1881 and 1909 five railroads laid tracks to Butte, tying the city to the east and west coasts, to Salt Lake City and points south, and north to Canada (map 1). By June 1916 thirty-four passenger trains terminated, originated, or passed through Butte every day. Railroads exported the metallic wealth of Butte and imported thousands of immigrants, prodigious quantities of food, consumer goods that rivaled the stock of New York City department stores, traveling theater groups, evangelizing reformers, and campaigning politicians.[7]

Butte became a rowdy town that inspired pungent description from novelists, journalists, and travelers: notorious, drab, dingy, ugly, noisy, naked, and barren, but also young, animated, shrewd, generous, jubilant, democratic, and cordial. The foul sulphurous fumes spewing from smelters or floating from open heaps of roasting ore repulsed travelers to the burgeoning metropolis in the 1880s. Dense smoke compelled residents to walk the streets with sponges or rags tied over their mouths and noses, carrying lanterns to find their way in the middle of the day. Although some residents complained about the smoke, capitalist William A. Clark claimed healthful benefits, asserting that the fumes were a disinfectant that killed germs and that the measure of arsenic in the smoke gave Butte women their beautiful, pale complexions. Ann Pentilla remembered that the byproducts of mining had a different cosmetic effect. She recalled that "your face would be pitted from the chunks of sand" blown from tailings piles. In Butte, however, health and beauty were secondary considerations, and the *Butte Miner* expressed the majority's opinion when it declared, "The thicker the fumes the greater our financial vitality."[8]

From 1890 to the eve of World War I, Butte enjoyed a rollicking adolescence. Few doubted that the riches of the Hill were limitless, and although there were always bust times when the price of copper was down, just as surely boom times would return. These were the years of the War of the Copper Kings and the consolidation of the Anaconda Company, of increasing copper production and high wages, of construction of a thriving central business district on the Hill—"uptown Butte"—and streetcar suburbs on the valley floor. New immigrants—Finns, Serbs, Croatians, and Italians—augmented colonies of Irish and Cornish miners, and the geography of ethnicity and class became clearly demarcated. The city reveled in its

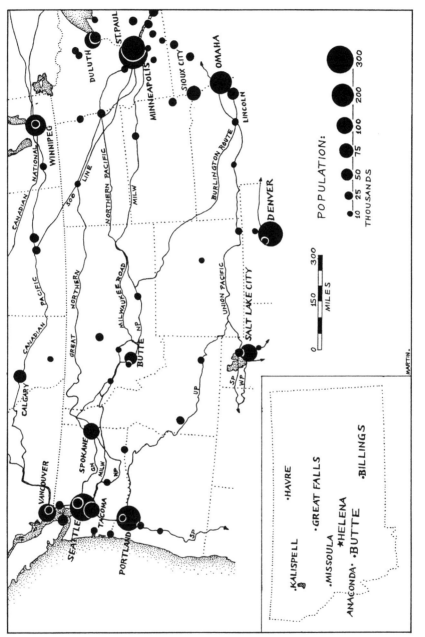

Map 1. Urban Density and Railway Main Lines of the Northern Tier, 1920

reputation as a wide-open town. Miners kept saloons, restaurants, gambling halls, and the red light district bustling twenty-four hours a day. Gertrude Atherton, a writer who set her novel *Perch of the Devil* in Butte in 1914, captured the optimistic spirit of the prewar days when she wrote that Butte "has the jubilant expression of one who coins the very air, the thin, sparkling, nervous air, into shining dollars, and, confident in the inexhaustible riches beneath her feet, knows that she shall go on coining them forever."[9]

Butte's hub was the corner of Park and Main streets, the center of the business district (map 2). Some of the city's most impressive buildings anchored the intersection. An elegant seven-story office building, designed by Cass Gilbert and housing the Daly Bank and Trust Company, claimed the southwest corner across the street from the Rialto Theater and kitty-corner to the ornate Owsley Block (individual business buildings in Butte were often referred to as "blocks"). Streetcars, part of the county's thirty-eight-mile rail transit system, met at the corner, bringing shoppers to town from the suburbs, picking up children and families headed out to the Columbia Gardens amusement park, and carrying weary miners home after work.[10]

By 1917 automobiles challenged streetcars and the existing army of horse-drawn wagons, buggies, and hacks. Although eleven livery stables still operated in Butte in 1917, the automobile was destined to prevail, and by the mid-1920s no stables remained. The streetcar system persisted until 1937, when it too conceded victory to the automobile and bus. Automobile dealerships multiplied during the 1910s, peaking at twenty-eight in 1918. Car dealers proclaimed the triumph of the automobile when the government proposed a 5 percent tax on cars during World War I. In protests to their congresswoman, Jeannette Rankin, dealers declared their willingness "to stand our share of war cost but why discriminate against automobiles; they are necessities not luxuries."[11]

Although mining dominated the economy, a wide variety of mercantile and small manufacturing enterprises—food wholesalers, breweries, department stores, warehouses, brick works, and iron foundries—provided the amenities of urban life and the goods and services necessary to make Butte a regional economic center. Well-heeled consumers could indulge in French wines at the Lisa grocery, have a fur coat altered at Klingbell's taxidermy, purchase silver service and jewelry at any of two dozen jewelers, select finery for a costume ball from Madame Robinson, or acquire an oriental carpet from Joseph David. There were dozens of butchers and grocers

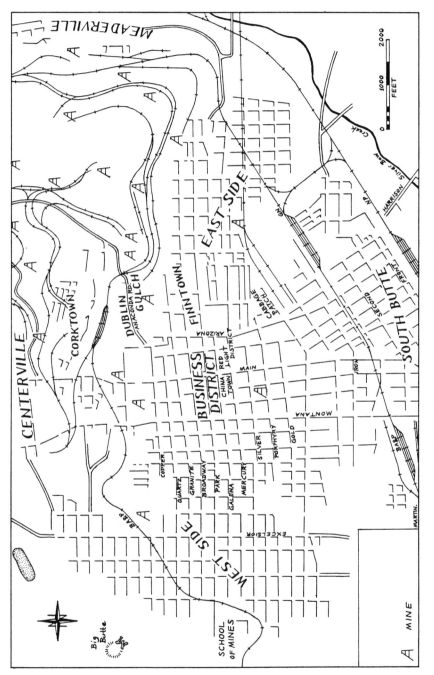

Map 2. Neighborhoods on the Butte Hill in 1939

who would deliver food to the door. The Imperial Macaroni Company manufactured pasta and soups. Vincent Truzzolino provided tamales, wholesale and retail, and a handful of noodle parlors served Chinese food or delivered dishes by messenger. Symons Dry Goods Company—cash only—employed a small army of young women who ran cash from the customer to the cashier's office and brought back change. Hennessy's Department Store was famous for providing everything from miners' overalls and plain groceries to furs, china, and furniture.

Uptown Butte also housed a wealth of commercial amusements. Confectioneries accommodated cigar counters, newspapers racks, and ice cream parlors that catered to courting couples, maids and children, gossiping businessmen, and shoppers seeking refreshment. In 1917 fourteen theaters drew people uptown for vaudeville and movies. Off-shift workmen filled saloons, billiard parlors, and gambling halls. Chinatown, just a block southwest of Park and Main, beckoned thrill-seekers, attracted by exaggerated stories of gambling, opium dens, and white slaves. Visitors were more likely to encounter vegetable sellers, silk traders, and Chinese on their way to devotions at the joss house or the Chinese Baptist Mission. Directly east, across Main Street, hundreds of prostitutes worked in the red light district, a warren of wooden cribs interspersed with substantial brick parlor houses.[12]

On most nights, a large proportion of Butte's population could be found congregated in one of the city's many labor or fraternal halls. Butte had been nicknamed the Gibraltar of Unionism because nearly all wageworkers in Butte before the war were union members, their solidarity inspiring workers throughout the West. Forty-four locals listed themselves in the 1917 city directory. Cab drivers and horseshoers, musicians and decorators, butchers and barbers, newsboys and theater ushers, sheepshearers and telephone operators, and chambermaids and iron molders all followed the lead of miners by unionizing. When men from the Butte Miners' Union organized the Western Federation of Miners in 1893, Butte became a center of the western labor movement.[13]

Many people also belonged to a variety of associations; nearly every organized fraternal group in the country had a chapter in Butte. By the advent of World War I, the Masons, Elks, Odd Fellows, Good Templars, Knights of Columbus, Ancient Order of Hibernians, Sons of St. George, and Scandinavian Brotherhood, among others, had built impressive halls. Most fraternal organizations had ladies' auxiliaries, and women also formed a plethora of independent literary and cultural clubs, for example, the Homer Club, the Drama Study Club, the West Side Shakespeare Club, and the Plant and Pray Garden Club. Women also founded local branches of the Woman's Christian Temperance Union and the Florence Crittenden Rescue Circle. In addition to ethnic and fraternal societies, Butte boasted dozens of civic, religious, professional, and athletic associations for the entertainment, pleasure, and comfort of the city's men and women.[14]

. . .

It was always difficult to know just how many people were bustling around Butte. Miners were notoriously transient, and political boundaries and the methods of census-taking disguised meaningful figures. When people referred to Butte, they usually meant the metropolitan area that included the densely settled neighborhoods outside of but contiguous to the city limits. Thus, census figures for Silver Bow County, which apart from Butte contained only a few villages, are a much more accurate reflection of the Butte population than those for the city itself. William A. Kemper, president of the Butte Land and Investment Company, calculated through his own inquiries and a survey of construction, that although the census bureau had underestimated residents of the city at thirty-nine thousand in 1910, the R. L. Polk Company, canvassing for its 1916 city directory, was "inclined to flatter" with its claim of a metropolitan population of a hundred thousand. His reckoning of the 1916 populace in Butte and the adjacent suburbs was approximately eighty-five thousand, and he qualified even that, noting, "with conditions changing so rapidly, it must be, at most, a guess." Even with such qualifications, until 1930 Butte remained the largest city between Spokane and Minneapolis and north of Salt Lake City, making it not only a copper metropolis but also a regional trading center.[15]

A large percentage of Butte's highly mobile population was foreign-born. One analyst of the census concluded that between 1890 and 1930 Butte was the most ethnically diverse city in the intermountain West. The celebration of George Washington's birthday in 1920 graphically demonstrated that fact. The Daughters of the American Revolution welcomed guests to the YMCA, where Welsh singers, the Daughters of Scotia, and Swedish, Norwegian, Slavic, Italian, and Polish musicians played and sang and then listened to speeches by representatives of thirty-three nationalities. Although major seaport cities are usually considered the loci of the country's immigrant population, in fact those cities funneled streams of people to the hinterlands. Between 1870 and 1910 the percentage of European-born people who lived in the mountain states was higher than that in the nation.[16] Montana for most of the twentieth century harbored the greatest number of these mountain states' immigrants, who were drawn to the "treasure state" by its mines and smelters.[17]

Between 1890 and 1930, 20 percent or more of the region's Irish lived and worked in Butte and Anaconda. Turn-of-the-century Butte was "one of the most overwhelmingly Irish cities in the United States." In 1900 Irish immigrants and their children accounted for a quarter of the county's population, a higher percentage than in any other American city at that time. By 1910 immigrants and children of foreign or mixed parentage made up 70.2 percent of Butte's population. Ireland, England, and Canada contributed the largest number of immigrants to Silver Bow County in 1900, 1910, and 1920. In 1900 Germans, Scandinavians, and immigrants from the Austro-Hungarian Empire formed the next most numerous cohort. In the first decade of the twentieth century Finns and Russians poured into the state. By 1920 almost a third of the region's Finns resided in the Montana coal and copper mining counties of Carbon, Cascade, and Silver Bow. By that same year, mines and merchants in Butte employed and served significant numbers of Yugoslavs, Italians, Greeks, Czechs, and Poles. After World War I the Irish still wielded influence, but the city's ethnic amalgam had grown richer and more complex.[18]

Butte's population was overwhelmingly young and predominantly male. In 1900, 88 percent of the population was younger than forty-five; fewer than 1 percent was older than sixty-five. The figures had scarcely changed in 1910. By 1920, 78 percent of Butte's residents were still younger than forty-five, and only 2.2 percent was older than sixty-five. Most of these young urbanites were men. In 1900 there were 147.7 men to every 100 women in Butte, ten years later the ratio was 132.4 to 100, and in 1920 it was 119.6 to 100. One significant change concerned the growing number of married men. In 1910, 52 percent of Butte men were single; in 1920, however, only 42 percent of those older than fifteen were unmarried, a figure that held steady in the 1930 census.[19]

Butte's population resided in a web of neighborhoods radiating from the uptown hub of commercial activity (map 3). Booms in the copper market caused frequent housing shortages and subsequent flurries of building. In 1906 the *Butte Miner* reported accommoda-

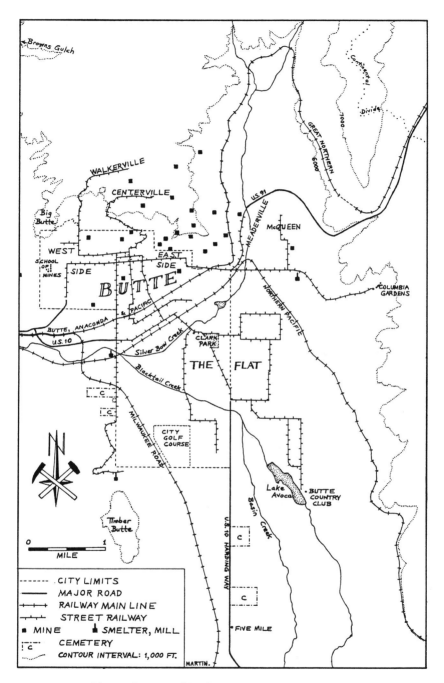

Map 3. Butte and Its Environs in the Late 1920s

tions so sparse that transients were spending the night in Turkish baths and visitors were sleeping in chairs. Butte's contractors were busiest between 1915 and 1918, when the city issued more than three thousand building permits. Immigrants jammed into new walk-up flats, and bungalows shot up in Butte's middle-class neighborhoods. Mary Clapp was pleasantly surprised by the oak floors, beveled plate-glass windows, commodious bookcases, and especially the white-tiled bathroom and built-in tiled ice box she found in her West Side bungalow. "No wonder I never thought of Butte as a mining camp," she recalled. "No wonder I imagined that every light down the hill shone from the window of some bungalow as rich in possibilities of home happiness as our own."[20]

The West Side, home to Butte's upper and middle classes, was an attractive neighborhood of rambling Victorian houses, Queen Anne cottages, and craftsman bungalows. Businessmen, lawyers, doctors, teachers, and skilled workers resided there. So did some of Butte's wealthiest citizens. Daniel Hennessy, the "Merchant Prince of Montana," built his mansion on the corner of Park and Excelsior. His next-door neighbor was Cornelius Kelley, who became president of the Anaconda Company in 1918. Fellow ACM executives William D. Scallon and John D. Ryan also built their residences on the heights of Excelsior Avenue.

North and east of the business district neighborhoods bore a different configuration. Dublin Gulch, Corktown, Centerville, and the independent town of Walkerville lay to the north and northeast, encompassing the parishes of St. Mary and St. Lawrence O'Toole. The streets and alleys of these working-class neighborhoods connected like the seams of a crazy quilt, curving to edge around headframes, hoist houses, and mine dumps. Here were some of Butte's most famous and most lucrative mines: the Anaconda, Neversweat, Diamond, Mountain View, High Ore, Parrot, Speculator, and Mountain Con. Small wood-frame cottages huddled around the mine structures. Many of the deep mines were "hot boxes" where sweat quickly bathed a working man. As soaking wet men stepped off the mine cages into the frigid air of Butte's winter, clouds of steam enveloped them and a chilling walk home in icy clothes invited pneumonia. Until streetcars made it possible to commute to the mines and until employers built "drys"—buildings in which men could shower and change into dry clothes after work—workers built their homes as close to the mines as possible.

Dublin Gulch, as one would expect, was overwhelmingly Irish. As Julia McHugh recalled, "Most of the families were Harringtons,

Murphy, Sullivan, etc., and all the fathers and mothers were John or Mary." Residents coined nicknames such as Mary Black Pete, Mary-up-to-Paddy's, and Mary Cal to distinguish one Mary Harrington from another. Strong neighborhood ties were evident in fiercely contested football and baseball games with other neighborhoods and in the close scrutiny of boys from outside the Gulch who came courting. Julia McHugh's mother exhibited her loyalty to the neighborhood in a confrontation with the coal deliveryman. Once, when the coal wagon had a hard time backing up to the coal bin window and "the horses were slipping on the ice and the driver was swearing at the crazy people who would live there, Ma said, 'I'll have you know I wouldn't give up my house for Con F. Kelly's on the West Side.'"[21]

In a crescent just southeast of the red light district lay the Cabbage Patch, a hodgepodge of cabins and ramshackle buildings full of "batching" and "housekeeping" rooms. In its confines working-class poor rubbed elbows with drug addicts, older prostitutes, bootleggers, and criminals. The Patch was "notorious" for its "third class saloons, its cheap restaurants and its cheaper flop houses, flanked by employment offices for transient labor."[22]

The East Side, crammed with walk-up flats, fourplexes, and rambling boardinghouses spread out north and east of the Cabbage Patch. "It was teeming with people and it seemed like all families had kids," remembered John Onkalo. "In fact, the houses were almost skin to skin, and boy, there was kids all over in the neighborhood." Children absorbed the ethnically based rivalries of their parents, venting them in street fights. Catherine Hoy identified with a gang of Irish boys from Dublin Gulch who would "go down to Finntown and all those places to fight. . . . Of course, we had the advantage. Anaconda Road was on a hill and Finntown was down below us there on Granite and we could pelt rocks down there but they couldn't put the rocks up."

Finntown was the East Side's dominant ethnic neighborhood, although the streets encompassed in the mental map of residents were not settled exclusively by Finns. Onkalo described the area close to the Pennsylvania Mine "like an English colony," and many Swedes lived along East Galena Street. But Finnish immigrants and their institutions flavored the neighborhood. Saunas and the good food served in Finn boardinghouses drew working men and women from all over the city to Finntown. The community built Finlanders Hall in 1902, and for several decades it hosted parties, dances, and plays as well as the offices of the Industrial Workers of the World and the Finnish Workers Club. Finns worshipped at the Holy Trinity Finnish Lutheran church and at the evangelical Finnish Mission church.[23]

The East Side also attracted a small enclave of Lebanese, at that time known as Syrians. These immigrants made their living as merchants, often selling groceries and fruits, sometimes carpets. Syrian women, carrying large suitcases filled with handmade aprons, housedresses, and other notions, peddled their goods door to door. The Syrian Peace Society, organized in 1908, was the first Syrian fraternal lodge in the country. In its hall on East Galena Street immigrants held wakes, weddings, receptions, and English classes.[24]

Serbs, Croatians, Slovenes, and Montenegrins also lived on the East Side and in Dublin Gulch. These southeastern European immigrants were subjected to intense discrimination. In 1910 the *Butte Evening News* inflamed public opinion with accusations that "bohunks" were "driving the white men slowly but surely out of the camp." Ann Pentilla remembered students cruelly teasing Slavic children: "When we went to school they would make fun of us, they called us 'the garlic eaters.' At recess nobody wanted to stay behind us because we smelled from garlic. My mother flavored everything with garlic. And now everybody uses it, but in those days just Slavic people and the Italians used garlic." Slavs created a rich organizational life in their neighborhoods. Social and fraternal lodges, such as the Serbian Montenegrin Federation, the Montenegrin Literary Society, the Serb-Yugoslav Unity Lodge, and the Circle of Serbian Sisters, eased the transition to life in the United States. Serbs worshipped in the onion-domed Serbian Orthodox church, and Roman Catholic Croatians continued to celebrate the pre-Lenten *mesopust,* a festival culminating in the burning or beheading of a straw effigy, signifying the exculpation of the community's sins.[25]

Further east lay the suburbs of Meaderville and McQueen. Meaderville, which in the 1920s and 1930s became famous for its restaurants, speakeasies, and nightclubs, began as a settlement of Cornish and Italian miners and smeltermen. McQueen lay huddled at the foot of the mountains bordering the east side of the valley, north of the Pittsmont smelter and about two miles from uptown Butte. Settled primarily by immigrants from the Austro-Hungarian Empire and England, McQueen also sheltered newcomers from Scandinavia, Germany, and France. The gathering places of this overwhelmingly Catholic community were the Jesuit-built Holy Saviour church and several Slavic saloons: Brozovich Brothers, Jurmick's, Petrovich's, Raenovich's, and Krizman's.[26]

All of these neighborhoods ranged across the Hill. "The Flat" was the valley floor stretching south, where new suburbs developed in the 1910s to accommodate the growing population. Streetcars enabled men and women to get to work on the Hill and to live on the Flat in comfortable bungalows set in small yards, a luxury found uptown only on the West Side. A commercial district grew up on Harrison Avenue. Lake Avoca, with boats for rent and beer gardens for refreshment, attracted pleasure-seekers from all parts of the city. In 1909 the ten-year-old Butte Country Club moved to a site next to the lake and laid out a new golf course. By the late 1910s the Flat had enough residents to warrant construction of several grammar schools.[27]

Butte's working-class neighborhoods were vigorous, fascinating districts, but they were also overcrowded, unsanitary, and noisy. In a memoir of the East Side Frank Carden evoked the cacophony that was an ever-present part of the landscape. Northern Pacific steam locomotives with "bells ringing and whistles blowing" shunted cars between coalyards and the warehouse district. Blacksmiths, machinists, and boilermakers noisily executed repairs and maintenance work at the nearby Great Northern Railway roundhouse. Steam-driven vibrators launched booming attacks on frozen ore in the Belmont Mine's ore bins, breaking it up to be dropped into cars of the Butte, Anaconda and Pacific Railway. Stationary steam engines running mine hoists and turning the creaking sheave wheels at the top of gallus frames sometimes operated twenty-four hours a day to serve three shifts of miners.[28]

East and West Sides were different worlds in early-twentieth-century Butte. West Siders had horses and buggies and then automobiles. East Siders walked or took the trolley. West Side children had store-bought toys; those on the East Side improvised with scraps of wood and metal they found or stole from the mine yards. A daughter of a shift boss stuck out like a sore thumb in Dublin Gulch. With only one sibling and a father who made more money than most of his neighbors, she got "new shoes, dresses, coats, caps, scarves, and all for school" rather than the hand-me-downs with which most children made do. Workers and their children organized their social life according to a complex web of class and ethnicity. Catherine Hoy observed that for the most part, everyone in her neighborhood lived according to unspoken yet collectively acknowledged norms: "They didn't try to outdo the other one. If you did, you got into trouble . . . if they thought you were a little richer than they were, they wouldn't associate with you. They'd think, 'What the heck, she's too rich for me.'"[29]

■ ■ ■

Hardrock mining was an industrial pursuit, one of the most dangerous occupations in the world. Hardrock miners engaged in underground extraction of metallic ores that required drilling and blasting; the term distinguished such workers from placer miners and
coal miners. Large-scale extraction and processing of metallic ores
required enormous amounts of capital, complex technology, and
thousands of wage laborers. By 1900 more than five thousand Butte
men worked for wages as underground miners. In 1916, the peak
year of copper production before World War II, 14,500 men, almost
one-fifth of Butte's population, toiled in the mines.[30]

In no other metal mining district of the United States was such a
small area mined so intensively, and the peculiarities of Butte's geol-
ogy made mining the Hill unusually treacherous. Deep shafts, high
rock temperatures, and faulted, fractured ground set the stage for
underground fires, falling rock, and suffocation. When Dr. R. R. Sayers of the U.S. Public Health Service and Daniel Harrington, a mining engineer with the U.S. Bureau of Mines, visited Butte's deepest
level in 1921—3,800 feet down in the Steward Mine—the water temperature was 113 degrees Fahrenheit, the rock temperature 108
degrees, and the air temperature 107 degrees, with a relative humidity
of 100 percent. The following year, after the installation of ventila-
tion, the air temperature still steamed at 92 degrees.[31]

As mines went deeper conditions generally deteriorated. The
temperature rose, more water poured into the workings, and the
ground shifted more often. Helen Raymond recalled that men
dressed differently for work in different parts of the Hill: "Some
places they had to wear water resistant clothes 'cause the water
dripped on them and the copper water would make sores on your
body. And then there were places it was so hot that they couldn't
wear hardly any clothes." Heat and humidity also magnified the
odors of the underground. Toilet cars were not used widely until
1916 and locomotives did not replace the last mules until 1923, so
the smells of human and animal excrement mingled with those of
sweat, blasting powder, rotting food, and tobacco.[32]

The fact that the most common cause of death in Butte mines
was a fall of rock underscored the instability of the ground and the
unpredictability of working conditions. Even the most cautious
could be caught by unsound ground. The possibility spawned the
term *duggan*, a reference to any precariously placed rock that could
fall on a miner. As one worker explained, "They called it 'Duggan'

because Larry Duggan used to be the undertaker. And if one of those came down and got you, you was headed for Larry Duggan's undertaking parlors."[33]

Social and economic forces aggravated the physical dangers and discomforts of mining. Until the 1890s experienced miners—native-born men who had worked in Michigan or the West's other mining districts or immigrants from the United Kingdom—constituted the majority of Butte's underground work force. Irish and Cornish miners, who had learned their trade in their countries' copper and tin mines, easily transferred their skills to Butte. The southern and eastern European immigrants who began arriving in Butte during the final decade of the nineteenth century were agricultural workers who had no mining skills. Bosses often assigned them to dangerous sites that veterans avoided through seniority. Butte mines had no apprenticeship system, and novices tackled treacherous work without training. New immigrants, who could neither speak nor understand English, could not heed the advice that experienced miners gave them, and prejudice against "bohunks" sometimes meant that they did not receive proper warnings. In the early twentieth century the two most dangerous metal mining regions in the world were the American West and the South African Transvaal. Both had predominantly immigrant labor forces.[34]

The miners' habit of transience also contributed to high accident and fatality rates. Few men spent their lives in growing familiarity with one mine, and that lack of familiarity meant more accidents. Miners quit if they thought they were working in too dangerous a place, if they disagreed with a shift boss, or if they could find a more comfortable place to work. John Onkalo's search for a "nice mine" was common. He worked at the Mountain Con, the Belmont, the Leonard, the Steward, the Emma, "and the Anselmo, I worked up there for a few months. That was the nearest I could see to the Orphan Girl. The Orphan Girl was my favorite mine but the Anselmo was the closest to being like the Orphan Girl. . . . It wasn't as hot and the air seemed like it was pretty good. A nice mine to work in."[35]

Some men, Hanford Toppari, for example, looked back at decades of mining and wondered, "Why in the hell did I ever go down there?" Others found the mining process fascinating. In "The Hard Rock Man" Butte poet Berton Braley described a miner who decided to quit the trade, get a job on top, and find a wife. But when a friend invited him to examine the progress made on a particularly tricky tunnel he succumbed again to "the hard rock fever" and declared, "Fer the hard rock's callin' louder / Than the longin' for a home." Other men appreciated the independence mining offered. Shift bosses, often supervising too many men, visited work sites only every two days. Lunch breaks stretched into card games, and although poor supervision contributed to the neglect of safety measures it also gave miners a sense of self-rule. Under the contract system, in which miners were paid by the amount of rock they broke or removed during a shift, supervision was even more relaxed.[36]

Between 1860 and 1920 new technology transformed the underground. Machines replaced hand drilling and tramming, and these innovations spurred management to demand ever more and faster production. Shift bosses, responsible for delivering ore, tried to strike a balance between protecting miners' lives and protecting their own jobs. Despite the Anaconda Company's efforts to prevent injuries through an elaborate "safety first" program inaugurated in 1914, the message miners received was "rock first safety second." Witnesses, ranging from nurses at St. James Hospital to shift bosses, testified that Butte's accident rate would have been much lower had it not been for the "rush for rock."[37]

Bone-crushing accidents and mine fires claimed the lives of at least 559 Butte miners between 1914 and 1920, but many more fell victim to the mines' most insidious killer, rock dust. Before the 1920s dry power drilling predominated in the Hill. Dry drilling filled the air with rock dust containing a high density of quartz or free silica. Breathing silica caused scarring of lung tissue, resulting in silicosis or miner's consumption—the dreaded "miner's con." In 1916 federal investigators examined 1,018 miners and found that 42 percent of them had silicosis. Acute silicosis developed after only one to three years of work in an atmosphere heavily permeated by dust and accounted for the unusually high number of deaths among young miners. To Julia McHugh, growing up in Dublin Gulch, it seemed the miners all died in their thirties and forties. Her father survived until fifty-two, but "he was like an old man." Silicosis's weakening of the lungs left miners vulnerable to tuberculosis and pneumonia. Although ACM tried to blame miners' high rates of tuberculosis on unsanitary living conditions, the figures spoke for themselves. Between May 1913 and May 1914, 152 Butte citizens died of tuberculosis. Only five of them were women. An investigation of the thirty-four male victims who were not miners at the time of their deaths revealed that they had indeed all worked in the mines and had taken jobs as teamsters, janitors, and watchmen only when they could no longer work underground. A decade changed little. In 1923 eleven women and children died of tuberculosis in comparison to 137 men who succumbed to pulmonary disease.[38]

In 1925 federal investigators reported that in the nine years they had been monitoring Butte mines many improvements had been made: all the mines had installed ventilating fans; wet drilling, designed to keep down rock dust, was the rule if not always the practice; some long-smoldering fires that had generated poisonous fumes had finally been extinguished; and ACM was maintaining a first aid, fire-fighting, and mine-rescue training program. Still, persistent problems remained, chief among them the use of open-flame carbide lamps on miners' hats, which had ignited deadly mine fires in the past. The Bureau of Mines recommended the substitution of storage-battery lamps, but they were not adopted until the 1930s. It was only in 1946 that ACM recognized silicosis as an occupational disease and agreed to compensate its victims. Accident rates remained high, with no significant drop until 1942. As Victor Segna, an Italian immigrant who began working in the mines in 1922, said, "Once you got on that cage, you never knew if you'd come out of there. You never knew it. You got on there and you got down there, you may come up and you may not."[39]

Miners gambled with their lives daily, but they did not dwell on the dangers of their occupation. Instead they looked to the potential of mining as a steady job and, even in the twentieth century, as an opportunity for sudden riches. Many underground miners still roamed the nearby mountains in the summer, prospecting and staking claims in search of gold. A spirit of gambling optimism pervaded early Butte, and wageworkers often invested their paychecks in "promising" mining ventures. As one daughter of a confectionery store owner recalled, "everyone" speculated in mining, and most, like herself, could paper a wall with useless stock certificates.[40]

In 1920 miners still made up 40 percent of Butte's male work force, and most women in the city were wives and daughters of miners, carpenters, blacksmiths, machinists, pipe fitters, and other working men associated with the mines. As in virtually all American communities, the census masked the income-producing activities of many women. Wives took in boarders, laundry, and mending to supplement the family income. Widowed mothers resorted to a vast array of nonwage work they scheduled around caring for their children. Ann Pentilla recalled one widow, a midwife, who "had a cow and she baked bread and she used to take in washing and then the children would deliver the washing. And that's how she raised her children." When John Cavanaugh's father died, his mother kept

three or four boarders, baked bread that his aunt sold in her grocery, and worked as a domestic servant. Butte women also engaged
in wage work in just about the same numbers as women in other
parts of the country. In 1920, 21.1 percent of women more than
ten years old in the United States were gainfully employed. In Butte
that percentage was 22.7, only a shade more than the 22 percent
who had worked for wages in 1910.[41]

Butte's economy was western in the sense that it depended upon
natural resource extraction, a type of industry which, in the nineteenth and early twentieth centuries, employed a minuscule number of women. Yet it also paralleled eastern cities. Pittsburgh, for
example, was another metropolis dominated by heavy industry—
iron and steel—that employed an almost exclusively male labor
force. In these communities shaped by the extraction or processing
of metals, the vast majority of female wageworkers labored in the
service sector. In the West the manufacturing concerns that hired
women tended to be on a smaller scale than those in the northeast.
The textile mills and shoe factories that employed so many eastern
women were scarce west of the Mississippi. Julia McHugh's first job
was wrapping butter with about sixteen other girls at the Blanchard
Creamery. Other Butte girls started working at the C.O.D. laundry
when they finished eighth grade. And a few made pasta at the Imperial Macaroni Company.[42]

In 1920 the most common work for women in Butte was still as
domestic servants. The label *servant* encompassed a wide range of
jobs: bucket girls who packed miners' lunch pails, dishwashers and
chambermaids in boardinghouses, and cooks and maids in private
homes. Nellie Tweet, from Ireland, described her typical routine
when working for a West Side family: "Everything was on schedule.
Monday was wash day. Tuesday was ironing and Wednesday was kind
of pick up everything, you know. And Thursday we usually did a lot
of cooking. Friday, then, was big cleaning day: the beds had to be
changed, the rooms all vacuumed and cleaned and dusted and everything. And the kitchen had to be scrubbed and the bathroom.
Course, in between, the bathroom, the sink, and everything had to
be washed every day. But the floor, just on Friday." Nellie also answered the telephone and the door, served all the meals, and cared
for her employers' daughter when they went out.[43]

By 1920 the feminization of clerical work, which had restructured
women's work nationwide, had caught hold in Butte. In 1910 the
most common local occupations for females, following that of servant, were boardinghouse keeper, teacher, prostitute, and dressmak-

er. By 1920, however, stenographer, typist, cashier, bookkeeper, and accountant closely trailed servant and teacher. The increase in ready-to-wear clothing pushed dressmaker into thirteenth place in a table of occupations. Many girls, such as Olga Sontum, attended the Butte Business College to improve their employment opportunities. Olga's father had died when she was fourteen, and her mother did not speak English very well, so she became the head of the household. Cleaning houses after school, Olga earned $2 a week and "run home as fast as I could with it to my mother. I never thought of spending it." She soon quit public school, however, and went to the Business College, hiring on as a bookkeeper at Lutey Brothers Grocery when she was sixteen. Ann Pentilla also attended the college, hoping to achieve a better job. She worked during the day as a cashier and attended night school, finally getting a bookkeeping job at a laundry, where she eventually earned $35 for a six-day week, a far better wage than the $5 a week she had been paid clerking in Symons Department Store.[44]

Butte's female wage earners, like their male counterparts, were organized into unions that protected their interests. Saleswomen belonged to the Butte Clerks' Union, laundry workers to the Laundry Workers' Union, and teachers to the Teachers' Union. The first local of telephone operators in the United States was organized in Butte in 1902 to raise wages and reduce the twelve-hour day. In 1903 these women successfully negotiated union recognition, a nine-hour day, and a $50 per month wage. The Women's Protective Union (WPU), all female and founded during the early 1890s, originally organized boardinghouse and restaurant workers. In the twentieth century it extended its jurisdiction over janitresses, theater ushers, carhops, and cocktail waitresses. The WPU had a reputation for strictly enforcing work rules. The officers were known as implacable adversaries of employers who mistreated union members. Business agents negotiated grievances but would also take after a boss with a broomstick if he gave their "girls" a hard time.[45]

Union women worked and played together. When union meetings adjourned, groups of women went out for ice cream or to a show. In 1917 clerks from the shirtwaist department at Symons rented a box at the Empress Theater and capped the evening with dinner at the Butte Hotel. Val Webster remembered that when she worked at the Union Grill, she and two other waitresses became such fast friends that even though they worked staggered shifts they would wait for each other to finish work and then go out together—dressed alike—to dances at the Winter Garden.[46]

■ ■ ■

By the eve of World War I the contours of modern Butte were in place. Neighborhoods coalesced along lines of class and ethnicity, business and entertainment districts flourished, and ideology and custom demarcated arenas of behavior for workers and bosses, and men and women. Butte was a workers' city. Miners and the carpenters, blacksmiths, engineers, machinists, cooks, waitresses, laundresses, and boardinghouse keepers who supported their work dominated the city's work force, its streets, and its social life.

When Butte miners worked, they commanded the highest wages in the American mining industry, and mining paid well. In 1914 metal miners earned an average of $932, whereas all workers' average yearly wages were $639. For more than thirty years, an Irish union leadership, strong Irish associations like the Ancient Order of Hibernians, and Irish management of the Anaconda Company cooperated to provide steady jobs for workers and profits for ACM. During the thirty-five years from 1879 to 1914 there were no miners' strikes in the Gibraltar of Unionism.[47]

In the early 1910s the harmony between the Anaconda Company and the Butte Miners' Union began to crumble. New management practices initiated in New York took away a good deal of the control traditionally wielded by Irish shift bosses; the influx of inexperienced workers from southern and eastern Europe caused tensions underground; and a new generation of Irish workers, who looked to Ireland and to groups more radical than the BMU for political direction, created splits in Irish associations and in the union. Butte rode the wave of municipal socialist reform that propelled radicals to mayoral seats in several U.S. cities during this period. In 1911 Butte citizens elected Lewis Duncan, a socialist, as mayor. Duncan's victory polarized local politics and drove the Anaconda Company to unprecedented heights of fraud, bribery, intimidation, and violence aimed at destroying the radical movement, containing the labor movement, and gaining control of city, county, and state politics. In 1914 tensions within the BMU came to a head, and one faction dynamited the Miners' Union Hall. That outburst of violence led to the impeachment of Mayor Duncan, the imposition of martial law, and the effective end of the Miners' Union. Butte miners would work in an open shop for the next twenty years.

As war erupted in Europe in August 1914, conflict also came to Butte, where the war years were profoundly disturbing. Between

1917 and 1921 the city suffered a series of blows that strained the fabric of community. U.S. entry into the war in April 1917 prompted demonstrations against the draft, a horrific mine disaster rocked the city, a long strike taxed the resiliency of those worn down by tragedy and uncertainty, the flu epidemic decimated families who had already suffered death from war and mining accidents, and depression cloaked the city when the war was finally over. In 1920 when federal census takers canvassed Butte, only 60,313 residents remained in Silver Bow County. A remarkable exodus of nearly one-third of the metropolitan population had taken place over the course of four years, and thousands more left in 1921. A severe depression in metal markets forced the Anaconda Company to announce a complete suspension of mining as of April 1. The shutdown laid off 6,500 workers; copper production that year was a mere forty-eight million pounds, only 13 percent of 1916's output.[48]

The events of these years would affect men and women differently. Men experienced death, defeat, and a concerted attack on their primary social institution, the saloon. Women faced not only the hardships of the home front, but also new opportunities for work and achieving reforms that seemed to hold out the promise that Butte could be converted from a man's town to a more family-oriented city.

In January 1917, Benjamin B. Thayer, vice president of ACM, assessed 1916 for the *Engineering and Mining Journal*. It had been a year of "unprecedented activity." All mining companies had operated at full capacity, and even small properties, shut down prior to the outbreak of war in Europe, had resumed mining. Copper production in Montana topped 352 million pounds, valued at more than $96 million. Miners and merchants reaped the benefits of a bullish market for copper, and Thayer testified "that never in the history of Butte has there been experienced such a period of prosperity." Had he submitted a report for 1917 the tone would surely have been different. Labor strife plagued the city, and copper output had plummeted by more than seventy-five million pounds.[49]

Tragedy triggered the strike of 1917. On the night of June 8, flame from a carbide lamp ignited the oil-soaked insulation of a power cable being lowered down the Granite Mountain shaft. Fire roared down the shaft and into the connected Speculator Mine, filling it with deadly smoke and gas. Of the 167 miners killed, only two were burned; the others suffocated. In terms of lives lost, it was and still remains the worst hardrock mining disaster in American history.[50]

On June 11 the miners struck, setting off a war between a company determined to produce copper for the wartime market and a work force kindled by tragedy. A litany of grievances inspired the miners. Speed-up practices designed to get "the rock in the box," combined with an influx of immigrant miners who could not understand English, had made underground conditions more unsafe than ever. The rustling card system, a method of screening employees instituted by the Anaconda Company in 1912, was seen as un-American and undemocratic. New unions had arisen to replace the Butte Miners' Union, but the company would deal with none of them. Inflation gave the lie to so-called wartime prosperity.

In addition to direct strike action, workers pleaded with their congressional representative to intercede on their behalf with the federal government. Their representative was Jeannette Rankin, who in 1916 had become the first woman elected to the U.S. House of Representatives. Upon Rankin's election, Elizabeth Kennedy, wife of a shift boss and an influential member of many of Butte's women's clubs, wrote to congratulate her and express the hopes of many Montana women: "I am especially happy in your election because I feel that the women of Montana can depend on their woman representative to achieve legislation for their benefit, hitherto unaccomplished by men." Rankin served all Montanans, and many men wrote to express their opinions, offer advice, and seek help. But women felt a special affinity to "their representative" and wrote to her in great numbers to speak for themselves, their families, and their community.[51]

The first issue upon which women called for help was the 1917 strike. Elizabeth Kennedy, a staunch supporter of the strikers, wrote to Rankin at the behest of the strike committee, explaining their grievances. Miners demanded a federal investigation of the Speculator fire, the elimination of the rustling card system and blacklisting, and redress for the *excessive high* cost of living in this town." As Kennedy made clear, the rustling card system ranked first among miners' grievances.[52]

Instituted in December 1912, the rustling card was a permit to look for work, "to rustle a job on the hill." On the surface the system appeared innocuous. Job-seekers filled out an application with basic biographical information, including citizenship status, marital status, whether the applicant could read and write English, where his family resided, whether he had ever worked for ACM, in which mine he had worked, and the date he left that job. ACM then sent an inquiry to his last employer, guaranteeing confidentiality and asking whether the information provided was correct. If the employer verified the information and the company had no objection to the background revealed, the applicant received a card that permitted him to approach a mine superintendent or shift foreman for work.

The *Engineering and Mining Journal,* speaking for the mining companies, could not understand miners' opposition to the system and argued that "each holder of a rustling card ought to feel proud of being in the possession of such a certificate of character and merit." Although the card may indeed have started out only as a way to keep track of employees, by 1917 miners saw it as curb on their political rights. The company admitted the rustling card's role in keeping "undesirables" out of its mines. In 1917, L. O. Evans, ACM counsel, declared that it had become apparent to company officials that many radicals and members of the Industrial Workers of the World were working in the mines. In order "to do any part of its duty to the community and to itself," the company needed a mechanism for identifying and eliminating them. By "knowing its employees," the company could not only keep "undesirables" off the payroll but also deny workmen's compensation to many immigrant miners and their families. The Montana workmen's compensation bill, passed in 1915 after a long struggle, excluded alien immigrants and their families from any compensation in the case of injury or death, thus greatly reducing company expenses.[53]

The men and women who wrote to Jeannette Rankin in 1917 manifested an intense awareness of class divisions and a desperate wish to have the world outside of Butte realize their plight. People testified to ACM's control of the government, business, and the press, and to its use of the Industrial Workers of the World as a scapegoat for all the city's labor troubles—thus turning miners' real grievances into the wild ravings of unpatriotic radicals. To the laboring men and women of Butte, ACM was the foe of democracy, not the Wobblies or striking miners. And Butte, not France, was the immediate battleground in the struggle for democracy. Catherine J. Penney, married to a miner, condemned the rustling card as "a most formidable weapon for intimidation" and noted that the psychological effect of the system, combined with a captive press, meant that "thinking men and women feel their intelligence is being insulted; free press and free speech exist but in name . . . any one who dares to voice his sentiments, can and will be punished through the 'Black List.'" Penney concluded, "We want at home the real democracy that our sons are fighting for in France."[54]

The skyrocketing cost of living during wartime, aggravated by strike conditions, posed special challenges for working-class women. Ethel Yates, whose husband was a janitor for the ACM-owned Butte, Anaconda and Pacific Railway, wrote to Rankin that "we women, whose husbands are earning very very small wages are almost in despair because it is such a struggle to feed and clothe our families decently." A miner's wife who declined to sign her name claimed that the Employers' Association had ordered all retailers to stop giving credit to the strikers. Mrs. Thomas Burns seconded her, noting that "hundreds of miners familys are living from the support of the union," whose resources were rapidly diminishing. "If we are compelled to hold out much longer it will cause great suffering to the little innocent children." Mertie J. Bowen, a real estate agent for a Helena-based company, reported difficulty collecting payments due on property and noted that all the city's real estate offices experienced slow sales throughout the war years.[55]

Under such conditions it was difficult for strikers to hold firm, and throughout the fall of 1917 men trickled back to work. The *Engineering and Mining Journal* reported that the mines were operating at 70 percent of normal production by November. Still, labor remained scarce, and the *Journal* observed that for the first time employers were compelled to "hustle" for men. Striking miners, with a fine sense of irony, suggested the establishment of a rustling card system for employers. Finally, on December 20, 1917, the Metal Mine Workers' Union, the main union stepping into the breach created by the destruction of the BMU, declared the strike over.[56]

The following year was quiet, due in part to the fact that federal troops, who had arrived in Butte in August 1917 and were to remain until January 1921, continued to patrol the roads leading to the mines. In February 1918 ACM created the position of labor commissioner to handle individual grievances. The first appointee was Thomas J. Chope, a diplomatic choice because he had started out as a miner in 1903, later served as a union officer, and, as a mine foreman, had compiled one of the best safety records in the company. With the strike over, ACM made some concessions. By July 4, 1918, miners were earning $5.75 a day, a 50 cent increase from July 1917.[57]

Even with this raise, miners' wives found it hard to make ends meet. They combated the high price of goods by "rustling" coal and wood when they could, saving cash for food. Children climbed up on railway coal cars and threw handfuls of coal down to their mothers and siblings, who bagged it and dragged it home. Discarded wood from the mines was also fair game. In McQueen, where many families raised hogs, chickens, and rabbits, children trudged to the Leonard Mine with their slop buckets and called out to the miners to throw them their lunch scraps so they could feed their livestock.[58]

The one thing workers and the *Engineering and Mining Journal* agreed on was the fact that merchants were gouging consumers. The *Journal's* Butte correspondent reported that every time miners received a wage increase, "every restaurant, boarding-house keeper, lodging house, grocer, barber, laundry, and even saloons, advance their prices correspondingly, some going the raise in wages a little better." Merchants represented by the Employers' Association were the worst offenders, and miners claimed "that the mining companies, if they had the interest of their employees at heart, could prevent this graft." Miners were not the only ones who blamed the mining companies. A woman from the Associated Charities told a federal investigator that when people voted for bonds to build a city market to combat the high price of groceries, John Gillie, manager of ACM, appeared before the city council to protest this cost during wartime. Only after the spur of a state-sponsored investigation into the cost of living did the city help construct a market.[59]

In 1919 a team of state investigators documented Butte merchants' opportunism. Charles Goodenberger, manager of the Silver Bow Motor Company, unabashedly confessed to taking advantage of the wartime economy to make an excessive profit selling gasoline. When the interviewer asked him what special circumstances warranted his making an 8½ cent per gallon profit when the average was 2 cents, he answered, "Nothing at all." And when the interviewer continued, "You took advantage of the opportunity?" Goodenberger replied, "Yes and made lots of money too." Grocer E. A. Ames testified that he could buy groceries in Tacoma, ship them to Butte, and still sell them at a lower price than if he bought them from the wholesale houses in Butte. The committee also discovered that some businessmen had recorded liberty bonds as expenses to show a smaller profit.[60]

Disappointed with the actions and inaction of Butte men, the city's women decided to attack high food prices through the Butte Housewives' League. The league bypassed middlemen by arranging for farmers to ship carloads of produce to Butte and then marketed the goods directly to consumers at the railroad depot. They sold a shipment of potatoes for 75 cents per hundred pounds below the retail price and planned to do the same for butter, eggs, and poultry. The indomitable Elizabeth Kennedy was president of the league and employed the Butte Women's Council to organize women in a domestic war for food conservation and lowered prices.[61]

Two delegates from every women's club in the city made up the Women's Council, and they investigated the food distribution system in Butte. Women monitored wholesalers who apparently tried to dispose of edible food in attempts to decrease supply and drive up prices. As Kennedy explained to the Cost of Living Investigating Committee, women's watchfulness often took on dramatic aspects. One afternoon Mrs. Mazie, a member of the league, telephoned Kennedy to report that a teamster was apparently hauling a wagonload of asparagus to a hog ranch or the incinerating plant. Mrs. Mazie and a companion had spotted the load when the driver stopped for a drink in a nearby saloon. The women climbed up onto the hubs of the wagon to examine the contents and discovered that the asparagus was still good. Kennedy immediately called the city health office and asked for the use of a car. Mr. Harris, the city chemist, responded, and the two of them followed the driver for miles but did not catch up with him. Harris, presumably acting on additional information, later discovered sixty crates of asparagus at a local hog ranch, a great deal of which was indeed fit for human consumption. Kennedy and her colleagues similarly tracked crates of strawberries to the city incinerator and wagons of watermelons to the hog ranch. They complained vociferously to wholesalers and established an effective "neighborhood watch" on the waste of food.[62]

When watching proved less than effective, women employed the boycott. At a meeting of the league, women decided to boycott eggs until merchants lowered their price. Each member pledged to enroll three friends in the boycott. Women exchanged recipes for eggless pudding and entertained with eggless cake. Merchants dropped their prices to the women's satisfaction a month later but then threatened to raise the price of potatoes. In turn women promised a house-to-house campaign to boycott potatoes and began trading potatoless recipes. When wholesalers attempted to derail the city market by refusing to sell to market vendors, the league circumscribed them by patronizing mail order houses.[63]

The Butte Housewives' League was not the only women's group mobilized during the war years. America's entry into World War I infused new energy into Butte's women's voluntary associations and widened their focus of attention. Established groups embraced war work and new organizations formed with patriotic agendas. The

Women's Patriotic League of Silver Bow County, founded in April 1917, coordinated the efforts of the county's women's clubs. Associations as diverse as the Lutheran Guild, Welsh Aid Society, and Pythian Sisters devoted hours to rolling bandages and knitting socks and sweaters. The Masonic Temple and Hennessy's Department Store donated space for Red Cross work, and by November 1918 the women of Silver Bow had manufactured more than 750,000 bandages and dressings and a prodigious number of pajamas, shirts, pillows, sheets, and knitted articles. Women stopped serving refreshments at meetings in order to conserve food for the Allies, and they turned the educational segments of their meetings to wartime topics. They listened to programs on canning, victory gardens, wartime mothers, women's work in European hospitals, the history of the Red Cross, and the transportation of foodstuffs during war.[64]

Women's groups were also concerned over the apparent shifting morality that wartime conditions created. News stories such as that of Jewell LeClair, a "slender girl with the leer of the west in her eyes," who reportedly used a Red Cross uniform to gain "an intimate acquaintance with several soldiers and sailors," alarmed the Woman's Christian Temperance Union (WCTU). In addition to donating money, knit goods, and hospital supplies to the war effort, the WCTU attempted to teach young women "what harm may result from . . . seeking the company of soldiers outside of their homes." The WCTU sought to protect the moral well-being of young men as well. "Serve them chocolate instead," they advised when they discovered that $400 of the $420 Butte women had raised and donated to enlistees from Butte at Camp Lewis, Washington, had been spent on tobacco. In each of the thousands of comfort bags sent to Montana soldiers, WCTU members included a Testament and a "packet of good temperance literature." Other women's groups joined the WCTU in petitioning the city council—to no avail—to close saloons while soldiers embarked for the war.[65]

When the call for Red Cross workers went out, a group of African American women organized their own unit and named it after a member of Butte's black community, Dr. Frank Pearl, who was serving overseas. After demobilization the group decided to continue meeting as the Pearl Social Club. Their purely social agenda was short-lived, however. Like black women's clubs across the country, the Pearl Club worked to increase respect for African American women and improve conditions for all blacks in Butte. In 1920 it joined the National Association of Colored Women, and in 1921 it invited Montana's other African American women's clubs to form a state federation. Drawing upon the theme "Lifting as We Climb," the Pearl Club called upon these women to unite in "an organization to do our part in solving the problems that confront us as a race." Launched under the motto "Unity and Perseverance," the Montana State Federation of Negro Women's Clubs proceeded to study topics such as "The Negro Woman in Business and Industry," "Interracial Understanding," "Fear," and "The Achievement of the Negro." In addition to analyzing the problems African Americans faced in Montana, the federation moved to solve them. It sponsored antidiscrimination legislation, attacked segregation in Montana communities, and supported the activities of the NAACP.[66]

While many Butte women served on the home front as volunteers, others were catapulted into men's jobs during the war years—at least temporarily. These positions gave them a basis for comparison, and traditional women's work did not fare well. Monitoring the status of women during the war, the WCTU found that Montana women were doing "all sort of work," farming, driving trucks and streetcars, and working for the railroad. Overall, they reported, "'Uncle Sam' makes a good boss." Anna Whitney, hired by the Northern Pacific Railway as a car cleaner, told an interviewer that she preferred the work to domestic service: "It pays considerably more money and I am more independent. I may go home with a smudgy face, but that's easily washed off. The girl who works all hours for a private family cannot say her soul is her own. When I'm through with work, I'm absolutely my own boss."

Anna Whitney, not troubled by the male antecedents of her work, wore overalls on the job and tried to persuade her fellow workers to turn in their skirts for more practical clothing. But other car cleaners laid claim to their new jobs by keeping them in a traditionally female frame of reference. Lillie Wilson declared that "engine wiping is like house cleaning and a man doesn't know anything about it. . . . We may not be able to 'doll up' and look as nice as the girls who work at less strenuous trades, but we make enough to outdress them on occasion if we want to." The running of elevators also fell to feminine hands during the war. The *Anaconda Standard* judged woman operators far superior to typical "elevator boys" who slid into the basement for cigarettes and "indulged in familiarities" with patrons. Well-behaved "elevator girls" also gave Butte a chance to snub its nose at New York, where female operators were reported to be habitual gum-chewers and outrageous flirts.[67]

Women's financial acumen impressed Butte's business community. By 1920 Butte banks had launched a campaign to encourage women to open accounts, reportedly because during the war the "eyes of bank officials were opened . . . to the level-headed manner in which the average woman conducts her business affairs." Women in business offices found themselves taking on new duties and responsibilities as their male supervisors went off to war. Beatrice Bray, bookkeeper and stenographer for the real estate firm Reynolds and Sypher, single-handedly kept the business going during the war. Even after the armistice, when she left for a better position, she lent her support to the spunky young woman who succeeded her. Bray admired her successor for standing up to the men in the office who called her a "contrary little cuss" when she refused to work overtime without pay.[68]

Bray's compatriot was one of a long string of young Butte women who defended their rights in the workplace. In 1881 the paper commented that Butte waiting girls "often exhibit plucky spunk or what is denominated and better understood as 'sand.'" An incident in one of the city's cafes prompted the paper's remarks. When a waitress refused to perform a task outside her regular duties and her boss cursed her, she smashed his nose with a syrup pitcher and then, for good measure, threw a plate in his face. The fact that women workers had organizations behind them undoubtedly encouraged their assertiveness.[69]

Young business women did not have a union, but in December 1920 they formed a club to support their interests. Fifty young women met at the Chamber of Commerce to organize a Business Girl's club to strengthen "ties of social intercourse among the girls of the commercial world." Club members' self-image changed over the years, as reflected in modifications of the organization's name. First, they became the Women's Commercial Club, and in 1925 the Professional and Business Women's Club, which eventually affiliated with the national organization of Business and Professional Women.[70]

Women fought the company, merchants, and unfair employers to protect themselves and their families during the war. But in the autumn of 1918 a deadly foe against which women had no defense attacked the mining city. The influenza pandemic of 1918 struck that season, peaking in October, when city health officials reported 3,500 cases. Schools closed and were turned into hospitals, and teachers served as nurses. A quarantine shut down saloons, theaters, bowling alleys, and pool rooms. Ore production fell because of the number of miners incapacitated by the virus. Hundreds died. Beatrice Bray kept her boss apprised of the situation through her letters. On October 29 she reported that twenty-three people had died the previous day, "the highest toll of a day in Butte yet. . . . hospitals are full, so full, in fact, that one poor woman and her four children had to be cared for at the jail until there was room in a ward somewhere . . . it takes about a page for funeral notices now." The *Great Falls Tribune* reported that Butte "undertakers no longer garage their 'dead wagons,' but leave them in the street as calls are so frequent."[71]

On November 8 the County Board of Health lifted the quarantine, judging that the worst of the epidemic was over. Three days later, on November 11, the mine whistles signaled the armistice, and joyful hordes packed the streets to celebrate. By November 14 the epidemic was raging again, but the city council and mayor defied the Health Board's orders to close all schools, churches, businesses, and amusements. Bray and others attributed officials' defiance to the lobbying of saloon keepers. The influenza epidemic killed more than 640 people in Silver Bow County, nearly 1 percent of the county population. By comparison, 681 Montanans were either killed in action or died from war wounds in World War I. More than a third of the flu-related deaths in Montana—one of the hardest-hit states in the nation—occurred in Silver Bow County.[72]

▪ ▪ ▪

Butte's celebration of the armistice was short-lived. Peace meant a drop in the demand for copper, and by the end of 1918 several mines had closed. Shorty Felt, a mucker who had been too old to join the service and had worked in Butte throughout the war, recorded the first months of 1919 in his diary. Shorty had been mucking at the Berkeley Mine since May 1918. On January 4, 1919, a sign posted in the timekeeper's office announced a reduction in hours. "It is fierce," wrote Shorty, "how the company are laying off men and closing down the mines . . . I thought we was going to have all kinds of prosperity after the war, but it dont look much like it." The mines laid off single men first, preserving jobs for returning veterans and married men, but even veterans found it tough to get work. When Preston Ramsey came back to Butte he "couldn't buy a job in this town. The place was closed down tighter than hell." Finally, on January 24, Shorty, too, was let go. At first he tried to sleep late and enjoy his "involuntary vacation," but he met with "poor success." The next few months were a nightmare of drinking, rustling, and intermittent work; the diary breaks off abruptly on June 24.[73]

On February 6, 1919, the day shipyard workers initiated the Seattle General Strike, ACM announced a dollar a day reduction in wages, and five other mining companies followed suit. The following day miners began to walk off the job, but the strike folded in less than two weeks. Labor relations remained tense throughout 1919. However, the next major confrontation did not occur until the following year, when the Metal Mine Workers' Union and the Industrial Workers of the World called for another strike on April 19, 1920. Again they demanded a raise in wages and abolition of the rustling card. How the melee began remains confused, but on April 21 mine guards on the Anaconda Road opened fire on pickets, killing one man and wounding sixteen others. All were shot in the back as they fled, seeking to escape the unexpected attack. No one was arrested. In the case of Tom Manning, the murdered miner, the coroner's jury—loaded with allies of the ACM—brought in the verdict that Manning had died "from the effects of a wound caused by a .32–caliber bullet fired from a pistol in the hands of some person to this jury unknown." The strike collapsed three weeks later with no gains for the workers and strict enforcement of a new blacklist. The Anaconda Road massacre marked the last direct battle between the company and the miners until 1934, when the National Recovery Act gave the Butte Miners' Union the outside backing it needed to reorganize.[74]

Thus, by 1920 miners, the single largest occupational group in Butte, were defeated, demoralized, and working under an open shop. The company had crushed every effort to organize since the destruction of the BMU in 1914. The hated rustling card was still in effect, and in the wake of the events of 1920 the company added new questions to test workers' sympathies toward the IWW. The Anaconda Road massacre symbolized the consolidation of ACM power. Commentators in the 1920s described the "copper collar" that encircled Butte: "Like the Lord God Almighty in His universe, the Anaconda Copper Mining Company is everywhere. It is all, and in all. Its titular Mercy Seat is on the sixth floor of the Hennessy Building at the intersection of Main and Granite streets, but it is enthroned in the heart, brain and wallet of every man and woman from Nine-Mile to Stringtown, from the Main Range to Whisky Gulch."[75]

As the 1920s began, Butte was a different city from the prewar metropolis. Anaconda's efforts to weed out "radicals" through the use of the rustling card and the blacklist focused upon single, transient workers, "giving way to the married or those with dependents, thus leaving the more conservative of the miners." What company policy did not achieve, depression did.[76]

For Butte men, the legacy of the war years was a smaller work force, chastened by defeats at the hands of ACM, cynical about the meaning of democracy, a bit more cautious, and a little less confident about the certainty of a prosperous future. Montana men had rallied to the call to arms and were proud of their participation in the Great War, but there, too, patriotism, had cost dearly. Montana exceeded the rest of the nation in enlistment rates and draft quotas for the armed services. In part this was enthusiasm; nearly twelve thousand Montanans enlisted. But confusion over Montana population estimates set disproportionately high draft quotas, and nearly twenty-eight thousand more men were compelled to serve. Montana thus sent nearly forty thousand men, almost 10 percent of its population to war. Idaho, with a population roughly similar, sent half that number.[77]

By contrast, Butte's female work force was slightly larger, and although dominated by maids, waitresses, and other service workers, it had also been infused with the energy of women who had stepped into men's shoes during the war. Women did not keep nontraditional jobs after the armistice, and Butte, remaining a mining town, never offered much more than service work for women. Nonetheless, women wageworkers' wartime experiences had forced them to become more worldly, more assertive, and more comfortable in the public arena. Following a 1920 strike by the Women's Protective Union, every cafe and restaurant in the city signed a union contract. Women earned $17 to $18 a week, certainly less than most men's wages but "significantly above the $14 a week estimated as the necessary minimum for a single woman." Women who earned wages were joined by housewives who had enlisted in war work and the food conservation movement. Both groups took heart from Jeannette Rankin, who became an example of what women could achieve and a public voice for their concerns. In the postwar years women would continue to claim greater public territory in the city.[78]

After 1920 Butte struggled to redefine its character. The cycle of boom and bust would continue, and with it a feeling of impermanence that encouraged a tendency to live for the day. But the city had to deal with the social and psychological effects of the war years. Butte had a solid history as a single-man's town—shaped by male workers, male entertainments, and male politics. But demography and changes in gender roles catalyzed by the events of the war years pushed against that tradition. More and more, families characterized Butte's population, and women more assertively sought to shape the community.

During the war years public attention was not focused on recreation and leisure, but after 1920 many of the wrangles over how to recreate Butte centered on those issues. Between 1920 and 1940 some men and some women, informally and in organized ways, sought to change wide-open Butte. Supporters of Prohibition faced a losing battle against alcohol, but Prohibition did encourage more heterosocial habits of drink and eroded the male monopoly on public drinking. Young women, partaking of the commercial pleasures of urban life, forced a redefinition of respectability. Although men often blamed women for changes in previously all-male arenas of leisure, the company also began programs to encourage a greater integration of families into Butte's recreational life. Women's clubs and fraternal organizations attempted to provide wholesome recreation for men, women, and children, in contrast to Butte's more typical pleasures, which many felt crossed the line into vice. During the 1930s New Dealers hoped to institutionalize public recreation. The war years sobered Butte, and in the following two decades its residents would seek to reconcile the city's raucous past with the needs of a changing population and a seemingly less optimistic future.

NOTES

1. Hutchens, *One Man's Montana*, 172–77.

2. Howard, "Boisterous Butte," 316.

3. In the late 1970s before underground mining ceased in Butte, the Hill produced—in 1984 dollars—more than $22 billion worth of copper, silver, and gold. On Butte geology, see McClernan, "Sixty Million Years of History."

4. On the holdings of Anaconda, and for a variety of interpretations of the War of the Copper Kings and early Butte history, see "The Top 100 Industrials"; Marcosson, *Anaconda*; McNelis, *Copper King at War*; Glasscock, *The War of the Copper Kings*; Malone, *Battle for Butte*. Wheeler is quoted in Wheeler, *Yankee from the West*, 77.

5. Malone, *Battle for Butte*, 15–17.

6. Chadwick, "Montana's Silver Mining Era"; *Geologic Atlas of the Rocky Mountain Region*, 304–5; Federal Writers' Project of the Work Projects Administration, *Montana*, 139.

7. Malone, *Battle for Butte*, 28; *Official Guide of the Railways*, June 1916, 629, 640–41, 713, 733, 796.

8. Foy and Harlow, *Clowning Through Life*, 184–85. Clark is quoted in Bigart, *Montana*, 80; Ann Pentilla, interview by Ray Calkins and Caroline Smithson, Butte, 27 April 1979, 43–44; *Butte Miner* quoted in Wyman, *Hard Rock Epic*, 16.

9. Atherton, *Perch of the Devil*, 57.

10. Carden, "A Walk from 228 S. Gaylord Street," 8; Swett, *Montana's Trolleys-II*, 23.

11. *Butte City Directory*, 1917, 1918. On the abandonment of Butte's street railway system, see Myers, "The Butte Rail Connection," 36; and Kwitny, "The Great Transportation Conspiracy," 20. M. H. Coyne to Jeannette Rankin (hereafter cited as JR), 5 May 1917, Jeannette Rankin Papers (hereafter cited as JR Papers), box 11, file 3, Montana Historical Society Archives (hereafter cited as MHSA).

12. Sanborn Map Company, *Insurance Maps of Butte, Montana*, 1900, 1916.

13. On the development of Butte's labor movement, see Frisch, "The 'Gibraltar of Unionism.'"

14. *Butte City Directory*, 1917.

15. Kemper, "Butte," 14–15.

16. In this analysis the mountain states are Arizona, Colorado, Idaho, Montana, Wyoming, Nevada, New Mexico, and Utah.

17. *Anaconda Standard*, 22 January 1920, 17; Winsberg, "European Immigration to the Mountain States."

18. Winsberg, "European Immigration to the Mountain States," 105; Emmons, *Butte Irish*, 13; U.S. Department of the Interior, Census Office, *Abstract of the Twelfth Census*, 106; U.S. Department of Commerce, Bureau of the Census, *Thirteenth Census*, 2:1158; U.S. Department of Commerce, Bureau of the Census, *Fourteenth Census*, 3:586. All census statistics cited in the Census Bureau's published reports refer to the city of Butte; figures were not given for Silver Bow County. In 1920 census supervisor James H. Faulds complimented Butte enumerators but said, "They have experienced more difficulty in securing the necessary information in Butte, owing to the attitude adopted by a number of landladies and landlords, who have refused to give them any information whatever. Butte is the worst place I have had in this respect." *Anaconda Standard*, 23 January 1920, 1.

19. U.S. Department of the Interior, Census Office, *Abstract of the Twelfth Census*, 109; U.S. Department of Commerce, Bureau of the Census, *Thirteenth Census*, 2:1147, 1150; U.S. Department of Commerce, Bureau of the Census, *Abstract of the Fourteenth Census*, 131, 175, 258; U.S. Department of Commerce, Bureau of the Census, *Fifteenth Census*, 3, pt. 2: 25, 30. Figures on marital status refer only to Butte city; marital statistics are not available for the county population, except for 1930, when 42 percent of the men in the county were also listed as single.

20. On housing in Butte and neighborhoods' social composition, see Murphy, "Report on a Survey of Historic Architecture on Butte's West Side"; and Martin and Shovers, "Butte, Montana." Mary Brennan Clapp's remarks are found in the *Anaconda Standard*, 4 February 1923, pt. 2, 1.

21. McHugh, "Gulch and I," 4, 15; Catherine Hoy, interview by Ray Calkins and Caroline Smithson, Butte, 11 May 1979, 20–21.

22. Sanborn Map Company, *Insurance Maps of Butte, Montana,* 1916; Ostberg, "Sketches of Old Butte," 114. For other descriptions of the Cabbage Patch, see *Montana Standard,* 21 April 1940, 1, 10; and Writers' Program, Work Projects Administration, *Copper Camp,* 267–71.

23. John Onkalo, interview by Ray Calkins, Butte, February 1980, 7; Hoy interview, 20–21; Edward Sullivan, interview by Laurie Mercier, Butte, 25 February, 10 March 1982; *Anaconda Standard,* 6 April 1902, 8.

24. Pentilla interview, 16–17; *Montana Standard,* 28 August 1977, n.p.

25. *Butte Evening News,* 24 July 1910, 9, 31 July 1910, 9; Pentilla interview, 15–16, 33–34; *Anaconda Standard,* 15 February 1920, 5; unreferenced clipping, MHSL vertical file. Butte was not unique among western mining towns in its discrimination against Slavic immigrants. See, for comparison, Kosso, "Yugoslavs in Nevada."

26. *Montana Standard,* 29 July 1973, 17, 20 November 1978, 1.

27. Murel L. Roberts, interview by Ray Calkins, Butte, 8 August 1980, 23; "Observing Thirty Years with the Present Butte Country Club House," 18 August 1945, 1–3. For development of the Flat, see Ore, "Suburban Schools in Butte, Montana."

28. Carden, "A Walk from S. Gaylord Street," 17–18.

29. McHugh, "Gulch and I," 2; Hoy interview, 24–28; Olga Sontum, interview by Ray Calkins, Butte, February 1980, 11, 15. This attitude of not outspending one's peers reflects the early-nineteenth-century "traditional" culture that Gordon and McArthur describe in "American Women and Domestic Consumption" and suggests its persistence in twentieth-century working-class culture.

30. Wyman, *Hard Rock Epic,* 14; Shovers, "Miners, Managers, and Machines," 58.

31. U.S. Department of Commerce, Bureau of Mines, *Review of Safety and Health,* 15.

32. Shovers, "Miners, Managers, and Machines," 24, 43; Helen Shute Raymond, interview by Laurie Mercier, Butte, 9 October 1981.

33. U.S. Department of Commerce, Bureau of Mines, *Review of Safety and Health,* 24; Calkins, comp., *Looking Back from the Hill,* 32.

34. On the background of miners, see Emmons, *Butte Irish;* Shovers, "Miners, Managers, and Machines," 35–37.

35. Onkalo interview, 2; Clarence Miller, interview by Ray Calkins, Butte, 13 June 1980, 16.

36. Hanford Toppari, interview by Ray Calkins, Butte, 1 May 1980, 2, 7; Braley, *Songs of the Workaday World,* 119–20; Shovers, "Miners, Managers, and Machines," 17, 21–22. Andrew "Shorty" Felt's diary records how the pace of work differed from day to day, depending on where in the mine a miner worked and how frequently bosses visited. A copy of the diary is in the BSBA and chronicles about six months in 1919.

37. On technological changes in hardrock mining, see Shovers, "Miners, Managers, and Machines"; Wyman, *Hard Rock Epic;* and Brown, *Hard-*

Rock Miners. Amy Lasatee to JR, 29 July 1917, JR Papers, box 2, file 5, MHSA; Elizabeth Kennedy to JR, 10 July 1917, JR Papers, box 1, file 8, MHSA.

38. Jim Harrington compiled data on death caused by mine accidents from Butte mortuary records, coroner's reports, and Bureau of Labor Statistics reports. My thanks to him for sharing his research with me. Shovers, "Miners, Managers, and Machines," 31, 73–77; McHugh, "The Gulch and I," 4; Butte City Health Department, "Report of the Health Officer, May 1914"; U.S. Department of Commerce, Bureau of Mines, *Review of Safety and Health,* 14–15. On the dangers of copper mining, see Lankton, *Cradle to Grave.* The following works discuss the efforts by miners' organizations and reformers to recognize silicosis, establish the links between it and tuberculosis, and provide appropriate treatment: Price, *Fighting Tuberculosis;* Derickson, *Workers' Health, Workers' Democracy;* Derickson, "Industrial Refugees"; Rosner and Markowitz, *Deadly Dust.*

39. U.S. Department of Commerce, Bureau of Mines, *Review of Safety and Health,* III-V, 6, 8; Shovers, "Miners, Managers, and Machines," 34, 79, 105; Victor Giuseppe Segna and Louise Zanchi, interview by Russ Magnaghi, Butte, 3 May 1983.

40. Dorothy A. Martin, interview by Mary Murphy, Butte, 23 May 1988, 36. The persistence of gold-seeking by industrial workers is dramatized in Dallas, *Buster Midnight's Cafe.*

41. Pentilla interview, 10. John Cavanaugh, interview by Ray Calkins, Butte, May-June 1980, 2–6, 27. See Murphy, "Women's Work in a Man's World," for a discussion of men's and women's occupations in Butte. National figures are found in Amott and Matthaei, *Race, Gender, and Work,* 305; and U.S. Department of Commerce, Bureau of the Census, *Fourteenth Census,* 4:247.

42. On women's work in western cities, see Locke, "Out of the Shadows." For a discussion of women's work in Pittsburgh, see Kleinberg, *The Shadow of the Mills,* 144–55. See also McHugh, "The Gulch and I," 8; Carden, "Come Wander Back with Me," 28–29.

43. U.S. Department of Commerce, Bureau of the Census, *Thirteenth Census,* 4:214–18; U.S. Department of Commerce, Bureau of the Census, *Fourteenth Census,* 4:246–51; Nellie Tweet, interview by Claudia Claque Tweet, Butte, 24 July 1982.

44. U.S. Department of Commerce, Bureau of the Census, *Thirteenth Census,* 4:214–18; U.S. Department of Commerce, Bureau of the Census, *Fourteenth Census,* 4:246–51; Sontum interview, 4–5, 13, 17; Pentilla interview, 3, 13.

45. On the telephone operators union, see Norwood, *Labor's Flaming Youth.* On the Women's Protective Union, see Val Webster, interview by Mary Murphy, Butte, 24 February 1980; Blanche Copenhaver, interview by Mary Murphy, Butte, 21 February 1980; Aili Goldberg, interview by Mary Murphy, Butte, 29 February 1980; and Cobble, *Dishing It Out.*

46. *Anaconda Standard,* 14 January 1917, sec. 2, 8; Webster interview, 8–9.

47. Wage statistics are in U. S. Department of Commerce, Bureau of the Census, *Historical Statistics of the United States,* part 1. On Butte's labor history up to 1920, see Emmons, *Butte Irish;* Calvert, *The Gibraltar;* Frisch, "'The Gibraltar of Unionism'"; Gutfeld, "The Murder of Frank Little"; Gutfeld, "The Speculator Disaster in 1917"; and Gutfeld, *Montana's Agony.*

48. *Anaconda Standard,* 30 March 1921, 1; Department of Agriculture, Labor and Industry, *Montana Resources and Opportunities Edition* 3 (August 1928): 182.

49. *Engineering and Mining Journal,* 6 January 1917, 12 (hereafter cited as *EMJ*); Department of Agriculture, Labor and Industry, *Montana Resources and Opportunities Edition* 3 (August 1928): 182.

50. On the Speculator fire, see Department of the Interior, Bureau of Mines, *Lessons from the Granite Mountain Shaft Fire, Butte.* Statistics on mine disasters are found in Department of the Interior, Bureau of Mines, *Major Disasters at Metal and Nonmetal Mines.* The number of men killed in the Speculator fire is reported differently in a variety of sources. I am using the figure, 167, calculated by Jim Harrington from his extensive review of sources, including death certificates, mortuary records, newspaper accounts and obituaries, and coroner's reports.

51. Josephson, *Jeannette Rankin;* Elizabeth Kennedy to JR, 15 November 1916, JR Papers, box 3, file 5, MHSA; also see Anna L. Rogers to JR, 3 August 1917, JR Papers, box 1, file 9, MHSA.

52. Kennedy to JR, 23 June 1917, JR Papers, box 1, file 8, MHSA.

53. Evans is quoted in *EMJ,* 15 September 1917, 466. Also see Brissenden, "The Butte Miners and the Rustling Card," 764, 772; and Merz, "The Issue in Butte." On the fight for worker's compensation in Montana, see Shovers, "Miners, Managers, and Machines."

54. Affidavit, Catherine J. Penney, n.d., Montana Attorney General Records 1893–1969 (hereafter cited as Atty Gen Records), box 7, file 8, MHSA. Also see Susie Yundel to JR, 14 June 1917, JR Papers, box 2, file 7, MHSA; T. E. Warner to JR, 10 September 1917, JR Papers, box 1, file 10, MHSA; and Leon P. Gratiot to JR, 29 August 1917, JR Papers, box 1, file 9, MHSA. On Anaconda ownership of the press, see McNay, Jr., "Breaking the Copper Collar."

55. Ethel Yates to JR, 20 June 1917, JR Papers, box 2, file 7, MHSA; "A Miners Wife" to JR, 3 September 1917, and Mrs. Thomas Burns to JR, 29 August 1917, JR Papers, box 1, file 10, MHSA; Mertie J. Bowen to Beattie Co., 2 June 1917, 3 July 1917, 1 August 1917, 1 August 1918, 4 April 1919, E. W. and G. D. Beattie Records, 1872–1935, MHSA.

56. *EMJ,* 3 November 1917, 813; Calvert, *The Gibraltar,* 110.

57. Calvert, *The Gibraltar,* 113; *EMJ,* 9 February 1918, 305, 16 March 1918, 529, 18 May 1918, 918; Brissenden, "The Butte Miners and the Rustling Card," 772; Frederick Laist to B. Butler, 17 July 1918, Anaconda

Copper Mining Company Records, 1876–1974 (hereafter cited as ACMCo Records), box 370, file 2, MHSA; *EMJ*, 28 July 1917, 185.

58. Hoy interview, 6; Pentilla interview, 1–2, 25–26; *Montana Standard*, 29 July 1973, 17.

59. *EMJ*, 29 September 1917, 577; unsigned letter to Mr. Barker, 1918, Atty Gen Records, box 7, file 8, MHSA.

60. "Report on the High Cost of Living," 160–61, 1041; *Anaconda Standard*, 25 July 1919, 1.

61. *Anaconda Standard*, 1 January 1917, 7 and 18 January 1917, 14. For a comparative look at consumer agitation during this period, see Frank, *Purchasing Power;* and Frank, "'Food Wins All Struggles.'"

62. "Report on the High Cost of Living," 1238–39.

63. *Butte Daily Bulletin*, 3 January 1920, 1–2, 23 January 1920, 6, 7 February 1920, 6, 8 April 1920, 1, 9 April 1920, 1.

64. American Legion, *Silver Bow County in the World War*, 64, 66. The minutes of the Marian White Arts and Craft Club reveal that war work or topics related to it occupied some of every meeting between 3 May 1917 and 3 October 1918. Marian White Arts and Crafts Club Records, BSBA. Also see Butte Woman's Club Yearbook, 1918–19, Woman's Club of Butte, Montana, Yearbooks, 1901–23, MHSA. On women's war work in neighboring states, see Murphy, "'If Only I Shall Have the Right Stuff'"; and Ruckman, "'Knit, Knit, and Then Knit.'"

65. *Butte Miner*, 25 December 1918, 3; *Woman's Voice* 4 (July 1917): 1, 5 (January 1918): 4, and "Report of the Thirty-fifth Annual Meeting of WCTU," 16.

66. *Proceedings of First Session of the Montana State Federation of Negro Women's Clubs*, 22, 3; programs for 1923, 1938, 1940 conventions, Montana Federation of Colored Women Records, 1921–78, MHSA; Montana Federation of Colored Women, Historian's Reports, 1922–56. The historians' reports are in the possession of Lucille Thompson of Bozeman, Montana. My thanks to her for sharing them with me. See also *Club Histories District II: Montana Federation of Women's Clubs*, 1964; and Lena Brown Slauson, interview by Mary Murphy, Butte, 2 December 1987.

There is as yet no body of work relating to black women's clubs comparable to that documenting white women's clubs. Lerner's "Early Community Work of Black Club Women" appeared in 1974, and other scholars have begun to address this lacuna. See, for example, Brady, "Kansas Federation of Colored Women's Clubs, 1900–1930"; Dickson, "Toward a Broader Angle of Vision"; and Neverdon-Morton, *Afro-American Women of the South.*

67. *Woman's Voice* 6 (December 1918): 3; *Anaconda Standard*, 7 September 1919, sec. 2, 1.

68. *Butte Miner*, 12 December 1920, 6; Beatrice Bray to George Sypher, 23 November 1918, 9 June 1919, Beatrice Bray Papers, WMM.

69. *Daily Miner*, 15 March 1881, 3.

70. *Butte Miner,* 4 December 1920, 3 and 19 September 1925, 5.

71. George Jackson to L. A. Leskey, 21 November 1918, Jackson to Benton Welty, 2 November 1918, Jackson to Theodore P. Nickson, April 1918, all in ACMCo Records, box 348, file 9, MHSA; American Legion, *Silver Bow County in the War,* 64; Lillian Beamish, interview by Laurie Mercier, Thompson Falls, 29 July 1982, and Beatrice Bray to George Sypher, 29 October 1918, 4 November 1918, 9 November 1918, "Thanksgiving," and 23 November 1918, all in Beatrice Bray Papers, WMM. The *Great Falls Tribune* is quoted in Mullen and Nelson, "Montanans and 'The Most Peculiar Disease,'" 55.

72. Beatrice Bray to George Sypher, 14 November 1918, Beatrice Bray Papers, WMM; Minton, "Population Control"; Shore, comp., *Montana in the Wars,* 69.

73. Andrew "Shorty" Felt diary; Preston K. Ramsey, interview by Ray Calkins, Butte, 26 March 1979, 11.

74. On the Anaconda Road massacre, see Calvert, *The Gibraltar,* 117–23; Walter, "Who Murdered Tom Manning?"; Gutfeld, *Montana's Agony,* 78–79; and Shutey, "The Butte Labor Strike of 1920."

75. O'Dane [Reuben Maury], "Hymn to an Oasis," 195.

76. *EMJ,* 12 July 1919, 69.

77. There is disagreement over the exact number of enlistees and draftees. See Malone, Roeder, and Lang, *Montana,* 268–69; American Legion, *Silver Bow County in the War;* Shore, *Montana in the Wars,* 69; Montana News Association insert, 31 October 1918. The American Legion estimated that 4,624 men and women from Silver Bow County served in some capacity.

78. Cobble, *Dishing It Out,* 69, 118.

2

Habits of Drink

The bottles consumed in Butte on a week-end, when empty would build a stairway from the top of its highest peak to the utmost depths of hell. —BILLY SUNDAY

Late one evening in 1922, as federal prohibition officer Ben Holter drove along Nettie Street in Butte, his car broke down. He asked to use a telephone at a nearby house, but his attention quickly shifted from the stranded car to "demon rum." The woman who answered his knock, Maud Vogen, aroused Holter's suspicions when she denied having a telephone, although one sat in plain view. Returning a short time later, accompanied by two police officers, Holter's hunch paid off—they found Vogen and another woman tending a twenty-gallon still and a quantity of whiskey and mash. A few days after Vogen's arrest, police apprehended her husband Andrew, who was living at another address, on the assumption that he had been in charge of the bootleg operation. Subsequent investigation, however, revealed that Maud and Andrew Vogen had not been living together as husband and wife for some time. Maud Vogen was "in sole charge" of the still, and the woman with her at the time of her arrest was her mother.[1]

In the 1920s Butte women made, sold, and drank liquor in unprecedented fashion. Decades later a Butte woman recalled the many evenings she donned her flapper finery and headed to the dance halls, where she and her friends shimmied to jazz tunes and slipped outside to share a pint of moonshine. In 1929 Butte judge Dan Shea proposed a city ordinance calling for police matrons in all the city's dance halls, his action prompted by the number of women carrying whiskey flasks into the popular night spots.[2]

Until the advent of Prohibition, drinking in Butte was governed by clearly defined and understood social rules. Saloons were male preserves, and they reflected the ethnic and occupational strata of the community. Any woman who drank in a saloon was assumed to be a prostitute at worst, "loose" at best. When reputable women drank, they did so at home. Prohibition rattled these traditional patterns. It curbed some drinking, but more significantly it changed the drinking habits of youth and women. Blatant flouting of the law during Prohibition created new social spaces for drinking, and women began stepping up to the bar along with men, albeit in speakeasies and night clubs rather than in the old corner saloons. Prohibition accelerated the advent of heterosocial night life as new watering holes welcomed young couples and groups of women as well as men.

Prohibition also allowed ethnic groups and women to capitalize on the underground economy by launching new businesses in the manufacturing and sale of liquor. Women cooked liquor on the kitchen stove to supplement family incomes. Husbands and wives running blind pigs, moonshine joints, and "home speaks" competed with saloons hastily converted into soft drink parlors. A few women operated profitable roadhouses. In the 1920s judges and juries, whose previous contact with female criminals had been almost exclusively with prostitutes, were confounded by grey-haired mothers appearing in their courts on bootlegging charges. In all aspects of the liquor business, women moved into spaces that had once been reserved exclusively for men. Prohibition allowed women to rewrite the script of acceptable public behavior and transform one arena of commercial leisure bounded by rigid gender roles.

Drinking in the late nineteenth and early twentieth centuries was one of the most gender-segregated activities in the United States. No one denied that women drank. Some researchers estimated that women comprised between one-tenth and one-third of problem drinkers during the period. As saloons became more popular, however, men began to drink in public, commercial arenas, whereas women were relegated to drinking at home. Increases in working-class income and free time, coupled with a search for relief from the monotony of ever more regimented work, led to the growth of public saloons for male workers. More and more frequently, men went "out" instead of patronizing "kitchen grog shops," traditionally operated by women. Women, meanwhile, stayed at home, losing both the income from their small businesses and the companionship of husbands and male neighbors. Thus, social drinking became divided by gender. Even in Butte, the wide-open town of the northern Rockies, change awaited Prohibition.[3]

■ ■ ■

When people described Butte as a wide-open town, they meant that a man could buy a drink, place a bet, or visit a prostitute at any hour of the day or night without worrying about being arrested. It is doubtful that the majority of the population ever approved of prostitution, and many had reservations about gambling. Drinking, however, was such an accepted institution that it took a national movement to present any challenge to its dominion. As it happened, Prohibition's effects in Butte were quite different from the designers' intent.

Montanans voted on statewide prohibition in November 1916. Most neighboring states had already gone dry. The referendum passed with a comfortable margin of 58 percent of the vote, only three urban counties dissenting: Deer Lodge, the site of the smelter city Anaconda; Lewis and Clark, home of Helena, the state capital; and Silver Bow. In fact, Silver Bow County neatly reversed the statewide referendum, with 58 percent of its voters opposing the measure, the largest vote against Prohibition in the state. The real strength of the prohibition movement rested in the rural counties, several of which passed the referendum by 60 to 70 percent. Silver Bow County's vote against Prohibition was hardly surprising. Butte was the largest city in the state, and drinking was an integral part of its male-dominated, immigrant culture. At the time of the referendum Silver Bow County had three breweries and more than 250 saloons. In 1915 the county had collected $227,904 in property taxes and license fees from saloons, 84 percent of the amount it collected from the county's largest taxpayer, the Anaconda Company.[4]

Saloons were endemic to the urban culture of the nineteenth and early twentieth centuries as centers of male conviviality; on the mining frontier they were multifunctional institutions. Often the first nonresidential buildings constructed, saloons predated fraternal lodge halls, hotels, churches, schools, and city halls. Men used them as banks, employment agencies, and post offices. One of the most striking examples of saloons' chameleonlike quality was Denver's Apollo Hall. Opened in June 1859 as a saloon and billiard parlor, two months later it debuted as a hotel, and the following month there was a grand opening ball, with dancing and five-dollar dinners. In October it became Denver's first theater, and on Sundays it sheltered churchless Presbyterians. In 1860 Denverites met there to draft the municipal constitution for the town government.[5]

As other urban institutions developed, most saloons shed their many skins and returned to their original form as places where men drank, talked, and argued. However, in newly minted western cities saloons were more likely to accommodate billiards, gambling, and prostitution than were more strictly regulated eastern taverns. Saloons in poor and immigrant neighborhoods often continued to hold workers' savings in their safes, to distribute foreign-language newspapers, and to let people from the neighborhood use their toilets. One saloon in Butte, known as a hobo retreat, served only beer and whiskey, always had a pot of stew on the stove, was festooned with clothes drying after a wash in back-room tubs, and served at night as a flophouse.[6]

Despite their many community functions, western saloons were first and foremost places for men to drink and socialize. A cross-cultural study of North American and Argentine frontier saloons referred to both as "theaters of excessive machismo." On their stages men played out ritualized roles of masculine culture: camaraderie and conflict, communality and competition. The denouement was often violence. Strong cultural links between manliness and drinking existed in both societies, as evinced in nineteenth-century Idaho, where a man was scarcely able to do business if he was "a lemonade son of a bitch."[7]

Taking a drink was also a public proclamation of a boy's entry to manhood. In his autobiographical novel *Singermann,* set in early-twentieth-century Butte, Myron Brinig charted young Michael Singermann's journey to adulthood. On the day he first donned long pants at age thirteen, Michael marched into the corner saloon, went straight up to the bar, and ordered a beer. Chastened because the bartender refused to serve him, he was about to retreat in humiliation when a man at the bar bought him a schooner. As Michael took his first sip, "The beer ran down his throat, into his stomach, down his thighs and seemed to love the feel of his long pants. Beer was good now that he was drinking it in his long pants. It was a man's drink, filling a man with a golden glow, lighting little torches all over his body until he was aflame for life." Drinking became Michael's rite of passage, and he soon adopted his companion's stance, "with one foot on the brass rail, his left elbow propped up on the bar, his right hand holding the schooner of beer."[8]

Although the law forbade the presence of minors in saloons, parents often sent their children to the bar with a pail, smeared inside with lard to keep down the foam, to be filled with beer and brought home. Pat O'Leary stopped at the back door of Stripey's saloon every night, handed over his money, and bought a bucket of beer for his father and a Hershey bar for himself. Newsboys and messengers, hoping to earn a few cents running errands, plied their trade in saloons. Frank Carden remembered accompanying his father on rounds of Saturday chores and persuading him to take him to the Atlantic Bar for a liverwurst sandwich, a glass of milk, and a chance to watch the goings-on. These childhood forays contributed to young boys' socialization into the masculine club of the saloon. Mike McNelis realized early on that the measure of man, at least by a saloon's standards, had more to do with size than age. A boy was old enough to drink "if you were tall enough to put the money up on the bar."[9]

In Butte, the masculine nature of the saloon grew not only from a long tradition of American drinking habits and the frontier experience but also from patterns brought over from Europe, especially from Ireland, the country that provided the single largest group of immigrants to Butte. Historians and other investigators have observed that Irishmen traditionally used drinking as a safety valve for sexual tensions, the depressions of poverty, the frustrations of parental authority, and their hatred of the English. As long as he did not threaten his family's income, a hard-drinking man was admired by his peers or treated with maternal affection as "the poor boy." In the local tavern or shebeen a man's status was secure, unchallenged by his father and unthreatened by women. Drink became a symbol of courtesy, friendship, and equality. The ritual of treating reinforced the bonds that tied men together. Both married and single men belonged to a "bachelor group" that spent evenings in the shebeen, demonstrating that sexual divisions were far more significant than those between old and young or married and single. One historian has noted that when the Irish-American Catholic Church attacked whiskey and took up the temperance cause it was like pulling "the keystone from the arch which was traditional male culture."[10]

Drinking was interwoven with spontaneous and ritualized aggression in Irish male culture. In Irish folklore, whiskey brought power and victory, and it was often after a few rounds that Irishmen attacked informers, landlords' agents, or other enemies. "Faction fights" and "patterns" were two examples of ritualized violence.

Patterns began as devotional feast days, which evolved into days of revelry, drinking, and fighting. Faction fights had their genesis in battles between extended clans, but by the nineteenth century they had become forms of popular recreation. In Butte the legacy of faction fights may well have been recreational brawling in saloons. In the mining city, although Irish still sparred with Irish, more often they would tackle other ethnic groups. After school boys would run down to the saloon to watch regular confrontations between Cousin Jacks (Cornish miners) and the Irish. One remembered, "The Irishmen were great big guys. The Cousin Jacks were rather short, but they were muscular. They were pretty evenly matched, one for size and the other for muscles." Every fifteen or twenty minutes a gang would "come boiling out" the back door of the saloon on to the sidewalk. "They'd fight across the street as far as the curb, and then they'd stop and they'd all go back in again and drink some more beer. I used to watch them day after day."[11]

In Butte, a death in the Irish community involved two stages of social drinking: at the wake and after the funeral. Home wakes were common throughout the 1930s. They had taken on the form of entertainment in Ireland at the end of the seventeenth century and continued in America as a vivid example of the separation of the sexes in all tasks, including grieving, and of the primacy of liquor in nearly every aspect of men's lives. Women would prepare the body and lay it out in the front room, and neighbors would cook and bake until the house was full of food. During the depression some people watched the newspapers for death notices and attended wakes just to get a good meal. After offering condolences to the family in the front room, the men would leave the women to weep while they adjourned to the kitchen, where they would start drinking to the memory of the deceased. "'Well, let's drink to good old Pat or good old Catherine,' or whoever it was. So we'd have a drink for good old Catherine: 'Well, he was a pretty good guy' or 'she was a pretty good wife'; 'always a good mother and she never quarreled with her husband'; 'he never beat his wife.' All the nice things they'd say about him, of course." After about the third round, the men would start telling stories, then jokes, and then they would begin to sing. "Then a woman would come out, and she'd say, 'Sh-sh. Haven't you got any respect for the dead?' And, of course, everybody would quiet down for five minutes, maybe, and then somebody would say, 'Let's have another drink,' and it would keep going." Wakes were long ordeals. "For the men, it was a lot of fun. For the women, it was a sorrowful, tedious, dragged-out affair."[12]

Mourners rented horses and buggies or later drove their cars to the cemeteries down on the Flat for burials and then raced to one of the nearby roadhouses to continue drinking. A few brought the food left from the wake and had a picnic. As Catherine Hoy recalled, "All the men . . . were pretty good drinkers. Well, you weren't Irish unless you were a good drinker. They were good drinkers. They'd come home. Waited for the next funeral to take place."[13]

In 1916 at least 29 percent of Butte's saloonkeepers were either Irish or of Irish descent, and they formed the largest single ethnic group among that occupation. Perhaps not coincidentally, what other communities called a boilermaker—whiskey with a beer chaser—was known in Butte as a Sean O'Farrell. Folklore contends that the drink was served only at shift changes and only to men carrying their lunch buckets, proof they had spent the day or night in the mines: "The whiskey is to cut the copper dust from their lungs, and the cooling beer is to slack the thirst accumulated during eight hours in the 'hot-boxes' . . . two makes a new man of the miner and calls for a third for the new man."[14]

Naturally, the Irish were not the only ethnic group with established drinking patterns transplanted to Butte. Far fewer Italians were saloonkeepers, but the community was well known for its homemade wines and grappa, a potent brandy. Slavs, Germans, Finns, Greeks, English, and French all kept and patronized saloons. Like the Irish church, the Slavic church made no moral objection to drinking. But in other respects Slavic and Irish drinking habits differed. Some Slavs, too, drank heavily on ceremonial occasions such as weddings and christenings, and those bouts of drinking often led to brawls, but they did not drink at funerals. Unlike Irish women, who did not socialize in Irish shebeens or American saloons, Slavic women occasionally patronized ethnic saloons in America, which resembled Eastern European inns that had doubled as shops and served both sexes. Accustomed to light wines and liquors, and having taken to beer "like ducks to water," many Slavic immigrants, especially industrial workers, drank daily.[15]

When Saima Myllymaki, who was Finnish, came to Butte her first impression of the East Side was of a dirty city where the miners did "a lot of drinking." In 1905 immigrants formed the Swedish-Finnish Temperance Society, and in 1919 members attested that the advent of Prohibition had no effect on their work. Some of the Finns' East Side saloons had reputations for being rough and clannish. One night John Onkalo pulled the leg of a non-Finnish friend who wanted to see some of the infamous "joints." "I told him, 'Boy, it's pretty rough in those joints. You got to be careful when you go there. Man, sometimes somebody'll get killed off on the spot and they just drag them over to the wall and they just let them lay there until the joint closes and then they might call the authorities down to pick them up afterwards, or else they might drag them outside and let the authorities find them.'" Such warnings did not deter his friend, so they proceeded to a Finn bar where three drunks happened to be laying along the wall. "He was looking at me and I says, 'Yeah, they're probably gone. They'll just let them be there until it gets quiet and then just haul them out. It happens here all the time.' So he really thought it was an awful wild place."

Onkalo's joke had a tragic echo one night in 1914 when Jacob Nikkila and Manu Piri had a "friendly wrestle" out in the street after leaving a saloon. Nikkila knocked Piri to the ground, and Piri pulled a gun and shot Nikkila twice. Badly wounded, Nikkila made it back to his boardinghouse, but the other boarders ignored his moans, "because he usually came home drunk" and made a fuss. It was not until the next day that Nikkila showed a fellow roomer his injuries, too late for help. Jacob Nikkila died that evening.[16]

While Old World customs influenced New World drinking, living and working conditions in Butte also drove men to saloons. Myron Brinig captured the feelings that many miners probably shared when he described the appeal of the saloon: "When you dig for copper all day in the moist drifts underground, and you come up, and there is no sunlight, no waves beating against a rocky shore, why, a saloon, is a heaven then." When miners finished work and headed home, they frequently traded one unappetizing environment for another. The lack of sanitation in the densely packed neighborhoods was a serious problem. Throughout the early 1910s, the county and city health departments reported filthy alleys full of refuse and rotting food, unkempt animals, and privies dangerously close to houses. Garbage, standing water, and dead animals were such a problem at one vacant East Side lot that neighbors kept their windows closed to minimize the stench.[17]

The majority of miners returned not to family homes but to cabins where they "batched" with a few other men, furnished rooms in the upper stories of commercial buildings, or boardinghouses. In addition to the families who took in one or more boarders, there were fifty-three boardinghouses and 379 buildings providing furnished rooms in Butte in 1916. Some boardinghouses were modest, harboring a dozen or so men who slept and ate there and serving food to a few more. Others were massive business ventures.

In 1919 the Florence, known as the Big Ship, had three hundred beds. Boardinghouses provided some sociability during their family-style meals, but for thousands of men who lived in furnished rooms mealtime meant a quick trip to a cafe or restaurant. Men who worked all day in the dark underground were reluctant to retire to small, inhospitable sleeping rooms. A County Board of Health study demonstrated that the physical environment of some working-class saloons was far healthier than that of the men's boardinghouses. It was not surprising that men sought the warmth, lights, and company of saloons, cigar stores, or fraternal lodges in uptown Butte.[18]

Butte's drinking establishments ranged from "saw-dust joints" to places such as the Atlantic, which had a bar a block long and fifteen bartenders working each shift. Saloons were working-class institutions, but within their ranks hierarchies and divisions based on ethnicity, occupation, and income prevailed. Electrical workers congregated at the Park saloon; smeltermen favored the Atlantic. Pedestrians passing Tickell and Spargo's on West Broadway delighted in the harmonizing of Cornish and Welsh singers. The *Anaconda Standard*, reviewing Butte's saloon business on the eve of Prohibition, revealed its prejudice when it compared uptown, established saloons, where "the talk is never loud and where order always maintains itself," to rougher places on the East Side that were owned by "Finlanders and other foreigners" who served poor liquor and scarcely noticed fights. Saloon ownership reflected Butte's settlement patterns. Americans, English, Germans, and Irish owned the bars in the central business district. In Centerville and Dublin Gulch, proprietors were Irish; on the East Side, Finns, Slavs, Germans, and Irish dominated; and in the suburban enclaves of Meaderville and McQueen all but two saloons were run by Italians or Slavs. Journalist Byron E. Cooney, in a homage to Butte saloons, observed, "Everyone who drank at all had their own pet saloon. Personally I felt very much at home in all of them."[19]

On the other end of the scale from even the plushest workingman's saloon was Butte's Silver Bow Club, organized by William A. Clark and several colleagues in 1882 and incorporated in 1891. In 1905 the club bought a lot adjacent to the courthouse, hired Montana's most prominent architects, and built a four-story edifice replete with massive fireplaces, murals of English country life, copper and leaded glass chandeliers, and a bar decorated with stained glass panels of lush grapes and sinuous vines. Members paid an initiation fee of $50 and, between 1915 and 1920, annual dues of $60. The club served meals and had a well-stocked cigar counter, but its main source of revenue was the bar.[20]

Established members nominated and sponsored prospective members, and the process naturally led to an enrollment of Butte's upper crust. A sample of names drawn from the roll books between 1915 and 1920 reveals lawyers, bankers, doctors, the presidents and managers of Butte's largest businesses, and half a dozen ACM executives. If further proof was needed to demonstrate the gulf between members of the Silver Bow Club and patrons of Butte's saloons, it was evinced during the labor strife in 1914. When martial law closed the saloons, the club remained open through the private intervention of Gov. Sam Stewart.[21]

The Silver Bow Club admitted women for special events, the most lavish of which was the annual New Year's Eve dance. In 1914 the clubhouse was decorated with "magnificent quantities" of American Beauty roses, holly, and palms. Mary Kelley, wife of ACM vice president Cornelius Kelley, outshone the other women in a dress of silver with a girdle of gold cloth, marten trim, and a silver headdress. Vaudeville performers entertained upstairs while members danced downstairs, and supper was served at the turn of the year. In 1917 the ballroom was darkened at the first stroke of midnight, a curtain was drawn aside, and flashing electric lights illuminated "1917" flanked by two pointing dolls.[22]

■ ■ ■

The female guests of the Silver Bow Club no doubt sampled its wine cellar, but for the most part public drinking outside the country's largest cities remained a male privilege until Prohibition. Even in freewheeling Butte, as Aili Goldberg declared, "You just didn't see a woman in a saloon." Alma and Lillie Muentzer were born above their father's brewery and saloon. Alma recalled that the Butte Brewery and Saloon had a "little room in case the ladies wanted anything. . . . [but] it was never used much because women at that time didn't go to bars." Lillie remembered that the California Bar featured "booths for ladies," but she also noted, "You weren't a lady if you went in." Throughout the West, the only women to frequent saloons openly were prostitutes. As the custom became entrenched, any woman who entered a saloon was assumed to be of dubious character. Men in Denver capitalized on the universality of that assumption to taunt female reformers. When women of the Woman's Christian Temperance Union (WCTU) tried to enter saloons to record the condition of drinkers, they were met by guards who shouted, "Whore!"[23]

In 1907 Montana institutionalized the taboo against women drinking in saloons. That year the Republican-dominated state legislature enacted a program of progressive legislation designed to protect the physical and moral health of Montanans. Abolishing the "wineroom evil" targeted prostitution and garnered nearly unanimous legislative support. Winerooms—the partitioned areas in which some saloon owners permitted women to drink—were considered incubators of prostitution. The new law banned women from saloons and compelled saloon owners to dismantle any accommodations designed to provide space for female drinkers. It also instructed proprietors to remove signs that advertised a ladies' entrance or a private entrance and demolish winerooms, private apartments, or screened areas. Butte complied with the state legislature and passed a complementary city ordinance the same year.[24]

Although the law barred women from saloons, it was not designed to stop them from purchasing alcohol. Women who never drank in saloons commonly bought liquor there. Catherine Hoy recalled that neighborhood women in Dublin Gulch either went themselves or sent their children to the back doors of saloons for buckets of beer. Many Slavic women, who apparently preferred wine, would also have a little glass at home. Women's drinking habits, barely recorded by historians, were widely recognized by contemporaries. Indeed, during the campaign for Prohibition in Montana at least one dry advocate chastised "mothers in Butte who won't vote for prohibition because you want to have beer on your own tables in your own homes." Until the reconstruction of social drinking during Prohibition, reputable women, with few exceptions, continued to drink at home while men drank in public.[25]

■ ■ ■

Factions for and against Prohibition in Montana paralleled divisions in other states. The WCTU and the Anti-Saloon League led the dry forces. Enrollment in Montana's WCTU, founded in 1883, peaked during the prohibition campaign of 1916. Like the WCTU in other states, the organization fought not only for temperance but also for suffrage, increased education, and other measures designed to improve the lives of women and children. In 1907 the WCTU joined the Anti-Saloon League in a Dry Federation and deemphasized many of its other programs in order to devote its energy to the crusade against liquor. Agricultural counties and many businessmen wanted a dry Montana, whereas urban centers and organized labor preferred to keep it wet. The Anaconda Company trod carefully, perhaps fearing to alienate its work force. Editors of the company-owned newspapers promoted the virtues of abstinence without specifically endorsing Prohibition. When push came to shove, however, the company supported the drys for economic reasons, citing evidence of increased efficiency and decreased accidents during the period when saloons were closed under martial law.[26]

Drys failed to convince Silver Bow voters of the advantage of their position in the 1916 state prohibition election, but they could take heart that more sober heads prevailed throughout the state. The battle for national prohibition was yet to be won, however, and Butte women tied their white ribbons to the banner of patriotism to promote their cause. In June 1917 Mrs. C. J. Nepper, president of the Butte chapter of the WCTU, chaired a mass meeting in which women called for prohibition as a means of food conservation mandated by the war. In letters to Jeannette Rankin, Butte women avowed their intention to boycott Herbert Hoover's "registration of housewives for conservation of food" until Congress curbed the wastefulness of brewers and distillers, who made women's use of grain appear negligible. Wrapped in new patriotic rhetoric lay persistent arguments. Nepper wrote, "What good would it do a woman with a drinking husband to save a few ounces of flour when the husband would waste more in one visit to the saloon." Lulu Wheeler, wife of U.S. district attorney Burton K. Wheeler, concurred, "It will be useless for Mr. Hoover to appeal to us house wives to take the bread away from our children and let the brewers and distillers have it to make the fathers drunk. We will use more wheat instead of less if that is to be the case." M. H. York of Anaconda summed up the WCTU's attitude: "We want to be loyal, but we want to be right."[27]

When Prohibition took effect, the WCTU continued its efforts by urging officials to enforce the law. State president Anna Herbst pledged to the state attorney general that the WCTU would be vigilant in tracking down bootleggers. "You can always depend on our women, they are fearless," she reminded him. Young Rose C. Bresnahan, "a woman tax-payer" and in later years head of the women's division of the Montana Works Progress Administration, demonstrated that spunk. Disgusted with the flagrant disregard for the law in Butte's sister city Anaconda, she and a companion called on county attorney David H. Morgan to complain. Morgan referred them to the sheriff, who invited the pair to accompany him on his rounds. After some delay, which Bresnahan was sure enabled word of their approach to circulate among soft drink parlor owners, the sheriff met the ladies and took them to several of the converted saloons.

Far from reassuring them of the innocence of such places, their inspection revealed "suspicious looking and smelling bottles with the labels soaked off" stored behind the shelves of soft drinks. Nonetheless, the women were unable to prove their suspicions. As Bresnahan explained, "As we had not expected to go slumming when we started out, neither of us had cash with us. I asked the sheriff to lend me some money but he would not do so therefore I couldn't buy a sample bottle." Bresnahan and her compatriots continued their siege against law breakers. When she felt that Sam C. Ford, the new Republican state attorney general, was not doing enough to enforce the law, Bresnahan pledged to persuade Republican women to join an alliance with "a goodly number of my Democratic women friends" and vote against him.[28]

The WCTU's campaigners waged a losing battle. On their program in 1920 was the question, "Does Prohibition Prohibit in Butte?" Reluctantly, they had to answer no. By 1923, 156 of the 250 saloons operating in Butte in 1916 and 1917 were in the same locations, under the same proprietorships and thinly disguised as soft drink parlors. The city directory advertised another forty-four new soft drink parlors, and it is impossible to estimate the number of clandestine speakeasies. Frank Carden observed that "the saloons all stayed open and dispensed 'bootleg' whiskey, homemade wine and homemade beer, brandy, gin . . . if they were raided by Federal officers they would just pause long enough to get in another stock of liquor and start over again." As federal judge George M. Bourquin proclaimed, "Shabby, dingy holes in the wall, labeled 'soft drink parlors' do not fool anybody, least of all the court," especially when they were in the same location as former saloons. Clearly, such parlors were not operated for the sale of ice cream and pop, nor did they cater to women and children.[29]

The WCTU lost strength in the 1920s. Butte, the largest city in the state, with the greatest "liquor traffic," never had the most active local union. Only ninety-four Butte women wore white ribbons in 1917. Bozeman, an agricultural community of approximately six thousand, had 148 members. By 1920 Butte counted only fifty-six stalwarts. Throughout the 1920s membership declined across Montana, as did the WCTU's ability to raise funds and lobby effectively. During its 1926 campaign against repeal of statewide Prohibition, the WCTU raised less than half the money it commanded in 1916. The persistence of the liquor traffic frustrated not only the volunteers of the WCTU but also those officials charged with enforcing Prohibition.[30]

In May 1923 federal prohibition enforcement officer Addison K. Lusk outlined the problems he faced in Montana to Gov. Joseph M. Dixon. The 550–mile border that the state shared with wet Canada had only two customs stations. Two lines of the Great Northern Railway ran into Canada, and rail officials made no attempt to prevent the shipping of liquor to Montana in cars of coal and lumber. The vastness of the state made it impossible for his force of thirteen or fourteen men to enforce the law effectively. When Lusk described the urban situation, he wrote with exasperation, "It is not necessary to say that Great Falls and Butte are bad and that Helena is nothing to boast of. Confidentially I may say that in these three towns the police authorities do absolutely nothing to prevent the sale of liquor." In fact, affidavits by enforcement agents attested that a former police chief ran the Cyrus Noble saloon, patronized by uniformed and plainclothes detectives.[31]

In 1920, after federal Prohibition had taken effect, U.S. Military Intelligence officer Maj. A. S. Peake, stationed in Butte because of the strike situation, reported "a great deal of liquor" available in the city and more drunkenness "than one would expect in view of the prohibition amendment." Statements from county attorneys across the state showed varying rates of success prosecuting Volstead Act violators. From November 1920 to November 1922, Silver Bow County's attorney won convictions in 59 percent of his liquor cases. Only 105 cases were prosecuted at that time, however, compared to 271 in Cascade County and 168 in Lewis and Clark, both with smaller populations. Despite almost daily newspaper accounts of confiscation of stills and illegal liquor, law enforcement officials were not collecting evidence sufficient to convict. Even when they did, Butte juries remained unsympathetic to the law. In 1928 Judge Bourquin replaced a jury that had been hearing prohibition cases and admonished the twelve new men to bring in verdicts in accordance with the evidence: "I don't want men sitting in the jury box who have no regard for their oaths. We have had two such juries and I don't want anymore if we can escape it."[32]

By July 1920 agents realized that moonshining was becoming standardized. In preparing an exhibit of confiscated equipment for district court they noted that such makeshift apparatus as washtubs and ice cream freezers had been replaced by copper stills of standard manufacture and increasing size. In November an explosion brought authorities to a house on Dakota Street, where they found two stills, one capable of running seventy gallons, the other forty. In 1923 agents confiscated 3,500 gallons of mash and a seventy-gallon still near Columbia Gardens. Some moonshiners built elaborate plants, run by steam boilers, that turned out hundreds of gallons each day. Toward the end of the decade neighbors in Dublin Gulch "stoutly maintained" that the house at 417 Ridgely had been vacant for some time, despite the odor of moonshine that permeated the air for a two-block radius. When federal agents raided the place they found two hundred-gallon stills, one still warm, but no one to arrest.[33]

Confusion and rivalry among the city police, the county sheriff's office, and federal agents contributed to the lack of enforcement. Corruption also played a role. In 1920 Jack Melia, head of the county attorney's dry squad, was accused of selling $10,000 worth of confiscated liquor. Although city police chief Jere Murphy denied charges of police collusion with moonshiners, there was a general belief that Prohibition "brought about an awful lot of graft, payoffs." One source alleged that the federal revenue agent took kickbacks through "a woman friend." A bootlegger agreed that the agent provided protection for many of the bootleggers and sabotaged other officials' attempts at enforcement in order to preserve his power and income. It was a commonly held belief that bootleggers serving time in Butte jails "lived the life of Riley." In effect, they organized the equivalent of a private club while they were incarcerated. Each paid the sheriff a dollar a day, and he looked the other way while they ordered daily groceries, had friends bring in kegs of whiskey, and set up their own housekeeping routines and rules of behavior: "If anybody got drunk they didn't get no more whiskey. And if they ate too much of the food and got into the larder in between meals they were fined. . . . And so it run real smooth. It was a gesture of protest against the law." In 1929 the newspaper reported that eighty-eight bootleggers had settled into the county jail, "with a phonograph tearing off jazz tunes and with bedroom slippers on their feet."[34]

Despite blatant disregard for the law, Prohibition, especially in its early years, did cut down on the number of drunks in Butte. Although not a day went by in 1918 without at least one charge of drunkenness, according to police court records seventy-two days passed without such charges during 1919. A high of seven such cases occurred on one day in 1919, but there had been many days with more than a score of arrests for drunkenness in 1918. Still, many drinking habits remained unchanged. Speakeasies continued to serve after-shift Sean O'Farrells, substituting moonshine and home-brewed beer. Before Prohibition, saloons simply put in a stock of soft drinks to shield their liquor and continued business as usual—

at slightly higher prices. Chief Murphy, who offered a typology of drunks he regularly picked up—"the Saturday night drunk," "the crying jag drunk," "the singing jag drunk," "the automobile dodger," "the fighting drunk," "the flirtatious drunk," "the profane drunk," and "the hell-roaring drunk"—noted that a new type had appeared with Prohibition: drunks suffering from alcohol poisoning caused by bad liquor.[35]

By 1926 a majority of Montanans agreed with Helen Raymond, who thought, "It was a shame they ever had [Prohibition] because I think it broke down a morale of the people that would never have happened if they didn't have it. 'Cause once you think you can break a law, you're in worse shape than if you'd never done it." Montanans judged the noble experiment a failure, and in 1926 voters repealed their state prohibition law with 53 percent of the vote. Silver Bow County tallied 73 percent in favor of repeal, the largest majority in the state. Voters reinforced their decision in 1928, when they defeated a referendum to reenact state prohibition. By 1932 nearly all support for Prohibition in Montana had eroded. A *Literary Digest* poll found 80 percent of Montanans in favor of repealing federal Prohibition. Of all westerners only Nevadans felt more strongly—88 percent of them supported repeal.[36]

Unfortunately, no records remain to document whether women were actively involved in the 1926 state repeal movement, although they did join the effort to roll back federal Prohibition. Those who believed that Prohibition had failed and created more problems than it solved founded the Women's Organization for National Prohibition Reform (WONPR) in 1929. By 1933 the group claimed a million and a half members, more than three times the numbers of the WCTU. The WONPR was organized by many women who had crusaded for temperance. Although their involvement in the repeal movement might at first seem contradictory, their actions were a continuation of a desire to protect young people, women, and the family from the ill effects of unrestrained, excessive drinking and its social consequences. After almost a decade of Prohibition, these women were appalled by the manifest disrespect for the law and the corruption, crime, and hypocrisy that a society dry in name only seemed to have fostered. Fear for the morals of their children impelled many WONPR members, who came to believe that egregious violations of the Volstead Act were more harmful than licensed drinking. At least under old laws saloonkeepers selling liquor to minors could lose their licenses. Under prevailing conditions no sanctions effectively prevented adolescents from buying liquor.[37]

Montana's WONPR leaders did not consider theirs to be a particularly active branch. As Mrs. W. A. Simons, state co-chair, noted, by the time the group was created, Montana was wet: "We have had a referendum twice and each time voted for states rights, and of course . . . our state officials do not pretend to enforce Prohibition in Montana." She concluded "we don't need to work." Mrs. Simons, the daughter of a Methodist Episcopal South clergyman, led the state WONPR along with Mary Kelley, whose husband was by this time president of the Anaconda Company; Mrs. L. O. Evans, wife of the company's general counsel, was vice-chair. Four of the state organization's six officers were from Butte. Despite Mrs. Simons's conclusion that Montana women did not need to work for repeal, she and her co-workers did enlist fifteen thousand women in the organization. Elizabeth Kennedy, vice-chair of the Silver Bow County chapter, submitted a petition in support of repeal carrying more than seven thousand women's signatures.[38]

The leadership of Kelley, Evans, and Kennedy suggests that all spectrums of Butte society believed Prohibition had failed. Kelley and Evans, of course, represented the company's point of view. Kennedy, a staunch supporter of labor and a member of many Butte women's clubs, had often found herself opposing the company. By the late 1920s all had apparently agreed that regulated liquor sales were preferable to the current free-for-all.

With the passage of state repeal in 1926, federal agents became entirely responsible for enforcement, and their efforts at times seemed farcical. In 1928 the newspaper reported a "dry sleuth" who had adopted a disguise designed to entrap young Butte fraternity men. Bartenders noted that raids often followed the appearance of a hatless young man "flaunting white flannel trousers and black coat or corduroy pants and skin-tight sweater [with] hair . . . greased back from forehead and smile of sophistication . . . spread on his face." The alleged agent would gain the confidence of Butte youths "whose entry to the drink parlors is never questioned," buy them drinks, and leave. Shortly afterward, a raid would commence.[39]

■ ■ ■

Prohibition did not change the habits and economy of uptown drinking. Contrary to its intent, it created economic opportunities for people who had never been involved in the liquor business. At one end of the bootlegging chain were children who collected empty bottles outside dance halls and sold them back to moonshiners, or who discovered bootleggers' stores and pilfered a few bottles of liquor to sell on their own. Italians, who had traditionally made wine for their own families, expanded production for commerce. The commission houses ordered freight-car loads of grapes—the largest anyone remembered was thirty-four cars—and had them brought directly to a siding near Meaderville. As one bootlegger recalled, "Them Italians would just pack the grapes off, anywhere from a few boxes to a ton or so at a time, depending on how much money they had. Take them home and make wine." Italians who lived in Brown's Gulch, northwest of the city, also made wine and grappa. Dorothy Martin, who taught school in the Gulch, recalled that a sudden cloudburst would sometimes flood a bootlegger's cache, and barrels of wine and grappa would come rolling down by the schoolhouse.[40]

It may well have been profits from bootlegging that led to the creation of a zone of restaurant-nightclubs in Meaderville during the late 1920s and early 1930s. These nightclubs bore little relation to pre-Prohibition saloons, and it was within their walls that a new heterosocial nightlife evolved. The first clubs opened during the last years of Prohibition, and, by the time liquor again became legal, they were local institutions. The Rocky Mountain Cafe, Aro, Golden Fan, Copper Club, and Pera Cafe, among others, attracted all classes of men and women for drinking, dancing, gambling, and one- or two-dollar multicourse steak and chicken dinners served with spaghetti and ravioli. As in New York City's cabarets, the design of Butte clubs gave women social and physical protection. They offered privacy and distance not provided in open barrooms, where there were few tables or chairs and where patrons freely mingled and jostled one another. In the Rocky Mountain Cafe, for example, booths lined the walls around a central dance floor, and the gambling operation was in a back room. Many people patronized the clubs exclusively as restaurants without sampling their other attractions. Meaderville's nightclubs also created an atmosphere in which women felt comfortable drinking and gambling, if they so chose. As one customer observed, "Meaderville's night clubs lack the vigor, the hairy chests and the call of the wild that you'll find in the city. Women may gamble side by side with their men and loll at the bars with them." Unlike saloons, where women were welcome only at the backdoor, nightclubs encouraged women's attendance and trade.[41]

Butte's roadhouses also had female patrons and in some cases female proprietors. In 1919 prohibition officer Larry Houchins took his wife to the Three Mile House—presumably as his "cover"—

where they drank highballs and were entertained by male and female performers. Nell Taylor owned the Three Mile House and relied on the stock of bootleggers. She apparently owned at least one other roadhouse run for her by a "damn good looking woman" who made an extra profit for herself by buying and selling moonshine and passing it off as bonded whiskey, unbeknown to Nell Taylor. Lucille Howard, another female proprietor, owned a "generously patronized roadhouse" called the Bungalow. Built in 1910, the resort had a ballroom, two parlors, a barroom, and kitchen on the first floor and thirteen rooms upstairs. Howard bought the place from its original owner in 1921 and continued to run it in wideopen, pre-Prohibition style—so successfully that it was closed twice by federal abatement. She later traded her investment for an apartment house in Seattle. Nell Taylor was running the Bungalow in 1928 when it caught fire. She rescued the piano, phonograph, and jukebox before it burned to the ground.[42]

While the Meaderville clubs and roadhouses provided a variety of entertainment, more common throughout the city were home speaks, which marked a return of kitchen grog shops, run by women or families. Mike Erick and his wife, for instance, owned a small dance hall and soft drink parlor that catered to fellow Slavic immigrants. Mr. and Mrs. Charles Martin, African Americans, ran a home speak on New Street. Pat O'Hara sold beer and moonshine in his cabin, which he denied was a dance hall although he did admit that his customers sometimes danced to the music of a phonograph.[43]

Bootlegging provided a new vehicle for women, especially widows and wives, to supplement their incomes. Slavic women began making wine and selling it to boarders with their dinners. Many working-class women in Dublin Gulch, on the East Side, and in gulches outside the city had their own stills or cared for family stills while their husbands were at work. One of the most elaborate outfits confiscated, a three-hundred-gallon-capacity still, was operated by eighty-year-old Lavinia Gilman. The court gave Kate Farlan, a "gray-haired mother" convicted of manufacturing liquor in her home, a suspended sentence on condition she obey the law for one year. Shortly after sentencing, agents found another still in her house. Mrs. Michael Murray, who had two children and claimed she could not work outside the home, confessed to being the "cook" in an operation in which her husband and a friend marketed her liquor. Widow Nora Gallagher told police she set up a still on her kitchen stove in order to outfit her five children for Easter. Police arrested women selling liquor and beer in grocery stores and boardinghouses and others attempting to destroy incriminating evidence by dumping liquor and mash into cellars.[44]

Home bootlegging was, for the most part, a working-class practice, but at least a few middle-class women set up their own stills, presumably more for the thrill than from any economic need. Arriving home one day to find a peculiar odor in the house, Dr. Carl Horst traced it to the basement, where he discovered that his wife had assembled a still. He demolished it over her protests, allowing her to keep a gallon for her ladies club. The public did not expect the middle class to manufacture their own liquor. When police found a still "within a stone's throw of the classic halls of the School of Mines and surrounded by residences of men of high standing in the community," it was "an astounding revelation."[45]

The independence of female bootleggers challenged male notions of women's place. Police and judges had long experience with prostitutes and woman drunkards, but bootlegging women were beyond their ken. When police arrested Susie Gallagher Kerr along with two men, she admitted that the seized still was her operation, but the police preferred to believe that the men were in charge. The judge who tried Lavinia Gilman felt her son was the "real culprit" and hoped that he would come forward to save his mother. The younger Gilman apparently did not share the court's chivalrous attitude and never appeared. Judge Bourquin, a staunch upholder of the law, did not like to commit women to jail, but in the case of twice-caught Kate Farlan he felt compelled to carry out the court's order and reluctantly locked her up for six months.[46]

Many writers who commented on women in speakeasies during the 1920s and 1930s portrayed them as silly or comic. But caricatures of well-to-do young flappers or matrons, their high heels hooked over brass rails in smoky speakeasies, trivialized an important and, for some, disturbing change in women's behavior and values. Butte author Reuben Maury, writing in *Scribner's Magazine* in 1926, captured the anxiety of a mining city mother whose daughter seemed to care more for "comfort and an automobile and an able bootlegger" than for the prospect of marriage and children. Mothers feared that their daughters were eschewing domesticity for frivolity.[47]

Men shared the uneasy feeling that more was at stake than a woman having a drink. Indeed, male writers' caustic remarks about ladies lunching in speakeasies were a defensive response to women's invasion of traditional male territory. As one scholar of drinking habits noted, men defined the use and abuse of alcohol as a male privilege, a symbol of power and prestige. What bothered them was not that women drank, but that they drank in public commercial institutions. Not only the anti-saloon thrust of the prohibition movement but also the heterosociability of new watering holes seemed to spell doom for the saloon, that long-cherished male bastion. As one journalist remarked, men found in saloons a "release from reality—from laying brick and driving nails and adding figures and paying rent, and sweetest of all, from the hateful virtues of a woman's world."[48]

Women who made whiskey and patronized speakeasies were breaking both custom and the law. Their actions were deliberate and self-conscious. For working-class women, bootlegging was a logical extension of the many kinds of home work they had traditionally undertaken to supplement family income. It admittedly carried some risks, but it presumably offered greater rewards. For unmarried women—both working and middle class—drinking and visiting speakeasies were open acts of rebellion; "nice girls" did not do such things.

The speakeasy culture that gave more freedom to young women became associated with other symbols of independence, such as smoking cigarettes and bobbed hair, not necessarily connected to drinking. These gestures in some ways became rites of passage for young women during the 1920s. Peer pressure and the lure of the forbidden were clearly at work. Alma Muentzer Hileman recalled that none of her girlfriends drank until Prohibition, "then everybody ha[d] to taste and see what it [was]. . . . That's the first that any of us ever knew what a highball and all that stuff was. And we were born in a brewery."[49]

Many daughters deliberately violated long-held conventions defining respectability and tested the strength of familial bonds. Both Helen Harrington and Dorothy Martin spent a considerable amount of time preparing their parents for the day they came home with bobbed hair. Dorothy's father had initially dissuaded her from having her hair cut when he told her that only prostitutes wore bobbed hair. She persisted, but it was only after her mother saw that nearly all Dorothy's friends were having their hair cut that she was allowed to get a bob. As she came home from work each day for several weeks Helen Harrington told her mother that she was going to have her hair bobbed. Her sister remembered the day she finally did: Helen came home and said, "'Ma, I got my hair bobbed,' and Ma never looked at her. Finally after a while, she peeked over her 15–cent-store glasses and all she said was, 'I guess you'll be going to the roadhouses next.'"[50]

Josephine Weiss Casey did go to the roadhouses. Wearing her "pretty dress," she and her boyfriend and two or three other couples would drive over from Anaconda to eat, drink, and dance in the Meaderville clubs. For a dollar they could get a chicken dinner and two highballs; the third was, by custom, on the house. Other nights after a movie they would go to a speakeasy that served "the best gin fizzes in the world." It was not just the quality of the liquor but the fact that "swanky drinks" were served in "tall nice glasses" in a place "packed, packed and not all [with] kids like us" that made the evening so tantalizing.[51]

The speakeasies often seemed mysterious and thrilling for young women. Dorothy Martin recalled that going to the clubs "was probably the most daring and frightening thing that I did." She remembered climbing down a ladder to get in one place. "You couldn't see through the smoke because everybody smoked. And I thought, 'Oh, boy, what a wonderful place for tragedy.'" But Dorothy didn't like liquor, and she ended up dumping her drinks in the spittoon when no one was looking. Clearly, it was not alcohol but adventure that drew her and perhaps many of her peers to the "downright honest-to-God bootleg joints."[52]

The Meaderville nightclubs eventually challenged women's traditional forms of leisure. In the late 1930s the Daughters of Norway engaged in a considerable discussion over the relative merits of having their annual picnic or going to a Meaderville cafe for a ravioli dinner. Ravioli triumphed over tradition, and the women had such a good time that they made it an annual event. Club minutes record their pleasure: "We all had a glorious evening, an evening that will live in our memory for a long, long time; after a hi-ball or two, Mrs. Sontum got hot clear down to her feet, & [if] that wasn't enough, she also emptied their slot machines." In an addendum to the minutes the secretary noted, "It was moved and seconded that we should take the dollar Mrs. Larsen & Mrs. Langstadt gave us to treat ourselves to some wine, which we did."[53]

Prohibition's new speakeasies, nightclubs, and roadhouses catered to couples and sanctioned and encouraged drinking women. Young women who ventured into these new institutions knew they were crossing a divide between an old set of assumptions about behavior and morality and a new code they were creating. Some faced the divide with a bittersweet knowledge of the price of innovation. As Dorothy Martin recalled when she finally had her hair cut, "I kind of cried myself when I looked at me with my short hair. But, it was done."[54] The actions of Dorothy Martin, a schoolteacher, Helen Harrington, a shop clerk, and hundreds of other young women forced changes in the public perception of female drinking. Female patrons of speakeasies were neither "loose women" nor "floozies." They were "good" women, and they compelled people to acknowledge that they could retain their respectability while taking a drink in public.

There is great irony in Prohibition. The law had, in effect, created a vacuum of rules, and women exploited the opportunity to slip into niches in the economy of liquor production, distribution, and consumption. Women had been in the vanguard of the prohibition movement, a movement designed to restrict male behavior by abolishing the vice-ridden retreat of the saloon and curbing male drinking. Yet a decade after legislative success, some of the very same women led the campaign for repeal of the Eighteenth Amendment, having concluded that some kind of regulated liquor trade was preferable to moral anarchy. Much to their dismay, drinking had become an equal opportunity vice during Prohibition. True, many saloons closed their doors forever and the consumption of alcohol did decrease. But during Prohibition men and women reconstructed social drinking habits, and the greatest change was women's newfound penchant to belly up to the bar.

Unforeseen by proponents and opponents, Prohibition effectively created new social spaces in speakeasies and nightclubs, which allowed a redefinition of sex roles in one of the most gender-segregated arenas of leisure—getting together for a drink. Behavior followed structural change. Public drinking was not on the list of rights that twentieth-century feminists demanded. Indeed, the seemingly frivolous activities of young women in the 1920s dismayed some feminists who saw them diverting energy from politics. The reorganization of drinking did increase women's autonomy, however. Whether they spent an evening drinking and dancing with their boyfriends, husbands, or members of their ladies club, doors that had been closed to them now opened in welcome. Prohibition provided women with new economic opportunities, greater choices of public leisure, and a chance to broaden the definition of reputable behavior. Young working women would continue to push against other barriers, forcing the community to reenvision gender relations in the mining city.

NOTES

1. *U.S. vs. Maud Vogen,* Judgment Roll 928, U.S. District Court, Montana, 11 November 1922, U.S. District Court, Montana, District of Montana

Criminal Register and Dockets, Record Group 21, National Archives, Pacific Northwest Region, Seattle. Between 1920 and 1934, 134 Butte women were prosecuted in the district court for violations of the Volstead Act.

2. Anonymous letter to John Hughes, 27 September 1982, (Hughes was an archivist at the BSBA and received this letter in response to a column he wrote on local history); *Montana Standard,* 11 April 1929, 1.

3. Lender and Martin, *Drinking in America,* 117; Kennedy, "The Saloon in Retrospect and Prospect," 206. Brennan discusses the growth in the diversity of public drinking places in *Public Drinking and Popular Culture in Eighteenth-Century Paris,* 14–19. Duis discusses gender-segregated drinking along public and private lines in *The Saloon,* 105–7. Rosenzweig describes the demise of kitchen grog shops in *Eight Hours for What We Will,* 41–49, 63.

4. Bahin, "Campaign for Prohibition," 94–96, 130, 57; *Butte City Directory,* 1916; *Butte Miner,* 11 December 1915, 6.

North Dakota had entered the union with Prohibition in its state constitution; Washington and Oregon went dry in 1914; Idaho in 1915; and South Dakota in 1916. Only Wyoming lagged behind Montana, finally voting dry in 1919. Timberlake, *Prohibition and the Progressive Movement, 1900–1920,* 166.

5. On the multifunctional nature of western saloons, see Putnam, "Prohibition Movement in Idaho," 54, 403; West, *Saloon on the Rocky Mountain Mining Frontier,* 131–32; Noel, *City and Saloon,* 13, 65; Brundage, "The Producing Classes and the Saloon," 30–32; and Burk, "The Mining Camp Saloon," 385.

6. West, *Saloon on the Rocky Mountain Mining Frontier,* 131–32; Kingsdale, "The 'Poor Man's Club,'" 265; Noel, *City and Saloon,* 65; Writers' Program, Work Projects Administration, *Copper Camp,* 83.

7. Slatta, "Comparative Frontier Social Life," 158–59; West, *Saloon on the Rocky Mountain Mining Frontier,* 19–21; Putnam, "Prohibition Movement in Idaho," 10.

8. Brinig, *Singermann,* 292–93.

9. On children in saloons, see Noel, *City and Saloon,* 89; Stevenson, "Saloons," 571, 577; and "The Experience and Observation of a New York Saloon-Keeper," 311. Pat O'Leary, interview by Ray Calkins, Butte, 22 July 1980, 17–18; Carden, "A Walk from S. Gaylord Street," 6–7; Mike McNelis, interview by Alice Finnegan, Anaconda, 18 October 1985, 8.

10. On Irish culture and drinking, see Bales, "Attitudes toward Drinking in the Irish Culture," 157–87; Barrett, "Why Paddy Drank," 155/17–166/38; Clark, *The Irish Relations,* chap. 4; and Babor and Rosenkrantz, "Public Health, Public Morals, and Public Order," 265–86. On treating, see Hoke, "Corner Saloon," 311–21. Stivers discusses Irish bachelor culture in *A Hair of the Dog,* 76–97. The quotation about the church is from McDannell, "'True Men as We Need Them,'" 24.

11. Calkins, *Looking Back from the Hill,* 78.

12. Ibid., 70–71.

13. Edward Sullivan, interview by Laurie Mercier, Butte, 25 February, 10 March 1982; Catherine Hoy, interview by Ray Calkins and Caroline Smithson, Butte, 11 May 1979, 8.

14. *Butte City Directory,* 1916. On the ethnicity of saloon owners, see Duis, *The Saloon,* 164–70; Noel, *City and Saloon,* 53, 57; Barrett, "Why Paddy Drank," 154/17; and Rosenzweig, *Eight Hours for What We Will,* 49–50. On the Sean O'Farrell, see Writers' Program, Work Projects Administration, *Copper Camp,* 250; and Hand, "The Folklore, Customs and Traditions," 161. In *Shadow of the Mills,* 224–25, Kleinberg recounts that Pittsburgh's industrial workers believed that boilermakers settled their stomachs, cleared dust from their throats, and overcame exhaustion.

15. Balch, *Our Slavic Fellow Citizens,* 95, 365–69. On Slavic drinking habits in Montana, see Zellick, "Fire in the Hole," 24–26.

16. Saima Myllymaki, interview by Laurie Mercier, Stanford, 19 March 1982; *Butte Miner,* 28 December 1919, 10; John Onkalo, interview by Ray Calkins, Butte, February 1980, 19; *Anaconda Standard,* 24 January 1914, 4.

17. Brinig, *Wide Open Town,* 6, 15–16; Silver Bow County Board of Health, "Report on Sanitary Conditions in the Mines and Community"; Silver Bow County Board of Health, "Report Showing Results of Inspection of Dwellings, Hotels, Rooming Houses"; *Annual Reports of the City Officers, City of Butte for the Fiscal Years Ending April 30, 1908–09; Annual Reports of the City Officers, City of Butte for the Fiscal Years Ending April 30, 1910–11; Annual Reports of the City Officers of the City of Butte, Montana, Fiscal Year Ending April 30, 1912.*

18. *Butte City Directory,* 1916; *Butte Miner,* 17 June 1928, 1; Florence Hotel voucher record, 1919, ACMCo Records, MHSA; Emmons, *Butte Irish,* 152. For a comparable situation regarding boardinghouse life and patronage of saloons, see Rosenzweig, *Eight Hours for What We Will,* 56.

19. Duffy, *Butte Was Like That,* 41, 47; Writers' Program, Work Projects Administration, *Copper Camp,* 74; Butler, "Impressions of a Hobo," 205; *Montana Standard,* 25 October 1959, 9B; *Anaconda Standard,* 14 January 1917, pt. 2, 1; *Butte City Directory,* 1916; Cooney, "The Saloons of Yester-Year," 64. Several Butte saloons are described in North American Industrial Review, *Montana,* 16, 24, 25, 40, 78, and Burke depicted the flavor of Butte saloons in 106 verses in "The Saloons of Old Time Butte," in *Rhymes of the Mines,* 65–75.

20. Hopwood, "History of the Silver Bow Club"; Cigar and Liquor Inventory, November 1916–December 1917, ACMCo Records, MHSA.

21. Silver Bow Club, Roll of Members, 1915–1920, ACMCo Records, MHSA; Bahin, "Campaign for Prohibition," 42.

22. *Anaconda Standard,* 4 January 1914, pt. 2, 8 and 1 January 1917, 5.

23. Aili Goldberg, interview by Mary Murphy, Butte, 29 February 1980, 18; Alma E. Hileman, interview by Ray Calkins, Butte, 27 June 1980, 7; Noel,

City and Saloon, 112. Peiss specifically notes the absence of reputable women from saloons in *Cheap Amusements,* 20–28. On this topic, see Powers, "Decay from Within," 115; Hapgood, "McSorley's Saloon," 15; Melendy, "The Saloon in Chicago," 300; and Hoke, "Corner Saloon," 313–15. In *Steppin' Out,* Erenberg discusses the rise of New York cabarets at the turn of the century as places where reputable, well-to-do women could drink in public. Cabarets were not, of course, common outside the largest American cities.

24. *Laws, Resolutions and Memorials of the State of Montana Passed at the Tenth Regular Session of the Legislative Assembly,* 434–37; Carroll, comp., *The Revised Ordinances of the City of Butte, 1914,* 463–64. Roeder discusses the Progressives' thinking in "Montana in the Early Years of the Progressive Period," 202–5. Other cities and states passed or attempted to pass similar laws; see Putnam, "Travail at the Turn of the Century," 15–16, and Duis, *The Saloon,* 254. In at least two cases, Butte did try to enforce the law. In 1912 the city revoked the liquor license of the Canteen saloon for violating the city ordinance, and in 1917 sheriffs arrested the owners of a roadhouse for permitting females to frequent the establishment. "Petition of Centennial Brewing Company, Re revocation of Liquor license at 27½ West Granite St.," *Butte Miner,* 6 April 1917, 7.

25. Hoy interview, 10–11; Ann Pentilla, interview by Ray Calkins and Caroline Smithson, Butte, 27 April 1979, 53; McNelis interview, 6; *Butte Miner,* 10 April 1916, 6.

26. Alderson, *Thirty-Four Years,* 14. Bahin discusses the role of the ASL in Montana in "Campaign for Prohibition." Arguments for and against Prohibition are reflected in telegrams from the Silver Bow Trades and Labor Council and other parties to Jeannette Rankin (hereafter cited as JR), Jeannette Rankin Papers (hereafter cited as JR Papers), box 6, files 11, 12, and 13, MHSA. The ACM position is expressed in *Engineering and Mining Journal* 102 (July 1916): 70.

General works on the prohibition movement and attempts to enforce the law include Burnham, "New Perspectives"; Clark, *Deliver Us from Evil;* and Kerr, *Organized for Prohibition.* For works on prohibition in western states, see Official Records of the National Commission on Law Observance and Enforcement, *Enforcement of the Prohibition Laws,* vol. 4, *Prohibition Surveys of the States.* Studies of prohibition enforcement were conducted in several northern Rockies states, including Colorado, Wyoming, and Idaho. Unfortunately, no study was conducted in Montana; however, reports of these states provide valuable insights into the problems of enforcement in the West. Also see Bailey and McPherson, "'Practically Free from the Taint of the Bootlegger'"; Papanikolas, "Bootlegging in Zion"; Clark, *The Dry Years;* Fahey, *Rum Road to Spokane;* McCullough, "Bone Dry?"; Jones, "Casper's Prohibition Years"; Wilson, *Honky-Tonk Town;* O'Brien, "Prohibition"; Ostrander, *The Prohibition Movement in California;* and four studies by Rose, "Booze and News in 1924," "The Labbe Affair," "'Dry' in Los Angeles," and "Wettest in the West."

27. *Butte Miner,* 24 June 1917, 6; Mrs. C. J. Nepper to JR, 18 June 1917, JR Papers, box 6, file 3, MHSA; Lulu W. Wheeler to JR, 27 June 1917, JR Papers, box 2, file 7, MHSA; and M. H. York to JR, 15 July 1917, JR Papers, box 7, file 1, MHSA. For the WCTU position on wartime prohibition, see Gordon, *Woman Torch-Bearers,* chap. 6.

28. Mrs. A. C. Herbst to S. C. Ford, 4 January 1919, Montana Attorney General Records (hereafter cited as Atty Gen Records), box 16, file 7, MHSA; R. C. Bresnahan to S. C. Ford, 2 January 1919, Atty Gen Records, box 16, file 7, and 25 September 1919, box 16, file 3, MHSA.

29. *Butte Daily Bulletin,* 10 January 1920, 4; *Butte City Directory,* 1916, 1917, 1923; Carden, "A Ride on an Open Trolley," 9; *Butte Miner,* 3 May 1923, 6.

30. "Report of the Thirty-fourth Annual Meeting of WCTU," 14; *Woman's Voice* (October 1920): 9 and (October 1919): 4; Bahin, "Campaign for Prohibition," 105.

31. Addison K. Lusk to Gov. Joseph M. Dixon, 16 May 1923, Montana Governors' Papers, 1893–1962, box 32, file 15, MHSA; affidavits in Atty Gen Records, box 7, file 11, MHSA.

32. "Intelligence Report for Troops on Strike Duty," 25 April 1920, U. S. Military Intelligence Reports: Surveillance of Radicals in the United States, 1917–1941, microfilm collection; "Report of County Attorneys for two years from November 30, 1920 to November 30, 1922 on liquor cases," Atty Gen Records, box 15, file 16, MHSA; *Montana Standard,* 20 December 1928, 18.

33. *Butte Miner,* 23 July 1920, 6, 23 November 1920, 5, and 6 May 1923, 10; *Montana Standard,* 5 January 1929, 5; James Blakely, interview by Ray Calkins, Butte, 15 November 1979, 3.

34. *Butte Miner,* 31 October 1920, 1, and 3 June 1921, 5; Helen Shute Raymond, interview by Laurie Mercier, Butte, 9 October 1981; Blakely interview, 5–6; McNelis interview, 6; *Montana Standard,* 5 January 1929, 2. On the difficulties that local, state, and federal officials had working together on enforcement, see Hacker, "Rise and Fall of Prohibition," 99, 103; Anderson, "Speakeasy as a National Institution," 117, 120; and Brown, *Mabel Walker Willebrandt,* chap. 3.

35. Analysis of the police court's records appears in *Anaconda Standard,* 16 January 1920, 6; Writers' Program, Work Projects Administration, *Copper Camp,* 250–51; and *Anaconda Standard,* 3 February 1920, 14. Studies indicate that national alcohol consumption declined significantly during Prohibition. See Lender and Martin, *Drinking in America,* 138–39; and Kyvig, "Sober Thoughts," 12–13.

36. Raymond interview; Bahin, "Campaign for Prohibition," 133; Waldron and Wilson, *Atlas of Montana Elections,* 114; *Literary Digest,* 30 April 1932, 7.

37. On the WONPR, see Kyvig, *Repealing National Prohibition.* See also Kyvig, "Women against Prohibition," 474; Kyvig, "Thirsting after Righteousness," 8; and Brown, *Setting a Course,* 191.

38. Root, *Women and Repeal,* 197; "Proceedings of the First Annual Convention of WONPR, 1930," "Report of Second Annual Conference of WONPR, 1931," and "Report of the Third Annual Conference of WONPR, 1932," all in Papers of the Association against the Prohibition Amendment and the Women's Organization for National Prohibition Reform, microfilm reels 12 and 13; Elizabeth Kennedy to James E. Murray, 16 February 1936, James E. Murray Papers, box 816, file 7, K. Ross Toole Archives, University of Montana, (hereafter cited as UM).

39. *Montana Standard,* 12 September 1928, 1.

40. Calkins, *Looking Back from the Hill,* 15–17; Blakely interview, 4; Camille Maffei, interview by Russ Magnaghni, Butte, 4 May 1983; *Montana Standard,* 4 November 1962, 1B; Dorothy A. Martin, interview by Mary Murphy, Butte, 23 May 1988, 29–30.

41. Teddy Traparish scrapbook, Teddy Traparish Papers, BSBA; *Montana Standard,* 4 November 1962, n.p.; Calkins, *Looking Back from the Hill,* 71. Quotation is from Davenport, "The Richest Hill on Earth," 53. On the rise of restaurant-nightclubs after the repeal of Prohibition, see Erenberg, "From New York to Middletown." On economic gains made by Italians during Prohibition, see Mormino, *Immigrants on the Hill,* chap. 5. On business aspects of bootlegging, see Haller, "Philadelphia Bootlegging."

42. Agents' reports, 19 December 1919, Atty Gen Records, box 20, file 2, MHSA; Blakely interview, 27–28; *Butte Miner,* 9 September 1928, 1, 14.

43. *Butte Miner,* 31 July 1922, 1 and 27 August 1922, 6; *Montana Free Press,* 21 January 1929, 13. Hilder notes "home speaks" as a phenomenon of the West in "New York Speakeasy," 591.

44. Pentilla interview, 54; *Butte Miner,* 23 November 1924, 6; *Montana Standard,* 28 December 1928, 1; *Butte Daily Post,* 14 March 1921, 1; *Anaconda Standard,* 26 March 1921, 5 and 23 December 1928, 19; *Butte Miner,* 4 December 1920, 3 and 5 September 1928, 5. In *Ardent Spirits,* 252, Kobler relates the concern of a priest in Pennsylvania who attributed women's unfaithfulness and penchant to run off with star boarders to tending home stills.

Local statistics on arrests for violating Prohibition are not particularly revealing. Police records for Butte do not include arrests made outside the city limits and thus exclude much of the metropolitan area. In the middle of 1921, it appears that officers began recording liquor offenses under the heading "maintaining a nuisance." This masks meaningful understanding of arrest figures, because maintaining a nuisance also encompassed bill posting on poles, depositing rubbish on the streets, and slaughtering cattle without a permit, as well as a plethora of other offenses. Nonetheless, analysis of arrests that can definitely be identified as liquor-related reveals that in the three years following enactment of state Prohibition (and before record keeping changed), women made up between 7.7 and 10.3 percent of those arrested. City of Butte Police Blotters, 1919, 1920, 1921, BSBA.

45. Betty Horst, unrecorded interview by Mary Murphy, Butte, 23 May 1988; *Butte Miner,* 3 July 1924, 5.

46. *Butte Daily Post,* 9 April 1927, 11; *Butte Miner,* 23 November 1924, 6; *Montana Standard,* 28 December 1928, 1. Bourquin usually placed on probation female first offenders who pleaded guilty. *Montana Standard,* 18 May 1929, 1.

47. Maury, "Home," 640. According to the New York City Investigating Committee of Fourteen, in 1925 the number of women seen in places that sold illegal liquor was "astounding." Cited in Mowry and Brownell, *The Urban Nation,* 25. On women in speakeasies, see Allen, *Only Yesterday,* 211; Hilder, "New York Speakeasy," 591–601; Banning, "On the Wagon"; and Tarbell, "Ladies at the Bar."

48. Gusfield, "Status Conflicts and Changing Ideologies," 102; Hoke, "Corner Saloon," 322.

49. Hileman interview, 32. Burnham identifies the Prohibition era as a watershed for the adoption of many "bad habits" into mainstream American culture in *Bad Habits.*

50. Martin interview, 8–9; McHugh, "Gulch and I," 20–21. The press contributed to the notion that the fashions of the 1920s were linked to prostitution. For example, a prostitute, who charged her husband with assault after he broke her jaw for not earning enough money on the street, was described as "a pretty girl with bobbed hair and dressed in the style of a flapper." *Butte Miner,* 29 August 1922, 6.

51. Josephine Weiss Casey, interview by Alice Finnegan, Anaconda, 18 May 1989, 17.

52. Martin interview, 30–31; Casey interview, 17.

53. Minutes, 3 January 1939, Daughters of Norway, Solheim Lodge No. 20 Records, BSBA.

54. Martin interview, 9.

Streetcars at the corner of North Montana and Broadway streets in front of Sutton's Theater and the First Baptist Church around 1900. (Courtesy of the World Museum of Mining)

Tracks of the Butte, Anaconda and Pacific and the Northern Pacific Railways traverse the Hill just below a Butte street named Clear Grit Terrace, 1909. (Photo by John L. Maloney; courtesy of the Montana Historical Society)

The headframe of the Neversweat Mine looms above workers' houses in Finntown, 1939. (Photo by Arthur Rothstein; courtesy of the Library of Congress)

The headframe of the Mountain View Mine and the High Ore electric substation mark the skyline above the West Colusa Mine and a Meaderville neighborhood, 1939. (Photo by Arthur Rothstein; courtesy of the Library of Congress)

Backyard of a house in Centerville, ca. 1912. This photo was part of the
County Board of Health report documenting sanitary conditions in the
community. (Courtesy of the Montana Historical Society)

Children playing marbles in Finntown, 1916–17. Mine dumps and alleys
were children's playgrounds. (Courtesy of the Butte–Silver Bow Public
Archives)

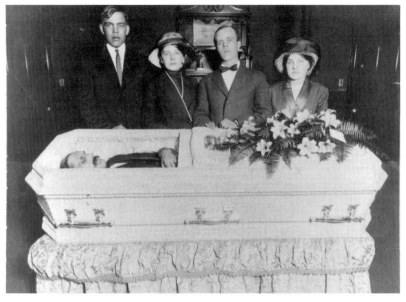

Family mourns a Finnish miner, killed in a mine accident on his last shift, ca. 1914. (Courtesy of the Butte–Silver Bow Public Archives)

First convention of the Montana Federation of Negro Women's Clubs, held in Butte, 1921. (Zubick Studio photo; courtesy of the Montana Historical Society)

World War I Red Cross volunteers from the Maccabees Review Number 20 in Anaconda, 1918. (Courtesy of the Anaconda–Deer Lodge Historical Society)

The office and store of Dr. Huie Pock, Chinese physician and merchant. (Courtesy of the Montana Historical Society)

One of Butte's Chinese families poses for a formal portrait. (Gibson Studio photo; courtesy of the Montana Historical Society)

Timbering in a stope at the Pittsmont Mine, 1918. (Bureau of Mines photo; courtesy of the National Archives)

Men setting up compressed air drills at the 1900-foot level of an unidentified mine. (Photo by N. A. Forsyth; courtesy of the Montana Historical Society)

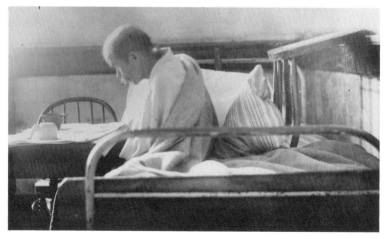

A patient in the county hospital. This photo was also part of the County Board of Health report, ca. 1912. (Courtesy of the Montana Historical Society)

A Butte saloon in the days before Prohibition. (Courtesy of the World Museum of Mining)

Men gathered in an uptown cigar store. (Courtesy of the Montana Historical Society)

The Montana WCTU campaigned for Prohibition in Columbus's 1916 Fourth of July parade. (Courtesy of the Montana Historical Society)

A woman sits on the porch of her Butte house. (Courtesy of the Montana Historical Society)

Murray Hospital's graduating nurses pose on the hospital roof in 1921. (Courtesy of the Butte–Silver Bow Public Archives)

Salesclerks in Hennessy's Department Store. (Courtesy of the Montana Historical Society)

The girls' Central High School basketball team—the "Maroon Maidens"—in 1931. (Courtesy of the World Museum of Mining)

The queen and her court at Butte High School's junior prom in 1927—bobbed hair all. (Reprinted from the *Butte High School Yearbook;* courtesy of the Butte–Silver Bow Public Archives)

Courting couples pose in front of an automobile dealership. (Courtesy of
the Butte–Silver Bow Public Archives)

3

Manners and Morals

Montana women are self-reliant, provided they get a chance.
—MARY O'NEILL

Early in June 1920, a distraught Butte mother reported to the police that she had been unable to get in touch with her daughter for more than a week. Margaret had moved into a room uptown a month before but had kept in regular contact with her family. When the police investigated, they found Margaret in a rooming house on the edge of Chinatown. She was registered as the wife of a man named Chong Wing but was apparently living as his "paramour" in exchange for the $6 a day she needed to support her cocaine habit. Wing was arrested, tried, and convicted of contributing to Margaret's delinquency, although he did not provide her directly with drugs. Those she purchased in a Chinese cafe on South Arizona Street. During the trial Margaret testified that she had been frequenting Butte's Chinese restaurants for six months and had made friends with a circle of young women, whom she subsequently learned were drug users. Margaret was arrested on charges of vagrancy but released in the custody of her mother.[1]

Such sensational reports of female delinquency, involving drink, drugs, and sex, alarmed Butte parents and civil and church authorities in the 1920s. Were young women in the post–World War I period abandoning the morals of an older generation? Without a doubt, the experiences of World War I, combined with the defiant ambience of the Prohibition era, nurtured a revolution in public manners, a revolt led by a vanguard of young working women. But did changes in dress, cosmetics, dancing styles, and even drinking habits signal a profound shift in women's values and convictions about what their role in society should be?

Before World War I, challenges to the model of "true womanhood" that dominated middle-class culture and stood as a public measure for propriety came from two directions. First, "new women," educated, articulate, and often politically active, challenged the truism that woman's proper—and most fulfilling—role was as wife and mother. Many new women consciously chose a single life, or a life with another woman, and a career other than homemaking. Through their examples and writings, these women sought legitimacy for an alternative model of womanhood. On a different front, working-class urban women challenged ideals of true womanhood by embracing a heterosexual and heterosocial culture outside the home. Working-class women in America's larger cities had a long tradition of enjoying the commercial pleasures urban life offered. Many female workers, desiring the somewhat costly pleasures of cafes, dance halls, and theaters, dated men who paid their way, and in return they sometimes provided social and sexual favors. Reactions to their pursuit of amusement varied, depending upon the mores of their families and their religious and ethnic communities. However, by the middle-class standards most frequently held by contemporary observers of urban life—editors, reformers, and employers—working women's actions bordered on the promiscuous. Not until the 1920s did this working-class social style gain acceptance within the middle class.[2]

After the war it became harder and harder to say what was and was not ladylike and distinguish between immorality and frivolity. It is impossible to order the importance of various factors leading to that state. Greater opportunities for women to leave home and go to college; a wider variety of jobs in the white-collar sector; and the national distribution of technological delights such as movies, radios, Victrolas, and automobiles that generated new fashions, dances, and styles of courtship all contributed to changes in women's behavior. The war experience and ensuing depression inspired a feeling of disillusionment, recklessness, and immediacy. One English writer noted that the war gave birth to a "grimly humorous generation which from childhood had both expected and experienced the seamier side." The effect may not have been as extreme in the United States, but certainly the popular culture of the 1920s had its dark side. The exuberance of jazz melodies often masked bleak lyrics; the romantic thrill of frequenting speakeasies was based on breaking the law; and boxing, one of the decade's most popular sports, was brutal and corrupt.[3]

Change occurred most obviously and quickly in large metropolitan areas, cities that had jobs that attracted girls from surrounding farms and small towns. These urban migrants lived in furnished room districts on their own. Or, if they lived at home, they sought their pleasures in places that were perhaps a trolley ride away from their own neighborhoods and the judgmental gazes of parents and neighbors. Most of America, however, was not like Chicago or New York City. In small and middling cities—like Butte—there were fewer of the new commercial amusements, and few places women could go where someone would not know them or their families. Quite simply, most women lacked the anonymity that emboldened their urban sisters.

Anonymity had two meanings in urban life, however: passing unnoticed and remaining unidentified. In the nineteenth century, citizens learning to navigate the treacherous currents of urban life strove for public anonymity. They went about their business, minding their own business. The prescriptions for a woman's deportment, especially, claimed that she could avoid insult or unwelcome attention by dressing and acting as inconspicuously as possible. If she did not, she invited propositions and laid herself open for comparison to a prostitute. Clearly, this type of anonymity was not part of the code of public manners that many young Butte women adopted after the war. Comfortable enough with urban life and claiming new spaces within it, their public demeanor was designed to invite notice.[4]

Yet acting boldly was a far cry from becoming a female delinquent such as those exposed in the Butte newspapers. Butte women lived in a geographically small city of closely knit neighborhoods, many governed by a rigid Catholic morality. In style women may have eschewed public anonymity, but the fact that they could not easily lose themselves in an urban crowd, combined with limited income and religious and family proscriptions, circumscribed their behavior.

It was unusual to find many new women or working-class trendsetters outside large metropolitan areas before the war. The bonds of cultural conformity were tighter in small towns and cities where anonymity was often impossible, where the eyes of family and neighbor monitored women's behavior, and where tongues too easily labeled amusements immoral. Change took place more slowly in the hinterland. In Butte we can chart the expansion of the boundaries of womanly behavior during the late 1910s and 1920s. Although increasing numbers of young women attended dance halls, in equal numbers and often, the same women spent evenings at the movies and at church-sponsored card parties. In the 1920s most of Butte's young women anticipated a future that comprised a few years of paid work before marriage and children. There were only a handful of "new women" in Butte, but there were many young working women. In the years between school and marriage, when they earned and could control their own incomes, they claimed for themselves new rights in the workplace, on the streets, and in arenas of commercial leisure. In the process they redefined the parameters of respectability.

■ ■ ■

The first significant challenge to the ideals of true womanhood in Butte came from a nineteen-year-old native-grown iconoclast named Mary MacLane. Mary was the child of failed fortune. Her father had made some money in the California gold rush but died when she was eight. Her mother married another adventurer, who took the family to Butte in search of his fortune. On the eve of Mary Mac-Lane's departure for Stanford University, her stepfather confessed that he had lost the family's money in a mining speculation and could not afford to send her to college. Restless, unemployed, and trapped in Butte, Mary spent her days walking through "sand and barrenness" and confiding her thoughts to her diary. In 1902 she sent this handwritten text to a Chicago publisher. Herbert S. Stone issued the manuscript as *The Story of Mary MacLane* and sold eighty thousand copies during its first month in print. The Butte Public Library banned the book, and a daily paper denounced it as "inimical to public morality." The *New York Herald* pronounced Mary mad and demanded that paper and pen be denied her until she regained her senses. The *New York Times* advised a spanking.[5]

What could a teenage girl in Butte, Montana, have written to provoke such responses? In an age when legs were referred to as limbs, Mary boasted of her strong woman's body; in an era of moral absolutes, she claimed that right, wrong, good, and evil were mere words. In defiance of all the strictures of true womanhood, she pronounced that she was neither high-minded nor spiritual, but "earthly, human, sensitive, sensuous, and sensual." Mary longed for fame and romance and a man to seduce her. She wrote, "As the world views such things it would be my ruin. But as I view such things it would not be ruin. It would be a new lease on life." She prayed that she would never become "that abnormal merciless animal, that deformed monstrosity—a virtuous woman." Most of all Mary craved "Experience":

> It is not deaths and murders and plots and wars that make life tragedy.
> It is Nothing that makes life tragedy.
> It is day after day, and year after year, and Nothing.
> It is a sunburned little hand reached out and Nothing put into it.[6]

Mary used her royalties to leave Butte and move to Greenwich Village, where she acquired a taste for cigarettes and martinis, attended the theater and prizefights, and reveled in the company of other free-spirited women. She returned to Butte in 1909 to remain for seven years, haunting gambling dens and roadhouses and writing another autobiographical book. Mary was a figure of both scorn and fascination, outrageous enough to become part of Butte's pantheon of characters but also considered a dangerous influence on women. She drank, gambled, and "liked rowdiness when she happened to be in the humor." She wrote about male lovers and her physical attraction to women, but little is really known about her sexual life. Betty Horst recalled the time her father, Butte's health officer, rented a hack to take his wife to a roadhouse for dinner. As they walked through the bar toward the dining room, they passed Mary sitting at a slot machine, smoking and drinking. She invited Mrs. Horst to join her. Mrs. Horst accepted. Her shocked husband continued into the restaurant. When it sunk in that his wife actually knew Butte's notorious female writer, Dr. Horst got up and drove home. In 1910 the *Butte Miner* invited Carrie Nation to comment on the phenomenon of Mary MacLane. Nation pronounced Mary "the example of a woman who has been unwomanly in everything that she is noted for" and admonished residents not to let their daughters read her books.[7]

Mary MacLane was unusual by any definition of early-twentieth-century womanhood, but she was not alone in contesting orthodoxy. Women in business and politics challenged stereotypes of women's proper place, seeking to exert female influence in commerce and government. Brash, high-spirited working-class women assaulted conventions of feminine behavior, especially outside the workplace. Susceptible to the power of movies and the advertising industry, mass-marketers of glamour and romance, these women aspired to more than food and shelter, and they demanded that their behavior, rowdy though it sometimes was, be counted respectable.

Women who wanted to make changes in Butte faced a paradoxical cultural heritage. On the one hand, they drew on the precedent of the independent behavior of pioneer women. Pioneers were the heroes of Montana, honored for surviving the hardships of the overland trail and frontier conditions. In 1934, when Mary L. Alderson was preparing her manuscript "A Half Century of Progress for Montana Women," she queried her former companions in the suffrage and temperance movements about what they considered the most significant accomplishments of Montana women. Nanita Sherlock, assistant commissioner for state lands, replied that the survival of the pioneer spirit was Montana women's greatest heritage. A decade earlier, Mary O'Neill, a Butte businesswoman and political activist, chastised a national representative of the League of Women Voters for treating Montana women condescendingly, like a bunch of "rubes." O'Neill championed Montana women, claiming "they are of the spirit of the pioneers who . . . established civilization in centers and are gradually building a great state." In 1932 Grace Erickson, wife of Gov. John E. Erickson, disclaimed her title of "first lady." She argued that the "first ladies" of Montana were not the wives of the state's governors, members of Congress, and senators, but the women "who went into the mining camps and the forest and the newly added agricultural areas of this state, braving privation, hardship and often grave peril, to erect homes, rear families and help to build a new commonwealth."[8]

As Erickson implied, groundbreaking did not necessarily mean greater freedom from the canons of ladyhood. Women pioneers were admired for the fact that they survived the overland journey as ladies and brought special civilizing traits to the frontier. Obituaries in the 1910s and 1920s eulogized early female settlers of Montana as "pioneer matrons," often recounting their contributions to frontier community-building. Changes in ladylike conduct made the journey to Montana very slowly. Anna Appelman had to return to the East to take a small step forward. While in New York, Anna decided "to break a provincial tenet" of the West that women not lift their skirts for a public shoeshine. When one shoe was finished, she heard a familiar voice say, "'Now you would not get a shoe-shine on the streets of Butte,'" and looked up to see William Scallon, onetime president of the Anaconda Company, observing her. She recalled, "I think he enjoyed my confusion."[9]

Butte women had a right to be confused. The strictures of domesticity seemed clear, but women also had the example of trailblazing political campaigners to follow. Populist Ella Knowles lost the 1892 election for state attorney general by only five votes, leading the party's ticket. Thanks to Jeannette Rankin and her cohort, Montana enacted universal woman suffrage in 1914, and Rankin's successful bid for Congress two years later also encouraged women's political activity. Nevertheless, Butte was a small, male-dominated city with provincial ideas about women's seemly behavior, ideas that governed everything from the etiquette of shoeshines to appropriate jobs. In 1917 the city's women's clubs pressured the government to create a position for a woman police officer. Fifty women applied for the job. The city hired none of them. Officials consulted applicants' fathers and brothers, who put a halt to their relatives' job search.[10]

Butte had inherited the dichotomous ideology permeating late-Victorian and Edwardian-Anglo culture that viewed woman as either "good" or "bad." According to this scheme, good and bad women occupied different universes and rarely if ever came into contact with each other. But in the reality of the American mining West, a combination of demography and geography brought the moral and immoral cheek to cheek. In early mining camps women were a minority, and frequently the first and most numerous female migrants were prostitutes. As the classic jingle related, "First came the miners to work in the mine / Then came the ladies to live on the line." In prairie towns "the line" might be literally across the tracks, off the beaten path of shoppers and casual strollers. But in mining towns like Butte, often perched precariously on hillsides or nestled in narrow gulches, town builders did not have the luxury of the prairies' wide-open spaces. Butte cribs and brothels started out on the main east-west avenue of Park Street, and the red light district eventually consolidated just two blocks south of Park and Main. Butte was not unique. In Helena, another Montana mining town, the Catholic orphanage and school, built on a hill above the main gulch, had a bird's-eye view of the red light district. The press also kept the activities of prostitutes in the public eye. About the only coverage working women received in western newspapers involved accounts of prostitutes' attempted suicides, arrests, fights, or other escapades.[11]

Prostitution was one of the most common occupations for women in Butte in the early twentieth century. When a reforming state attorney general shut down the red light district in 1917, the *Anaconda Standard* estimated that four hundred women would be affected: 350 in the district and another fifty who worked in roadhouses out in the county. Even the most sheltered girl could not help but have some knowledge of her "other" and perhaps wonder at the differences between them. In rare instances she might even admire the moxie that prostitutes shared with suffragists and pioneers. When George D. George was arraigned on white slavery charges for transporting Joyce McDonald from British Columbia to Butte for immoral purposes, McDonald filed a claim of ownership for the automobile he had been using as a taxi. She alleged that she earned every penny of the money that bought the car while working in the district, and she demanded that the automobile be turned over to no one but herself or her lawyers.[12]

Red light districts conveniently segregated women defined exclusively by their sexual activity from those who endangered their claims to womanliness if they exhibited any hint of public sexuality. In Butte this distinction was so integral to the definition of womanhood that the city ordinance regulating vagrancy distinguished "women" from "lewd and dissolute female persons." Restricted districts were circuses of commercialized sex, and Butte's shocked even an experienced prostitute from Chicago. Madeleine claimed she had never seen the seamy side of the underworld until she arrived in Butte, where it was underfoot at every step: "Here was no kid-gloved vice with a silken veil across its face, but vice naked, raw, and rampant. The noxious fumes from the smelter became as pure ozone when compared with the vitiated moral atmosphere." A Butte journalist likened the district to "a street leading into hell," and in 1916 a committee from the Law and Order League of Chicago, passing through en route to the West Coast, judged it "a disgrace to American civilization."[13]

Butte residents had mixed emotions regarding the district. Sordid it might be, but it seemed necessary in a town full of single miners. There was even a touch of braggadocio in comparisons to New Orleans's Corduroy Row and San Francisco's Barbary Coast. The city, in fact, was proud of both its good and its bad women—as long as they remained separate. The red light district was designed to guarantee that, and both men and women shared the belief that the presence of the district protected good women. Helen Raymond, in speaking of the district during the 1920s, expressed the common opinion that Butte streets were safe for women despite the presence of so many rough men. With the red light district flourishing, men "knew where to get their pleasures."[14]

During the war years, mothers began worrying that the lines of the district were dissolving. In 1914 Butte's Socialist administration bowed to pressure from the Florence Crittenton Rescue Circle and agreed to give special police powers to its female field missionary, Amanda Pfeiffer. Pfeiffer patrolled the red light district looking for "erring" girls out for a night's excitement, whom she took home to their parents.[15]

In 1917, when Attorney General Sam Ford ordered all the restricted districts in the state closed, not all law-abiding Montanans thought it a wise reform. Prostitutes merely moved into previously respectable hotels and boardinghouses and carried on their trade, making it easier for local girls to enter the ranks of occasional prostitutes without the conspicuousness of moving to or working in the district. One Butte mother told Ford that his reform was "one of the worst things you could of ever done." She complained that before the district was closed her daughters were "good girls" who stayed at home and worked. "Now they are never home never work and always have plenty of money." E. J. J. Shea, a miner, shared the belief that the dispersal of prostitutes throughout the town would undoubtedly lead respectable women into immorality: "How can you expect women to be decent when moral profligates are roaming around." Only Violet Bruder, a prostitute in Butte, challenged the idea that it was her co-workers who corrupted society. She asked, "Were the morals of the frequenters of said district not degenerate, would there be any call for degeneracy?"[16]

A few citizens' letters to Ford revealed the connection people drew between consumerism and prostitution. T. L. Blackman contended that closing the districts was futile because it was not their presence that caused the downfall of women, but "booze, dancing, low wages, human nature, and show windows in all your big department stores." Parents feared that their daughters might be attracted to prostitution, not because they wanted sex with strangers but because they wanted money and the goods and entertainment it would buy. They suspected that the tenets of Judeo-Christian morality were not a strong enough defense against the allure of clothes, movies, dance halls, and the other enticements of a burgeoning consumer society.[17]

Young women could see both horror and glamour in Butte's red light district. Most prostitutes were "everynight workingman's whores" who sold their bodies for a dollar in dark, narrow cribs and made most of their income selling dollar-a-bottle beer. Transient, worn, often addicted to alcohol and drugs, they were tragic, exploited women. But Butte also sported several elaborate brothels whose inmates "were all beauties, or else they wouldn't be there." Parlor house girls charged higher prices and often served as companions as well as bed partners. They were famous for their fine wardrobes— clothing much nicer than department store clerks could afford. Ann

Pentilla recalled, "You could just pick them out because they were so outstanding, they were dressed so nice. And it wasn't gaudy, it was just beautifully dressed." Charlie Chaplin, who traveled through Butte, concurred: "If one saw a pretty girl smartly dressed, one could rest assured she was from the red-light quarter, doing her shopping. Off duty, they looked neither right nor left and were most respectable." Chaplin later argued with Somerset Maugham about the grotesque costume of Sadie Thompson in a production of the play *Rain*, stating that "no harlot in Butte, Montana, could make money if she dressed like that."[18]

In 1920, under the banner headline "Butte Store Named 'Little Redlight,'" the city's socialist newspaper charged that the low wages earned by department store cash girls—the young women who ran change between customers and the cashier—drove some of them to prostitution. Averring that Symons's cash girls, who made an average of $3.50 per week, could not support themselves unless they lived with their parents, investigators claimed to have positive evidence that some girls were "rustling" on the street. Symons's employees reported that the store routinely discharged girls after they served their apprenticeship, thus preventing them from becoming full-fledged clerks at union wages and forcing them into the streets to make a living. At Hennessy's Department Store investigators discovered two former prostitutes working—allegedly with the connivance of some managers—as "procuresses." The two enjoined salesclerks to go on joyrides to drinking parties out at the roadhouses, where they were turned over to men who had made prior arrangements with the former prostitutes. If the girls complained, they lost their jobs at the store. According to the investigators, it was Hennessy's employees who coined the nickname "the little redlight" for their place of employment.[19]

It is unlikely that many department store clerks turned to occasional prostitution to augment their wages. Ever since women had moved into low-paying public work, labor organizers and reformers had raised the specter of prostitution as the inevitable fate of underpaid female workers. Women certainly learned more about sex from their fellow workers than they did from their parents, however. Ann Pentilla recalled that neither she nor her sisters "knew enough about the birds and bees until we went to work." Butte's women workers were indeed conscious of the low wages they received and the discrepancy between what their paychecks bought and what the owning class enjoyed. One woman, Anna Rogers, described the life of shopgirls as "keeping body and soul together on a mere pittance while Mr. Woolworth can live in a mansion with every luxury." Undoubtedly, there were some women who did barter sexual companionship for entertainment they could not afford. But we do not know to what extent Butte's female workers welcomed joyriding, drinking parties, and arranged assignations. In all probability it was a highly visible minority.[20]

What many studies have revealed is that working girls' actions—whether forced, welcomed, or hazarded through ignorance—appeared to parents, the press, and moral guardians in the church to blur the line between prostitute and lady. As Dorothy Martin and Helen Harrington could attest, unladylike conduct, such as smoking, dancing, and wearing short skirts and short hair, inevitably elicited comparisons to prostitutes. Frederick Lewis Allen observed that in many minds of the decade, "Short-haired women, like long-haired men, are associated with radicalism, if not with free love." Many young Butte women donned the accouterments of the jazz age simply for fashion and fun. Others embraced them as declarations of independence. Parents and other figures of authority were often exasperated and disturbed, yet they were not alone. The allure of new fashions and new freedoms, seemingly linked to consumer culture, transcended ethnic and national boundaries. Mexican-American families in Los Angeles suffered the same intergenerational tensions sparked by young women's adoption of new styles of dress and cosmetics and freer attitudes toward sexual relations. African women in the Zambia copperbelt, once they moved from their villages to mine compounds, assumed European dresses of fashionable cut, coveted goods such as tea, sugar, and bread, and began hosting dances and tea parties. Their activities vexed husbands, who were expected to provide more money for European-style amenities, and mine managers, who interpreted women's cultural innovations as dangerous demonstrations of independence.[21]

■ ■ ■

During the war, society applauded young women's willingness to trade in their skirts for overalls and do the jobs that needed to be done. But their after work activities were frequently censured. Complimented as prudent savers of their meager paychecks, young women were chastised as spendthrifts of morality. Critics singled out their penchant for dancing and frivolous clothes, interpreting both as evidence of weakened moral fiber. Mrs. George Rose, a traveling evangelist, reminded Butte women that "in years gone by" telling daughters "that a thing was unladylike" was enough to make them desist. However, "now the motto seems to be 'Be a good sport.' Modern fashions, exposed necks, bare arms, yes, even exposed legs . . . you say they are worn innocently, with no thought of appeal to the lust of men. I wish I could think that this were so."[22]

The Butte press regularly published articles on other communities' attempts to police women's dress, perhaps hoping that someone in Butte would emulate them or that girls would take heed of warnings such as that issued by Denver high school boys, who proclaimed a boycott on bobbed hair, low-cut waists, flimsy hosiery, rouged lips, and "cheeks that bloom like a drugstore blush." Even one prostitute considered Butte's shopgirls "overdressed." The outcry against young women's new look was premature, because not everyone adopted the provocative fashions. Judging by yearbook photographs, bobbed hair did not appear with any regularity at Butte High School until 1924. In 1923 Mary Josephine McGrath reigned as prom queen, a "true Irish type of beauty" praised for not being "the flapper type." The girl voted most beautiful in the school was a freshman who had long ringlets adorned with silk flowers and bore a stronger resemblance to Mary Pickford than Clara Bow.[23]

Many Butte working women, however, felt that fashionable clothes and using cosmetics were a sign of coming of age. Just as in other parts of the country, the acceptance of cosmetics and the increasing commercialization of beauty made its way to Butte. In 1917 there was no such thing as a beauty parlor in Butte, but by 1931 there were twenty-eight, and the city had enacted an ordinance to regulate them. Even more than fashionable hair styles and cosmetics, however, working women sought new clothes. Dresses did not have to be elaborate, just store-bought. Bernice Knierim recalled that one of the first things she did when she got a real job was to buy "a decent dress. . . . It was a flowered dress with kind of a lace trim, nothing fancy. But I felt like I was a millionaire in it." Bernice had never had a new dress; her mother sewed all her clothes. "I don't care what you say, a homemade dress is a homemade dress. And a boughten dress is a boughten dress."[24]

To Ann Pentilla, her first pair of high heels signified that she was grown. With few material possessions, often with no thought of or chance for education beyond grammar or high school, beauty— including sleek apparel—was one asset that young women could cultivate. Julia McHugh, who remembered being "old" before she got a "boughten" dress, had no qualms about spending her money on clothes: "In those days, our redeeming feature was our 'good looking' legs and we would pay any price for hose. When I worked in the Wiz Way sorting onions, I would have on my black patent leather pumps and $2.50 hose—this on $40 a month. We were quite vain." For single, wage-earning women, store-bought clothes became a symbol of independence. Not only could women pay for their own clothing, but they could also choose its cut, color, and fabric and present to the world an image that they had chosen, not their parents, guardians, or school authorities. Mary MacLane recognized that women's dress was a stage for expression and improvisation. In her 1917 book *I, Mary MacLane,* she acknowledged that only a few women could express themselves through acting, painting, politics, or other work. "But there's not one—from a wandering Romany gypsy, red-blooded and strong-hearted, to an over-guarded over-bred British princess—who doesn't express what she is in the clothes she wears and the way she wears them. Her clothes conceal and reveal, artfully and contradictorily and endlessly."[25]

The shorter, looser, skimpier clothes of the postwar period allowed women greater comfort and mobility and apparently sent a message of disturbing sensuality and, in some cases, threatening athleticism to those who preferred to think of women as the "weaker sex." In a 1926 short story by that title, a man nervously contemplates the postwar generation of "sailboat-handling-she-Vikings," "skiing Valkyries," and "diving Venuses." In an effort to curb this Amazonian threat, Montana's Catholic church took up the battle against short skirts. Bishop John P. Carroll visited Butte churches and enlisted Catholic women in a league to combat indecent dress and immoral dances. The bishop received an enthusiastic response from women, who pledged in the name of Mary Immaculate "to maintain and hand down the traditional and proverbial purity and modesty of Catholic womanhood."[26]

Churches played a major role in Butte women's social life. In 1917 the mining city boasted forty-seven churches, missions, and synagogues. The most powerful of all the denominations was the Roman Catholic. With nine churches in 1917 and a tenth built in 1921, Catholics had the largest church membership in the metropolitan area. Approximately fifteen thousand men, women, and children belonged to Butte's Catholic parishes in 1917. Methodists, who had eight congregations, mustered little more than a thousand.[27]

Apart from urging women to resist new dress and dance styles, what did the Catholic church have to say about the apparent moral revolution of the 1920s? Although copies of Butte priests' sermons no longer exist and the transactions of the confessional remain private, parish magazines of the late 1910s and 1920s presented the

Church's position on many of the social and moral concerns of the day. The *Catholic Monthly* featured local parish news and occasional writings by parish priests or the bishop, but the bulk of articles were national columns reprinted in every parish magazine. Marriage, divorce, birth control, flirting, prize fighting, movies, and gambling were all subjects of discussion in the 1910s and 1920s.

In 1917 the Church exhorted women to wear simple dress and warned of the sin of flirting, which was defined as "simply, deliberately, and wantonly acting in a way to attract the attention of particular persons of the opposite sex." Women who flirted had lost "all sense of decency." The fact that flirting often took place on the public street compounded the offense, for it led to comparisons with "abandoned women, seeking for custom." However, the Church did not couch all of its advice in terms of warnings. In several essays on the sacrament of marriage, authors explained the virtues that Catholic men and women should possess to ensure a happy and holy marriage. In 1923 an essayist described "true manhood" as the "practice of certain virtues, nobility of aim, cleanness of living, unswerving honesty, respect for women." As a counterpart, the "predominant virtue expected from a woman [was] chastity," accompanied by "habits of modesty, reticence, decorum." Those virtues could best be expressed in a marriage in which the man was breadwinner and the woman was homemaker and mother. The Catholic church, then as now, opposed all forms of artificial birth control and believed that "ideal conjugal love require[d] children." On this issue, the Church was persuasive. When Margaret Sanger planned a speaking tour in Montana in the 1930s, local organizers advised her not to bother with Butte. "Butte would be futile, I'm afraid," wrote Belle Winestine, "on account of the great preponderance of citizens who are opposed to even *listening* to birth control propaganda, on account of religious convictions."[28]

While the Church sponsored councils for women that engaged in fund-raising and charitable works, it emphasized that those activities should not interfere with a woman's work at home. Some essays expressed fear that women's education would lead them away from their proper place as homemakers. One priest challenged the notion that educated women made better wives than their less educated sisters. He ridiculed "women's emancipation" and asked, "Will history record the 'century runs,' 'golf games,' 'women's conferences' where stupid theories are discussed and homes neglected?" Many Catholic women, however, disagreed. They supported Catholic education for women and in the late 1920s, raised scholarship money for girls. Some drew lessons from the Federation of Women's Clubs and the League of Women Voters, noting that Catholic women's councils could mobilize their members to vote when issues of importance to Catholicism appeared on the ballot.[29]

Messages in the *Catholic Monthly* targeted women as the guardians of virtue. Men, too, were admonished to be pious and pure, but less frequently and with less urgency. The moral well-being of the family was put in women's hands. Although both young men and young women could be tempted by immoral dances, immodest dress, and obscene movies, it was the job of mothers—not fathers—to help them resist such temptations. This was hardly unique to Catholic ideology. In 1923, Butte Methodists held a series of public sermons on the sanctity of the home. A Dr. Clifford urged mothers to teach their daughters to sweep and sew so they would stop "fussing with cosmetics, following the movies, and marathoning to jazz music."[30]

■ ■ ■

Jazz had moved upriver from New Orleans in 1917, when the U.S. Navy shut down Storyville and musicians dispersed throughout the country. Recordings of the Original Dixieland Jazz Band sold millions and inspired thousands of musicians, black and white, good and bad. Even in Butte, groups of young men formed their own jazz bands, such as the Whirlwinds, while the Butte High music teacher forbade the addition of a saxophone to the orchestra because it was "too sexy." In a 1924 short story, Butte's Myron Brinig denoted the disturbing change wrought by "grandsons of the pioneers [who] twisted and wriggled to the jazz melodies of eccentric bands." It was the link between sex and jazz that alarmed parents. When the Original Dixieland Jazz Band made its debut in New York, *Variety* reported, "There is one thing that is certain, and that is that the melodies as played by the Jazz organization . . . are quite conducive to making the dancers on the floor loosen up and go the limit in their stepping." That possibility must have appalled dance reformers, who had in the previous decade struggled to clean up the "tough dances," which celebrated physical contact. Butte parents' concern that dancing led to immorality was perhaps understandable when they read in the newspaper that the latest popular tune was a "twinkling fox-trot" with the title "Snake Hips," or that the new band of all Butte boys playing at the Winter Garden was "sweet—lowdown and hot." From World War I to the mid-1930s prostitutes made blatant the connection between sex and jazz by propositioning men with the phrase, "How about some jazz?"[31]

Dancing was among the most popular forms of entertainment in Butte during the 1920s and 1930s, and there were dance halls to suit every mood: roadhouses with somewhat shady reputations, neighborhood speakeasies with small dance floors, the very respectable Winter Garden, and the romantic Columbia Gardens' pavilion, festooned with Japanese lanterns. All the fraternal lodges sponsored dances and rented their halls to other groups when they needed the space. Organizations as diverse as the Swedish-Finnish Hall, the Odd Fellows, the Butte Muckers' Athletic Club, the American Legion, and the Walkerville Social Club hosted "flower and basket" dances, marathons, and walkathons to raise money and entertain their members. Dances were occasions for dates; Pat O'Leary, who loved to dance, took his fiancée to the Winter Garden three times a week. But many men and women attended with friends of the same sex and waited to see what pairing might develop at the dance hall.[32]

While many lodge dances were patronized exclusively by members of the same ethnic associations, at public dances young people from many ethnic groups and all parts of town mingled. One young woman, who danced whenever she could, loved best the schottisches and polkas at the Scandia and Finn Halls. Murel Roberts, too, remembered going to Slovak and Finn dances with his friends: "We'd go to them and we'd have a great time because of the way they danced. They didn't take their partner and dance, you'd dance a little ways and then you'd stop and . . . then you'd go around again and stop. Oh boy! . . . we'd have a lot of fun." Julia McHugh and her girlfriends from Dublin Gulch were all "swell dancers," and they shimmied and spun at the Sacred Heart school basement every Wednesday, at the Hibernia Hall on Friday, the Rosemont on Saturday, the Winter Garden in the winter, and Columbia Gardens on Sundays in the summer. They "knew kids from all parts of Butte . . . so as soon as we arrived, we would be asked for a dance and we would be four or five ahead. No dancing with the same guy all night. We didn't go on dates, but . . . someone would take us home."[33]

Not everybody went right home. One woman remembered a night when "the boys 'took' a car. An old Ford. The doors on it and the floor boards missing in the back seat. No breaks, we practically used our feet. . . . It was a wild ride coming down Harding Way. . . . Maybe we kept late hours but we shore had fun."[34]

It was just such adventures that perturbed clergy and reformers. Authorities across the nation worried about the effect dance halls had on girls—presumably boys could fend for themselves. This attitude prevailed in Butte as well. In 1914 the Rev. E. J. Groeneveld, surveying "the amusement problem," declared that "the dance hall is to the girl what the saloon is to the man. The public dance hall, with its promiscuous gathering, is an extremely dangerous institution." Dance halls could be perilous, although the more common danger was sudden violence, not seduction, especially when alcohol was present. Drinking was not allowed inside the dance halls, but there was usually a saloon or speakeasy downstairs or next door. Miners recalled that on weekend nights at the Butte honky-tonks you could "drink all you wanted to and dance and fight and everything else." Fights often erupted over the "everything else," which included sexual foreplay, not always with one's date. Lisle Scanland had grown up going to country dances with his family and "knew what went on outside the dance hall." He warned his girlfriend, "'You go to a dance with me, I don't care who you dance with in the hall, but, if you go out of that door, you either go out with me or you don't go out that door—unless you're with a girl.'" In his opinion, "Jealousies was created in the dance hall."[35]

At times jealousy and rowdyism got out of hand. On the night of July 30, 1922, shots rang out at a small dance hall adjacent to a soft drink parlor on Second Street. In the aftermath of the shooting none of the participants, all Austrian immigrants, would talk to the police. But it was rumored that six men had quarreled over a pretty eighteen-year-old girl. One died from his wounds.[36]

Butte's ordinance governing dance halls embodied all the elements advocated by national dance hall reformers: each concession had to be licensed; its license could be revoked if disorderly or immoral activities took place on the premises; no liquor was to be sold or served; and minors under eighteen had to be accompanied by a parent or guardian and sign a register with their names, ages, and addresses. But enforcement of the ordinance was fitful at best. Citizens complained to the state attorney general of Sunday dancing, drinking, and fighting at Butte dance halls. Lax enforcement stemmed in part from administration of the ordinance. In most cities the police force, specially appointed inspectors, or private agencies working in cooperation with the police were in charge of dance hall inspection. But in Butte, as Josephine Roche and Ella Gardner, investigators from the U.S. Children's Bureau, discovered, any city official was eligible for the unpaid position. In 1923 a committee from the League of Women Voters requested that the city assign a woman to the job and give her a salary. The mayor partially obliged, delegating the task to the assistant county probation officer, who inspected the halls in addition to her regular full-time job. Roche and Gardner were dubious about her performance. In response to their observation that they had found at least a dozen girls under sixteen at the dances they attended, she replied that she knew and that she permitted the girls to stay and dance until 10:30: "'I think it's better for them to be there where we know what they're doing than to send them out on the streets.'" She did not believe that the girls went home when they were expelled from the dance halls and felt that it was wiser to keep an eye on them than to turn them out on the street, where they would pick up men and go to roadhouses. Roche and Gardner doubted that permitting the girls to dance until 10:30 would make them any readier to go home.[37]

Despite their reservations, Roche and Gardner reported that Butte's dance halls generally operated in an orderly fashion. Each had a bouncer who ejected drunken men, and the dancing was "no different from that in other cities." The roadhouses, however, were "rough places" and, according to the local police, all too accessible to girls who went out in automobiles after town dances. The investigators supported Butte's chief probation officer, David O'Connor, in his complaint (which echoed authorities in other cities) that it was negligent parents who were responsible for most juvenile delinquency. O'Connor believed that ninety-nine out of a hundred parents could take better care of their children. Roche and Gardner reported, "Some of them came to him wondering what in the world to do with their children, assuring him that their girls, 'never used to be like this,' while all the time . . . 'the kid is sitting there trying to vamp the cop.' She [the girl] did not learn so much in a minute, he said, and if parents were on the job they would understand. In most cases, however, 'if any of those young girls who chase around every night got in before 3 A.M. they beat the old folks home.'"[38]

In 1923 the *Butte Daily Post* reported that the county was "going after Butte dives . . . until disreputable 'joints' where youth is permitted to have its fling in its innocence and ignorance, are cleaned out. If the older ones that should know better want to go the route, let them hop to it, but they will not be permitted to smirch the young people." The provocation for what would turn out to be a short and narrowly focused "clean-up" of joints was a police raid on a New Year's Eve party at the Silver City Club, which turned up white women "dancing with negroes to the jazz music of a colored orchestra," and white men "jazzing it" with black women. Although the club, located on the edge of the red light district, was known as a hang-out for prostitutes, a gambling joint, and a place to buy dope and bootleg liquor, the police had previously ignored it. What was different and disturbing about this party was that the dancing women were not "denizens of the underworld," but white stenographers, clerks, and shopgirls, daughters of respectable Butte families. None of the girls was arrested. Instead, the county attorney began proceedings to close the club. The issue was not settled then. In 1927 the tale of white women frequenting a roadhouse operated by blacks again made the front page. The paper claimed dancing was the attraction, and a judge threatened to close the place. The tiny number of African Americans in Butte—in 1920 only .5 percent of the population—and the fraction of them who patronized the Silver City Club or roadhouses could scarcely threaten the morals of overwhelmingly white Butte. However, they provided a convenient scapegoat for the police. Racism had consistently figured in opposition to jazz music and dance. In 1927 *The Maroon,* the annual of the boys' Catholic high school, contrasted the modesty and grace of Irish step dancing—albeit originated by pagans—with jazz dance, the "unsightly wriggling of some uncivilized Mid-African tribesman."[39]

Fears that young women's capers would land them in real trouble seemed justified when residents scanned the daily police reports. In 1920 the *Anaconda Standard* reported that annually nearly a thousand women spent time behind bars in Butte. The majority served time for drunkenness, vagrancy, and "incorrigibility." In 1918 Mrs. A. J. Steele wrote to the state attorney general seeking to have her daughter put in the Good Shepherd Home until she was twenty-one and had "regain[ed] her health vitality and self-respect." Miss Steele drank and used drugs, and her parents sought her redemption. Her mother blamed the girl's condition on her frequent visits to public dances, noodle parlors [the colloquial name for Butte's Chinese restaurants], and "every 'dive' in town." The state of young womanhood appeared to worsen as the decade progressed. In 1922 a seventeen-year-old girl pleaded guilty to incorrigibility and was committed to the Good Shepherd Home until she reached twenty-one. A regular at the dance halls, when she did not come home one night her mother called the probation officer, Mrs. O'Neill. O'Neill found her in a rooming house in bed with her sister-in-law and an unidentified man. In 1929 a series of raids on "resorts" in the central business district uncovered a score of girls drinking and dancing with customers "on a commission basis."[40]

In 1926 a bizarre case threw into relief the jumble of fears and expectations some Butte residents had about women's changing roles. On November 23 Jacques Moret, considered "'one of the gang' among a number of young men of the city," was arrested while standing on the corner of Park and Main, smoking a cigar and ogling girls. Moret was not arrested for loitering, but for impersonating a man. Jacques, in fact, was a twenty-three-year-old woman. Moret claimed to be a private detective in town working on a case, but she refused to divulge the name of her agency. She had been in the city for two months, dressed in "sheik's garb," gambling, squiring women to the Meaderville night clubs, and playing piano in a dance hall. When interviewed, she said she had worn male dress since she was thirteen and had "seen more life because of wearing men's garb than a thousand women have seen attired in dresses, but I have done no wrong."[41]

A large crowd, including many women, packed the police court when "Jack" was tried. Her attorney, former mayor William H. Maloney, argued that she had violated only an obsolete statute forbidding persons to appear in public "in a dress not belonging to his or her sex." He claimed that if Moret were subject to arrest merely on the basis of her apparel, then so was every female theater usher and a majority of women who rode in automobiles. Maloney concluded that Moret's attire was far more modest than that worn by the average woman on the street and had "goods enough to make flapper dresses for a dozen women." Judge Daniel F. Shea, however, took a broader interpretation of the law and stated that there was a "decided difference" between a woman who dressed in mannish fashion and a woman who tried in every manner to give the impression that she was a man. For Shea, the issue was not trousers versus skirts, but the boundaries of gender. He fined Jack $50—suspended if she donned garb "in keeping with her sex"—and ordered the police to arrest her every time she appeared publicly in men's clothing.

Moret's disguise as a "sheik" was audacious. In 1921 sheik mania gripped the country after 125 million movie fans watched Rudolph Valentino sweep across the screen in *The Sheik*, a film version of a 1919 desert romance novel. During the early 1920s the persona of the sheik evolved in response to the perceived danger of increasingly independent women. He stood in opposition to the emasculated, effeminate "modern man" who kowtowed to flappers and new women. The sheik ransomed the threatened masculinity of the early twentieth century, embodying the "virile, sensual male, a priapic, violent lover who masters females by sexual prowess and physical force." He was more than a match for the "politically emancipated, economically independent and sexually uninhibited" woman of the postwar world. Butte's strong reaction to Moret's male attire was perhaps compounded by the fact that the style she adopted seemed to signal that not only did she wish to act as a man, but also that she was preempting the very persona that men had adopted in response to uppity women.[42]

Jack was not easily dissuaded from her habits of ten years, and within the week she was in jail again. Overstepping the bounds of the court's order, the police arrested her in her room at the Grand Hotel in the company of a nineteen-year-old cabaret singer. The girl was in bed; Jack was attired only in BVDs. Jack claimed that she had rescued the singer from a "notorious resort" in Butte and was awaiting the arrival of Jack's wealthy mother, who was going to take the girl to Denver and "start her right along the road of life." Jack's mother never showed up, and Moret ended up serving out her sentence in jail.

Jacques Moret's antics, recounted on the front pages of Butte's dailies, undoubtedly provided hundreds of Butte readers nothing more than a titillating story and a good laugh. They certainly unsettled some, however, and her arrest and prosecution illuminated Butte's gender system. Jack had close male friends in the city who declared they had no idea she was a woman. The cabaret singer, who presumably knew the truth, only commented that Jack was a most attentive companion, "thoughtful at all times," "hiring taxis for short distances," and a "wonder at ordering dinners." While vowing that she would continue to wear men's clothing if she had to carry her case to the Supreme Court, Jack also claimed feminine sensibilities and announced her intention of alerting the Federation of Women's Clubs to the filthy condition of the jail. She pointed out the irony that prostitutes were fined $10 for their activities, whereas she was fined $50. Both her fine and the front page headlines accorded to Moret's escapades, in comparison to the routine arrest and fining of prostitutes, underscored the fact that prostitutes' sexual transactions were an accepted part of the city's heterosexual practice. Prostitutes knew their place and were accredited members of the female pantheon; Moret was not. When Daniel Shea sentenced Jack, he was enforcing Butte's gender code. His judgment that her "masquerade detracts from the feminine genuineness of a woman" demonstrated that women's manners and morals were tightly braided.

▪ ▪ ▪

If we accept the perspective of the press, male employers, and some parents, it appears that young Butte women in the 1920s were intent upon destroying long-held social, moral, and even racial standards. But from the point of view of working women themselves, their activities were hardly revolutionary. Compared to young women in Chicago and New York City, Butte women played out a muted sexual revolution; their activities constituted more of a "sensual revolution," to borrow Lois Banner's phrase. Recent studies of women "adrift" may present a skewed idea of the sexual revolution in the United States because of the unique set of circumstances at work in large cities. By 1900, more than 20 percent of Chicago's working women boarded apart from family or relatives. That number increased steadily, and by 1930 approximately forty-nine thousand women were "adrift" in Chicago. These thousands of female workers shaped the landscape of the "furnished room district," where women, out from under the watchful eyes of parents and neighbors, pursued both urban pleasures and dangers in relative anonymity. In most U.S. cities this was probably not the case. In 1920, the watershed year in which more Americans were registered living in urban (defined by the Census Bureau as a concentration of 2,500 or more people) than rural areas, only three cities—New York, Chicago, and Philadelphia—had more than one million inhabitants. Of the 288 cities with a population of twenty-five thousand or more, 196 of them had fewer than seventy-five thousand residents. The experiences of Butte women—living in a metropolitan area of sixty thousand—more likely reflected the lives of the majority of American urban women than did the experiences of those residing in Chicago, New York City, or Philadelphia.[43]

Butte women were, for the most part, enmeshed in a web of familial and neighborly relations. The 1910 census reveals that only a small proportion of single working women over fifteen did not live with their immediate families or relatives. By far the largest number who boarded were servants, but even then most were the only servants in private homes where they had limited free time and employers monitored their behavior. Butte's economy offered few opportunities for female workers other than domestic service, teaching, clerical work, and prostitution. Industrial work or manufacturing was practically nonexistent. Records of the city employment agency disclose that the only real demand for female workers was from people seeking servants. Although more women worked in clerical jobs in 1920 than they had in 1910, servant was still the most common occupation for Butte women at the beginning of the decade.[44]

Butte's small size and women's living arrangements circumscribed their activities. Unlike New York City, where observers noted that patronage of dance halls was "hardly ever local" and men and women drifted from hall to hall in which "nearly everyone [was] a stranger to everyone else," Butte did not have that many dance halls or that many strangers. As Julia McHugh recounted, by the time she and her friends from Dublin Gulch were old enough to attend dances, they knew kids from all over the city. Girls found in disreputable roadhouses by the police were taken home to their parents, not brought to jail.[45]

This broadening of friendships from a neighborhood circle to the city at large was partly because children went to grammar schools within their neighborhoods but adolescents went to one of two high schools, Butte High or [Catholic] Central High School. For many students this was the first encounter between the East and West Sides, and the meeting was not always friendly. Attending Butte High was a powerful Americanization process for the children of immigrants. David Emmons observed that adult male immigrants from Ireland who came to work in Butte rarely had to leave Dublin Gulch. Their homes, the mines in which they worked, their saloons, and the Hibernian Hall were all in the neighborhood. They lived in a "little Ireland," with scant knowledge of other immigrants or native-born Americans. Their children, however, became integrated into a larger urban culture. The Lynds uncovered a similar phenomenon in Middletown, noting that the homogeneity of neighborhood, class, and ethnicity was lost when teens from all over the city entered the same high school. They concluded that a spectrum of cultural experiences tangled in the forum of high school, causing uncertainty and tension for both parents and their children but exposing all to a wider range of ideas and values.[46]

Indeed, one wonders what might have been in the minds of some Butte girls as they watched the senior high school play of 1924, *Fanny and the Servant Problem.* Fanny, a pretty chorus girl, marries an English earl, only to discover upon arrival in her new home that all of his servants are her family members. The play, of course, has a happy ending, but it must have stirred the thoughts of students from Butte's working and middle classes, some of whom worked as domestics after school and would continue to do so after graduation, whereas others in their class were destined for college and "good" marriages.[47]

While the actions of overall-clad girls hanging around soft drink parlors and young vamps "jazzing it" in roadhouses drew the attention of reformers, many young women quietly spent their leisure in innocent pleasures revolving around church, family, and lodges.

Butte was probably more like Middletown than New York City in its attitude toward new sexual mores. When the Lynds explored Middletown's sexual customs in the mid-1920s, they found the taboo against premarital sex "as strong today as in the county-seat of forty years ago." Catherine Hoy and other girls knew the limits of acceptable sexual play. One woman's mother told her "not to let the boys fool around." So she "kissed a lot" but was not about to do anything that might lead to the censure dealt an unwed mother. Catherine stated that very few single women got pregnant. "They knew their bounds—in fact, they knew that the fathers and mothers would kill them." Yet she did not feel restricted. "We were allowed to mingle. We didn't think anything of going with the boys back and forth to school. They'd come to our house and stay there. We had an old phonograph, and we played that old phonograph, danced." Even in the dance halls, young women policed themselves. As Mae Mucahy recalled, "If you went in a dance hall and you seen a girl with a cigarette or taking a drink, you'd get in another corner, way way down in another corner. That was a no-no."[48]

Although dating was on the rise in the 1920s, young women often entertained themselves in their own company or with their families. Ice skating, movies, camping trips, card parties, and picnics provided an array of inexpensive leisure activities. Independent stenographer Beatrice Bray loved to go for automobile rides, especially in some gentleman's new car, but most of her free time was taken up with church and lodge work, and her dearest wish was to attend the Shriners' convention in Portland. For Nellie Tweet, going to card parties at the Catholic church in the company of other servants was a real treat. Their employers bought tickets to support whatever charitable cause was being promoted and then passed them on to their servants, who welcomed the chance to win towels and linens for their future homes. Alma Hileman's parents forbade her and her sister to go to the dance halls, but she remembered, "You had your home parties and theaters and you had your little friends that you went out with." One of the most enjoyable and cheapest forms of entertainment was to walk uptown with other girls, window-shopping and stopping to flirt, just seeing and being seen.[49]

Ethnic and religious celebrations provided other opportunities for entertainment for young people and their families. Olga Sontum recalled that all the Norwegians would gather together and walk to the top of Big Butte to greet Midsummer Day. Serbians observed Serbian Christmas and Easter with rounds of visiting, special services, and meals. The Welsh celebrated St. David's Day on March 1, and the Scots observed Robert Burns's Day on January 25. The Irish staged plays, banquets, and parades in honor of St. Patrick's Day. Lodges and unions held picnics and dances. Until 1914, when the Miners' Union collapsed, Miners' Union Day was the summer's main event. All union members in the city paraded through the uptown, and then workers and their families adjourned to Columbia Gardens for a day of games, contests, picnicking, and dancing.[50]

Daughters of immigrants or of marriages between an immigrant and a native-born American formed the single largest category of female workers in Butte in 1920. These young women's experiences in high school and in the workplace often created a desire to participate in activities frowned upon by their immigrant parents. Ann Pentilla remembered that her father, born in Yugoslavia, was very strict. He forbade her and her sisters to wear cosmetics. Nevertheless, when the girls left the house to go to work, they stopped to make up their faces because "everybody was." Still, they carefully wiped off their lipstick and powder before returning home. Two of Ann's sisters worked as live-in servants and were able to sneak out to dances without her father's knowledge, but she and her other sister "never went around too much." When they did get out, strict rules governed their conduct. She and her sister were mortified one New Year's Eve when their father came to collect them from a lodge party because they had not come home promptly at midnight.[51]

Many immigrant parents tried to balance Americanization with the preservation of their native culture. The process often reversed traditional paths of knowledge between parents and children. Mary Trbovich's mother sent her children to Sunday school so they would learn Serbian, and they in turn taught her to read and write English. In a study of Chinese immigrants in Butte, Rose Hum Lee cites the case of a woman who described herself as "a prisoner for ten years in a land that was hailed for its individual freedom." By custom she was forbidden to leave her home. When her children were grown, they defied their father and took her uptown to see the city. As a gesture of independence she began discarding her Chinese dresses and accumulating a Western wardrobe in spite of her husband's disapproval.[52]

When women had money for entertainment, they were more likely to spend it on a movie ticket than on admission to a dance hall. By 1931 there were more than seven thousand theater seats in Butte, and when a new show opened at the Rialto the ticket line clogged the sidewalk for a block. Catherine Hoy recalled that for the clerks at Symons, sitting through a double feature with a sack of popcorn or candy was the "height of our amusement." Nellie Tweet went to the movies and out for ice cream not with a beau but with the young daughter of her employers, and Julia McHugh's eldest sister regularly escorted her siblings to the show. Although they might not attend movies with boyfriends, it was the vision of heterosexual romance that attracted young women. George Hodge, a strict Methodist from Cornwall, forbade his daughter Inez to dance, but he let her attend the movies. Inez went to the show every week and loved the romances best because she "could just sit there and dream." Mary MacLane once told an interviewer that she had "paid 15 cents on several thousand afternoons in the far wilds of my native Butte in order to translate me from the somber colors of myself to the passionate prisms of life as presented by various directors." Mary later entered the dream-making business herself, writing and starring in a 1917 silent film, *Men Who Have Made Love to Me*. Although they never achieved her success, many of Butte's young women shared MacLane's desire to be transported from the daily life of a mining town to the romantic environs portrayed on the screen.[53]

Scholars of film have analyzed the content and appeal of the movies of the 1920s and 1930s and speculated about their effect on fans. All agree that it is impossible to measure the behavioral influence of the films but suggest that it was considerable. Mary Ryan refers to films as "handmaidens to the modern preoccupation with intimate heterosexual relations." The Lynds recorded schoolteachers' opinions that movies contributed to youths' early sophistication and a relaxation of social taboos. Elizabeth Ewen, in her study of immigrant women and the movies, found films to be "manuals of desire, wishes and dreams," presenting the consumer society as a new ideal, a new definition of "American." Several studies revealed that by the 1920s movie stars had replaced politicians, businessmen, and artists as youths' favorite role models. As Rose Hum Lee discovered in Butte, movies penetrated even the most traditional of immigrant communities. Chinese women adopted the hair and clothing styles of film stars, subscribed to movie magazines, and avidly discussed movie stars' roles and love lives.[54]

Irish maids, Croatian bookkeepers, Serbian clerks, and Chinese schoolgirls—each awaited her own Rudolph Valentino or envisioned herself on the silver screen. Stardom did not seem outside the realm of possibility. Mary MacLane, of course, had made a movie, but she was too eccentric to be taken seriously. Violet Bowen, however, a Butte girl who made good in Hollywood, fed youthful fantasies. In

September 1926 the *Butte Miner* informed its readers that Bowen was about to have her back insured for $100,000. The previous June she had won a bathing beauty contest in Dallas, in August she received a silver cup for having the most perfect athletic figure in Los Angeles, and a month later she won the Los Angeles "perfect spine" contest. Bowen starred in western pictures, acknowledging that her background had helped her career because Montana cowpunchers had taught her to sit a horse.[55]

Like movies, beauty contests also fed romantic fantasies. Summer visitors to Columbia Gardens cast their votes for the Pansy Queen. One traveler through Butte in 1919 met Emma Harrington, an aide to the city auditor, and, smitten, sent her photograph to a national weekly, along with a check for $100 and a challenge for anyone to find a more beautiful girl. In 1928 the VFW announced that it would sponsor a Miss Butte contest. Contestants had to be sixteen and of good character. The Miss Butte contest had a distinctly western flavor. The winner received not only a new Graham-Paige sedan but also a trip to Tulsa, Oklahoma, and a chance to become Queen Petroleum. As it turned out, the winner was not the most poised, charming, and beautiful girl in Butte, but the one who sold the most tickets to the "Siege of 1918," a fireworks drama presented by the VFW to outfit its new drum corps.[56]

The Miss Butte contest was emblematic, for romance ran up against reality time after time for young women of the 1920s. Even the films of the period bore a mixed message. Although they touted the independence of wage-earning flappers, they made it clear that this was but a short phase of a woman's life. Glamorous heroines were "hot" but "chaste at heart" and always preserved their virginity until marriage, which was, after all, the point of all that flirtation. Women's true happiness came when she outgrew her youthful fling and married. *A Woman's Woman,* which played in Butte in 1923, dramatized the tug-of-war between independence and family. The story revolves around an apron-clad mother whose "pies are a delight" but whose old-fashioned ways are an embarrassment to her husband and children. With their encouragement she "steps out," but family life disintegrates as she increasingly revels in her new world. Finally, she sacrifices her own ambitions to "again become the home builder." Three years later *Dancing Mothers* reversed the denouement of *A Woman's Woman.* In this case, the woman, mother of a spoiled flapper and wife of an unfaithful husband, walks out, not to return. But *Dancing Mothers* was an anomaly. It was an unusual movie for the 1920s, and the studio was so nervous about its reception that it filmed another conclusion, a "happy" ending, more appropriate "for regular audiences outside the bigger towns."[57]

Like the film flappers who found happiness in marriage to men of their own class, Butte's young working women looked forward to marriage to miners or other working men. Marriage was both a joyous event and a sobering moment. Some women, like Ann Pentilla, took advantage of their economic independence and delayed marriage. Ann, the last of her sisters to marry, mused, "I think when you're young . . . you don't care whether you marry or not . . . you have a good job, buying your own clothes and you're independent and you don't care." Others shared Catherine Hoy's opinion that if a woman was nineteen and unwed, people considered her a spinster.[58]

The weddings of many working-class women were modest affairs, and the realities of housework and children quickly dampened the romance of courtship. Saima Myllymaki remembered that after she married and began a family her husband went on contract work in the mines. At the end of his workday he was so tired that "there was no such a thing as wanting to go dancing." Julia McHugh shopped for her wedding dress on her lunch hour, and a few days before her wedding discovered that her parish priest intended to kill two birds with one stone by graduating the eighth-grade class at her wedding mass. She moved the ceremony to Friday, necessitating a change in the wedding feast. Guests toasted the newlyweds with moonshine and dined on tuna and cheese. She and her sister spent the morning of her wedding day cleaning the house, and after the reception she and her husband Tom drove to Great Falls for a brief honeymoon. They had to be back Sunday night for Tom to go to work. The end of girlhood came to Anne Sloan when she married in 1929. "We eloped and ran away to Helena," she recalled. Her father was against it. She was his only daughter and he wanted her to get an education and become a teacher. But his hopes came to naught. "It was cold that day in Helena. . . . We had a touring car, a Chalmers touring car that had California curtains. . . . About froze to death because the old car didn't have a heater in it. We were going to stay in Helena a couple of days [but] it was so cold and we were short money, so [we] went back to Butte . . . and I stayed there [at home] and my husband went to work that night."[59]

When daughters became wives and mothers they had to negotiate with husbands, rather than parents, the disposition of money, work, and leisure. Marriage brought a new set of pleasures, responsibilities, and choices. A rich Butte folklore concerning wives' infidelity, and occasional newspaper accounts of women's adultery, suggest that not all sexual experimentation ceased with marriage. Birth control allowed women choices in and outside the bonds of marriage. Catholic Butte frowned upon birth control and abortion, but some women chose to limit their families' size. Montana's birth rate declined steadily from 1915 to 1933. Throughout the interwar years there was at least one abortionist working in Butte.[60]

The generation of women who came of age during World War I and the 1920s brought new experiences to their adulthood. Some had stepped into men's shoes during the war, gaining a sense of self-confidence and a taste of economic independence. Nearly all had participated to some extent in the revolution of manners and morals that accompanied the war and the following decade. Yet few opted for roles other than wife and mother.

■ ■ ■

Of all the leisure activities that engaged young women in the 1920s, the one that attracted the least attention by concerned authorities was perhaps inherently the most revolutionary. Window-shopping and sidewalk flirting typified the changing nature of urban life in the 1910s and 1920s and the role women played in that change. Dallying in front of display windows, women announced themselves as independent wage-earners and consumers. Their dress, their assertive presence on the sidewalk, and their flirtatious manners proclaimed their right to share the street—and by extension movie theaters, dance halls, restaurants, and nightclubs—with men and to do so on their own terms. Never as outrageous as Mary MacLane, still, their defiance of Victorian standards of modesty and manners inspired concern and protest. Behavior that at one time was labeled immoral, and even psychotic, became merely frivolous, and eventually the norm, as it was adopted more and more widely.[61]

Butte's young women gathered their notions of womanhood from a variety of models—pioneers, prostitutes, and politicians. As daughters of a mining city, they knew the perils and pleasures of a boom-and-bust town. They were often rowdy and exuberant, absorbing the devil-may-care atmosphere of Butte. Yet, the trappings of flappers draped the frames of women who sought husbands, families, and stability. Most went on to marry and had little time for dance halls. New concerns occupied their energies, and they had to learn to deal with men on a different basis. Men would also have to learn to deal differently with women during the 1920s and 1930s, together forging a community more responsive to the needs of both sexes.

NOTES

1. *Butte Daily Bulletin*, 7 June 1920, 5 and 8 June 1920, 6; *Butte Miner*, 8 June 1920, 6 and 9 June 1920, 5; *Anaconda Standard*, 6 June 1920, 2, 8 June 1920, 5, and 9 June 1920, 5. See also Odem, *Delinquent Daughters*.

2. On changing gender roles in the 1920s, see Baritz, "The Culture of the Twenties"; Critoph, "The Flapper and Her Critics"; Fass, *The Damned and the Beautiful;* Filene, *Him/Her/Self;* Freedman, "The New Woman"; Freeman and Klaus, "Blessed or Not?"; Hall, "Disorderly Women"; Hewitt, "Patterns of Female Criminality"; Lemons, *The Woman Citizen;* McGovern, "The American Woman's Pre-World War I Freedom"; Pumphrey, "The Flapper"; Smith-Rosenberg, "The New Woman as Androgyne"; Sochen, *The New Woman;* and Yellis, "Prosperity's Child." On urban working women's amusements, see Stansell, *City of Women;* Peiss, *Cheap Amusements;* Peiss, "Commercial Leisure"; Meyerowitz, *Women Adrift;* and Schudson, "Women, Cigarettes and Advertising."

3. Allingham, *Traitor's Purse*, 151–52.

4. Kasson, "Civility and Rudeness"; Kasson, *Rudeness and Civility.*

5. For biographical material on MacLane and reactions to *The Story of Mary MacLane*, see Wheeler, "Montana's Shocking 'Lit'r'y Lady'"; Rosemont, "Marvelous Mary MacLane"; Mattern, "Mary MacLane"; Atherton, *Adventures of a Novelist*, 491–92; Miller, "'Hot as Live Embers'"; and Pruitt, ed., *Tender Darkness.*

6. MacLane, *The Story of Mary MacLane*, 32, 17, 46, 109, 268, 74, 70.

7. Mattern, "Mary MacLane," 60–61; Atherton, *Adventures of a Novelist*, 491; Betty Horst, interview by Mary Murphy, Butte, 23 May 1988; *Butte Miner*, 6 March 1910, 18.

8. Alderson, "A Half Century of Progress for Montana Women," 77–81; Mary O'Neill to Marguerite Wells, 26 May 1923, League of Women Voters Papers, series 2, box 8, Library of Congress (hereafter cited as LWV Papers); *Montana Standard*, 2 November 1932, 3.

9. Appelman, "Montana," 101.

10. *Anaconda Standard*, 5 February 1920, 7; Butte City Council Records (18 April 1917), 17:19.

11. Writers' Program, Work Projects Administration, *Copper Camp*, 175; Petrik, *No Step Backward*, xviii. Other studies of western prostitution include Butler, *Daughters of Joy, Sisters of Misery;* Goldman, *Gold Diggers and Silver Miners;* and Murphy, "Women on the Line."

12. According to the 1910 census, 3,005 females ten years old and over worked for wages in the city of Butte, forming 22 percent of the female population ten years and older. The occupations employing the largest number of women were servant (641 women, or 21.3 percent of the female labor force); boardinghouse and lodginghouse keeper (303, or 10 percent); and teacher (278, or 9.2 percent). The published census figures do not list prostitute as an occupation, but the manuscript census revealed 260 women working in prostitution, which would have made prostitution

the fourth most common occupation for women in the city in official numbers. U.S. Department of Commerce, Bureau of the Census, *Thirteenth Census,* 4:214–18; *Thirteenth Census, 1910, Montana,* vol. 16, *Silver Bow; Anaconda Standard,* 13 January 1917, 1, *Butte Miner,* 5 December 1916, 5.

13. On the usefulness of red light districts, see Harvie and Bishop, "Police Reform in Montana"; and Murphy, "Women on the Line." Carroll, comp., *Revised Ordinances,* 461; *Madeleine,* 221, 220; Writers' Program, Work Projects Administration, *Copper Camp,* 180; Wilson, *Honky-Tonk Town,* 2.

14. Writers' Program, Work Projects Administration, *Copper Camp,* 177; Helen Shute Raymond, interview by Laurie Mercier, Butte, 9 October 1981. See also, "Butte Research July 1946" notebook, Joseph Kinsey Howard Papers, 1927–1954 (hereafter cited as Howard Papers), box 1, file 13, MHSA; and Olga Sontum, interview by Ray Calkins, Butte, February 1980, 6.

15. *Anaconda Standard,* 4 January 1914, 6.

16. Harvie and Bishop, "Police Reform in Montana," 56; *Anaconda Standard,* 14 January 1917, 2; Mrs. T. J. Fleming to S. C. Ford, 1 July 1919, Montana Attorney General Records (hereafter cited as Atty Gen Records), box 24, file 30, MHSA; Mrs. O. Caffery to S. C. Ford, 3 October, 1917, and E. J. J. Shea to S. C. Ford, 31 October 1917, Atty Gen Records, box 20, file 3, MHSA; *Anaconda Standard,* 10 January 1917, 5. Butte's red light district remained closed for only a short time. Although large numbers of women did leave on January 14, 1917, in February a "tax payer" wrote to Ford to say some of the major houses in the district were still operating, and in May another "war" on the district was declared, targeting many "dives" where prostitution flourished. "A Butte Tax Payer" to Attorney General, 18 February 1917, Atty Gen Records, box 20, file 3, MHSA; *Butte Miner,* 11 May 1917, 1.

In 1927–28 and again in 1932–33 the American Social Hygiene Association conducted a survey of prostitution in fifty-eight cities, including Butte. Basing their evaluation on flagrancy of operation, activities of third-party exploiters, methods of operations, rates, ways of attracting customers, attitude of officials and the public, and special environmental factors encouraging or discouraging prostitution, they rated Butte "bad" in 1928 and absolutely unimproved in 1933. Johnson and Kinsie, "Prostitution in the United States."

17. T. L. Blackman to S. C. Ford, 24 January 1917, Atty Gen Records, box 20, file 3, MHSA.

18. Jean Jordan, personal reminiscence, 1976, BSBA; Ann Pentilla, interview by Ray Calkins and Caroline Smithson, Butte, 27 April 1979, 30–31; Chaplin, *My Autobiography,* 128. Tandberg summarizes research on prostitutes and clothing in "Sinning for Silk."

19. *Butte Daily Bulletin,* 9 February 1920, 1, 4, 11 February 1920, 1, 4, and 17 February 1920, 1, 3; *Anaconda Standard,* 17 February 1920, 2.

20. Pentilla interview, 22; Anna L. Rogers to Jeanette Rankin, 3 August 1917, Jeanette Rankin Papers, box 1, file 9, MHSA. See Benson, *Counter*

Cultures, for a discussion of saleswomen's wages and controversy about their working conditions and morals. Kessler-Harris reviews the alleged link between low wages and prostitution in *Out to Work,* 103–5.

21. Allen, *Only Yesterday,* 2; Ruiz, "'Star Struck'"; Parpart, "Household and Mine Shaft." See also Taylor, "Mexican Women in Los Angeles Industry."

22. *Butte Miner,* 10 April 1916, 6.

23. *Anaconda Standard,* 5 February 1920, 4; *Madeleine,* 209; *The Mountaineer,* 1924, and *The Mountaineer,* 1923, 78–79, 165.

24. *Butte City Directory,* 1917, 1931; Butte City Council Minutes (1 October 1930), 18:835; Bernice Knierim, interview by Diane Sands, Glasgow, 3 August 1987. On the adoption of cosmetics and the growth of the beauty business, see Peiss, "Making Faces."

25. Pentilla interview, 22; McHugh, "Gulch and I," 4, 8; MacLane, *I, Mary MacLane,* 25–26.

26. Arthur Stringer, "The Weaker Sex," *Saturday Evening Post,* December 18, 1926, 11; *Anaconda Standard,* 16 February 1920, 2, 23 February 1920, 1, 24 February 1920, 5, and 26 February 1920, 13. See Banner, *American Beauty,* for a discussion of the influence that sports had on women's clothes of the 1920s.

27. *Butte City Directory,* 1917; *Celebration of the Gift of Faith,* 59–64.

28. *Helena Catholic Monthly,* 1 (March 1917): 38, 1 (July 1917): 23, 7 (July 1923): 23, and 13 (May 1929): 9–12. Birth control was apparently an issue of much concern in the 1920s. It, more than any other issue relating to sexuality, drew the attention of the magazine's writers. Belle F. Winestine to Edna Rankin McKinnon, 4 February 1937, Margaret Sanger Papers, box 149, reel 96, National Committee on Federal Legislation for Birth Control, State File, Montana, General Public, Library of Congress.

29. *Helena Catholic Monthly* 1 (June 1917): 22–25 and 11 (October 1927): 12. On the discrepancies between Catholic ideology and Catholic women's behavior, see Mercier, "'We Are Women Irish,'" 38.

30. *Helena Catholic Monthly* 8 (February 1924): 3; *Butte Miner,* 7 May 1923, 5.

31. On the history of jazz, see Shaw, *The Jazz Age,* and Stearns, *The Story of Jazz.* Art Chappelle, unrecorded interview by Mary Murphy, Butte, 29 July 1988; Dorothy A. Martin, interview by Mary Murphy, Butte, 23 May 1988, 8; Brinig, "The Synagogue," 261. *Variety* is quoted in Stearns, *The Story of Jazz,* 155. *Butte Miner,* 11 May 1923, 2 and 6 September 1928, 5; Winick and Kinsie, *The Lively Commerce,* 41. On styles of "tough dancing," see Peiss, *Cheap Amusements,* 100–104. On dance reform, see Perry, "'The General Motherhood of the Commonwealth,'" and Perry, "Youth, Community Morality, and Censorship." One reformer in New York claimed that 70 percent of the city's fallen girls were ruined by jazz. Cited in Mason, "Satan in the Dance-Hall."

32. Pat O'Leary, interview by Ray Calkins, Butte, February 1980, 18. For an account of dancing's popularity in an English industrial community, see Wild, "Recreation in Rochdale."

33. Murel L. Roberts, interview by Ray Calkins, Butte, 8 August 1980, 23–24; McHugh, "Gulch and I," 8.

34. Anonymous letter to John Hughes, 27 September 1982, BSBA.

35. *Anaconda Standard,* 19 January 1914, 8; Gus Koski, interview by Kathy Tureck, Geyser, 23 September 1982; Lisle Scanland, interview by Laurie Mercier, Corvallis, 22 June 1983.

36. *Butte Miner,* 31 July 1922, 1 and 2 August 1922, 3. On the immoral atmosphere of dance halls, see Nye, "Saturday Night at the Paradise Ballroom," and Johnson and Kinsie, "Prostitution in United States."

37. Carroll, comp., *Revised Ordinances,* 416–19; L. A. Foot to Larry Duggan, 31 July 1925, Atty Gen Records, box 26, file 19, MHSA; U.S. Department of Labor, Children's Bureau, *Public Dance Halls,* 23, 31; *Butte Miner,* 27 January 1923, 1, 2. On other cities' efforts at regulation, see Gullett, "City Mothers, City Daughters," and Phelan, "Our Dancing Cities."

38. The actual field report on Butte no longer exists in the records of the Children's Bureau; parts of it were reprinted in the *Butte Daily Post,* 9 April 1927, 1, 11.

39. *Butte Daily Post,* 3 January 1923, 1; *Butte Miner,* 3 January 1923, 6; *Anaconda Standard,* 16 April 1927, 1; *The Maroon,* 1927, 62.

40. *Anaconda Standard,* 15 February 1920, sec. 2, 1; Mrs. A. J. Steele to S. C. Ford, 1 April 1918, Atty Gen Records, box 7, file 21, MHSA; *Butte Miner,* 19 November 1922, 23; *Montana Standard,* 7 February 1929, 1. Women dancing and drinking "on commission" testifies to the presence of taxi-dance halls in Butte. This type of dance hall raised the sharpest concerns among reformers. See Binford, "Taxi-Dance Halls," and Cressey, *The Taxi-Dance Hall.*

41. All quotations and material on Moret in this and following paragraphs are from newspaper articles: *Butte Miner,* 24 November 1926, 1–2, 25 November 1926, 1–2, 29 November 1926, 1–2, 30 November 1926, 7, and 2 December 1926, 2; *Butte Daily Post,* 26 November 1926, 1. On crossdressing, see D'Emilio and Freedman, *Intimate Matters,* and Garber, *Vested Interests.*

42. Melman, *Women and the Popular Imagination,* 24, 89–90.

43. Banner, *American Beauty,* 264; Meyerowitz, *Women Adrift,* 4–5; Reynolds, ed., *New World Atlas,* 134. See also, Meyerowitz, "Sexual Geography and Gender Economy."

44. U.S. Department of Commerce, Bureau of the Census, *Fourteenth Census,* 4:369; 1910 Manuscript Census. The analysis of the employment bureau was made by the *Anaconda Standard,* 7 January 1914, 9.

45. Mason, "Satan in the Dance-Hall," 180; U.S. Department of Labor, Children's Bureau, *Public Dance Halls,* 33–34.

46. Emmons, *Butte Irish,* 77; Lynd and Lynd, *Middletown in Transition,* 175–80. Central High School was a coeducational institution until 1927, when separate Girls Central and Boys Central were created. Flaherty, *Go with Haste into the Mountains,* 72.

47. *The Mountaineer,* 1924, 123.

48. Lynd and Lynd, *Middletown,* 112; Anonymous letter to John Hughes, Butte, 27 September 1982, BSBA; Catherine Hoy, interview by Ray Calkins and Caroline Smithson, Butte, 11 May 1979, 17; Mae Mucahy, interview by Gary Stanton, Butte, 28 August 1979.

49. Beatrice Bray to George Sypher, 2 July 1918, Beatrice Bray Papers, WMM; Nellie Tweet, interview by Claudia Claque Tweet, Butte, 24 July 1982; Alma E. Hileman, interview by Ray Calkins, Butte, 27 June 1980, 9; Pentilla interview, 29–30. In his study of leisure in Pittsburgh, Couvares notes that dance halls and skating rinks were especially popular because they permitted physical contact between the sexes. See "The Triumph of Commerce," 143–44. On the development of adolescents' dating in the 1920s, see Modell, "Dating Becomes the Way of American Youth"; Rothman, *Hands and Hearts;* and Bailey, *From Front Porch to Back Seat.*

50. Sontum interview, 36; *Anaconda Standard,* 20 February 1920, 9 and 14 January 1917, 11.

51. U.S. Department of Commerce, Bureau of the Census, *Fourteenth Census,* 4:369; Pentilla interview, 12, 21–22. On the conflict that American patterns of consumption and leisure caused between immigrant parents and children, see Ewen, *Immigrant Women in the Land of Dollars.*

52. Mary Trbovich, interview by Mary Murphy, Butte, 4 November 1987; Lee, *The Chinese in the United States,* 193.

53. *Butte City Directory,* 1931; Carden, "A Walk from S. Gaylord Street," 5; Hoy interview, 14–15; Tweet interview; McHugh, "Gulch and I," 15; Inez Shifty, interview by Mary Murphy, Butte, 14 October 1987; Wheeler, "'Montana's Lit'r'y Lady,'" 31.

54. Ryan, "The Projection of a New Womanhood," 372–84; Lynd and Lynd, *Middletown,* 267; Ewen, "City Lights"; Fishbein, "The Demise of the Cult of True Womanhood." On the emulation of movie stars, see Banner, *American Beauty,* who discusses in detail the influence of the theater on American fashion and behavior. On Chinese women's reaction to movies, see Lee, "Social Institutions of a Rocky Mountain Chinatown," 10.

55. *Butte Miner,* 13 September 1926, 6.

56. *Butte Miner,* 8 August 1922, 2, 21 September 1919, 8, 29 July 1928, 1, 11, and 13 September 1928, 1. See Banner, *American Beauty,* on the development of beauty contests.

57. Ryan, "Projection of a New Womanhood," 373–74; *Butte Miner,* 2 May 1923, 5; Fishbein, "'Dancing Mothers.'"

58. Pentilla interview, 32; Hoy interview, 17.

59. Myllymaki interview; McHugh, "Gulch and I," 11; Anne Sloan, interview by Laurie Mercier, Butte, 28 July 1983.

60. On adultery in industrial communities in general and Butte in particular, see Bancroft, "Folklore of the Central City District"; Bodnar, *The Transplanted;* Davidoff, "The Separation of Home and Work?"; Duffy, *Butte Was Like That;* Hand, "Folklore of Butte Miner"; and Andrew Vázsonyi, "The

Cicisbeo and the Magnificent Cuckold." Montana's birth rate is charted in Montana State Board of Health, *1954 Annual Statistical Supplement,* table 1, 3. The only study of abortion in Montana is Sands, "Using Oral History to Chart Illegal Abortion."

61. Elizabeth Lunbeck discusses the turn-of-the-century development of the psychiatric diagnosis, "the hypersexual female," as a response to working women's seemingly inexplicable rowdy and sensual behavior in "'A New Generation of Women.'"

4

Born Miners

To live you had to fight. —SONNY O'DAY

In her reminiscences of life in Dublin Gulch during the first three decades of the twentieth century, Julia McHugh related the time she, her sister Lil, and her husband Tom attended a baseball game between Centerville and the Gulch. "We all hated Centerville and everything they did," she wrote. "We hadn't seen an umpire behind the plate before, especially with the face mask and all on. So I said, 'Leave it to Centerville to be different. They have two catchers.' No response from Tom." Then she noticed that the Gulch catcher and pitcher were over on the side throwing the ball back and forth: "'The game must not be very interesting. Crnich and Goodman are just playing catch.' So Tom said, 'They are only warming up.' Lil said, in such surprise, 'Warming up on a swell night like this.' That did it. Tom said, 'I'll see you after the game,' and away he went." As McHugh's story illustrates, efforts to turn traditional male pastimes into heterosocial activities did not always succeed. Nonetheless, by the late 1920s, men and women were adapting to each other's presence in more and more places of commercial and sporting leisure, reconfiguring the recreational landscape of the mining city.[1]

When Josephine Roche and Ella Gardner surveyed the city's recreation in 1927, they concluded that Butte was "typically a man's world." Simply looking at the streets of Butte bolstered their opinion. Working men garbed in blue overalls, serge coats, and soft caps, businessmen attired in three-piece suits, and gamblers adorned with flashy jewelry filled cafes, dance halls, saloons, and shops. During shift changes the streets swarmed with men. Ed Sullivan, looking out the windows of his Corktown house, watched thousands of miners going to and from work until "the road would be black with men." Catherine Hoy remembered getting "lost in the shuffle" when caught on the road at the changing of shift. More than men's physical presence dominated the city. Their desires and ambitions shaped work, politics, and leisure. Elizabeth Kennedy and her colleagues in the Good Government Club were "disgusted" with the succession of city administrations that catered to men's pleasures by sanctioning the red light district and ignoring the welfare of the city's young women.[2]

Custom and economics sustained a public culture of masculine diversions and militated against the establishment of exclusively female centers of commercial leisure. There were no women's saloons, gymnasiums, theaters, and gambling halls. Women's lack of wages discouraged such development, as did their roles as mothers, homemakers, and moral guardians. To be sure, women could be found in movie theaters and dance halls, but male companions often paid their admissions. Once inside, there was little on which to spend money besides popcorn. The milieu of the dance hall or theater was not that of the saloon, where treating signified comradeship, nor the gambling hall, where one needed ready money or good credit to participate in the action.

Nevertheless, changes precipitated by Prohibition and women's incursions into commercial leisure accelerated in the mid-1920s and 1930s. More and more women began to appear in the formerly all-male arenas of gambling rooms and prizefight audiences. Much like the geography of drinking that emerged during Prohibition, heterosocial gambling took place in new establishments. On the national level, sports promoters had begun to recognize the potential profits in women spectators and actively encouraged their attendance at baseball games and prizefights. The trend passed to Butte as well. This is not to say that all men readily welcomed women at the faro tables, in the bleachers, or at ringside or that a strong single male culture did not persist. Nonetheless, the creation of a heterosocial culture demanded not only the incursions of women but also the participation of men.

By the 1920s the patterns that shaped manhood as well as womanhood in Butte were changing. Just as women garnered their models of womanhood from a variety of sources, so did men. Working-class masculinity or manliness was intimately related to work and its skills, to camaraderie, and, at least in Butte, to the quality of "toughness." Butte men had to be physically and mentally tough to withstand the rigors of mining, both above- and belowground. To take care of oneself and one's partner underground and ward off any foes aboveground required skill, physical strength, and trust. Although miners worked under an open shop in the 1920s, the legacy of unionism, brotherhood, and solidarity was strong. Miners may not have been organized, but they were surrounded by union men and women in all the other trades of the city. These were traditional influences that shaped notions of manliness, harkening back to the first days of Butte. In the 1920s they were joined by new, less work-related models of masculinity. Increasingly, public attention was devoted to men's role as father and husband, to notions of marriage based on companionship, and to the idea that fathers and sons should be "pals." Fathers were advised to take an active role in the rearing of their children, especially of their sons, not only within the privacy of their homes but also by becoming Scout leaders and athletic coaches.[3]

These ideas fell on receptive ears in Butte. By 1920, for the first time since the city was founded, a majority of men were married and either fathers or potential fathers. They by no means gave up the prerogatives of power, yet times were changing. Even the Anaconda Company, which had been conspicuous by its absence in the social life of Butte, sponsored family events and encouraged women and children to take an interest in their fathers' work and employer. By the early 1930s, and even more so by the end of the decade, journalists, who loved to pass through Butte and churn out stories about its wild and woolly social life, described a more subdued community not exclusively tuned to the pleasures of single men.

■ ■ ■

The most obvious model of manhood was the hardrock miner. His was a physically demanding, hazardous life. The thousands of miners who lay buried in the cemeteries on the valley floor were never far from men's minds. As he took a bath at his boardinghouse, a miner in *Wide Open Town* ruminated on the cycle of life and death in Butte: "Every miner who had ever lived at Mrs. Costello's had left a part of himself behind in that tub, a part of his experience in the mines and in Silver Bow. Some of the dirt rims had been left there by men now dead, men who lay in the cemeteries south of the town, mere dirt themselves now, men who had sweated and sworn and wenched. You could see a thousand men, one after another, bathing in that tub, for a thousand days."[4]

Men in Butte dealt with the possibility of death every day. Certain days were especially dangerous. On June 13, 1919, Shorty Felt confided to his diary, "Friday and the 13th in combination to feel shaky about. But nothing happened but hard work. Well, a working man should always be superstitious and suspicious too." Many miners shared the superstition that the underground would kill any man who tried to quit it. Some would leave without notice to escape that last deadly shift. Sixty-five years after the Speculator fire, Ed Sullivan still felt the horror and weariness of that orgy of death: "They took the bodies out of there so fast, they'd take them to the funeral homes and they weren't big enough to take care of them. They had them in the halls and everything—the bodies. Go there and see them. . . . I'm getting old."[5]

The dangers of mining cemented bonds of male friendship. Under the contract system, men worked in partnerships where the pressures of speed and productivity demanded harmony and trust. Hanford Toppari had known his partner since they were children. Their closeness encouraged them to challenge the company when they felt they were being cheated on a contract. As Toppari said, "We were a couple of rounders. I shouldn't ought to say it, but I will. We never took no shit from Anaconda in any way. But we stood up for our rights. If we figured we were right we stayed right there and batted."[6]

In 1925 the *Anode,* the Anaconda Company's safety magazine, published the poem "Damon and Pythias" by Dan Holland, a timekeeper on the Hill. Alluding to the Roman myth in which two friends pledge their lives for each other's safety, the poem is a tribute to a friendship between two men, "born miners," that began in the mine and flourished aboveground. Mike was from County Cork; Jan from Cornwall. The poem recounts the many ties of male camaraderie. Mike and Jan work together, drink together, bail each other out of jail, fight over politics, nurse each other in sickness, quell each other's loneliness, and are bound together even in death:

They sleep now in the graveyard and their spirits hover near,
That friendship which was classic has been told from year to year.
A broken fence divides their graves o'er which new grasses trail.
—Here's Jan who hailed from Truro town;
—There's Mike from Doneraile.[7]

The motif of twining vines that unite lovers in their graves is common in prose and poetry, but no women appear in the saga of Mike and Jan. Their work and their social lives revolve around each other and other men. The poem is undoubtedly emblematic of the lives of many Butte laborers.

Butte indeed encouraged its boys to grow into "Mikes" and "Jans." At an early age boys learned to work, to fight, to organize, to claim the streets as their own, and to seek the company of other males. In the 1910s a rising concern that boys were learning all their survival skills on the streets led to the establishment of Boy Scout troops and boys' clubs. Both Centerville and Meaderville had boys' clubs that coached youths in sports and fair play. The Meaderville Young Men's Club opened a gym in the Leonard Mine yard in 1914 and hired an athletic director who gave physical culture instruction every night. The club had a basketball team and in 1916 staged the state's first Amateur Athletic Union wrestling and boxing tournament. In December 1910 Butte's Troop Number 1 became the first scout troop chartered in Montana. Twenty years later, the city had eighteen. A shortage of scoutmasters in 1919 led Benjamin Owen to appeal for one hundred volunteers from the city to train Butte's share of "America's manhood."[8]

Many boys' training came through work rather than play. Murel Roberts felt his childhood "was more business than pleasure." As soon as school let out, he and his brother ran to the newspaper office to buy papers to hawk on the streets. On Sundays they rose at 3 A.M. to get the Sunday editions. Newsboys were a fixture of city streets, and in Butte, as elsewhere, they were aggressive entrepreneurs. Bill McKernan recalled that buying a paper sometimes entailed becoming the third party in a territorial battle: "You'd walk up the street and you'd go to buy a paper off of one kid and the other one would come up and push him away. And then there'd be a fight. One kid would say, 'This is my corner,' and the guy'd say, 'Well, this is my customer.'" Newsboys also fought each other in the alley outside the newspaper office, jockeying to get their papers and be the first to hit the streets.[9]

The public liked to think of newsboys as figures drawn from Horatio Alger, learning young the lessons of free enterprise. In fact, they were often training to be future union men. Butte newsboys were organized. In 1903 city leaders founded the Butte Newsboys Club to provide educational and recreational opportunities for the youngsters. Boys attended lectures, concerts, and picnics and celebrated the club's tenth anniversary with a banquet, speeches by a former county attorney and the president of the WCTU, and a 120–pound birthday cake. The boys also used the club as a labor union and organized strikes in 1914 and 1919. The 1914 strike protested the *Butte Daily Post*'s cut of subscription rates below the newsboys' wholesale price. Newsboys of the socialist *Daily Bulletin* led the 1919 strike, seeking to stop distribution of the *Daily Post,* which carried adverse reports on the start of a miners' strike. Thus, early on Butte boys learned to employ direct action in defense of their rights and their turf.[10]

In a city with virtually no neighborhood parks, streets, alleys, saloons, and gambling halls became children's playgrounds. By the time boys reached puberty, there was little about street life that they did not know. While Murel Roberts stood on the corner hawking his papers, his younger brother ducked into gambling halls to "shoot a snipe"—pick up somebody's cigarette butt to smoke. Marie Paumie ran the Parisian Dye House and had most of the residents of the red light district as her customers. Nevertheless, she would have been shocked had she discovered that when her grandson delivered cleaning to a Mercury Street prostitute the woman would "take the paper bag off, look it over, take off the dress she had on, stand there stark naked, put on the clean one and give me the dress she had on."[11]

Boys acting tough challenged teachers and police. Schoolboys uniformly wore black cotton stockings, short pants, a suit coat, and a cap. But John Sconfienza and a few of his friends refused to "dress up" for school and wore older boys' attire: copper-toed shoes and overalls. They were sent home, but they did not care: "We wasn't going to be sissies. We were tough guys." Toughness and street smarts sometimes pushed boys' activities over the line from play to crime. In 1920 a gang of about twenty boys confessed to being members of a short-lived "Stealing Club." They each contributed a nickel initiation fee and then went on a week-long spree, breaking into a warehouse, two stores, and a pawnshop before members were caught. They took cases of candy and gum, a revolver, watches, and some jewelry. Another gang burglarized the apartment of a retired deputy sheriff and stole his collection of revolvers, reselling them to other boys for ten cents apiece. The ringleaders of each gang were only ten years old. For these children the border between play and crime became permeable. High-spirits and daring each other to perform risky deeds appeared to motivate them as much as profit-seeking.[12]

Gangs of older youths reaped pleasure and profit from threatening citizens. In 1928 a couple of policemen, posing as lovers in a

parked car near Lake Avoca, arrested two men who had been labeled the "petting party bandits" for their modus operandi of holding up parked couples. W. J. Rodgers, twenty-four, confessed to four
similar jobs and laughingly explained, "We had to do something for
a thrill, and it was lots of fun." Gangs loitered outside vacant buildings and busy cafes, verbally insulting and sometimes physically as-
saulting men and women. One morning a gang of fifteen boys
jumped a man returning from mass and beat him unconscious before bystanders broke them up. When Officer Frank K. Mutch told
a group of young men to "move on" outside a cafe in Meaderville,
they attacked him, inflicting a compound fracture of one leg and
severe abrasions. In 1931 the city council passed a motion urging
law officers to make a special effort to police male loiterers, but the
force did not have the manpower to patrol all the gangs' territories.
Frank Mutch was a painful reminder of the fate that could await a
patrolman who confronted them alone.[13]

Yet gangs did not always get their way. James Blakely recalled a
confrontation between a fellow miner and the notorious Overall
Gang, who "used to be tough up there on North Main Street." A few
gang members had stopped the miner on his way home from work
and demanded all his money. He gave them fifty cents, and the next
night the gang tried the same thing. But the miner had given all he
intended. "So they started to gang him," and he retreated until he
backed up to a picket fence. "As they came near him he knocked
them all one after another down off the sidewalk . . . then they started to run at him and he pulled off one of these pickets and, boy,
he just started to swing it. And the nails was sticking that far out of
the picket, you know, where he pulled it off, out of the two-by-four.
They never bothered that man any more. They never did, boy."[14]

Butte men fought for a variety of reasons and seemingly for no
reason at all. They fought in self-defense, they fought over women,
they fought over real and imagined insults, and sometimes they
seemed to fight for fun, as in the recreational brawls between Cornish and Irish drinkers. The problem with fighting as sport was that
a scuffle that began as a physical expression of rivalry or boisterousness could escalate to bloody, brutal combat. Men who learned the
elements of fisticuffs as boys on the street received further instruction in saloons and soft drink parlors as adults, and they added
knives, guns, baseball bats, iron rods, and brass knuckles to their
arsenals. John Onkalo recalled that "knife-happy" men were eager
to pass on their skills. "Some old Finn was telling me one time,
'When you handle a knife to use on somebody, you hold your thumb

on the blade depending how badly you want to work them over. If you just want to scrape them a little you hold your thumb so just a little bit of the point is sticking out from your finger. Boy, that's when you gash them. If you really want to give it to them, why give it to them handle and all.'"[15]

Jean Jordan, sports reporter for the *Miner* recalled no boxing match as memorable as some of the barroom and back-alley fights he witnessed, where "all the rules were thrown aside." One night in 1918 when police responded to cries for help from John Theis's saloon, they found blood-spattered walls, a free-for-all in progress, and John Higgins lying unconscious on the floor. Higgins died from head injuries, and Theis, standing at the bar with an upraised baseball bat, was arrested for murder. Although some brawls appeared to have ethnic overtones, such as the time when a group of young Irishmen assaulted three men of Italian and Slavic descent, police often could uncover no reason for street brawls or fights in soft drink parlors.[16]

Some men enjoyed the role of troublemaker and after a couple of drinks could not seem to keep the peace. Murel Roberts remembered one night when he and two friends were drinking in the basement of the Braund House on the East Side. Eventually they went upstairs to the dance hall, but kept on drinking. One of his companions, Jim, was a "troublemaker" who "just couldn't keep his mouth shut, popping off all the time. Finally we got in a fight with a bunch of Finns. We went outside, we took Jim outside to try to beat some sense into him." Instead of retreating, Roberts, Jim, and his companion returned to the hall, and "when we went in they were waiting for us. They beat the hell out of us. They had a pool table in there and balls. They took those billiard cues and they took the small stick and hit us over the head with them . . . my body was black and blue from that." The men finally escaped and took refuge in another saloon, whose patrons, incensed at what had happened, headed to the Braund House, ready to resume the fight. "We went in the front way and they [the Finns] went out the back way and they started shooting so we didn't follow them." Alcohol, toughness, and camaraderie—if little common sense—governed their actions that evening.[17]

Undoubtedly, more men were spectators at fights than participants. As Murel Roberts said, "Butte was sports-minded," and men took their sport where they could find it. Not everyone joined in the melees, however; it was more common to clear an area for the combatants, choose sides, and cheer on favorites. Some of the most vicious barroom spectacles men watched were between prostitutes. Jean Jordan recounted contests in which women used their finger-nails to gouge faces and grabbed handfuls of hair to pound their rivals' heads on the floor. Not until the loser was unconscious, fre-quently with a concussion and sometimes a fractured skull, would the crowd pull the women apart and stop the fight.[18]

■ ■ ■

In the late nineteenth and early twentieth centuries, the West be-came a haven for prizefighting, which had been declared illegal in the rest of the country. Nevada and California hosted championship fights, and Butte, one of the region's largest cities and a stopover point on train routes east and west, became a venue for many bouts. As one boxing historian has written, there was no sport "more confined to the realm of men" than boxing, and none more popu-lar in Butte. In fact, the first moving picture shown in Butte was a film of the Corbett-Fitzsimmons heavyweight championship match fought in Carson City, Nevada, in 1897. In 1899 James Murray, a banker, secured the film and hosted a private screening for his friends.[19]

Technically, prizefighting was illegal in Butte. An ordinance passed in 1890 banned prizefighting, boxing matches, and fighting contests with or without gloves. The ordinance may have been prompted by the tragic consequences of a prizefight held the year before. On December 15, 1889, George H. Ward and John Gallagh-er met at a roadhouse west of Butte to settle a personal dispute by means of a bareknuckle finish fight governed by the London Prize Ring rules. Ward was a carpenter, and Gallagher a miner. Each had about ten supporters so factions would be even if a brawl erupted. The two men fought for four-and-a-half hours, 105 rounds. In the forty-eighth round Ward broke Gallagher's arm, but Gallagher con-tinued to fight. In the ninety-eighth round Gallagher knocked Ward senseless, but the fight went on for seven more rounds until Ward finally collapsed. He died of his injuries the following day. At the coroner's inquest witnesses testified that during the last seven rounds Ward's seconds had held him on his feet, hoping he would revive. Friends spirited Gallagher out of town, and although the county attorney issued a blanket warrant charging all involved or present with first-degree murder, no one was ever convicted.[20]

Neither Ward's death nor the city ordinance that imposed a fine rather than a jail sentence for fighting stopped well-attended pub-lic fights. Moreover, promoters took advantage of a provision in the law authorizing the mayor and city council to issue permits for "scientific sparring" under the auspices of any reputable athletic club, a subterfuge that had been eliminated in many eastern states. Montana boxing historian Frank Bell termed the opening years of the twentieth century "a period of pugilistic frenzy for the mining city." A bout between Battling Nelson and Aurelio Herrera on Labor Day in 1904 drew six thousand fans to a specially constructed open-air arena on the Flat. The fight attracted men—and a few women— from every walk of life. "Politicians, society men, sporting men, and business men" sat "cheek by jowl" in the afternoon sun. The match ignited a passionate interest in boxing that continued through the 1930s, with Butte residents avidly following the national boxing scene as well as taking a proprietary interest in several local boxers.[21]

World War I did much to legitimate boxing in the United States. Boxers, lauded as models of morale and confidence, trained American troops in fitness. Sparring matches became one of the army's most popular recreational activities. On the home front, charity events, sponsored by women's auxiliaries, featured boxing matches. Some historians have noted that the prize ring became a satisfying, heroic, almost dignified arena of combat in contrast to the slogging horrors of an unheroic war. At the same time, the war seemed to release a bloodlust on the part of boxing enthusiasts. H. W. Whicker, a journalist, believed that spectators, once content with skillful exhibitions, now wanted lethal punches and blood.[22]

The new showmanship of the sport, staged in cavernous auditoriums and theaters, encouraged a gladiatorial atmosphere. Huge audiences screaming at the combatants urged boxers to greater brutality. The *Miner* reported of a 1922 card, "It was . . . a different kind of show, for, in place of the usual stellar boxing, every bout of the evening was featured by the kind of socking that brought the fans up shouting like a band of Indians on the war path." In 1924 the loser in a bantamweight match was "bruised crimson from his waist to the top of his head."[23]

Another change in boxing in the 1920s was that an increasing number of women were in the audience. The presence of reputable women was taboo at nineteenth-century fights. When Mrs. Robert Fitzsimmons appeared in her husband's corner in 1897, the press depicted her attendance as a sign of decadence. In the twentieth century, however, promoters, most notably Tex Rickard, courted women fans, rightfully calculating that their patronage would help legitimate the sport. A few women attended the Nelson-Herrera bout in Butte, and the *Miner* complimented their ladylike behavior although one woman rose and wildly waved her picture hat when Herrera floored Nelson in the fourth round. By 1922 the newspaper noted that all boxing matches were "generously sprinkled with women." It is also possible, however, that women's attendance at and enjoyment of boxing matches contributed to a general perception that the public as a whole was growing more bloodthirsty.[24]

Men were generally dismayed by having women at ringside; it may have seemed that one last unbreachable fortress of male leisure had fallen. Women who enjoyed boxing disproved men's belief that the sport was too brutal for feminine sensibilities. Some men found the fact that some women became emotionally involved in the passion of physical combat distasteful if not alarming. The presence of women urging bloodletting may have buttressed Whicker's belief that "the killer part became the rage" in postwar boxing.[25]

Still, despite its brutality, boxing was touted as the ideal way to instill manliness. Enthusiasts spoke of the grace, honor, and courage that adhered to boxers, and they played down the blood, bruises, hype, and fraud of commercial boxing. Boxers were marketed as heroes and role models. Skill and strength, necessary to a good boxer of any class, epitomized manliness. In an unpublished short story of the 1930s, Butte writer William A. Burke expressed a novice's admiration of an experienced miner by comparing him to a boxer: "It was a pleasure to watch that wizened up McCarthy work . . . he reminded me of a boxer. He never made an unnecessary motion, and I think he was the strongest and wiriest man I ever saw for his size. He sure could step around lively on those banty legs." As Elliott Gorn records, Ernest Thompson Seton, founder of the Boys Scouts of America, was comforted by the fact that he never met a boy who, given a choice, would rather be Leo Tolstoy than John L. Sullivan.[26]

States began legalizing boxing in 1920, opening the way for it to become "entertainment on a grand scale." More people saw Jack Dempsey—in Butte's eyes "the number one athlete" of the 1920s—in one of his films or on a vaudeville tour than in an actual fight. Dempsey came to Butte in 1921 in a show that featured a juggling act, a jazz band, dancers from the Ziegfield Follies, and Bea Palmer, alleged originator of the shimmy. After trading verbal jabs with his manager, Dempsey showed some of his training films and then sparred three rounds with a local middleweight.[27]

Butte entertainment impresarios capitalized on the boxing craze. Theater owners screened Dempsey's movies, and when the proprietor of the Winter Garden staged Dixie LaHood Night the whole family was invited to attend and participate. Namen "Dixie" LaHood, a successful young Butte bantamweight, shadowboxed, skipped rope, and sparred with another local fighter. There was an exhibition of child boxers and a challenge to women to stage a bout; the volunteers received gloves autographed by LaHood. Under the auspices of local boxing clubs and the newly formed American Legion, boxers from all over the West fought in Butte gyms and theaters. Butte athletic clubs, fraternal groups, and the YMCA all encouraged young boxers. The Knights of Columbus sponsored an annual Golden Gloves tournament. Within nine months of its creation in 1927, the Montana State Athletic Commission issued charters to seventeen boxing clubs, eight of them to American Legion posts. Disillusionment with fixed fights was one impetus for the establishment of the commission. In its first report to the governor members were pleased to recount that "sham or collusive contests are no longer perpetrated upon the public in this state, and thousands of people in all walks of life, including ladies, have been enabled to witness boxing contests amid decent and orderly surroundings."[28]

Local heroes inspired Butte boys and drew capacity crowds to the Empress and Broadway theaters. Joe Simonich, born in Walkerville in 1895, was the son of Slavic immigrants. His father, a miner, died in 1907; after Joe finished the eighth grade he worked at a series of odd jobs before enlisting in the army in World War I. During the war he distinguished himself on several fronts. He learned hand-to-hand combat in the Battle of the Argonne and in the boxing ring at Camp Lewis, Washington. When discharged, Simonich was a second lieutenant and the American Expeditionary Force's welterweight champion. Returning to Butte, he found boxing "going good," and his matches quickly became the main event in cards sponsored by the American Legion and the Manhattan Athletic Club. Simonich exemplified "the manly sport." In 1922, during the week before he fought a Fourth of July bout, the *Butte Miner* informed Simonich's fans that he had become a father and second baseman for one of Butte's Independent League baseball teams. He was known to put on a "class" show and firmly believed that dirty fighters would not last if the sport were governed correctly. During the mid-1920s Simonich's career took off, and under the moniker the "Butte Assassin" he fought all over the United States and Far East. In 1927 welterweight champion Pete Latzo agreed to a match if his title would not be at stake. Simonich won the bout and left the ring the "uncrowned welterweight champ." In 1931 he hung up his gloves and returned to Montana to run a ranch outside Butte and referee amateur bouts throughout the state. Simonich was one of the few boxers who managed to keep the showmanship and belligerence of the game in the ring and take from it his dignity and a little cash.[29]

Other Butte boxers had difficulty recognizing the boundaries of the ropes. Tally Johns, a Montana featherweight champ, "loved to fight" and instigated fights in bars, on the streets, and in the bleachers at football games. James Blakely recalled, "He always had a saying, 'I'll give you the first punch. Take it. Go ahead.' But they never got that first punch in." Known as "a tartar" in the ring, Dixie LaHood, the son of Lebanese parents, described himself as a "lifelong hard laborer." When he retired from boxing in 1933, he was elected constable of Silver Bow County. Some described his style of law enforcement as "colorful"; political opponents charged him with graft and excessive violence. Johns, Simonich, and LaHood all trained in small home gyms, with neighbors and family as sparring partners. Blakely, who attended every professional fight held in Butte from 1923 through "quite a few years" and knew Butte's boxers, compared Simonich's style to LaHood's: "Simonich was never out to hurt anyone . . . where Dixie LaHood, if he was training with his mother, he'd try to tear her head off."[30]

In Butte, excessive violence was not unusual. Miners and company guards pummeled each other during strikes, the Cabbage Patch and red light district were infamous sites of disorder, and the police force was noted for brutality. Boys learned early that fighting was a way to protect their territory and win respect. In a community noted for its charity to people in need, toughness and generosity combined in an ethic of working-class manliness. James Blakely summed things up when he spoke of Tally Johns: "Tally'd give you the shirt off his back and he'd fight a buzz saw."[31]

■ ■ ■

The elements of risk-taking, bravado, and excitement that attracted fight fans were also inherent in gambling, another of Butte's vaunted male pleasures. Describing the array of devices awaiting the gambler, a writer inspired by Butte's nightlife warned that "only strong character could withstand the temptations of Butte and maintain its strength and dignity." Those who waged campaigns to eliminate gambling in every decade of the first half of the twentieth century evidently felt that few men had the strength to resist those temptations.[32]

Gambling had deep roots in the mining city's male culture. In

1880 a report on "Saturday night in Butte" linked the psychology of mining to gambling, arguing that miners needed more intense thrills than other people did: "This excitement they are bound to have in one form or another, and if it is not to be found in the exploration of very promising looking croppings, the gaming table is resorted to as the best substitute."[33]

By the mid-twentieth century the connection between excitement and gambling was as strong as ever, but it extended to all segments of the population. When Bessie Towey Mulhern, an Irish immigrant and an "average country girl," arrived in Butte in 1939, she found the town "exciting," partly because of the easy gambling. "You would go to the store and there would be a slot machine and we'd put in a dime or whatever it was, a quarter. . . . Slot machines was all over. They were in the drugstores. I know I went down to the drugstore on Main Street one time and I put in a quarter and I hit the jackpot and the money was skidding all over the place." Had Bessie arrived ten years earlier she would not have had as much fun. Outside of the red light district, women were not welcome to risk their quarters gambling in Butte until the 1930s.[34]

Gambling was common in Chinatown and the red light district, and many saloons, pool halls, and cigar stores provided gaming tables. Gambling halls concentrated in the uptown business district and by the late 1920s and early 1930s were in Meaderville. Like saloons and brothels, gambling halls were not places for reputable women. Madeleine, the Chicago prostitute who found Butte's vice so appalling, fell prey to its gaming. While she was exploring the red light district on her first day in town, she overheard a loud voice announcing, "She is seventeen, gentlemen, and a black one." Already reeling from the horrors of the cribs, Madeleine believed she had stumbled upon an auction of women, only to discover a roulette game. After a companion introduced her to poker, she became addicted to gambling and spent many nights on the line playing "poker, roulette, faro, the races, or anything else on which money could be staked."[35]

Repeated attempts by state attorneys general to force Butte to comply with state laws prohibiting gambling left a record that both documents their failure and describes the nature of the game. During World War I, in the mid-1920s, and again during the 1930s, various administrations sent agents to Butte to gather evidence with which to prosecute gamblers. Officers seized and burned thousands of dollars worth of gambling equipment, and gamblers paid thousands of dollars in fines, but the persistence of men's desire to gamble and the willingness of others to accommodate them was the overriding lesson of this long campaign. After all, one journalist estimated that in 1930 gambling in Butte was a $2 million business.[36]

In 1927 investigators G. V. Elder and Ernest Loft visited twenty-two soft drink parlors and gambling houses to gather evidence for the state attorney general. They played blackjack, poker, English Hazard, panguingue, and craps. They bought lottery tickets in Chinatown and baseball pool tickets from high school boys. They bet on the Kentucky Derby. In only one place did they see a woman, and remarked upon her presence because it was so unusual. They could also have tried their hand at fan tan, roulette, faro, punch boards, and slot machines. Had they not spent all their time in uptown gambling halls, they could have wagered money on fifteen games at a charity circus sponsored by three fraternal lodges that hired Butte's most notorious gambler, Curley Darragh, to supervise. They discovered that gambling was endemic in Butte. Everyone played the baseball pool, including women. Conductors and brakemen on the Northern Pacific's Chicago to Seattle North Coast Limited bought batches of tickets and sold them to passengers. Bernice Knierim, home from college and "fooling around," bought a pool ticket and won $350. It financed her sophomore year.[37]

The chance of just such a win enticed working men to wager their pay and increasingly attracted women to the tables. Just as women did not breach the male sanctity of uptown speakeasies, they were not welcome in uptown gambling halls, but they were courted by the new nightclubs of Meaderville. Some astute gamblers, such as Curley Darragh, also built keno parlors specifically to cash in on women's trade. In 1937 a reporter interviewing a faro dealer who had worked in Butte for more than twenty-eight years found him vehemently opposed to women's presence in gambling houses. He believed gambling was "a man's game." Letting women into gambling houses caused a whole array of problems, ranging from sparking men's fights to endangering their homes. When women got into trouble in a gambling house, "The next thing you know her kids are in trouble" and soon her whole family was likely "to bust up. Keeping women out of the gambling rooms is only fair to the women who got to take care of the home. Besides no lady has any business hanging around crap tables and the like. Butte likes its women to be ladies." The dealer made an exception for keno, however, noting that "no lady is going to neglect her family and stop being a lady for a ten-cent racket."[38]

Women could play anything they wanted to in Meaderville, but the action there did not begin until the evening, and most women's opportunities to gamble came during the day when their husbands were at work and their children at school. Thus, for the most part, women patronized the uptown keno parlors. As one female patron of Darragh's put it, "The only places us women's got to rest our feet after shopping is some keno joint." She found men's concern for women's home responsibilities and reputations hypocritical: "If this was an honest-to-God open town like you think, and the Main Street places like Walker's wasn't for men only like they are, they'd have crap tables, blackjack, poker, chuck-a-luck, faro and that there panguingui game for women too instead of just skill ball, dart throwing and such keno games with a trained wheel now and then." The fact that these games of chance were not available to women had nothing to do with Butte women's character: "It ain't that us women here in Butte are sissies either. It's because they think if they give us anything but a ten-cent keno game there won't be any pork chops on the supper table." That judgment was the most infuriating, for she well knew that "when some men I know come out of some of them Main Street joints they ain't got enough money to buy a picture postcard of a pork chop." Clearly, men were worried not only about supper on the table but also about preserving one last male domain. As one bouncer asserted, "There's only a few men's towns left. And we aim to stay one."[39]

The claim that gambling women would abandon their household obligations may have been an excuse to keep women from men's space, but it also reflected men's own experience that gambling could harm family life. In the long run, gambling was a losing proposition for most players. Many men became addicted to it, and on numerous occasions working men lost far more than they and their families could afford. It was common practice for men to hand over their pay envelopes to their wives, who managed the household money. Gambling, as well as drinking, forced some women to take drastic measures to protect the household funds. Children met their fathers at the pay window and escorted them home or picked up their checks else they "spend it all over the gambling table." Occasionally, women successfully confronted the owners of gambling halls where their husbands had lost money. In 1919 Mrs. Philip Johnston, wife of a laborer at the Pittsmont smelter, marched into the Pioneer Club and demanded the $300 her husband had lost playing blackjack that afternoon. The owner apparently paid her. Several years later Bertha Olsen filed suit against the owners of Walker's to recover the $1,000 her husband had gambled away. The parties settled out of court for an undisclosed sum.[40]

Such incidents fueled gambling's opponents, who feared the effects of gaming on citizens' morals and families' welfare. Although concerted efforts on the part of ministers, some judges, and an ad hoc Law Enforcement League succeeded in closing down a few joints for a short time, foes of gambling faced the same problems that confronted dry forces. Even if they did not endorse gambling, the majority of Butte residents did not oppose it strongly enough to ensure its elimination. Thomas J. Davis, a lawyer and leader of the anti-gambling coalition, confessed to Attorney General L. A. Foot that many people complained of existing evils but few would sign affidavits. Foot himself had the experience of Butte witnesses telling him one thing and juries another. Davis also warned Foot that individual members of service clubs would support him but that he should not expect fraternal groups or the Chamber of Commerce to take an anti-gambling position.[41]

In such an atmosphere, charges of "fixing" flew back and forth between Butte and Helena. Citizens in Butte generally believed that the "fix was in" and at various times accused the mayor, city attorney, sheriff, county attorney, attorney general, city council, and police force of receiving payoffs and turning a blind eye to gambling. When Judge William E. Carroll ordered the deputy county attorney to raid three gambling joints that were running wide open in 1931, the order fell on the city's gamblers "as a bombshell." But little came of Carroll's dictum. The following year Alderman T. R. Morgan moved that the police committee of the city council call upon the chief of police to ascertain why gambling continued. His motion was roundly defeated. Police officers' claims that they could not get evidence that would stand up in court, the inability of prosecutors to get convictions, and the disregard of abatement orders all gave weight to the common belief that "anything can be fixed in Butte." Guy W. Bannister, an FBI agent, testified to Butte's toleration of vice when he addressed the Chamber of Commerce in the 1940s: "If the citizens of any community never raise their voices against the pattern in which they live, the pattern of adultery mixed with respectability, of graft mixed with time worn democratic slogans, of vice supporting charity and religion, and religion by inaction condoning vice, then you get the kind of law enforcement you deserve. It may not be the kind you want, but it is what you deserve."[42]

Many people maintained that the Anaconda Company supported vice as a way of controlling its labor force. Workers who spent their paychecks on games, drink, and prostitutes would necessarily return to the mines for more work and money. Some believed that men who dissipated their energy playing would have little left for organizing. The company's style was more a matter of acquiescence than connivance. Considering the political clout the company wielded and its close ties to the Butte police force, people generally believed that ACM would have suppressed gambling, drinking, and prostitution had those activities not been in the company's best interests. Because the company never supported anti-vice campaigns, Anaconda's "tolerance was generally recognized as having an element of calculation." As Sonny O'Day, a former prizefighter and a Meaderville club owner, observed, "It was the policy of ACM to keep the miners happy, keep 'em broke, keep 'em working."[43]

■ ■ ■

Much of Butte men's play—drinking, gambling, fighting, and sports—followed a pattern of male companionship, rough-and-tumble contact, and risk-taking that also shaped their work culture. Another side of social life was even more directly tied to work: activities sponsored by labor unions. Various unions staged smokers, socials, and picnics. The Miners' and the Clerks' Unions established libraries and reading rooms for their members. The clerks incorporated a Literary and Art Society for the purpose of "recreation, amusement and athletics." Nearly all the unions held balls and dances; some, like the Letter Carriers, issued public invitations in the newspaper: "Come spend an evening with the postmen." Others were private events, requiring the presentation of engraved invitations for admission and providing highly decorated dance cards for the ladies. Unions staged elaborate ceremonies to install new officers—"stag" affairs at which members were feted with food, drink, and entertainment. In 1914 the Butte Barbers' Union installed their officers and then enjoyed boxing bouts, a tumbling exhibition by the Centerville Young Men's Club, a dance act, and musical performances.[44]

During the summer many unions held annual picnics, but June 13, Miners' Union Day, was the city's greatest holiday. It celebrated the anniversary of the founding of Butte's first union, the Butte Workingmen's Union, established in 1878 and reorganized three years later into the Butte Miners' Union. The 1913 celebration marked the heyday of unionism before twenty years of an open shop for miners. Eight thousand union men and women marched in the annual parade through uptown Butte. A bearer carrying the American flag, followed by the president of the Miners' Union, led four divisions of marchers. The butchers sported white coats, pants, and caps, and sprigs of carnations pinned next to their badges. Five hundred clerks followed wagons of suffragists and a float designed by women laundry workers. The teamsters had groomed and beribboned 250 horses, arranging them in line by color. The teamsters themselves wore overalls and teamsters' caps, and many marched with their sons. In the last division, headed by the Irish Volunteers fife and drum corps, five thousand miners marched four abreast. After the parade, thousands of workers and their families adjourned to Columbia Gardens for an afternoon of picnicking, games, and an evening dance. No one missed work because the entire city shut down. All city and county offices, banks, stores, and mines closed for the holiday. Days before, the papers carried department store advertisements urging men and women to take advantage of "Miners' Union Day specials" and look their best for the holiday. It was a massive celebration of workers' pride.[45]

Miners' Union Day honored the city's work force; other events transformed mining skills into sport and elevated their champions to heroes of the working class. Hardrock drilling and mucking contests called upon men to demonstrate speed, strength, and skill and were one of the most popular sports in the mining West. Drilling contests faded away just before World War I. The introduction of mechanical drills made obsolete the knowledge of hand drilling. Mucking, the shoveling of rock into ore cars, did not change and continued to generate contests and champions.

In a drilling contest two partners hammered a sharpened steel into a granite boulder for fifteen minutes. The boulder was often mounted on a platform above the crowd to improve the spectators' view. The team that drilled the deepest hole in the allotted time won. The task was not as simple as it sounds. The pounding, done with a nine-pound sledge, required strength, speed, and accuracy. It also demanded great skill and coordination, as the partners, one swinging the sledge, the other holding and twisting the steel, switched positions and steels every minute—ideally without losing a stroke. Men trained long and hard for drilling contests, and professionals used custom-made hammers and steels. Victors often won several hundred dollars and cases of liquor in addition to any side bets that might have been laid. Walter Bradshaw, a Butte champion, estimated that he earned between $30,000 and $35,000 in his competitive career.[46]

"Rock in the box" was the cry accompanying the mucking contest. The object was to shovel a ton or half a ton of rock waste into an ore car in the shortest time possible. Mucking contests persisted into the early 1930s because there had been little technological change in that job. Although a favorite with the crowds, mucking contests never commanded the purses or the prestige awarded in drilling contests.[47]

Another enduring representative of miners' pride was the Butte Mines Band. Founded in 1887 by Sam Treloar and five other employees of the Boston and Montana Copper and Silver Mining Company, the Boston and Montana Band (later known as the ACM Band when Anaconda purchased the Boston and Montana, and finally as the Butte Mines Band) played for more than fifty years. Band members were all miners, and after one trip to Chicago, the press recorded its surprise that "so high class a musical organization could be assembled so far West and among a class of men who went beneath ground to earn their daily bread." The band became Butte's premier musical institution. It led most Butte parades, traveled throughout the West, greeted visiting dignitaries and returning veterans, and opened union balls and the baseball season. When Miners' Union Day was revived in 1935 the band led a mile-long parade of union members and then entertained thousands of picnickers with a concert at Columbia Gardens. In 1924 the Butte Mines Band took mining to vaudeville, signing on for an eight-week tour with Pantages vaudeville circuit. They carried an elaborate set depicting the underground, foreswore their band uniforms for regular digging clothes, and provided a lobby exhibit of a model headframe, ore samples, and mining machinery.[48]

Although work-related contests and exhibits continued into the 1930s, union-sponsored activities declined in 1914 with the demise of the Miners' Union. Miners' Union Day was not celebrated between 1914 and 1935. Having succeeded in establishing an open shop, the Anaconda Company now inaugurated several new programs aimed at winning the hearts and minds of its employees— and those of their families.

In 1914 ACM correctly anticipated the final success of a twenty-six-year lobbying effort to pass a Montana workmen's compensation bill. In response, the company initiated a "safety first" program designed to decrease the number of work-related accidents and the amount of compensation the company might be charged. Anaconda was the first American copper producer to inaugurate such a program, which entailed education, enforcement of existing safety regulations, monetary incentives, and the training of first aid and rescue teams. One arm of the program was the publication of the *Anode.*[49]

The company eventually extended its safety program to the community. Children had grown up playing on the mine dumps and in mine yards—hazardous playgrounds indeed. Dumps were laced with toxic mercury and arsenic. Tucking paper into stolen blasting caps made appealing firecrackers, but it also blew off children's hands. In the late 1920s ACM finally took steps to curb children being maimed. It instituted a stricter inventory control and sent a team consisting of an ACM safety engineer and a representative from DuPont to visit grammar schools and present an illustrated lecture on the dangers of playing with explosives. In 1931 company safety engineers taught first aid to the Ladies' Auxiliary of the American Legion, the Girl Scouts, and public school teachers.[50]

The *Anode* was the company's voice in the safety campaign, and the magazine had a consistent format throughout its life (1915–42). It always ran articles and illustrations on mine safety, the history and uses of copper, and various aspects of copper production. Jokes and anecdotes filled the bottom of pages, some meant to reinforce safety messages, others purely for amusement. The editor also encouraged employees to submit letters, poems, and stories and printed submissions that illustrated positive aspects of mining or taught safety lessons. Through the early 1920s the magazine was written primarily for an audience of single men. All the jokes that featured women were at their expense, and accounts of community activities were likely to be prefaced with remarks such as, "Even the married men enjoyed themselves, although their wives were present."[51]

By the mid-1920s this tone had changed as the editor began courting a family audience. There were still a number of dumbhousewife jokes, but there were also anecdotes featuring flappers and secretaries who fended off lecherous men with snappy retorts, and many more stories in which women knowingly wielded their sexual power to make men look foolish. More significantly, articles directly addressed women and children. Pieces appeared on fire prevention in the home, gas and electric appliances, vacation safety, household poisons, and the hazards of washing women's gloves in gasoline. Contests for children also appeared. Editors designed a fill-in-the-blank quiz on fire prevention and requested schoolchildren to submit essays on new uses of copper in order to draw employees' families into the company's embrace. In September 1925 the *Anode* published a short story entitled "Dad" by Lester Rudd, who mined at the Leonard Mine. The narrator of the poignant tale of a miner just buried by his lodge brothers appeals to children to appreciate their fathers while they are still alive.[52]

The shift toward a family audience reflected the company's realization that its labor force was changing to one composed of more married men. It was also part of a national movement of industrial welfare work. Clearly, by the mid-1920s Anaconda was trying either to temper its confrontational labor management policies or at least add another, more benign weapon to its arsenal of measures designed to control its employees.[53]

In addition to the safety campaign, Anaconda created Mines League baseball and an annual Miners' Field Day at Columbia Gardens to promote harmony among workers, their families, and management. A baseball commission representing all the mining companies in Butte launched the Mines League in 1920, and each company, or sometimes a pair of companies, sponsored a club. The clubs paid the ballplayers and also promised them mining jobs, which in 1923 paid $5.25 a day. The companies heavily subsidized the games. In 1920 admission was free; in 1921 only Sunday games cost twenty-five cents. League games attracted huge crowds. Indeed, in 1922 the Butte Electric Railway Company erected a grandstand and bleachers in Clark Park specifically for league games. Five thousand fans packed the stands to watch the mayor throw the season's opening pitch in 1925.[54]

Editors of the *Engineering and Mining Journal* felt that the league had great potential for creating accord between managers and miners. They reported that mine managers rubbed shoulders with muckers, and "all class distinction is eclipsed by the common desire to have the company's team victorious." As far as the *Journal* was concerned, the mining companies had created "a community of interest among mine executives and miners that may produce more beneficial results than are generally realized." Other observers were more cynical, but they speculated that the company's goal—less organization among workers—might indeed result. One Butte pundit wrote, "When the game was over, the crowd came up town, too hoarse to holler, too winded to argue, and too weary to waste time listening to the spellbinder on his soap box as he blatantly bellowed for reforms." Baseball four to six nights a week combined with available commercial entertainments could absorb all of a miner's free time. For instance, in 1924 a boxing match between Dixie LaHood and Billy Mascott was scheduled at 8:45 P.M. so fans could attend the league baseball game and still get uptown in time for the fight.[55]

In 1918 the Anaconda Company initiated an annual Miners' Field Day at Columbia Gardens to promote the Safety First Program and ease the tensions between the company and its employees that plagued the war years. The 1918 event attracted twenty thousand people. The editor of the *Anode* explained the company's agenda: "In such an industry as mining, where holidays are few and living is very strenuous, people are apt to forget to relax and consider the well being of their neighbors." He hoped that a day of field sports would cement "the people together in a happy considerate community feeling." In 1920, when labor relations had reached a nadir, the company pronounced Field Day a success because it recalled days before the labor strife of the war. "The crowd was typical of old-time Butte, the Butte of progress and prosperity, before the radical came to teach us how to live." As far as the company spokesman was concerned, "A lot of us went from the Gardens with the conviction that the tide had turned and Butte was coming to her own. As a get-together meeting between bosses and men the Field Day left nothing to be desired."[56]

Field Day activities included athletic contests for men, women, and children, a demonstration by the mines' first aid teams, a picnic lunch, and dancing in the pavilion in the evening. The field games were designed to draw upon men's work skills, play upon friendly rivalries, and even poke fun at bosses. Shot putting was restricted to blacksmiths, boilermakers, and machinists, and pole climbing to electricians. Mine carpenters and hoisting engineers challenged each other in the tug of war. Timekeepers and foremen's clerks competed in the three-legged race, and shift bosses and assistant foremen tried their luck at ladder-climbing. The mucking contest took center stage, as the drilling contest had done in earlier times. In 1928 William Vitti won by shoveling a thousand pounds of limestone rock into a mine car in one minute, forty-four seconds. Vitti, thirty-six, was one of the youngest men to win a mucking contest. In the past, the champion had often been more than fifty, proof that skill, not mere youthful strength, made a good mucker.[57]

Each year the planning committee introduced one or two new activities to maintain people's interest. In 1923 it staged a drilling demonstration for the benefit of those who had never been underground. As it turned out, the exhibit was swarmed by miners who had never seen a drill working in broad daylight. So many miners allowed their curiosity to overcome their "sense of chivalry" that no one else got to see the show.[58]

Men were the primary target of the company's goodwill, but ACM counted upon women for a large measure of the day's success. The company depended upon women to prepare the much-touted picnic lunches necessary to feed the crowds and create a family atmosphere. In 1918 the *Anode* curried women's favor by proclaiming,

"This lunch will be enjoyable as only Butte wives and mothers can make it." The sponsor's contribution was to arrange a place to check the anticipated well-laden picnic baskets so that the women would not have to carry them around all day. In 1920 the day's organizers again called upon Butte's women to provide the food that was such an important part of welding the community together and invite others to join their families. "You may not realize the good you can do by inviting some bachelor girl or boy to join you in the lunch. There is no loneliness more keenly felt than to be friendless in a crowd, nor is there a better cure for 'the blues' than to be invited by some good mother to join in the family picnic lunch." While Field Day planners delighted in their event, women must have contemplated the holiday with mixed emotions. Catherine Hoy recalled that as a child she looked forward to the day with excitement, but even then she was aware of the work her mother, grandmother, and neighborhood women—all mothers of six or eight children—put into preparing hams, chickens, and mutton, baking bread, pies, and cakes, and packing it all out to the Gardens on the streetcar.[59]

Field Day, although primarily a miners' holiday, also reflected the company's encouragement of family life. In 1919 planners added a baby review to the day's events, and five years later a baby clinic. With the help of public health nurses, mothers received advice on child care and their babies had a checkup. Healthy babies received blue ribbons. More children's activities—a dress parade for girls and their dolls, a pet show for girls and boys, and a safety poster contest for schoolchildren—appeared by the early 1930s. The *Anode's* yearly announcements of the day's program no longer boasted only of the social equality the day provided, but also noted that "best of all it is good for men to appear in public with their families." In 1926 a prize was awarded to the man and wife who paraded before the grandstand with the largest family. Perhaps in recognition of Butte's many remarried widows, the contest rules specifically stated that stepchildren could be included. The depression curtailed the company's public relations efforts, and the last Miners' Field Day occurred in 1931. When Miners' Union Day resumed, no one was interested in a company-sponsored field day.[60]

▪ ▪ ▪

A public male culture—shaped by the nature of work underground and the bonds partners forged there, by the continued majority of men in the general population, and by their economic dominance—persisted well into the 1920s. But it was a culture under siege. There were fewer and fewer single men in Butte. Prohibition and the rise of sexually integrated nightclubs threatened the male sanctity of the saloon, and women gambling and attending prizefights trespassed traditionally masculine domains. The demise of Miners' Union Day and the substitution of the company-sponsored Miners' Field Day chipped away at a structure of male pride erected on the bedrock of work skills and organization.

Nationally, the 1920s witnessed a revision in familial expectations. Increasingly, men were called upon to be "companionate providers." Marriage manuals, popular novels, and widely read magazines such as *True Story* translated the public sexuality of the decade into an ethic of mutual sexual pleasure within marriage and urged husbands to awaken their wives' desire. The increased availability of birth control contributed to the conviction that marital sex could be recreational, not merely reproductive. As barriers to women's attendance in places of commercial amusement fell, husbands and wives more frequently went out together instead of with companions of the same sex. A component of "masculine domesticity" was the belief that fathers should spend more time with their children, especially their sons. Acceptance of the concept of childhood as a distinct stage of human development, and one that needed appropriate recreational opportunities and parental supervision, fed the growing opposition to child labor. Organizations such as the Boy Scouts and Girl Scouts and the YMCA and YWCA created those opportunities for parents and children. All of these trends conspired to bind men more closely to family life and make family responsibility the measure of manhood.[61]

As Butte matured, the boisterous leisure of the mining camp, oriented toward the desires of single men, no longer satisfied all its residents. While the demand for traditional male pleasures endured and contributed to the persistence of Butte's reputation as a wide-open town—"a man's town"—many residents worked to make the community a place in which to raise families. As the twentieth century progressed, this task was shouldered, somewhat ironically, by fraternal lodges and women's voluntary associations. Originally formed for the pleasure of their members' company or as mutual benefit societies, these sex-segregated groups increasingly turned their attention to the welfare of the community, its institutions, and its children, regardless of gender. As Margery Bedinger, a journalist who passed through Butte in 1931, observed, "A new era is dawning. The movement for social uplift is subtly having its way with the virile inhabitants of Butte. There has been an eruption of service clubs of both genders within the last few years. Mr. Babbit has come to Butte at last."[62]

NOTES

1. McHugh, "Gulch and I," 21.

2. *Butte Daily Post,* 9 April 1927, 11; D. J. O'Connor to Ella Gardner, 16 April 1927, Children's Bureau Records, 68/20–88–8, National Archives. Gardner and Roche's judgment was based on their observations of the lack of an organized play program for girls comparable to the one boys had and the generally lax enforcement of the dance hall ordinance, which they thought necessary to protect girls' welfare. Hand, "Folklore of Butte Miner," 161; Duffy, *Butte Was Like That,* 43; Edward Sullivan, interview by Laurie Mercier, Butte, 25 February, 10 March 1982; Catherine Hoy, interview by Ray Calkins and Caroline Smithson, Butte, 11 May 1979, 2; *Butte Daily Bulletin,* 17 February 1920, 3.

3. Filene reviewed the literature on men's history up to the mid-1980s in "The Secrets of Men's History." Pleck and Pleck review the periodization of men's history in their introduction to *The American Man.* More recent works exploring the construction of masculinity are Hansen, "'Helped Put in a Quilt'"; Morgan, "Masculinity, Autobiography and History"; Rotundo, *American Manhood;* Rotundo, "Body and Soul"; and Rotundo, "Learning about Manhood." Marsh, in "Suburban Men and Masculine Domesticity," and Simmons in "Modern Sexuality and the Myth of Victorian Repression," discuss the rise of the notion of companionate marriage and participatory fatherhood. All of these works focus primarily on white middle-class men. McDannell's study of Catholicism and Irish-American manhood, "'True Men as We Need Them,'" is one of the few to address issues of working-class masculinity. Maynard also addresses this topic in "Rough Work and Rugged Men."

4. Brinig, *Wide Open Town,* 7.

5. Andrew "Shorty" Felt diary, 13 June 1919, BSBA; Carden, "Come Wander Back with Me," 27; Hand, "Folklore of Butte Miner," 16–17; Sullivan interview.

6. Hanford Toppari, interview by Ray Calkins, Butte, 1 May 1980, 16–17.

7. *Anode* 11 (September 1925): 11. On male friendship, see Ellis, "Men among Men," and Rotundo, "Romantic Friendship."

8. *Anaconda Standard,* 8 January 1914, 8; *Meaderville Volunteer Fire Department, Our Golden Anniversary; Montana Standard,* 23 February 1930, mag. sec., 8–9; *Butte Miner,* 19 November 1919, 6. On the development of the Boy Scouts and boys' clubs, see Macleod, *Building Character.* On changing attitudes toward boys' toughness, see Stearns, "Men, Boys and Anger."

9. Murel Roberts, interview by Ray Calkins, Butte, 8 August 1980, 21–22; Bill McKernan, interview by Mary Murphy, Butte, 9 September 1988.

10. Martin, "School for Struggle." The Newsboys Club disbanded in 1931. *Montana Standard,* 12 April 1931, 1. Nasaw, *Children of the City,* has wonderful material on newsboys in American cities.

11. Roberts interview, 19; *Montana Standard,* 17 January 1982, 18.

12. Carden, "Come Wander Back with Me," 16; John Sconfienza, interview by Ray Calkins, Butte, 27 June 1979, 6; *Butte Miner,* 4 June 1920, 1, 11 and 3 December 1921, 5. Katz addresses the appeal of property crimes "independent of material gain" in *Seductions of Crime,* see especially his chapter "Sneaky Thrills."

13. *Butte Miner,* 4 June 1928, 1–2, 26 December 1922, 5, and 18 March 1929, 1, 7; Butte City Council Minutes (13 July 1931), 18:988.

14. James Blakely, interview by Ray Calkins, Butte, 15 November 1979, 20–21.

15. John Onkalo, interview by Ray Calkins, Butte, February 1980, 18–19.

16. Jordan reminiscence; *Butte Miner,* 3 March 1918, 6, 25 July 1923, 2, and 13 February 1928, 5. Smith discusses the spillover of violence outside the rules of games in "What Is Sports Violence?"

17. Roberts interview, 23–24.

18. Ibid., 18; Jordan reminiscence.

19. Sammons, *Beyond the Ring,* 19–20, 24; Gorn, *The Manly Art,* 165; Bell, *Gladiators of the Gulches,* 90; *Montana Standard,* 18 March 1951, 5.

20. Carroll, comp., *Revised Ordinances,* 470–71; *Butte Miner,* 23 January 1921, mag. sec., 4; Coroner's Inquest, No. 474, Butte-Silver Bow County Courthouse.

21. Bell, *Gladiators of the Gulches,* 87, 89; *Butte Miner,* 6 September 1904, 2, 8.

22. Whicker's thesis is open to debate, but there are several indicators that support his opinion. Fights were bloodier and more deadly under the Queensberry rules, which governed twentieth-century boxing. Ironically, the rules were designed to make the sport safer, but their main effect was to make it easier to stage boxing as a commercial spectator sport. Required gloves protected fighters' hands but allowed men to hit harder and longer. The new three-minute rounds were nearly twice as long as rounds under old rules, and boxers who were knocked down had only ten seconds to recover instead of thirty. The ten-second rule encouraged clubbing blows to the head in order to induce brief bouts of unconsciousness and guaranteed that boxers would increasingly suffer damage to their faces, skulls, and brains. Sammons, *Beyond the Ring,* 49–50; Gray, "For Whom the Bell Tolled," 59–62; Gorn, *Manly Art,* 204. Sammons has an eloquent chapter on the physical costs of modern boxing. For another analysis of the connection between masculinity and boxing, see Haywood, "George Bellows's *Stag at Sharkey's.*"

23. *Butte Miner,* 15 November 1922, 8 and 9 April 1924, 9.

24. Sammons, *Beyond the Ring,* 54–55; *Butte Miner,* 6 September 1904,

8 and 31 August 1922, 8. On men and women's attendance at sporting events, see Guttmann, *Sports Spectators.*

25. Sammons, *Beyond the Ring,* 50, 55–57; McNamee, *You're on the Air,* 44.

26. William A. Burke, "Green Horn Miner," "Men at Work" file, WPA Records, MSU; Gorn, *Manly Art,* 247.

27. Sammons, *Beyond the Ring,* 59; Carden, "Come Wander Back with Me," 19; *Butte Miner,* 11 November 1921, 2.

28. *Butte Miner,* 5 April 1925, mag. sec., 6; "Parks-Recreation Class III B SBC," WPA records, MSU; "Report of the Montana State Athletic Commission for the Period Commencing April 9, 1927 and Ending December 31, 1927," 1–3, Montana Governors' Papers, box 38, file 6, MHSA.

29. Joe Simonich, personal reminiscence, 1976; *Butte Miner,* 2 July 1922, 22 and 5 September 1922, 9. Bell discusses Simonich's career in *Gladiators of the Gulches.*

30. Bell, *Gladiators of the Gulches,* 112–13, 133–35; Blakely interview, 22–25; *Montana Standard,* 14 December 1929, 1 and 14 February 1969, 1; *The Argus,* 12 August 1937, 1–4.

31. Blakely interview, 22. On police brutality, see Axline, "'This Is a Case for the Police!'"

32. Glasscock, *War of the Copper Kings,* 97.

33. *Butte Miner,* 3 October 1880, 3.

34. Bessie Towey Mulhern, interview by Laurie Mercier, Butte, 23 November 1981.

35. *Madeleine,* 210, 235.

36. Shepherd, "Sin in the Desert," *Collier's,* 42.

37. T. J. Davis to I. W. Choate, 26 October 1927, and F. H. Sarles to L. A. Foot, 26 April 1927, Montana Attorney General Records (hereafter cited as Atty Gen Records), box 7, file 9, MHSA; Carden, "Come Wander Back with Me," 17; Shepherd, "Sin in the Desert," 42; Bernice Knierim, interview by Diane Sands, Glasgow, 3 August 1987.

38. Davenport, "Richest Hill on Earth," 11. On women gambling in roadhouses but not uptown, see James, *High, Low and Wide Open,* 115–16.

39. Davenport, "Richest Hill on Earth," 9–10. Another man echoed the refrain that women playing keno in Curley Darragh's joint deprived men of their dinners: "At five o'clock, every day at five o'clock, you'd see the ladies streaming out of that place, going up to the delicatessen store and buying the poor miner a delicatessen supper." Quoted in Alma E. Hileman, interview by Ray Calkins, Butte, 27 June 1980, 27.

40. Roberts interview, 20; Report by Larry Houchins, 22 December 1919, Atty Gen Records, box 20, file 2, MHSA; *Butte Daily Post,* 15 April 1927, 7. On women's struggle to manage household income, see Roberts, "Women's Strategies."

41. T. J. Davis to L. A. Foot, 16 November 1927, and L. A. Foot to J. F. Murphy, 6 May 1927, Atty Gen Records, box 7, file 9, MHSA.

42. J. F. Murphy to L. A. Foot, 30 April 1927, and 8 May 1927, F. H. Sarles to L. A. Foot, 17 May 1927, L. A. Foot to F. H. Sarles, 18 May 1927, and I. W. Choate to T. J. Davis, 18 November 1927, all in Atty Gen Papers, box 7, file 9, MHSA. At the time of the judge's order, the Rocky Mountain Cafe, which had been raided recently—its roulette wheels, crap and twenty-one tables confiscated and burned—was in the process of constructing a new addition to house replacement equipment. *Montana Standard,* 18 August 1931, 1, 2; City Council Minutes (15 June 1932), 18:1179. Bannister is quoted in Howard, draft article, Joseph Kinsey Howard Papers, box 1, file 13, MHSA. On police corruption, see Axline, "'This Is a Case for the Police!'"

43. Hutchens, *One Man's Montana,* 174–75; Howard, draft article; Howard, "Butte: City with a 'Kick' in It," 307; Bell, *Gladiators of the Gulches,* 141–42.

44. *Butte Miner,* 2 April 1902, 5; *Anaconda Standard,* 15 February 1920, 7 and 2 January 1914, 6. For examples of other union-sponsored social events, see *Anaconda Standard,* 6 January 1914, 7 and 9 January 1914, 9, and *Butte Miner,* 23 July 1920, 5. For examples of invitations and dance cards, see Butte Labor History Collection, BSBA. In his study of nineteenth-century baseball Gelber uses the game to explore two theories of leisure, the compensatory theory in which leisure activities fill a gap in workers' physical, social, or psychological life, and the congruence theory, which posits that people participate in leisure activities that extend their work values. He concludes that the bulk of modern social science theory supports the congruence model and finds the simultaneous rise of baseball and business organization in the nineteenth-century substantiation of the theory. No play falls neatly into one or the other category, but the congruence theory seems applicable to many of Butte males' activities outside work. The predilection for male companionship, rough-and-tumble contact, and risk-taking are at play in the underground and in Butte males' most popular pastimes: drinking, gambling, fighting, and sports. See Gelber, "Working at Playing."

45. *Butte Miner,* 12 June 1913, 2, 13 June 1913, 1, 6, and 14 June 1913, 1; *Anaconda Standard,* 14 June 1913, 1; *Montana Standard,* 13 June 1935, 1 and 14 June 1935, 1, 2. In other communities the Fourth of July turned into a workers' celebration, much like Miners' Union Day. See Rosenzweig, *Eight Hours for What We Will,* 65–90, and Couvares, *The Remaking of Pittsburgh,* 50.

46. On drilling contests, see Young, Jr., *Black Powder and Hand Steel,* 50–56; Richie, "The Real Facts," 84–85; "When Drilling Contests Saw Titans"; and Frank Quinn Personal Reminiscence, 1976.

47. Young, *Black Powder and Hand Steel,* 49.

48. On the history of the Butte Mines Band, see Treloar, "Reminiscences of the Butte Mines Band," and *Butte Miner,* 10 March 1924, 3. The Chicago press is quoted in Freeman, *A Brief History of Butte,* 37.

49. Shovers, "Miners, Managers, and Machines," 85, 97–98.

50. Frank Jursnick, interview by Ray Calkins, Butte, 6 June 1979, 42; *Anode* 16 (June 1930): 16, 17 (March 1931): 10, and 17 (October 1931): 7.

51. *Anode* 6 (September 1920): 13.

52. For articles regarding home safety, see, for example, *Anode* 11 (April 1925): 1–3, 11 (May 1925): 1–4, 11 (September 1925): 1–4, 11 (October 1925): 15, 12 (August 1926): 16, 17 (March 1931): 2, 19 (October 1933): 3, and 11 (September 1925): 13.

53. On the rise of industrial welfarism or welfare capitalism, see Brandes, *American Welfare Capitalism,* and Gitelman, *Legacy of the Ludlow Massacre.*

54. "Players Agreements for Clark Ball Club," Elm Orlu Mining Co., ACMCo Records, MHSA; *Anode* 8 (May 1922): 16; Carden, "Come Wander Back with Me," 6; Quinn reminiscence; *Butte Miner,* 11 May 1925, 1.

55. *Engineering and Mining Journal* 114 (5 August 1922): 221 (hereafter cited as *EMJ*). The language that the architects of industrial welfarism employed in pursuit of harmony was universal across different industries. See examples in Brandes, *American Welfare Capitalism;* Duffy, *Butte Was Like That,* 59; *Anode* 9 (May 1923): 12; and *Montana Standard,* 30 July 1924, 9.

56. *Anode* 4 (June 1918): 6, 4 (August 1918): 1–2, and 6 (September 1920): 13.

57. *Anode* 4 (July 1918): 1–3; *EMJ* 126 (8 September 1928): 389.

58. *Anode* 9 (August 1923): 14.

59. *Anode* 4 (July 1918): 1 and 6 (August 1920): 13; Hoy interview, 15–16.

60. *Anode* 5 (July 1919): 1–2, 10 (July 1924): 4, 11 (August 1925): 5, 15 (June 1929): 1, and 17 (June 1931): 1; "Montana Maternity and Infancy Report, August 1927," Children's Bureau Records, 332/11–28–8, National Archives; *Anode* 12 (July 1926): 16–17.

61. In addition to Marsh and Simmons, who discuss concepts of companionate marriage and masculine domesticity, see Pleck and Pleck, *American Man,* 29–31; White, *The First Sexual Revolution,* chap. 8; and Griswold, *Fatherhood in America.*

62. Bedinger, "The Irrepressible Butte," 12. My thanks to Carrie Johnson for bringing this article to my attention.

5

Ladies and Gentlemen, Brothers and Sisters

It was a rough town to live in, but I loved it.
—BERNICE KNIERIM

I had always been interested in social service, and in Butte there seemed plenty of things one might do.
—MARY MEIGS ATWATER

Mary Hallock Foote, writer, illustrator, and wife of a mining engineer, claimed that "when an Eastern woman goes West, she parts at one wrench with family, clan, traditions, clique, cult, and . . . the explanation, the excuse, should she need one, for her personality." She advised herself and others, "The only way to come west happily is to embrace the country, people, life, everything as colonists do, jealously maintaining its superiority and refusing to see a blemish." Foote's admonitions applied not only to eastern women but also to all emigrants to the mining west who, with few exceptions, found it difficult to ignore the blemishes of their new home. Men and women alike responded to lack of kin, unfamiliar landscapes, and new and dangerous work by seeking—to use a geological term made famous by Wallace Stegner in his novel about Foote—an angle of repose, an equilibrium at which they could reconcile the lack of amenities they had known in the East or Midwest, or the familiarities of a European culture, with the opportunities of mining life. One response newcomers shared was to band together into voluntary associations that provided company and a means of molding their environment into a more familiar shape.[1]

In Butte, voluntary associations played a key role in supplying alternatives to "vice-ridden" commercial amusements. They shouldered the task of improving the quality of social and cultural life, they sought to fill the gap left by a city administration that refused to support community recreation, and they attempted to make Butte inviting to families. Through their influence Butte was exposed to art, music, gardens, and wholesome recreation. During World War I new groups, formed to serve patriotic purposes, joined the roster of associations founded during Butte's infancy in the late nineteenth century. In the 1920s, the peak years of voluntarism in Butte, they were augmented by such service clubs as the Kiwanis, Lions, Business and Professional Women, and the Exchange Club. Thus, dozens of cultural clubs, lodges, social improvement societies, ethnic fraternities, and church guilds reflected the class, racial, and ethnic diversity of the city. Groups occasionally worked together on communitywide projects, but for the most part they met in private spaces and pursued their own recreational needs and pet charities. Limited funds and parochialism frequently circumscribed each club's effectiveness, but cumulatively they made Butte physically and socially more pleasant.

The development of voluntary associations in western mining camps and western cities was originally an accommodation to life on the frontier as well as an expression of a national phenomenon. After the Civil War, America experienced an explosion of associational activity. New fraternal lodges and benefit societies such as the Knights of Pythias, the Woodmen, Foresters, Maccabees, Royal Arcanum, and dozens of others emerged as a response to industrialization and urbanization. Benefit societies sought to ameliorate the hardships of industrial work by providing sick and death benefits to members and their families. This vast network eased the strangeness of new places that an extraordinarily mobile work force confronted. "Brothers" and "sisters" could be found in lodge halls from east to west coasts and all points in between. Their rituals, bylaws, and customs afforded newcomers a cushion of familiarity.[2]

By the late nineteenth century women had formed auxiliaries to many of the fraternal orders and launched a nationwide movement of independent women's clubs, many of which congregated under the umbrella of the General Federation of Women's Clubs, which was organized in 1890. Urban, middle-class women, the first to enjoy the increased leisure resulting from the revolution in work and technology, formed the core of the women's club movement. Coming together for social pleasure and self-education, by the 1890s many had combined their original agendas with a concern for the bleak side of urban life. During the twentieth century, voluntary associations formed the backbone of many social reform coalitions.[3]

The life-cycles of voluntary associations mirrored the growth of communities and the social and economic development of their members. Associations were born, matured, and died as the need for them came and went. Sometimes members outgrew their organizations, and sometimes external political and economic factors caused their demise. Groups that originally formed as social enclaves—circles in which to ease the loneliness of emigration, cultivate business acquaintances, or recapture elements of a society left behind—frequently evolved into institutions that served their members' psychic and physical needs and the welfare of the greater community. Historians have observed that voluntary associations reinforced divisions in the population, because membership followed lines of race, class, gender, and ethnicity. Yet voluntary organizations also sought to integrate communities by tackling projects, such as sanitation, recreation, and beautification, designed to benefit everyone. Because most voluntary associations were initially formed to fill leisure time or pursue cultural uplift, their benevolent activities often reflected their original purpose and became recreational, cultural, or educational activities, especially on behalf of family life.

■ ■ ■

The first voluntary association organized in Montana seems to have been the Masons' Grand Lodge of Montana, established in Virginia City in January 1866. Freemasonry was the forefather of the many fraternal lodges that multiplied in the late nineteenth and early twentieth centuries until millions of Masons, Shriners, Odd Fellows, Pythians, Woodmen, Elks, Moose, and Eagles walked America's streets. Butte, Montana's fastest growing city, proved fertile ground for the cultivation of fraternal life. By 1900 there were lodges representing more than two dozen fraternal orders in the city. The Odd Fellows alone had eighteen branches, and the Masons closely trailed with fifteen.[4]

On the heels of their brothers, Butte women organized church groups, clubs, and auxiliaries to fraternal lodges. Within a decade of the city's incorporation, there were chapters of the Daughters of Rebekah and Order of Eastern Star, a Ladies Aid at the Mountain View Methodist Church, Ladies Home Missionary Society at the First Presbyterian, and St. John's Episcopal Sewing Guild, as well as a branch of the Woman's Christian Temperance Union. Although both men and women sought entertainment and companionship in clubs and lodges, voluntary associations were perhaps more important to women, if only because women had fewer opportunities for social recreation. Housekeeping was a lonely job and did not provide income or time for commercial pleasures. Excluded from places of working-class male camaraderie, working-class women met in church basements, neighborhood centers, or lodge halls rented for a modest fee. Middle-class women, without the financial resources to build private clubs comparable to those of men, turned their parlors into club rooms. Butte's large population allowed women's clubs to spring up to meet nearly every interest: reading, painting, singing, acting, sewing, or social and cultural uplift.[5]

The city's first independent women's group was the Homer Club. One February afternoon in 1891, Nettie Caspar invited some women of "kindred interests" to bring their darning to her home and read magazines. The women soon progressed from "mere" reading to preparing talks and conducting discussions. Deciding that they needed even further mental stimulation, Caspar, who had emigrated from Boston, wrote to a friend there, who responded with the entire study plan of a club headed by Edward Everett Hale. Thus the women embarked on a year-and-a-half study of ancient Greek history and the reading of the *Iliad* and the *Odyssey*. For the next thirty-two years they read their way through the classical literature, oratory, philosophy, and art history of Europe, America, India, Egypt, and the Orient. In 1925 they began reviewing contemporary literature.[6]

The women of kindred interests were Caspar's neighbors on the West Side. Educated and middle class, they found Butte bereft of music, literature, theater, and society. They were also the wives of the men who managed Butte. In 1912 members of the Homer Club included the spouses of Butte's mayor, the president and two professors at the School of Mines, the editor of the *Anaconda Standard,* the chief geologist of the Anaconda Company, five business owners, lawyers, physicians, a judge, a minister, and several other men in upper-management positions. During an era when a woman's status was largely determined by that of her husband, the Homer Club was Butte's elite women's group.[7]

Other clubs, such as the West Side Shakespeare Club, the Atlas Club, the Drama Study Club, and the Marian White Arts and Crafts Club, had members with more diverse economic backgrounds and more general interests. When the West Side Shakespeare Club outlined its purpose, it could well have spoken for any of the city's cultural clubs. The group met for "the mutual improvement of its members in literature, art, science, and the vital interests of the day." The women who belonged to these clubs included not only representatives of Butte's middle class but also the most financially secure of the working class. The Shakespeare Club met in the evenings because many of its schoolteacher members could not attend afternoon meetings. The Marian White Arts and Crafts Club had a membership that included a few wives of physicians and business-men and also women married to mine foremen, shift bosses, and skilled laborers.[8]

Because several of the West Side cultural clubs were exclusive—that is, their constitutions limited the number of members and re-quired the membership to invite and then vote upon new candi-dates—a few women met in 1897 to form a club whose membership was broader-based. The Woman's Club of Butte advertised for mem-bers in the newspapers and met in the public library. The founders' goal was to create a club "unlimited" in membership, "so broad and liberal in plan as to embrace every woman in Butte and vicinity of good moral character who was interested in a club for women only." Although its invitation was inclusive, the Woman's Club attracted a predominantly middle-class membership, with most of the women living on the West Side. It was, however, far larger than any of Butte's other women's clubs. In 1907, ten years after its birth and two years after it constructed a two-story Greek Revival-style clubhouse, the Butte Woman's Club had 225 active members. That year its course of study included the art of the Old Masters, scientific investigation of earthquakes, Tennyson's poems, practical cooking, juvenile courts, and modern Russian music.[9]

The skills women learned in their clubs, such as public speaking, organizing, and chairing meetings, prepared them for projects they would undertake once they broadened their definition of home to encompass the city as well as the bungalow. Many clubs embarked on self-improvement projects that also contributed to civic culture. The public library in which the Woman's Club met, for example, had been established by the Woman's Christian Temperance Union. Originally housed in a room of the county courthouse and super-vised by a member of the WCTU, the union later rented a larger facility in the basement of the Lewisohn Building and provided not only books but also games and other "YMCA features" well before a YMCA existed in the community. The union employed a man to oversee these operations but soon discovered that he was pawning books to buy whiskey. Loretta Groeneveld, who led the union's li-brary program, consulted with members and friends of the organi-zation and acquired a substantial donation from Charles X. Larra-bee, a businessman. Armed with money and the support of prominent men in the community, Groeneveld and the WCTU went to the city and proposed to donate Larrabee's $10,000 for books if the city would provide a building and maintain the library. In 1893 the new, two-story, brick and granite Butte Free Public Library opened its doors, a quarter of its reading room railed off and reserved for women. Soon, their section was embellished with the "Silver Bow Shield," a copper shield engraved with scenes representing the county and adorned with a gem and mineral-studded silver bow. All the minerals had been mined and processed in Silver Bow County, and the shield was designed and produced by women of the Silver Bow Columbian Association. After its display at the 1893 World's Columbian Exposition in Chicago, it was deposited in the library—both shield and building a testament to women's civic pride and commitment to public culture.[10]

The skills that Groeneveld employed in convincing the city to build and administer the public library were honed through club work. Five years after the founding of the Homer Club, Nettie Caspar recalled one of its first public programs. The club had arranged for dress reformer Annie Jeness Miller to speak at the library. Caspar recollected that neither she nor any other member of the club was confident enough to introduce Miller, and she asked a gentlemen from the audience to do so. But "I could do it myself now," she proclaimed, "and so could any of your members." Teaching women to speak in public was a major goal of women's clubs. The papers each member composed on her reading were formally presented and evaluated by those in attendance. In 1905 Mrs. W. W. Cheely, president of the Woman's Club, used a homely metaphor to explain clubwomen's activities: "A woman can be as deft with an oration as with an omelet, if she knows the ingredients of each, and has the heart for the work before her."[11]

Following the lead of the state and national federations of women's clubs, Butte organizations supported a variety of civic improvement campaigns and legislation designed to protect and educate women and children. The Marian White Arts and Crafts Club was typical. Between 1907 and 1916 the group raised funds for a girl's scholarship to the state university, endorsed the Pure Food Law, sought to raise the age of consent from sixteen to eighteen, supported the public playground movement, advocated the unsuccessful Montana Mothers' Pension Bill, and petitioned Butte's mayor for a woman police officer, in addition to its regular departmental work in literature, arts, and crafts. Such efforts mirrored those undertaken by women's clubs across America.[12]

■ ■ ■

Warren Susman has argued that the great common issue of the
1920s was community—its study and its fashioning. Certainly in
Butte a variety of organizations, from the Anaconda Company to the
Elks, appealed to the idea of community to heal the wounds of the
war years. But "community" in Butte was hard to pin down. The
unpredictability of the price of copper and the dominance of mining in the economy encouraged a fluid society. During boom times,
high copper prices meant high wages and good living conditions for
the working class, whereas a fall in the price of copper caused not
only layoffs of miners but also hardship for many members of the
middle class. Mining meant fortunes quickly made and quickly lost,
and people looked to qualities other than wealth to judge a person's
place in society. The single attempt to publish a Blue Book in Butte
is illustrative. In 1901 John Boyle O'Reilly made "every possible
effort . . . to secure a complete list of the prominent people of the
community, with special reference to those who figure conspicuously
in the social world." He also noted that "it will be found that the
lines have not been too closely drawn." Indeed, the book listed the
members of many of Butte's West Side clubs and also the women
of the Ethical Culture Club, a group of workers, mostly salesclerks
at Hennessy's Department Store, who met weekly for self-education.
Butte had little high society. When novelist Gertrude Atherton visited the city in 1914, she observed that all of its millionaires had fled
to New York or Europe to spend their gains. In their wake Butte
society was "rather interesting" but hardly typical, "for its history had
been too hectic, its conditions too unique, the wealth of certain of
its inhabitants too sudden and enormous." In consequence, "everyone" called on her, either out of hospitality or curiosity.[13]

The diverse membership of groups such as the Marian White Arts
and Craft Club demonstrated a heterogeneity seldom found in older
communities outside the West. A willingness to work on projects and
be a "brother" or "sister" was all that was required to earn a welcome
to many clubs. When the Elks held their annual picnic in 1920 they
emphasized that the festival was "every man's and every woman's"
and that all were welcome regardless of creed or fraternal affiliation.
Still, most organizations defined community in narrower terms, and
class divisions could not easily be overcome by appeals to brotherhood and sisterhood. Clubs' social entertainments reinforced a
sense of community based on class, race, and ethnicity as well as
whatever shared interest brought members together, and they were

a means of passing those values on to children. Although West Side clubwomen assisted the poor and visited working-class neighborhoods, they did not invite the subjects of their charity into their homes. Aili Goldberg recalled that there was "definitely a class distinction" in the city: "If you were from the East Side, you were from the East Side." When some of her relatives moved to the West Side, they called it Snob Hill. Speaking of West Side residents, her niece said, "It would be a rare day that you would be invited to anything [when] they had social functions at home." The social world of middle-class clubwomen was an insular one, revealed to the rest of the city through the columns of the society page.[14]

West Side society was the stuff of dreams compared to the gritty life of the East Side. Lydia Lowndes Maury Skeels recorded the pleasures available to the children of successful middle-class parents. Her father was a prominent lawyer and, until the depression of 1921, lucky in his mining investments. Between 1917 and 1920 he bought a summer cabin, a seven-seat Cadillac, and a piano. One year his wife, her mother, and the four Maury children spent a month at a hot springs resort, and Lydia and her sister Liz gave two or three dances for two hundred or so of their friends. Card parties, private dances, teas, and luncheons encouraged sociability among West Side families and set the standard of behavior for their children. Mother-daughter gatherings were common. When the Marian White Arts and Crafts Club hosted its annual scholarship tea, members' daughters—dressed in kimonos, Egyptian robes, or whatever costume suited that year's exotic theme—served the tea and, in a sense, their apprenticeships as clubwomen. The Woman's Club sponsored both a junior and senior girls' club in which young girls participated in supervised play and adolescents enjoyed music, folk dancing, lectures, and dances to which they invited neighborhood boys. Under the auspices of West Side clubs, women were able to offer their children alternatives to the dance halls and roadhouses patronized by working-class youths who did not have the resources for lavish private entertaining.[15]

■ ■ ■

Several middle-class voluntary associations—both women's clubs and men's service clubs—sought to bridge class lines between East and West Sides. They regarded their mission as the spreading of civilization, and they saw themselves as particularly suited to the task. As one contemporary explained, the burden of civilization fell upon the middle class because the upper class were parasites and the poor were too busy earning a living. This calling influenced associations' choice of projects, which they designed to be nonpartisan, noncontroversial, and capable of garnering communitywide support. Thus, when the Rocky Mountain Garden Club labored to beautify the industrial landscape, theater owners volunteered their movie houses for public slide presentations illustrating the transformative effects of shrubs and flowers. The club won the cooperation of the public schools and the management of Columbia Gardens for an Arbor Day pageant in which children played the parts of seeds, sunbeams, and spring showers. The Rotana Club's project to serve milk to underweight schoolchildren avoided controversy because teachers who distributed the milk did so in such a manner that the children did not know whose parents had paid for it and whose had not. Community efforts that helped the poor without humiliating them were well received.[16]

The most celebrated of Butte's communitywide charitable campaigns was the Joshers Club's annual provision of Christmas baskets to the needy. The club originated on Christmas Eve 1902 while a group of a dozen men warmed themselves at the bar of Green's Buffet. A messenger came in with a note for Billy Gemmell, then secretary-treasurer of the race track, who was known for being as gullible as he was generous. The message was a plea for help from a destitute family. Gemmell's companions thought it was a hoax, and when he left to investigate, they followed him, intending to have the last laugh when he arrived at a nonexistent address. But the address was real, a home where a widow and six children huddled over a fire kindled from their chopped-up furniture. Gemmell and "the boys" returned to Green's, passed the hat, collected a hundred dollars, and that night furnished the family with food, clothes, beds, and fuel. Thus was the Joshers Club born, and although the retelling may have embellished the founding, the club's subsequent work was more than deserving of a noble birth.[17]

For more than twenty-five years the Joshers provided food baskets to "those of our people who have been getting the worst of the 'breaks' in life." By the late 1920s the Joshers were orchestrating a citywide festival of charity. They staged a huge talent show each December to raise funds and solicited donations from businesses and individuals all over the county. Everyone pitched in. Anonymity was guaranteed to those who received baskets. People were encouraged to give members the names of individuals or families needing help. Ranchers outside of the city donated beef, and the Butchers Union volunteered to cut it. One year a man contributed forty ducks he had shot, and a woman gave a supply of homemade preserves. These special treats supplemented bags of onions, potatoes, rice, flour, sugar, coffee, tea, candy, several pounds of meat, and an array of canned goods. Teaming companies lent their trucks to the American Legion, who delivered the goods with the help of the Boy Scouts. The Joshers continued their work until the depression crimped even their efforts at private charity.[18]

In 1920 the Women's Auxiliary of the American Institute of Mining, Metallurgical, and Petroleum Engineers (WAAIME) forged a community in Butte. These women came together because they were married to mining engineers, not because they had common interests in art or literature or a common political perspective. Indeed, in 1923, when the Butte club's educational committee presented a report on bills pending in Congress, the ensuing discussion was so divisive that the club voted unanimously to exclude political questions from further programs. What these wives of mining engineers did share was the difficulty of homemaking in the snow and ice of the northern ranges and the blistering heat and sand of desert mining camps. They had all lived a transient life, and they appreciated the chance to be in one place long enough to form a club. The secretary of the AIME noted that in one year he had registered more than 2,200 changes of address for a membership of 3,300. When the Butte auxiliary hosted a Christmas party for members' children, its secretary reflected that "it was a great joy to have them all together and to imagine that in the future, scattered throughout the mining camps of the country, they will meet again and say to one another, 'Don't you 'member I played with you at the Christmas party in Butte in 1922?'"[19]

Members of WAAIME created an identity for themselves as "mining women." While the civic activities of most Butte women's clubs were interchangeable with causes in cities across the country, WAAIME tried to hone its work and entertainment to the specific needs of miners and their families. The club sent books to out-of-the-way mining camps and adopted patients at the Galen sanitarium, where miners recuperated from silicosis and tuberculosis. Members also turned their attention to the families of immigrant miners. WAAIME supported a kindergarten and sewing class at the East Side Neighborhood House and an Americanization class at the YMCA.[20]

WAAIME's members approached their work with immigrant families differently from the women's clubs that had sought to help immigrants at the turn of the century. At that time members of the

Associated Charities housed orphans in the Paul Clark Home and provided some social services for children whose parents were too poor to meet all their needs. Although on one level these women acknowledged that poverty in Butte was due to erratic employment in the mines, at heart they believed that it resulted from flawed character. Members saw their mission as preventing children from inheriting the weaknesses of their parents. They believed that their most important work was to save children "from beggary and vice." In order to do this, children "must be taught to feel the responsibility that their parents never felt; taught, if possible, the skill their parents never learned; given the character their parents never had." Women of the Associated Charities spoke in the voice of their class, looking down—with however many good intentions—at working-class families. They judged them by values that often had little to do with the realities of working-class life, and they made no attempt to understand the working-class, immigrant cultures they were trying to mold.[21]

Although WAAIME members inevitably viewed immigrant workers through middle-class lenses, these "mining women" also exhibited genuine interest in ethnic cultures. They invited women and children to perform traditional dances at their club meetings and looked forward to meeting immigrant families. During the depression, instead of distinguishing between the deserving and nondeserving poor and doling out charity accordingly, they purchased goods at a rummage sale on the East Side, the proceeds of which were distributed according to the residents' wishes. WAAIME believed this method of support would "help people to retain their independence." Two factors fostered the change in attitude of groups such as WAAIME: the flowering of ethnic associations, which promulgated a sense of community and forced Anglo-Americans to acknowledge the legitimacy of other cultures, and the professionalization of social work.[22]

WAAIME did not decide directly who deserved its help and who did not. Rather, it funneled much of its assistance through the East Side Neighborhood House, Butte's only settlement house. Begun in 1920 by the Board of National Missions of the Presbyterian church as "an adventure in social service," the house was run on a nonsectarian basis. Eventually supported by the church's Department of City, Immigrant, and Industrial Work, the staff carried out no church work except for Sunday school. Yet all clubs, classes, entertainments, and sports were conducted in "a Christian atmosphere and with Christian citizenship in view." A report in 1926 described the purpose of the house as promoting social uplift in a community that was "socially handicapped—that is in a congested industrial center inhabited largely by foreigners and other underprivileged folk and their children."[23]

The Presbyterian church established more than seventy neighborhood houses throughout the country, many in "deteriorated residential sections where no one would live but for the compulsion of economic necessity." When John Bailey Kelly, a national staff person, visited the East Side Neighborhood House in 1923, he was struck by the grim walk-ups of the East Side and the dusty, meandering streets that all seemed to converge on barbed wire-fenced mine yards. He observed, "If the spiritual state of the inhabitants corresponded in any way with their physical surroundings, this was an ideal place to locate such a center."[24]

Each month between three and four thousand residents of the East Side visited the neighborhood house. Most were children, for the house sponsored Girl and Boy Scout troops, a kindergarten, Campfire Girls, and a Friendly Mothers group. There was also a gym and lending library. In the evenings neighborhood clubs used the rooms for parties and dances. Kelly observed several children's activities on his visit and was impressed by the wide variety of ethnic backgrounds represented. Watching a polyglot group of girls pledge allegiance to the flag at the commencement of a Girl Scout meeting, he felt he was watching America's melting pot melt.[25]

The house combined traditional philanthropy with an emerging professional approach to social work and community-building. One of the first directors, Helen Crawley, was a graduate of Northwestern University and before coming to Butte had converted a saloon into a Christian neighborhood house in Michigan's Iron Range. The Board of Missions worked throughout the 1920s to make the house less dependent on national mission funding and more reliant upon local financing. By 1931 the East Side Neighborhood House's board of directors combined progressive reformers and the wives of Anaconda Company and Montana Power Company executives. There was little money in the East Side to support the neighborhood house; therefore, managers and board members courted the city's clubs. The neighborhood house's Women's Club served dinner to Rotana, and the director invited WAAIME to hold a meeting at the facility and regularly reported to various clubs' officers on the house's programs. By the 1930s Butte was contributing more than one-third of the cost of running the house. It permitted clubwomen a mediated glimpse of life on the East Side and assured them that their resources were being used appropriately.[26]

Reports throughout the late 1920s and early 1930s stressed the fact that the neighborhood continued to be a "rough and rowdy" place "where the amenities of social and religious culture are somewhat lacking." The church published stories of endangered children both to justify its work and to appeal for funds. In 1931 the *Presbyterian Reporter* ran a story describing work "typical" of the neighborhood house: A little girl had shyly asked the director's wife, Mrs. Vernon Brown, for a pair of shoes and was told that her mother should have accompanied her. When the girl replied that her mother was sick, Brown asked if her father could come with her that evening. "'No, was the reply. 'My Daddy is in jail; he shot my mother.'" Brown, of course, issued shoes, as well as other clothes and toys for the girl and her four siblings.[27]

The Board of Missions had hoped to accomplish more than merely providing entertainment and toys to immigrant children. When John Bailey Kelly walked through the East Side with Helen Crawley, he "read" a landscape of depression and violence. He was struck both by the many houses vacated by laid-off miners and their families and the intimidating fences erected to guard mine property. In Butte he saw "force enthroned as the solution of the problems of industrial society." What mission leaders hoped to accomplish through their work was to put sympathy "in place of suspicion, confidence in place of prejudice and cooperation in place of conflict." By 1929 the church believed that the house "was never more popular in the neighborhood than it is now, and was never rendering a larger service." But its good work was to last only a few more years. With the onset of the depression, Butte could not come up with its share of the house's funding, and the Board of Missions declined to proffer further support. Thus, in 1932, "with the greatest regret," the local board ordered the East Side Neighborhood House closed.[28]

▪ ▪ ▪

While many immigrant families enjoyed the facilities of the East Side Neighborhood House, almost every ethnic group in Butte had some kind of lodge, club, or association to look after its own. Some, like the Ancient Order of Hibernians (1884), the Cristoforo Colombo Society (1889), the Cornish Sons of St. George (1889), the Scandinavian Fraternity (1890), and the Sons of Herman (1896), were established early in the city's history. Many others, founded after 1900, reflected the later arrival of new immigrant groups, the organization of alternative lodges, or in some cases the eventual outreach of national organizations to Butte. The purpose of these associations was somewhat different from that of the cultural and service clubs of the Anglo-American middle class. Ethnic societies and Anglo-American clubs sought to protect and further the interests of their members. But ethnic societies rarely defined their interests as those of the entire community, whereas it was quite common for the Rotary or Rotana to declare that their work, protecting their interests, was done on behalf of Butte as a whole. Ethnic societies embraced both working- and middle-class members and pursued cultural as well as service goals, but only rarely did they address a population outside their ethnic constituency.[29]

Lodges provided economic security and social entertainment. The Ancient Order of Hibernians, for example, disbursed sick and death benefits and offered members the use of an employment committee to help them find work. Members also enjoyed an array of social programs. Once the group completed its weekly business meeting, the Irish-Americans spent the rest of the evening singing, drinking, smoking, debating Irish politics, and reciting poetry. The Daughters of Norway also combined the business of a benefit society with conviviality. Each meeting included a detailed report from the sick committee, covering everything from one member's bad corns to another's broken bones. The club reviewed claims carefully and distributed payment only upon receipt of a doctor's statement and review of the bylaws to make sure the injury was compensable. After taking care of business, the women settled down for refreshments and card playing.[30]

Many of the groups organized in the twentieth century had explicit cultural agendas set by their members' response to the United States. Some lodges formed with the dual purpose of preserving elements of traditional culture and smoothing the transition to American citizenship. The Daughters of Norway aspired "to preserve our memories and traditions, to maintain the honor of Motherland Norway by placing our ideals high and thereby bring forth the best in our character and make us better citizens of our adopted country." Montenegrin men, who had left Butte in the 1910s to fight in the Balkan Wars and World War I and then returned to the United States, founded the Montenegrin Literary Association. Prospective members had to swear that they would pursue citizenship; the club's purpose was to help them achieve that goal. The association's president explained that members were "not satisfied to accept the material benefits of this country, but they want to participate intelligently in its affairs." Butte Syrians formed a similar society to assist twenty immigrants through the naturalization process.[31]

Apart from dances, picnics, and fund-raising rummage sales and card parties, ethnic lodges also celebrated feast days of their nations' patron saints and honored citizens who had brought fame to their nationalities. Considering the number of Irish in Butte, St. Patrick's Day was naturally the grandest celebration of this type, "the day of all days" as Catherine Hoy proclaimed. The celebration began with a mass, the schoolgirls wore green bows in their hair, and everyone sported a shamrock. A parade followed and then a banquet in the church hall with "food, food, food and all the beer you wanted." No other ethnic holiday rivaled St. Patrick's Day, but many other saints were honored. The Cornish paid tribute to St. George, the Welsh to St. David, and the Serbs to St. Sava. Other lodges marked their native land's independence and the feats of their countrymen. Scots, for instance, celebrated Robert Burns Day, and Swedes saluted John Erickson, inventor of the ironclad warship.[32]

Theater was an especially popular form of cultural preservation and entertainment among ethnic groups. Finns staged many plays in Finlanders' Hall. Because the majority of Butte Finns were socialists and the hall was also headquarters for the Industrial Workers of the World and the Finnish Workers Club, it is not surprising that the plays "would invariably be political." Often they dramatized the struggle between Finland and Russia; Aili Goldberg remembered that there would occasionally be "a little bit of a love story," but always against a political background. Serbians also loved drama, although the women were more enthusiastic than the men and often had to play male as well as female roles. As Mary Markovich Trbovich recalled, the productions were usually "love plays where the man had to go to war and his fiancée waited for him to come back." She remembered one in particular in which a young woman who had married her lover just before he left for the war queried a returning veteran about the fate of her husband. After telling the woman that her beloved had been killed and then watching her tearful response, the soldier confessed that he was in fact her husband, made older by the war: "And everybody'd cry." Young women used drama to enact their romantic fantasies, such as the time they translated Cinderella into Serbian for a community performance.[33]

Theater was only one way in which lodges translated events in Europe to life in America. Immigrants closely followed developments in their own countries, and frequently occurrences thousands of miles away prompted local actions. The cause of Irish nationalism was the most obvious: Irish organizations in Butte sent hundreds of thousands of dollars to Ireland to fund the fight for independence. The depression after World War I took its toll on many organizations, the Irish orders included. But the Irish civil war dealt the killing blow. In Ireland those who supported the Irish Free State and those who rejected it killed and bloodied each other. In Butte they stopped supporting each other's businesses, stopped helping each other get jobs, and stopped speaking to each other. By 1922 only sixty Hibernians were on the order's rolls, a shell of the organization that had claimed more than six hundred members in 1905.[34]

More than a decade later, another European tragedy proved midwife to the birth of a new Butte group. In 1934, a month after King Alexander I of Yugoslavia was assassinated, Serbian women formed the Circle of Serbian Sisters. The murder of their king had stirred feelings of nationalism and a desire to band together for the preservation of Serbian culture. Maintaining and improving Butte's Orthodox church became the group's primary task; their fund-raising efforts helped build a new church and a parish hall. Like similar organizations, the circle had many social functions. Mary Markovich Trbovich recalled that her mother's one night out was when she went to circle meetings. Mrs. Markovich kept boarders—ten or twelve in three bedrooms—and often cooked for more who found rooms elsewhere. Circle night provided a welcome respite from a seemingly endless cycle of cooking, laundry, and housecleaning. Although she was never able to return to Serbia to see her parents, she found solace with the Serbian Sisters. The society of fellow exiles comforted many immigrant women who had accompanied or followed their husbands to America and left behind extended families.[35]

Like their Anglo-American middle-class counterparts, members of ethnic societies used their organizations to pass on to their children the values and standards of behavior they wished them to have. The Order of Vasa worked for the "preservation of everything Swedish that is fine and good," and adults taught American-born children traditional music, folklore, dancing, and the Swedish language. Lodges sponsored youth organizations that educated and entertained children, preparing them to become full-fledged members when they grew old enough. The Circle of Serbian Sisters began a group for unmarried girls who staged plays and learned Serbian songs. Only married women could join the circle itself, and when a woman wed her mother presented her for induction.[36]

Ethnic clubs also sought to preserve amity within their ethnic enclaves. The Daughters of Norway commented annually that the previous year had passed "in a very good Harmony" and hoped that the future would hold the same. As some immigrants prospered and moved away from the East Side, splits arose in the community. While speaking of class divisions in Butte, Mary Trbovich recalled that "even some of our Serbian families . . . didn't want to associate with any of us on the East Side because they thought they were better because they lived on the West Side." Supporting the church or joining the circle or men's lodge reminded immigrants of their common heritage and bridged growing class divisions.[37]

By the 1930s the insularity of many ethnic lodges had eroded. Immigrants adapted to American society, and in spite of their efforts their children did not learn native languages or embrace Old World customs. Minute books reflected the change. By the mid-1930s the Daughters of Norway, the Circle of Serbian Sisters, and the Cristoforo Colombo Lodge started recording their minutes in English instead of Norwegian, Serbian, and Italian. Associations began inviting other lodges to their social functions and inaugurated programs that depended on the participation of other neighborhood and ethnic groups. For example, in the early 1930s the Finnish Hall initiated the Finnish-American Athletic Club and played basketball with other clubs from various parts of town. Commercial entertainments also contributed to the integration of different ethnic groups, as witnessed by the decision of the Daughters of Norway in the late 1930s to substitute a ravioli dinner and gambling at a Meaderville cafe for their traditional summer picnic.[38]

■ ■ ■

Most of Butte's voluntary associations rejected political activity as a means of improving the city's quality of life. On the whole, Butte's volunteers preferred to "do it themselves" rather than become lobbyists for the public support of social welfare or public recreation. Few club members were like Elizabeth Kennedy, who in 1917 was president of the Butte Housewives' League, president of the Good Government Club, chair of the ways and means committee of the Woman's Club, and "a member of the other important women's clubs of Butte." She could often be found in the city council chambers, arguing for reform. Women's concerted activities during the cost of living crisis during World War I were the exception rather than the norm. The majority of club members were usually far more passive. Butte's women's associations traditionally limited their political expression to signatures on petitions or to one-time endorsements of measures that the state and national federations of women's clubs recommended. As Mary Brennan Clapp wrote in defense of the city's women's groups, "Butte literary clubs have been criticized for not taking part in civic work. But are they not wise to concentrate their energies on the line of work for which they are organized?"[39]

Men's service clubs, too, confined their attempts at civic improvement to projects such as scholarship funds, community Christmas trees, library donations, and Fourth of July celebrations. When they did enter local politics, it was usually on behalf of a relatively noncontroversial measure such as a traffic ordinance. Politics had the potential to destroy the harmony and social consensus that voluntary associations sought, and only a few groups, whose agendas were overtly political, were willing to face that possibility.[40]

Good Government Clubs and the League of Women Voters formed after the victory that made woman's suffrage clubs obsolete. The Montana Good Government Association was founded in 1915 to preserve the momentum of the suffrage campaign and victory. It transmuted into the Montana League of Women Voters shortly after the founding of the national organization in 1920. On the state level the Good Government organization was initially quite successful. In the first election after winning woman suffrage, the clubs helped to elect Jeannette Rankin to the U.S. House of Representatives, May Trumper to the office of state superintendent of public instruction, and Maggie Smith Hathaway and Emma Ingalls to seats in the state legislature. During the following legislative session, the Good Government clubs stationed lobbyists in the capitol and helped push through an eight-hour day for women, revisions in the Mothers' Pension Law, and the creation of a child welfare division in the Department of Public Health. But in Butte the Good Government Club's requests that the city hire a female social worker, do something about the appalling lack of public parks, and provide for wholesome recreation had no effect.[41]

Ironically, Butte's Good Government Club and the subsequent local League of Women Voters limited their effectiveness by encouraging the very political debates that other clubs sought to stifle. The history of the Montana League of Women Voters during the 1920s is a case in point. Mollie Vernon Rice of Butte was the state league's first president. Rice, a Michigan native educated at the Philadelphia Academy of Art, had taught art at Butte High School and served as chair of the arts division of the Marian White Arts and Craft Club for twenty-five years. She was married to Alonzo F. Rice, president of the Butte Business College and a member of the Rotary, Elks, and Chamber of Commerce. Mollie Rice was a conservative, and on several occasions she used her offices to promulgate her political views.

In 1920 the Butte league apparently did little to encourage voter turnout in the primaries until the "eleventh hour," when Rice organized a small group called the "Home Guards" and launched a vitriolic attack on the Nonpartisan League. She claimed that if the Nonpartisans won, Montana women "would be nationalized, the babies snatched from their mothers' breasts and placed under state care." Although few took her seriously, many were deeply offended that the president of the league had made "herself ridiculous by peddling prejudice based on absolute lies and vicious propaganda." On another front, the Butte Business College had consistently blocked attempts by various voluntary groups to offer free Americanization classes. Rice spoke vehemently against free classes, claiming at a Women's Council meeting that the community was under no obligation to educate all the ignorant Europeans who came to America and adding that they should pay for what they got. Rice's actions, informed as they were by free-market ideology, financial self-interest, and the bonds of familial loyalty, illustrated the controversy that could arise when voluntary associations tackled projects that conflicted with business, class, and family ties.[42]

With Rice at the helm, the Montana league was immobilized for nearly three years. The leadership accused the membership of socialism, bolshevism, and anarchism. When several women urged lowering the dues so they could broaden the membership, Rice refused, fearing the "radicals" would gain control and "attempt to make it a woman's party." Mary O'Neill, one of the so-called radicals, rebutted Rice's charges, dismissing them as "poppy-cock." She described Rice's opponents as "simply progressive women who believe in the innate love of Justice within the heart of Woman." O'Neill and her compatriots did not want a separate woman's party; many of them were committed Democrats and Republicans. They desired "an organization, capable of great good, working among the masses of women throughout the state."[43] Anticipating that she and her fellow officers would lose power in a new election, Rice resisted calling a state convention for three years. Stonewalled by her recalcitrance, other league members threatened to form a rival league unless Rice and her cohort resigned. This intense factionalism annoyed the National Board, who were generally frustrated by the highly decentralized organization of the league. During the early 1920s the board had problems with many state organizations, but none that quite paralleled the situation in Montana. Marguerite Wells, regional director and later president of the national league, confided to colleague Belle Sherwin in 1923 that she wished the

board could justify refusing the Montana group membership in the
national league. She believed that no one in the Montana League
of Women Voters was "either reasonable or well meaning." In lieu
of exclusion, she dispatched Florence Harrison, a former political
science professor, and Clara Ueland, the former president of the
Minnesota Woman Suffrage Association, to Montana and charged
them with helping reorganize the state league.[44]

When Florence Harrison and Clara Ueland arrived in Montana
in 1923, they assumed that women there were political innocents.
In fact, they met women who had been immersed in Montana politics for decades. Harrison and Ueland encountered divisions along
hardened partisan lines and were dismayed by the power struggles
within the State Federation of Women's Clubs. The factionalism in
the league, and within the Butte membership in particular, illustrated the deep class divisions within the city. Other national organizers had observed that the Montana league's leadership was "on the
side of corporate wealth" and used its position to stymie the more
progressive rank and file. Although Harrison and Ueland uncovered
no hard evidence to prove the allegations, they found many who
believed that Mollie Rice was controlled by the Anaconda Company or the Catholic church. Harrison wrote to Wells that she believed
"nothing would so assure the conservative element that the league
isn't a menace to society as a contribution from Mr. John Ryan." She
proposed that the New York league solicit a donation from Ryan,
who resided in New York and was Anaconda's chairman of the
board, and contribute it to Montana.[45]

Although recognizing that Rice and her fellow officers had nearly
destroyed the Montana league, Harrison, Ueland, and Wells shared
local leaders' fear of the rank and file and were reluctant to support the "reds." Nevertheless, in order to preserve a state league,
Rice was finally persuaded to step down amid much acrimony, and
a new slate of officers, inexperienced but "wildly enthusiastic," was
elected.[46]

Harrison and Ueland were appalled at placing the work and the
reputation of the League of Women Voters in the hands of Montana members, whom they characterized at various times as "crude,"
"wild," "radical," "idealistic," "like children," and "of no great social
standing." Montana women, in turn, resented the league's conde-
scending attitude toward them. Some hoped the League of Wom-
en Voters would take a more active role in progressive politics than
the petition signing and vague endorsements typical of the state's
women's clubs. The national league, however, sought to curb their

aspirations. When Belle Fliegelman Winestine said she thought the league should interest itself in the freeing of political prisoners, immigration, the Negro question, and birth control, Ueland labeled her "a zealot." Florence Harrison considered it ironic and "dangerous" that the chairperson of the citizenship committee was an "out and out socialist" and leader of the Finnish women in Butte. Evaluating the activities of Butte and Helena women in 1923, Harrison reported, "I'm simply so scared that they will go off on some wild measure that I have become practically a Taft Republican." Once the new slate of officers was elected, Ueland and Harrison warned regional headquarters that the reorganized league "must be guided all the time." Florence Harrison literally fled Butte, declaring she could not "endure this town."[47]

The Montana league disconcerted Harrison and Ueland, whose experience was mainly in the East and Midwest. Montana members were frequently working women or mothers who still had young children at home. Harrison was frustrated because "there is not among the present members of the League a single woman . . . who is a person of leisure." Fund-raising was problematic because there were few women "of social standing" who could appeal to fellow "well-off" citizens. Clara Ueland echoed the condescension that Butte clubwomen occasionally expressed toward immigrants when she wrote that Lulu Wheeler, wife of newly elected U.S. Senator Burton K. Wheeler, seemed "nice and intelligent" but "crude," apparently earning that judgment for having had the bad taste to bear five children. Their opinion, however, seems to have been shaped far more by class than by regional affiliation, and it was certainly shared by other Montanans. For example, in 1928, Annabel Long Edinger, a Montana member of the league from Divide, a small community south of Butte, tried to explain the Butte league's problems to national President Belle Sherwin. She wrote that Butte had only two classes, "the one, the miners; the other, the mine owners and the various professional groups and merchants." Edinger had little respect for the miners' leaders: "not the best type of labor leaders—intrigue and suspicion, etc. is always rampant." Unfortunately, from her point of view, "It is really rather too bad that the Butte League is entirely made up of this class." Edinger had apparently come from a wealthy background and revealed mortification at her current status when she wrote to Sherwin, "I have to confess—and it hurts very greatly to have to—we are ghastly poor."[48]

Eventually, internal politics stabilized. Wells even tempered her exasperation toward the Montana women with wry affection, and the Montana branch proved quite effective, despite the problems that national organizers perceived. Due in large part to the league's efforts, Montana became the fifth state in the Union to ratify the Child Labor Amendment in 1927, and the league was influential in implementing the state's maternal and infant care program under the Sheppard-Towner Act. Wells wrote to a colleague, "Montana was a terrible drag at first, but it bids fair to do us all credit. . . . The Montana people are unlike any others and the word 'pep,' which is a favorite of theirs, is certainly justified in their case." When the state league began planning a convention, they asked Wells to send a speaker, livelier than previous ones: "They want something that will give them chills and tears. They want something 'gripping that will make us feel that we can't sit still another minute, but we must get out and set the world right.' It is worth a great effort to give it to them."[49]

■　■　■

Curiously, Butte citizens exhibited little pep when it came to establishing one of the major resources that other early-twentieth-century urban-dwellers considered necessary to making their world "right"—public parks. Butte's lack of public parks and playground programs struck recreation specialists as highly unusual for a city its size. Children's Bureau investigator Ella Gardner observed that when she and Josephine Roche visited in the mid-1920s Butte had no director of parks and playgrounds and no program of supervised play. In 1930 the Chamber of Commerce invited L. H. Weir, field secretary of the Playground and Recreation Association of America, to survey the recreation situation in the city and recommend ways to improve it. As Weir put it, the story could be "quickly told." The city owned two parks: one was the municipal golf course, the other was a nature area five to six miles south of the city limits. A three-member parks and playgrounds committee of the city council had a $4,500 annual budget. With those funds they tried to maintain several privately owned sites, used in the summer as ball fields and in the winter as skating rinks. Weir noted that none of these areas met the minimum standards for a first-class park. His survey of public school playgrounds found that the vast majority had inadequate space and equipment. In fact, many playgrounds were reconstructed mine dumps without grass or water. Weir recommended that Butte adopt at minimum a $65,000 parks budget, a levy of roughly $1 per capita, a rate he claimed was the average funding level in other cities of Butte's size. During the course of his stay in

Butte he discovered that the city took in far more than $65,000 a year "from certain debased forms of the use of leisure time." It seemed only fair that some of that money be spent on wholesome recreation.[50]

Weir echoed complaints that some Butte residents made when he stated, "There is no place where the inhabitants can go for a short or a long period of rest and relaxation in an environment of natural beauty." In fact, he believed it would be hard to find "a city in all America that is so utterly devoid of beauty spots." Weir acknowledged that Clark Park and Columbia Gardens were beautiful parks, but not because of any effort on the part of the city. Both had been built and maintained by William A. Clark and then transferred to ACM management when Anaconda acquired Clark's properties. Lovely and heavily used, still neither was near the densely populated northern part of Butte. Clark Park was on the Flat, and Columbia Gardens was a long streetcar ride east to the base of the mountains.[51]

Better public parks had long been a goal of the indefatigable Elizabeth Kennedy. In 1917 she had written to Jeannette Rankin, describing hundreds of men loitering on sidewalk copings and building stairways because there was "not a park, even a block square, . . . not a seat provided by the public," in which men could rest "within a distance not requiring car fare to reach. . . . Is it any wonder" she asked, that "the saloons and picture shows are so crowded?" More than a decade later little had changed.[52]

Kennedy and a few of her supporters raised lonely voices in Butte. The absence of a public parks movement, in contrast to vociferous campaigns in other industrial cities, is difficult to explain. Perhaps Clark's support of two major parks, and subsequently that of the Anaconda Company, led citizens to believe that the provision of parks was a private matter. The boom-and-bust economy of mining is a more likely explanation, however. The history of mine closings and layoffs fostered a feeling of insecurity about the permanence of work in Butte and discouraged people from investing in the city's infrastructure. Despite Butte's persistence, many residents saw it as a place of transit and were likely more inclined to invest in goods they could take with them when they had to leave.[53]

Butte's political history seemed to reflect this attitude. When Charles A. Hauswirth was elected mayor in 1935 he gave a ringing inaugural address, stating, "It is doubtful if any city is in a more deplorable physical and financial condition" than Butte. Public buildings were a disgrace, pitifully few roads were paved or even graded, and the term *parks and playgrounds* was "a misnomer." He attributed these conditions not to deterioration during the depression, but to decades of neglect and "pie counter politics."[54]

For those who were committed to the arts and culture, Butte could be frustrating. Sam Treloar, leader of the Butte Mines Band, grew irate at the lack of concrete public support. People loved his band but would not build him a bandstand. He was still bitter when he wrote his memoirs, declaring that all other Montana cities had facilities for the entertainment and education of their residents, "While Butte the Metropolitan City of Montana, remains in the realms of bye gone days without Parks, Band Stand, Rest Rooms, and many other necessities for public conveniences." Butte boasted no art museum or natural history museum. The public library board was always scrambling for money and relied upon voluntary associations for funds to buy books. Circulation was correspondingly low, averaging less than one book per capita a year. In fact, during the 1920s the most popular place in the library was its third-floor meeting hall, where the American Legion staged boxing matches.[55]

The exception in Butte's otherwise gritty recreational life was the YMCA, which was unique in the service it offered. The first local stirrings of the YMCA movement occurred in 1906, when two hundred men organized a Young Men's Association and subsequently acquired a building in which they constructed a small gymnasium and billiard room. In 1916 a committee of prominent businessmen launched a building campaign, citing the fact that Butte was the largest city in the United States without a YMCA. Within ten days the committee raised more than $200,000. In October 1917 the cornerstone was laid. When additional funds were needed the following year, a second fund drive collected $190,000 in eight days, and in November 1919 the YMCA opened, the best equipped, it was claimed, in the Northwest. Bowling alleys, handball courts, a pool, a gymnasium, billiard and pool tables, two periodical reading rooms, a "substation" of the public library, kitchens, classrooms, a soda fountain, and a hundred bedrooms filled seven stories. Although many of the facilities were reserved for members, the library, soda fountain, and comfort stations were public.[56]

The relatively late development of the YMCA in Butte permitted it to escape much of the elitism and "muscular Christianity" of the original YMCA movement in the United States. The first YMCAs that emerged in the United States during the 1880s embraced the philosophy of the group's British founders, who merged Christian mission work and the self-improvement of white, middle-class youths. Butte's YMCA had a religious component, but it was markedly ecumenical. The task of the religious committee was to work with boys to make "Protestant boys better Protestants and Catholic boys better Catholics and Jewish boys better adherants [sic] to and defenders of the Hebrew faith." During its opening week, the YMCA hosted a housewarming, each night inviting a different group to tour the building and enjoy a specially tailored entertainment. The guest list revealed broad-based support. Contributors were feted the first night, but during the rest of the week fraternal lodges, miners, union members, foreign-language speakers, boys, and young men and women examined the facility. On miners' night the program included the presentation of gold medals to five men who had saved the lives of fellow workers during the Pennsylvania Mine fire in 1916 and the Speculator fire in 1917.[57]

The tone of Butte's YMCA was set by Sam R. Parker, who became the director in December 1920. Parker had worked for YMCAs since 1913 and came to Butte from Colorado, where he had run a program for the Colorado Fuel and Iron Company and supervised district work in the mining regions of Colorado and Wyoming. His familiarity with mining life enabled him to cater to the needs of the mining city. Parker recognized that although the institution's boards of directors and trustees were drawn from the city's business class, its constituents came from all classes. Indeed, more than 1,500 of the initial subscribers to the building fund were miners. Aware that Sunday was many working men's only day off, Parker opened the YMCA on the Sabbath and reaped a large attendance. In 1921 the YMCA initiated a free Americanization night school for immigrants, and by 1925 more than a thousand men and women had gone through the program. Whereas early YMCAs had only reluctantly inaugurated boys' programs and set high fees to discourage working-class youths from joining, the Butte YMCA provided boys' programs free of charge. Sustaining memberships subsidized children's programs. From the outset, the YMCA designed a nondenominational, cross-class program, and soon after opening was called upon to serve both sexes.[58]

The YMCA's founders had no intention of allowing women to use the facility. But attempts to raise money for a YWCA proved futile, and in 1920 women "demanded" the same privileges as men. The management acquiesced. The Butte YMCA was established during the years in which the national institution increasingly opened its doors to women, sanctioning coeducational programs as a way to encourage wholesome Christian heterosocial activity. The Butte YMCA instituted women's memberships and set aside times for their use of the pool and gymnasium. In 1921 a suite of women's club rooms was opened, furnished through donations of Butte businessmen, and soon many of the city's women's clubs met there. Sam Parker was especially pleased that many mothers took advantage of night-time gym classes, often accompanied by their daughters. Girls were the last to gain admittance to the YMCA, and their programs never matched those offered to boys. But the YMCA did host the Girl Scouts and Campfire Girls who supplemented YMCA-sponsored girls' activities. During the annual membership "round-up," men and women engaged in friendly rivalry to see which division could enroll the most new members.[59]

In effect, the YMCA filled the place that public playground movements did in other cities. Absorbing the functions of a municipal recreation program, it helped perpetuate voluntary associations' responsibility for community recreation. The YMCA's physical education director taught a playleaders course for schoolteachers and members of voluntary organizations, which sponsored their own children's programs and offered to supervise city playgrounds. The YMCA branched out from sports' programs under its own roof to organize team sports all over the city. Baseball, basketball, football, and ice hockey leagues began in 1925, and in 1926 a woman's baseball league took the field. YMCA personnel also formalized neighborhood teams and coordinated grammar school athletics into scheduled leagues.[60]

■　■　■

Voluntary associations were a crucial part of Butte society. Before the institution of publicly funded social welfare programs, they provided the most reliable safety net for the poor, the disabled, and the plain unlucky. For many, they were oases in a cultural desert. They permitted men and women "of kindred spirits" to assemble for comfort and pleasure. They were the single most important force in meeting the needs of women and children in a community whose commercial culture primarily served the desires of men. They were also one of the most persistent forms of gender-based leisure. Although men's and women's associations often cooperated with each other in civic projects and occasionally invited each other to social events, the single constant in the evolution of voluntary associations was that they remained single-sex groups. Clearly, both men and women wanted one part of their lives to be spent exclusively in the company of members of their own sex, and they protected that space and time with rules, regulations, and often elaborate rituals.

Associational activity in Butte peaked during the 1920s. Fraternal lodges enjoyed a boom in membership and ritual work: The Masons showed a steady increase in applicants throughout the decade, the Elks prospered and built a new hall in 1925, Rotary and Kiwanis tackled more and more projects, and in 1928 a group of young businessmen formed a branch of the Lions. Women's associations, too, fared well. Suffrage and growing business opportunities injected new life into such existing groups as the Women's Commercial Club and the Good Government Club, which reorganized under the guidance of national organizations like Business and Professional Women and the League of Women Voters. Groups such as the Pearl Club, WAAIME, and a branch of the National Council of Catholic Women emerged to address the postwar problems of their constituencies. Cultural clubs continued to promote art, literature, music, and crafts in private and public settings.[61]

Conditions would change in the 1930s. Clubs and lodges persisted, but membership declined and activities waned. The depression took its toll on dues-paying groups and private charities. People could not afford to give and to spend. To some groups' dismay, New Deal agencies took over the welfare administration they had been providing. But it was not only the depression that sapped voluntary associations. Even in the 1920s they had begun to face competition from new diversions. Movies and dance halls, which the middle class had greeted with suspicion, by the 1930s attracted nearly everyone. The YMCA itself created new forms of recreation, as did Mines League baseball and the cadre of Butte boxers showcased by the American Legion. The fact that women were welcome in nightclubs and speakeasies provided some with tempting alternatives to club meetings. One new technical innovation of the 1920s rivaled the potential entertainment value of clubs, dances, and ball games and kept men, women, and children at home. Radio captured the airwaves in 1922 and took Butte by storm in 1929, when KGIR, the city's first station, went on the air.[62]

NOTES

1. Paul, ed., *A Victorian Gentlewoman*, 23, 29; Stegner, *Angle of Repose*.
2. On voluntary associations and community development, see Clawson, *Constructing Brotherhood*; Doyle, *The Social Order of a Frontier Community*; Ferguson, *Fifty Million Brothers*; Gilkeson, Jr., *Middle-Class Providence*; Hewitt, *Women's Activism and Social Change*; and Meyer, "Fraternal Beneficiary Societies."

3. Thoughtful works on the women's club movement include Blair, *The Clubwoman as Feminist;* Blair, *The Torchbearers;* Boylan, "Timid Girls"; Conway, "Women Reformers and American Culture"; Freedman, "Separatism as Strategy"; Hall, *Revolt against Chivalry;* Martin, *The Sound of Our Own Voices;* McCarthy, ed., *Lady Bountiful Revisited;* Muncy, *Creating a Female Dominion;* Scott, *Making the Invisible Woman Visible;* Scott, *Natural Allies;* Sims, *Feminism and Femininity in the New South;* White, "The Work of the Woman's Club"; and Wilson, *The American Woman in Transition.*

4. Miller, *The Hands of the Workmen,* 21; Clawson, "Nineteenth-Century Women's Auxiliaries and Fraternal Orders," 40, 42; *Butte City Directory,* 1900. On the history of the Masons, see Clawson, *Constructing Brotherhood;* on the importance of fraternal lodges to men, see Carnes, *Secret Ritual and Manhood.*

5. *Butte City Directory,* 1889–1917. On women's clubs in Montana and other western states, see Cunningham, *The Woman's Club of El Paso;* Greenfield, "Shakespearean 'Culture' in Montana"; Jackson, "The History of Volunteering in Wyoming"; Sheehan, "'Women Helping Women'"; and Tubbs, "Montana Women's Clubs."

6. "Narrative History of Homer Club," 1, 4. See also Christie, "Women's Clubs of Montana."

7. Homer Club Yearbook, 1912–13, Homer Club Records, MHSA; *Butte City Directory,* 1913.

8. Christie, "Women's Clubs of Montana," 586; *Club Histories District II: Montana Federation of Women's Clubs,* 15; Marian Canavan, interview by Mary Murphy, Butte, 20 May 1987; Minutes, 14 April 1905, "E. S. Paxson," typescript, n.d., and Yearbooks, 1917–18, 1921–22, 1931–32, and 1939–40, Marian White Arts and Crafts Club Records, BSBA (hereafter cited as MWA&CC Records); *Butte City Directory,* 1917, 1923, 1931, 1940.

9. Christie, "Women's Clubs of Montana," 585–86; *Anaconda Standard,* 18 December 1898, 49; *Butte Miner,* 14 December 1905, 1; The Woman's Club of Butte Yearbook, 1906–7, MHSA; Martha Claire Catlin, research notes for the Butte Historical Society Building Inventory, BSBA.

10. Alderson, "Half Century of Progress for Montana Women," 9–11; Piatt, ed., *The Story of Butte,* 76, 79–80. Further information on the development of the library can be found in the "Butte Library—History" file at the Butte-Silver Bow Free Public Library. On the Silver Bow Shield, see Howey, "Description of Lady Manager's Organization and Fair Exhibits," typescript, Board of World's Fair Managers of the State of Montana Records, box 1, file 26, MHSA. On Montana's role in the Columbia Exposition, see Walter, "Montana's Silver Lady," and Rydell, "The Culture of Imperial Abundance," 205–10.

11. *Anaconda Standard,* 18 December 1898, 49; *Butte Miner,* 14 December 1905, 15.

12. Minutes, 5 December 1907, 2 February 1909, 5 February 1913, 3 April 1913, 21 January 1915, 4 February 1915, and 20 April 1916, MWA&CC Records, BSBA.

13. Susman, "Culture and Civilization," 109; O'Reilly, *The Butte Blue Book.* On the Ethical Culture Club, see Christie, "Women's Clubs of Montana," 587; *Anaconda Standard,* 10 February 1901, 15, and *Butte Miner,* 22 April 1906, 15. Atherton, *Adventures of a Novelist,* 489.

14. *Butte Miner,* 4 August 1920, 1; Aili Goldberg, interview by Mary Murphy, Butte, 29 February 1980, 34. On the use of clubs to strengthen and perpetuate class position, see Ostrander, *Women of the Upper Class,* and Lynd and Lynd, *Middletown,* 277–81.

15. Skeels, ed., *One American Family,* 2:392. On girls' club activities, see *Anaconda Standard,* 4 January 1914, 6, 11 January 1914, 7, 12 February 1920, 9, and 13 February 1920, 2; *Montana Standard,* 10 May 1929, 1; Minutes, 15 February 1917, 15 February 1923, and 7 March 1929, MWA&CC Records, BSBA; Dorothy A. Martin, interview by Mary Murphy, Butte, 23 May 1988, 13.

16. Bowden, "The Woman's Club Movement," 260; Knox, "The Redemption of 'Barren Butte'"; *Butte Miner,* 1 May 1923, 7 and 3 May 1923, 12; *Montana Standard,* 5 December 1928, 1 and 7 January 1929, 1.

17. On the history and activities of the Joshers Club, see *Montana Standard,* 25 November 1928, 1, 29; Writers' Program, Work Projects Administration, *Copper Camp,* 84–86; and Finlen, *Meet Some Folks,* 109–15.

18. *Montana Standard,* 25 November 1928, 1, 29, 20 December 1928, 1, 2, 21 December 1928, 1, 8, and 22 December 1928, 6; Finlen, *Meet Some Folks,* 115.

19. "Reports and Addresses, 1919–1926," Women's Auxiliary to the American Institute of Mining Engineers Records, Butte chapter, BSBA (hereafter cited as WAAIME Records); Spence, *Mining Engineers and the American West,* 327. WAAIME was established nationally in 1917; in 1920 the national president organized branches in Butte and Anaconda.

20. "Reports and Addresses, 1919–1926," WAAIME Records, BSBA.

21. Quotation is from "President's Annual Address, 3 January 1901," *Second Biennial Report of the Associated Charities,* 2 January 1902, 4. On the history of the Associated Charities, see *First Biennial Report of the Associated Charities of Butte, Montana,* 1 January 1900; *Second Biennial Report of the Associated Charities of Butte, Montana;* and *Third Biennial Report of the Associated Charities of Butte, Montana,* 1904. All of these reports are in the MHSL. The attitude of the Associated Charities toward the poor was quite common at the time. See, for example, Kusmer, "The Functions of Organized Charity in the Progressive Era."

22. "Reports and Addresses, 1919–1926," and "Annual Report, 1933," WAAIME Records, BSBA.

23. On WAAIME's support of the East Side Neighborhood House, see "Reports and Addresses, 1919–1926," and Minutes, 1930–1936, WAAIME Records, BSBA. For the origins and activities of the Neighborhood House, see *Butte Miner,* 6 March 1921, mag. sec., 6 and 20 August 1922, 21–22, and *Montana Standard,* 29 September 1928, 7, 29 January 1930, 5, and 19

July 1931, 3. Quotations are from *Minutes of the Synod of Montana*, 1926, 19, and *Presbyterian Reporter* 1 (June 1926): 5.

On settlement houses and voluntary associations, see Gittell and Shtob, "Changing Women's Roles in Political Voluntarism," and Daniels, *America via the Neighborhood*, 181–92. On the ideology of settlement house work with immigrants, see Carson, *Settlement Folk*. On other Presbyterian missions in the West, see Pascoe, *Relations of Rescue*.

24. Drury, *Presbyterian Panorama*, 262; Kelly, *Children of Copperland*, 3.

25. Kelly, *Children of Copperland*, 7–8.

26. Ibid., 5–6; *Presbyterian Reporter*, 5 (February 1930): 5; *Minutes of the Synod of Montana*, 1928, 13–14; *Minutes of the Synod of Montana*, 1932, 16; *Montana Standard*, 19 July 1931, 3. Members of the board of the Neighborhood House included a rabbi, an Episcopal priest, the lawyer who led Butte's anti-gambling crusade, the general secretary of the YMCA, and the wives of the assistant secretary of the Montana Power Company, the chief assistant geologist of the Anaconda Company, the general superintendent of the mines, and one of the company's most powerful lawyers.

27. *Presbyterian Reporter* 5 (February 1930): 4, and 6 (February 1931): 7.

28. Kelly, *Children of Copperland*, 10–11; *Presbyterian Reporter* 4 (February 1929): 5, and 7 (July 1932): 6–7; *Minutes of the Synod of Montana*, 1932, 16.

29. The dates of origin of many Butte clubs and lodges can be found in "State Encyclopedia Questionnaire, Silver Bow County," WPA records, MSU.

30. Emmons, *Butte Irish*, 109–12; Minutes, 1937–41, Daughters of Norway Records, BSBA.

31. A brief history of the Daughters of Norway is included in a cookbook they published; see *Kitchen Secrets of the Daughters of Norway*. *Anaconda Standard*, 24 February 1920, 2; *Butte Miner*, 22 May 1915, 5. When Butte Bohemians formed an association for all Slavic people, they launched it with a dance at the Swede-Finnish hall and announced that the group's purpose would be to host entertainments, lecture courses, and debates, and to promote the general welfare of Slavs. *Anaconda Standard*, 19 January 1914, 9.

32. Catherine Hoy, interview by Ray Calkins and Caroline Smithson, Butte, 11 May 1979, 18–19; "State Encyclopedia Questionnaire, Silver Bow County." On the political overtones of St. Patrick's Day, see Emmons, *Butte Irish*.

33. Goldberg interview, 20–21; Mary Trbovich, interview by Mary Murphy, Butte, 4 November 1987.

34. Emmons, *Butte Irish*, 398–407.

35. Trbovich interview; "Silver Anniversary of the Circle of Serbian Sisters, 1934–1959, Holy Trinity Orthodox Church," 1959, BSBA.

36. "State Encyclopedia Questionnaire, Silver Bow County"; Trbovich interview.

37. Minutes, 1937–41, Daughters of Norway Records, BSBA; Trbovich interview.

38. Trbovich interview; John Onkalo, interview by Ray Calkins, Butte, February 1980, 17; Minutes, 1937–41, Daughters of Norway Records, BSBA. For a comparative view of urban, ethnic associations during this time period, see Cohen, *Making a New Deal,* chap. 2.

39. Elizabeth Kennedy to Jeannette Rankin (hereafter cited as JR), 18 June 1917, Jeannette Rankin Papers (hereafter cited as JR Papers), box 1, file 8, MHSA; Clapp, "Highlights and Sidelights," part 2.

40. For examples of men's service clubs' projects, see articles on the Rotary Club in the *Butte Miner,* 8 June 1917, 7, and 22 February 1920, part 2, 9; and *Montana Standard,* 16 February 1930, 3.

41. On the statewide activities of the Good Government Clubs, see report by Mrs. Harvey Coit, n.d., National American Woman Suffrage Association (Montana) Records, 1913–19 and undated, MHSA. On Elizabeth Kennedy's fruitless efforts to achieve reform in Butte, see *Butte Daily Bulletin,* 17 February 1920, 3, and 18 February 1920, 1; *Anaconda Standard,* 9 January 1917, 7, and 13 January 1917, 7. On the Montana suffrage campaign, see Ward, "The Winning of Woman Suffrage in Montana," and Larsen, "Montana Women and the Battle for the Ballot."

42. Laura Way Mathieson to Mrs. James Paige, 10 November 1920, and Lila Rose to Marie Stuart Edwards, 15 November 1922, League of Women Voters Papers (hereafter cited as LWV Papers), series 2, box 1, "MTL-WV" file, LC. On women's involvement in the Americanization movement, see McClymer, "Gender and the 'American Way of Life.'"

43. Rose to Edwards, 15 November 1922, Florence Harrison to Marguerite Wells, 2 July 1923, and 31 July 1923, and Mary O'Neill to Wells, 26 May 1923, LWV Papers, series 2, box 8, "Mont-hist" file, LC.

44. Emma A. Ingalls to Paige, 24 December 1922, box 1, "MTLWV" file, and Wells to Belle Sherwin, 12 May 1923 and 14 May 1923, O'Neill to Wells, 22 May 1923 and 6 June 1923, and O'Neill to Sherwin, 31 May 1923, box 8, "Mont-hist" file, all in LWV Papers, series 2, LC. On the politics between the state leagues and the National Board of the League of Women Voters, see Lemons, *Woman Citizen,* 121; Black, *Social Feminism;* and Young, *In the Public Interest.* Black notes that the history of the state leagues has yet to be written, but a few studies do exist. See, for example, Donovan, "The Nebraska League of Women Voters"; Swenson, "To Uplift a State and Nation"; and Nasstrom, "'More Was Expected of Us.'" Unfortunately, the Montana League of Women Voters Papers include little substantive material before the 1950s, and it is impossible to trace the makeup of the league in the 1920s from national records. As Young notes, no "reasonably accurate" membership records for the LWV exist before 1930.

45. Executive Board of Montana League of Women Voters to Wells, 30 October 1922, Ingalls to Paige, 24 December 1922, Harrison to Wells, 24 June 1923, and 30 June 1923, LWV Papers, series 2, box 8, "Mont-hist" file, LC.

46. Harrison to Wells, 24 June 1923, LWV Papers, series 2, box 8, "Mont-hist" file, LC.

47. Clara Ueland to Wells, 24 June 1923, and Harrison to Wells, 24 June 1923, and 31 July 1923, LWV Papers, series 2, box 8, "Mont-hist" file, LC. Finnish women in Butte had organized a women's socialist club in 1906. See Frisch, "The Gibraltar of Unionism," 222–23.

48. "Report of Florence Harrison's Trip," n.d., Ueland to Wells, 24 June 1923, box 8, "Mont-hist" file, Annabel Long Edinger to Sherwin, 30 January 1928, box 77, "Montana" file, all in LWV Papers, series 2, LC. National organizers of the woman suffrage campaign commented in similar fashion upon Butte's class differences in the nineteenth century. See Larsen, "Montana Women and the Battle for the Ballot," 31–32.

49. Wells to Mrs. George Gellhorn, 13 December 1923, LWV Papers, series 2, box 8, "Mont-hist" file, LC.

50. U.S. Department of Labor, Children's Bureau, *Public Dance Halls*, 36–37; L. H. Weir, "Notes Concerning Parks and Recreation, Butte, Montana," 1930, National Recreation Association Records, box 41, "Butte" file, Social Welfare History Archives, Walter Library, University of Minnesota, Minneapolis. On municipal skating rinks, see *Montana Standard*, 16 December 1928, 11. On the typical activities of the Parks and Playgrounds Committee and the lack of playgrounds, see, for example, Butte City Council Minutes, vol. 18 (21 October 1931 and 18 November 1931), and vol. 19 (18 January 1933, 1 November 1933, and 6 May 1935).

51. Weir, "Notes Concerning Parks and Recreation," 21–22.

52. Elizabeth Kennedy to JR, 10 July 1917, JR Papers, box 1, file 8, MHSA.

53. On the relationship between industrialization and public parks, see Rosenzweig, *Eight Hours for What We Will;* Gilkeson, *Middle-Class Providence;* and Cranz, "Women in Urban Parks."

54. Butte City Council Minutes (6 May 1935), 19:505–6, 509.

55. Treloar, "Reminiscences of Butte Mines Band," 112, 130–31; Weir, "Notes Concerning Parks and Recreation," 31–32.

56. *Butte Miner,* 2 July 1906, 4, 30 May 1913, 6, and 23 November 1919, mag. sec., 4.

57. *Butte Miner,* 23 November 1919, mag. sec., 4; *Anode* 5 (November 1919): 8; *Butte Miner,* 25 November 1919, 1; *Anaconda Standard,* 24 November 1919, 3, and 26 November 1919, 11. One of the Butte YMCA's chief benefactors was a prominent member of the Jewish community, Joseph E. Oppenheimer, treasurer of Symons Department Store. He served on the original board of trustees along with the general manager of the Butte Electric Railway, the manager of the Butte Water Company, the manager of Western Iron Works, the vice president of the Murray Hospital, the manager of the COD Laundry, an attorney, the president of Butte Potato and Produce, the president of Lutey Brothers Grocery, and the vice president of the First National Bank. For a discussion of early YMCA work in America, see Macleod, *Building Character,* 72–76.

58. *Butte Miner,* 4 December 1920, 9, 23 November 1919, mag. sec., 4, and 31 October 1927, 5. Apparently the idea of subsidized memberships for boys started in Grand Rapids, Michigan, in 1916, but that YMCA did ask boys to pledge at least fifty cents every year. The Butte YMCA claimed it was the first YMCA to make no financial demands upon boys. *Anaconda Standard,* 24 November 1919, 3; *Butte Miner,* 23 April 1923, 11.

59. *Butte Miner,* 19 January 1920, 1, 12 April 1925, 8–9, 23 January 1921, 12, and 23 April 1922, 11; *Anaconda Standard,* 27 March 1921, 2; *Montana Standard,* 11 January 1929, 6, and 8 October 1930, 2. Another attempt to raise money for a women's building was begun in 1930 but came to naught. On the establishment of YMCA programs for women and girls, see Vandenberg-Daves, "The Manly Pursuit of a Partnership."

60. *Butte Daily Post,* 11 April 1926, 20–21; *Butte Miner,* 12 April 1925, mag. sec., 6.

61. *Butte Miner,* 3 October 1926, 2, 11 May 1925, 1–2, and 26 August 1928, 10; *Montana Standard,* 25 August 1929, 8, and 5 December 1928, 1; Miller, *Hands of the Workmen,* 76–79; Bagdad Temple Silver Jubilee, 1911–36, program booklet, Leggat Collection, MSU. Cott finds it "highly probable that the greatest extent of associational activity in the whole history of American women took place in the era between the two world wars, after women became voters and before a great proportion of them entered the labor force," see *The Grounding of Modern Feminism,* 97. Lemons concurs in *The Woman Citizen* and claims that the peak of women's effective lobbying for progressive reforms came between 1920 and 1925. Muncy, in *Creating a Female Dominion,* also supports this analysis.

62. Richardson, "Is the Women's Club Dying?"

The American Theater on West Park Street, featuring the 1922 film *Bobbed Hair*. (Schoettner Studio photo; courtesy of the World Museum of Mining)

Butte boxer Joe Simonich inscribed a photo for fellow pugilist Sonny O'Day. (Courtesy of the Montana Historical Society)

Prizes offered in keno games. The original caption for this photo read, "Gambling for housewives," 1939. (Photo by Arthur Rothstein; courtesy of the Library of Congress)

Men loiter outside the Arcade Bar & Cafe on the corner of Park and North Main streets, 1939. The basement housed a WPA recreation room. (Photo by Arthur Rothstein; courtesy of the Library of Congress)

Men surround the drilling contest at Columbia Gardens in 1923. (Courtesy of the Montana Historical Society)

The tug-of-war contest at Columbia Gardens in 1923. (Courtesy of the Montana Historical Society)

Members of the Neighbors of Woodcraft, Silver Bow Circle Number 239, a fraternal life insurance society, at their costume party in 1935. (Zubick Studio photo; courtesy of the World Museum of Mining)

Butte's Bagdad Temple Band of the Ancient Arabic Order Nobles of the Mystic Shrine in uptown Butte. (Zubick Studio photo; courtesy of the World Museum of Mining)

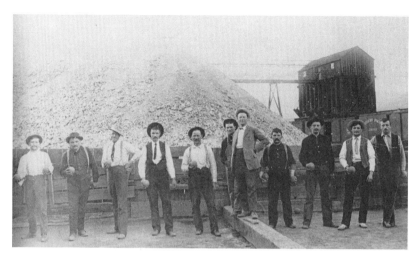

Italian men playing bocce in Meaderville. (Courtesy of the World Museum of Mining)

Miners with their lunch buckets pose in front of the Italian American Club on Main Street in Meaderville. (Courtesy of the World Museum of Mining)

Ed Craney and Emmett Burke host KGIR's "Night Owl" program, which aired in the mid-1930s. (Courtesy of the Montana Historical Society)

Local bands broadcast live from KGIR's studio. (Courtesy of the Montana Historical Society)

Local merchants displayed KGIR advertisements, such as this one for a broadcast of "Tony and Gus," sponsored by Post-Toasties. (Courtesy of the Montana Historical Society)

The Success Cafe on East Broadway, reputedly the smallest restaurant in the world—seating four customers—proclaimed its Democratic partisanship. (Courtesy of World Museum of Mining)

Women cutting out garments in Butte's WPA sewing room. (Courtesy of the National Archives)

Folk dancing sponsored by the WPA Recreation Project. (Courtesy of the National Archives)

A checker tournament for unemployed miners in a WPA Recreation Project game room. (Courtesy of the National Archives)

Children's art class sponsored by the Federal Art Project. The original caption noted that "complete individuality of thought and execution was given: copying was discouraged." (Courtesy of the National Archives)

6

Imagination's Spur:
Station KGIR

Through the radio . . . all isolation can be destroyed.
—STANLEY FROST

On February 1, 1929, Edmund B. Craney received the following telegram: "Was dead from the waist both ways till I tuned in on KGIR but now hot dog I could climb a cactus bush sixty eight feet high with a panther under both arms trim my toe nails with a forty-five when I reached the summit slide back to earth without a scratch hot dawg whoopee cmon have one with us fellas wine for the ladies n everything."[1] Radio station KGIR had arrived in Butte.

Radio performed a dual, sometimes contradictory function during the Great Depression. In a time of almost universal belt-tightening, the allure of the radio impelled people to buy receivers on credit, and commercial programming bombarded listeners with advertisements designed to increase their desire for consumer goods. But the radio also provided a source of comfort, news, and entertainment for the unemployed and underemployed who could no longer afford movies, vacations, restaurant meals, and other pleasures of the consumer society. A radio proved a substitute for many of the leisure activities people had to give up and prepared them to indulge more freely in mass consumerism once economic good times returned.

KGIR had other many-sided effects. Programs reinforced gendered patterns of leisure and work. Men gathered on street corners to hear broadcasts of prizefights; women sewed, cooked, and washed, listening to the "Women's Magazine of the Air." Yet the development of family entertainment and the station's support of civic organizations also fostered their aims of making Butte's leisure more family-oriented. The radio created a new social activity: gathering family and friends together to listen to music, comedy, and drama in the privacy of a home.

Through network programming, KGIR introduced Butte listeners to a developing national culture while at the same time continuing to broadcast local performers and shows. Broadcasts of traditional ethnic music won the loyalty of Butte's foreign-born and exposed the rest of the community to the languages and cultures of their neighbors. Butte's first radio station thus created an amalgam of news and entertainment that celebrated local talent and served community groups while delivering programs of national popularity and significance.

In the early 1920s and 1930s radio's effect was unknown. Observers predicted that it would both homogenize and democratize American society, diffusing education, culture, and a sense of national solidarity. Nevertheless, people clung stubbornly to their regional and ethnic identities, and class differences were not easily overcome by broadcasts of lectures and operas. Perhaps the most profound effect of radio was the beguilement of millions into the culture of consumption. KGIR brought all of radio's mixed messages to Butte.[2]

KGIR was Ed Craney's brainchild and Butte's first commercial station. Radio stations had been in existence in the United States for almost a decade before he established KGIR, and programming was about to undergo a revolution. In the first decade of broadcasting, sponsors were hesitant to make radio seem too commercial. On the contrary, they intended it to be educational and culturally enriching. By 1929, however, radio was entering what one scholar has called its "era of institutionalization." Broadcasting became explicitly commercial; radio networks formed, filling broadcast hours with programs developed by advertising agencies; and local control of content declined. Craney arrived in Butte on the cusp of this change.[3]

Until KGIR began broadcasting, the only radio signals emanating from Butte were those of amateurs; the one ham operator who did attempt public programming played records on the air for an hour or so each day. When Craney first visited Butte in 1927, he saw a potential market and applied for a commercial broadcast license. From the very start he had ambitious plans. Although other Montana stations preceded it, KGIR became the first to affiliate with a national network, the National Broadcasting Company (NBC), in 1931. Craney eventually turned KGIR into the flagship of a state-wide network of radio stations known as the Z-Bar, which he used to sell advertising more effectively and bring to Montana more diverse programming. Craney had social as well as commercial designs. He remained committed to local programming and attempted through radio to instill in citizens of Butte, and then of the Big Sky, a sense of themselves as Montanans rather than as isolated residents of an archipelago of small towns and cities.[4]

■ ■ ■

The nation's first radio station, Westinghouse's KDKA in Pittsburgh, broadcast the results of the Harding-Cox presidential election in 1920 and began regularly scheduled programs in 1921. Ham radio operators had conversed since before World War I, but their communication systems required building their own transmitters and receivers and mastering the continental telegraph code in which messages were sent and received. KDKA broadcast music and human voices. Those magical transmissions encouraged department stores to establish radio counters and propelled people into long lines in electrical shops where they bought parts to construct their own receivers. In *Middletown*, Helen Lynd and Robert Lynd noted the remarkable accessibility of radio in the early 1920s. Equipment could be purchased piecemeal, and a little skill and inventiveness provided new family entertainment. As the Lynds observed, "Far from being simply one more means of passive enjoyment, the radio has given rise to much ingenious manipulative activity." A Butte boy, demonstrating that resourcefulness, built his set by scavenging crystals from the mine dumps and earphones from pay telephone booths.[5]

Children's literature encouraged boys and girls to apply their mechanical skills to radio manufacture with the promise of subsequent adventure. The Stratemeyer syndicate, responsible for the Bobbsey Twins, Tom Swift, Nancy Drew, and the Hardy Boys books, launched a Radio Boys series and a Radio Girls series in 1922. In each story homemade radios proved essential to solving a mystery. The boys and girls traveled by automobile, boat, airplane, and ship to swamps, forests, icebergs, and islands to battle earthquakes, forest fires, sharks, and pirates. They championed the underdog, lent a hand to the government, escaped from thorny entanglements, and discovered buried treasures, all with the help of radios they had assembled. The Radio Boys series eventually encompassed more than a dozen volumes issued throughout the 1920s, but the Radio Girls series was less successful. Only four volumes were published, and in 1930 the books were reprinted, substituting "Campfire Girls" for "Radio Girls" in all the titles.[6]

"Radiomania" became a predominantly male sport. One writer and radio enthusiast claimed that landing an elusive station required the same "patience, ingenuity, and even skill" as landing a fish. Men considered building and operating radios to be a male activity that drew upon supposedly traditional masculine skills of mechanical cleverness and technical mastery. Some girls did take up amateur radio, but they were relatively few in number. Only a handful of women operators were listed in the early directories of *QST,* the magazine for wireless amateurs. Female operators were such a novelty that men often treated them like mascots. In a 1921 essay in *QST* a male amateur complimented Eunice Randall, the first woman with whom he had on-the-air contact, for having "the proper spirit for a real honest to goodness shemale radio bug." He then continued, "Other districts have had the honor of boasting an O.W. [signifying "Old Woman," the counterpoint to O.M., or "Old Man," the term by which amateurs addressed each other] long enough, by heck; we're going to have one of our own up here now."[7]

Early radio fans were attracted not so much by regular transmissions or even the content of programs as by the romance of distance. They caught the fever that caused so many amateur operators to stay up all night trying to make contact with stations in South America and Australia or ships near the Antarctic. Dorothy Johnson, a Montana writer who bought a second-hand tube set for $20 in 1923, attested, "What everybody wanted was distance. I was delighted with a lecture on raising baby chickens emanating from Lincoln, Nebraska; sometimes Pittsburgh came in loud and clear . . . once I even got Schenectady, New York." Radio manufacturers used the drama of distance to sell their products. One advertisement for Burgess batteries promised that with radio "brightening the long winter nights with music, special programs, messages and greetings from their 'home folks,'" the Canadian Mounties would never again be lonely on their assignment patrolling the "vast, wild area" of the northern wilderness. Radio telescoped the immense distances of the West, bringing to rural dwellers the sounds of the city, facilitating communication between towns and outlying ranches, and easing the loneliness of isolated lives. Edward P. Morgan, an Idahoan who eventually became a broadcast commentator in Washington, D.C., dated the start of his love affair with radio to his father's purchase of a

DeForest set in the mid-1920s. "My night sounds had been the sharp haunting bark of coyotes," Morgan remembered, "but now the boundaries of my world suddenly dilated far beyond the sagebrush hills of Idaho, and through the hissing swish of static, like a bell pealing in a snowstorm, came the sweet, wavering voices of KHJ, Los Angeles, KDKA, Pittsburgh, and, one enchanted evening, Havana, Cuba."[8]

Although entrancing, the signals from distant stations were irregular and spurred some Montanans to build local stations. Without the resources common in metropolitan areas, commercial radio in the state developed slowly and sporadically. Between 1922, when KDYS, Montana's first commercial station, debuted in Great Falls, and 1929, when KGIR went on the air in Butte, small stations opened in Havre, Missoula, Vida, Kalispell, and Billings. Many were shoestring operations and some were short-lived. KDYS broadcast for only eighteen months before going off the air. KGCX, which originated in Vida, population twenty-five, in 1926, eventually moved to Wolf Point, a town of fifteen hundred. Dallas Jensen, the station's operator, continued to augment his salary by working in the local drugstore. Programs depended on local talent and leaned heavily toward stock and grain market reports, coverage of school sports, updates on the weather, and direct messages to farm and ranch families.[9]

Throughout the 1920s commercial radio was distinctly noncommercial. Advertising agencies, sponsors, radio manufacturers, and broadcasters united in viewing the new medium as an educational tool, an avenue of cultural uplift. While jazz swept the country via phonograph records and hot bands playing in nightclubs and dance halls, radio stations played classical, or, as one critic called it, "potted palm," music. Advertisers felt they had no right to intrude uninvited into the family circle, where most people listened to the radio. WEAF, the nation's leader in sponsored programs, forbade offering samples, quoting prices, or describing products on the air. In fact, quoting product prices was not sanctioned until 1931. Radio's value to sponsors was to create goodwill and gratitude on the part of listeners. Sponsors limited advertising to modest announcements at the beginning and ending of programs, or they attached brand names to orchestras and performers, such as the A&P Gypsies, the Lucky Strike Orchestra, and the Best Food Boys. Owen D. Young, chair of General Electric and RCA, declared in 1926 that he considered the companies' new subsidiary, NBC, to be "semi-philanthropic."[10]

By 1929 the insistence on "sponsorship only" had faded, however. The advertising industry had mushroomed during the 1920s, and its successful cultivation of a consumer society fed its continued growth. Agencies realized that the intimacy of radio offered an unprecedented opportunity to personalize advertising, and they discovered that listeners did not mind commercials. Indeed, the audience often heard advertisements as part of the entertainment, and pollsters had found that what radio fans wanted was entertainment. The popularity of shows such as "Amos 'n' Andy," the "Eno Crime Club," and "Thirty Minutes of Sunshine" finally persuaded networks and advertising agencies that people desired comedy and drama as well as classical music and educational programs. Agencies began to design commercials as part of the show and listen to radio station managers who urged, "Ditch Dvorak. They want 'Turkey in the Straw.'" By the end of 1932 the days when advertisements were few, and the few were models of "decorum, courtesy and effectiveness," were over. A survey conducted in December discovered that air time devoted to commercials amounted to more than that given to news, education, lectures, and religion combined. As one analyst noted, "Until the arrival of television [radio] was the most persuasive, and accordingly, highly paid salesman in the nation."[11]

■ ■ ■

Radio in Butte bypassed the semiphilanthropic days of the 1920s. When the Symons Company of Spokane announced its intention to launch KGIR, the *Montana Free Press* reported that the station would be "frankly a commercial proposition . . . which proposes to derive an income through selling Butte merchants time on the air." Ed Craney, KGIR's manager, had been involved in the radio business for seven years when he came to Butte. Already an amateur operator when he graduated from high school in Spokane in 1922, Craney got a job running a radio parts store owned by Thomas W. Symons, Jr., a lawyer. As in many small metropolitan areas, the absence of good radio signals in Spokane made it difficult to sell receiving sets, so Craney and Symons started their own radio station in order to boost equipment sales. KFDC-Spokane went on the air in October 1922, one of the more than fourteen hundred stations that received licenses from the Department of Commerce in 1922 and 1923. Business picked up, and the two men expanded their sales to western Montana. It was during the course of his sales trips that Craney pinpointed Butte, "a real rip-roaring town," as a plum site for a new station.[12]

Craney received a license for KGIR in 1928 and began construction of the station late that year. He built studios on the third floor of Shiner's Furniture Store in uptown Butte and installed a 250–watt transmitter. Radio fans greeted Craney's actions with mixed emotions. Some feared that the new station would blanket signals from other major broadcasters. Like radio devotees in other parts of the country, Butte listeners reveled in picking up transmissions from KOMO-Seattle, KGW-Portland, and KPO-San Francisco. Butte newspapers published daily radio logs listing the programming of stations in those cities, as well as in Minneapolis, Oakland, Los Angeles, Kansas City, Denver, Milwaukee, and Salt Lake City. The Butte Radio Club, with a membership of three hundred, declared that it would take immediate action "to stop the nuisance" should the new signal interfere with their reception. The club's apprehensions proved unfounded, and it soon became one of KGIR's ardent supporters, three months later petitioning the city council to convert the arc lights illuminating uptown Butte to incandescent ones that would cause less interference with the KGIR signal. Radio fans had powerful allies in Judge William E. Carroll, "an ardent radio enthusiast," who introduced the measure, and Mayor Kerr Beadle, who requested that the Montana Power Company conduct tests to determine if the conversion would be beneficial. As a result, the city and Montana Power split the $12,000 tab for switching the uptown lighting system.[13]

Throughout January, 1929 Butte geared up for KGIR's premiere, scheduled for January 31. Shiner's offered a special price of $150, a markdown from $250, on "Freshman" radios, and the *Butte Daily Post* promised a free crystal set to any boy or girl who enrolled three new subscribers to the paper. Craney later claimed that radio dealers told him they sold three thousand crystal sets during the first week of broadcasting. He recalled, "You would find elevator operators with an earphone on their head listening to a crystal set all over town."[14]

On the night of January 31, Butte listeners tuned in to a recording of the "Star Spangled Banner" and the dedication of the station by the Catholic bishop, a Methodist minister, and a rabbi. Then followed twelve hours of musical selections and orations performed by men, women, and children from the Butte area, directed by three prominent Butte music teachers. Letters and telegrams sent to the station the next day testified to listeners' delight. One couple, who commented on their favorite performances, wrote, "We have had a radio for two years and get every station accessible to this territory and they [KGIR's performers] were as good as any we have heard."[15]

About a month after KGIR's debut, Craney arranged to broadcast Herbert Hoover's inauguration. It was KGIR's first hookup with NBC, and more than any other event it illustrated the radio fever that gripped Butte. Days before the broadcast a festive spirit infused the city as radio owners planned "inauguration breakfasts" so that friends and relatives could gather to eat, drink, and listen to Hoover's swearing-in. On inauguration day crowds massed outside the stores of radio dealers who had hung loudspeakers on their buildings. The Butte Radio Club and the Montana Stock and Bond Company hosted open houses for listeners. Restaurants and department stores aired the broadcast for the pleasure of diners and shoppers. Public and Catholic high school students listened in their auditoriums, and KGIR placed a receiver in the Ramsay rural school, eight miles west of Butte. Two thousand seventh- and eighth-graders heard the program over an Atwater Kent receiving set and loudspeaker installed in the Broadway Theater and cheered as the bands passed the reviewing stand in Washington, D.C. The following day the *Montana Standard,* which had absorbed most of the cost of the program, reported, "The inauguration was made actual, vital—something a great deal more than a remote happening . . . it was as if the listener here were standing among the throngs on the capital lawn."[16]

The inauguration broadcast boosted radio sales in the city. Orton Brothers Music Store, which had lamented that "the only difficulty in recent months has been to obtain a sufficient number of sets to supply the demands of our customers," announced the imminent arrival of a major shipment of new radios. A trainload of four thousand Majestic receivers, the "biggest single shipment of radio receivers ever routed to the northwest," arrived at the depot on March 23. Butte business directories had listed no radio dealers in the 1920s, but by 1930 five—and seven by 1934—served the city's fans. Still, despite the onset of radio fever, only 27.4 percent of Butte families owned radios in 1930. This was a low percentage for Montana, which itself lagged behind the rest of the country in radio ownership. According to the 1930 U.S. Census, 40 percent of American families had radios, but only 32 percent of Montana families owned receivers, with urban-dwellers slightly more likely to have a set than farm families and native-born whites considerably more likely to have a radio than immigrants or African Americans. Butte's low rate of radio ownership could have been due to the late development of a local station that provided strong broadcast signals. More likely it was tied to the economic depression that plagued the city in the 1920s with the drop in demand for copper. The salaries of metal miners had reached a national high in 1920 that was not matched until 1941. Butte miners, working under an open shop until 1934 and often working only part time in the 1930s, were in no position to make expensive purchases.[17]

Buying a radio was a major investment in the late 1920s and early 1930s. Early advertisements for radios usually placed them in plush drawing rooms of mansionlike homes. Publicists pitched their copy to an upper- and middle-class clientele—those citizens who added receivers to the list of durable goods, such as automobiles and furniture, that they purchased on installment plans. For example, a Freed Eiseman advertisement in 1926 characterized its product as "the preferred radio—in homes where leaders meet." A drawing published in *McCall's* in 1928 depicts a family lounging on a veranda overlooking a wooded lake. The father smokes a cigar, the mother holds a ping-pong paddle, the son sits cross-legged, balancing a canoe paddle on his knees, and the teen-aged daughter is languidly draped against a column. All are listening to a radio. The picture illustrates a story, "Summer Care and Use of the Radio Set," and declares that "dancing in the sand in bathing-suits to fox-trots picked up by a suitcase radio set seems to allure many."[18]

In Butte's poorer neighborhoods, listening to the radio was a community affair. For Christmas in 1929, the Kiwanis Club presented the East Side Neighborhood House with a Bremer Tully radio. It became an enormous attraction. Just as families and friends congregated to enjoy house parties with local musicians or dance to phonograph records, now they came together to listen to the radio. Craney recognized Butte's collective listening habits. Advertising KGIR's broadcast of the 1929 World Series, he described it as an opportunity for "radio parties."[19]

Seven companies accounted for two-thirds of the radios that the KGIR audience owned. The firms marketed models that sold, in 1929, for $44 to $300, with a few deluxe receivers ranging up to $1,750. The median price was well over $100. Winfred Slauson, a radio repairman and parts dealer, recalled that in the 1930s, even though smaller radios sold for less than $50, "that was quite a bunch of money." Slauson did not as a matter of course sell radios on time, but often during the depression money trickled in, "You might get part of it now and maybe hope to get the rest next month or so."[20]

■ ■ ■

Consumers traded indebtedness for the delights provided by the radio and the ability of KGIR to link Butte to a larger world in ways more intimate and immediate than newspapers, traveling theater, or even the movies. Yet KGIR also gave voice to many local citizens' talents and causes, making them celebrities. Radio exposed different groups within Butte to each other's music, language, and social activities. As Craney claimed, "We were the voice of Butte." The appeal of small stations lay in their local nature, in familiarity with advertisers, and in request shows on which listeners heard their names attached to the songs they had chosen and to the public service announcements for their clubs and civic groups. Commenting in 1940, a sociologist claimed that the atmosphere surrounding small stations was "much like that in poor neighborhoods, where there is still more personal contact among people than in wealthier, more depersonalized districts." When the Lynds revisited Middletown in the mid-1930s, they too discovered that the local radio station, similar in operation to KGIR, augmented "the 'we' sense among all elements of a no longer small-town community."[21]

Between 1929 and 1931, before KGIR affiliated with NBC and began receiving nationally syndicated programs, the station relied upon local talent whose performances supplemented the phonograph records and occasional transcriptions that formed the bulk of programming. In his quest to make listeners tune in, Craney and his small staff created fanciful promotions to multiply advertising revenues, increased coverage of local events, and groped toward a determination of listeners' pleasures. Craney's unfamiliarity with Butte led to some gaffes. A few months after opening, the station began a request hour. One night when Craney was hosting the program, his salesman Leo McMullen came in and asked what he was doing. Craney replied, "We're having request hour." "Request hour, hell," replied McMullen, "you're advertising every whore in Butte." "Gladys at 2 Upper Terrace" and "Dorothy at 8 Lower Terrace" had quickly discovered the commercial benefits of local broadcasting.[22]

For the most part KGIR drew upon reputable talent. Listeners delighted in local celebrities such as Howard Melaney, the "singing fireman" of the Northern Pacific Railway. In May 1929 KGIR observed National Music Week with a special choral broadcast of eighty-five Butte mothers and daughters. The Butte Male Chorus was another popular attraction. Originally, the chorus had sung on street corners, in fraternal clubs, and for the aged and ill. Now all of Butte could hear the harmonizing of these Welsh and Cornish miners. Even when he was playing phonograph records, Craney sought to engage the various ethnic listeners of the city. In July 1929 he featured a collection of records imported from China. The program was not expected to be "exactly enjoyable to American radio fans," but he hoped it would be educational to them and enticing to Butte's Chinese residents.[23]

The presentation of local talent became more regularized during the 1930s, when Symons Department Store sponsored an amateur hour. Ray Schilling, advertising manager for the store, decided to test the powers of radio. Symons scheduled a sale and advertised only on KGIR; nothing appeared in the newspapers. The response was overwhelming, and Schilling was converted. He and his brother then developed Butte's own amateur hour—a fad that swept the radio world in the mid-1930s. The show had other spinoffs. Art Chappelle played his accordion on the amateur hour, and shortly thereafter Craney approached Art's father, owner of Chappelle's Cleaning Works, to sponsor a fifteen-minute program of accordion music performed by his son. Art, who during high school had a band called the Whirlwinds and still moonlighted as a musician in addition to driving his father's delivery truck, happily obliged. Three times a week he stopped his truck at the KGIR studio, brought in his accordion, and performed a selection of polkas and waltzes. Often he played melodies popular with Butte's ethnic communities: an entire selection of Italian music or Irish, Polish, or Finnish songs. Art signed an occasional autograph, played requests, and was delighted when he dropped off someone's dry cleaning and they said, "I just heard you on the radio!"[24]

Butte radio fans did not always have their ear tuned to the Old World. According to Craney, Butte's favorite music was jazz, followed by old-time string band melodies such as those played by the Arkansas Travellers. The first wedding broadcast on Montana radio was that of William Harkins and Irene Shimin. The groom was leader of Harkins' Jazzadors, and the bride was pianist for the fourteen-member Butte band. Leo McMullen encouraged the couple to wed on the air as a promotion for their combo and for KGIR. Hundreds of congratulatory calls to the station confirmed the event's drawing power.[25]

KGIR's request hour exemplified fans' identification with the radio. More than any other program, it made listeners believe they had a personal connection to the station. Mrs. Henry Webking wrote, "The evening request program is the one most enjoyed in our home . . . our family and guests are quite thrilled as we sit at our radios in suspense and finally hear our request announced and played." George Hardesty compared the show to "sitting down to a cozy visit with unexpected friends, for it invariably brings familiar

names out of the ether. And more than names, it brings heart secrets, for do not the songs that impress us usually reflect our own
feelings." The request hour became part of adolescent culture, with
teens playing jokes on each other via the radio. Frank Carden recalled that a popular ruse was "to call in for 'I Love You Truly' and
use your name and the name of a person you were not too friendly
with which would really make you angry. You would try to figure out
who called in and get mad at them and it would not be that person
at all." Nellie Thompson attested to the show's popularity with everyone in her family, "from Grandma down to the small youngster."
Thompson admitted that she herself had requested a song and that
"it caused me to have a personal interest in that particular event. I
felt, when I heard my piece played, that after all, I have something
to do with the program."[26]

Beginning in 1929 Craney had appealed to NBC for "programs
of national importance" and sought affiliate status with the network.
He described the isolation of many Montana listeners who received
no station other than KGIR and whose newspapers reached them
only twenty-four to seventy-two hours after publication. NBC was
concentrated in the East. At the time of Craney's request it had
extended its service to only a few cities west of the Mississippi and
feared the unprofitability of a hookup in a small market like Montana. Craney persuaded Sen. Burton K. Wheeler to intercede, and
NBC, hoping to please an increasingly powerful politician, partially accommodated Craney. On November 28, 1931, KGIR affiliated
with NBC, although the network supplied only a partial roster of
programs to the station. Mayor Archie McTaggart lauded the event
in a radio address, stating that radio had removed the barriers of
time and space, and soon isolated farmers and the "legion of prospectors" who made Butte "the greatest mining city in the world"
would be able to enjoy "the world's outstanding artists and enter-
tainers, [and] all the world events that are making history today."[27]

Despite the new shows available through NBC, Craney continued
to solicit local talent sponsored by local advertisers and to balance
commercial broadcasting with community service. In the mid-1930s
KGIR aired "courtesy announcements" calling men back to work at
the St. Lawrence Mine, soliciting members for the Red Cross, and
advertising the annual policemen's ball, the Rocky Mountain Garden Club's flower show, the Knights of Columbus's carnival, and the
Miners' Union Auxiliary's card party, among many other events.
Police Chief Walter I. Shay got on the radio in 1935 to remind
motorists of the dangers of "motor madness." Shay also took the

opportunity to announce that social and financial standing would have no bearing on the dispensation of traffic tickets and that even lifelong friendship with the mayor would not get a ticket fixed.[28]

■ ■ ■

Although hundreds of Butte residents performed on KGIR, thousands participated in station-sponsored contests or wrote unsolicited letters. In 1930 Craney began conducting listeners' surveys to determine the average number of hours a day each radio receiver was turned on (in 1930 ten hours, in 1937 nine-and-a-half); how many hours it was tuned to KGIR (in 1930 seven hours, in 1937 eight-and-a-half); which programs were favorites and why; and what suggestions for new programs and new sponsors listeners might have. The responses that have been preserved reveal a wealth of detail about the likes and dislikes of Butte's radio audience, and the role that radio played in the lives of men and women during the darkest days of the Great Depression.[29]

Through polls and the success of a few new programs, broadcasters and advertisers across the country discovered that depression audiences wanted lighter fare than classical music and Department of Agriculture reports. Advertising agencies, who were producing most shows by the 1930s, experimented with transposing to radio many of the genres already present in popular literature—westerns, detective stories, and serialized melodramas—as well as developing fresh formats such as the amateur hour and quiz shows. The collapse of vaudeville in the early 1930s sent comedians and actors scurrying to radio studios. A relaxation of movie studios' strictures against their stars "cheapening" themselves by appearing on radio also permitted well-known screen stars to perform in radio dramas, creating a larger pool of dramatic talent.[30]

KGIR listener polls throughout the 1930s testified to the popularity of these new programs in Butte. Jack Benny, Al Pearce and His Gang, Ma Perkins, Ed Wynn, Pepper Young, Seth Parker, and Dr. I.Q. were perennial favorites. Radio—and KGIR was no exception—organized its programming around the sexual divisions of work and leisure. Daytime broadcasts were often directed at women, who tuned in during their household chores. Evening programs in the 1930s increasingly catered to the family audience, especially in the early evening before children's bedtime. Special news and sporting events sought to attract male listeners.[31]

In 1929 the *Montana Standard* and KGIR began a series of jointly sponsored special events that tied the novelty of radio to the traditional pleasures of male street life. In February KGIR began airing two evening news bulletins provided by the *Standard*, "prizefights, markets and all the indiscriminate events which make up the day's news in Butte and throughout the world." Prizefighting provided some of the most dramatic broadcast events of 1929. In May the station initiated a series of reenactments of famous fights of the past dating from the Sullivan-Corbett match of 1892 to the Dempsey-Willard fight of 1919. In a display that demonstrated Butte's relish of its new technology and testified to the popularity of boxing, the *Montana Standard* and KGIR teamed up to provide the widest coverage possible of the Stribling-Sharkey heavyweight elimination fight in Miami. Two telegraphic news services wired the *Standard* a blow-by-blow account, which was read directly from the news editorial offices over the radio. At the same time the fight was "megaphoned" to a crowd gathered in front of the *Standard* building. Bill McKernan recalled similar evenings when "there'd be a big crowd of guys there listening to the fights. . . . They'd be getting drunk and raising hell. There'd be a few fights. She was wild."[32]

On the other hand, programs aimed toward women assumed that they were at home and were homemakers. Advertising specially targeted women. In the days of commercial timidity, advertisers severely limited commercials during evening family time but decided that busy housewives, tuning in during the day, might find "a self-interested but tactful informational talk by an advertiser . . . a real service." In 1937 a list of prizes offered in a KGIR contest bore witness to the management's awareness of the domestic audience. Of eight trinkets offered, six were household items, such as kitchen skewers and tablecloths. The vest-pocket dictionary and radio map were presumably designated for the fewer number of male respondents.[33]

By the 1930s radio had become part of many women's daily lives, a companion that did more than lift the blues of the depression. Women's letters to the station reinforced managers' and advertising agencies' assessment of the female audience. Mrs. George McCoy wrote that the comedy of an early morning show, "The Gazooks," along with three cups of coffee, "make it possible to face the horrors of the new day with a smile." Nellie Sacry chronicled a day "beginning with the Gazooks—who help us get up better natured for you can't be grumpy when someone makes you laugh." Her eight-year-old son waited at the door with his coat on to dash out to school as soon as "Cecil and Sally" was over, and the "Music Box" accompanied dinner. Women appreciated the company that the radio provided while they were cooking and sewing. Mrs. Fred Everinghaus thanked the station for its fashion updates, because her family could no longer afford a newspaper and she liked to know about "the new ideas and styles for the up to the minute spring lady." Mrs. George Hardesty praised the sweet music that calmed her frayed nerves after a day of housework and made her "a better me, to meet my husband and family."[34]

The most controversial segment of radio programming oriented toward women during the 1930s were soap operas. Frank and Anne Hummert, members of a Chicago advertising agency, created a factory for the production of soap operas. They sketched out story lines and then supervised the work of armies of anonymous writers who fleshed out the episodes. The team created dozens of serials and by 1936 was churning out more than one hundred scripts a week for more than thirty sponsors. "Washboard weepers" had their detractors. Media critic John Crosby accused them of turning a generation of housewives into neurotics. Dr. Louis Berg, a psychiatrist, was the soaps' harshest censurer, claiming that the serials pandered to those who "lick their lips at the salacious scandals of the *crime passionnel.*" It was true that the serials rarely portrayed the typical lives of American housewives. Amnesia and paralysis, choosing among several wealthy suitors, or being accused of stealing an Egyptian mummy were hardly everyday problems for most. But the soaps were enormously appealing, and during their reign they dominated air time from 10 A.M. to 5 P.M. Their defenders believed that serials enlivened a housewife's day or made her problems—especially during the depression—seem not quite so bad. Two University of Chicago analysts claimed the soaps could be interpreted as morality plays, easily digested lessons in good and evil.[35]

A national study discovered that, despite the far-fetched story lines, women found the serials useful sources of information on interpersonal relationships, including the "dos and don'ts" of dating, marriage, and child-rearing. They saw in the characters reflections of people in their own families or put themselves in analogous situations and hoped to achieve happy endings. One young woman who followed a soap opera argument between a jealous boy and his girlfriend observed, "That is just like my boy friend . . . listening to the stories like that makes me know how other girls act and listening to the way the girl argued I know how to tell my boyfriend where he can get off at." A Butte woman echoed her remarks, writing to KGIR that her favorite program was the serial "One Man's Family" because "I have a younger brother like Jack and I have grown to understand his ways listening to Jack and Claudia talk. . . . I enjoy their family spats and arguments; they are so natural." "It gives us an insite of family life that many of us never had before" wrote another woman of the same program. And Mrs. Arthur Matteson concluded, "It is a thirty-minute picture of American life that might as well have been taken in Butte."[36]

Although KGIR may have reinforced sexual divisions of leisure that already existed in Butte, it also sought to further the work of the civic organizations that hoped to provide more family recreation in the city. In that process women who had involved themselves in public work gave new meaning to the term *municipal housekeeping.* Craney solicited local groups to stage their own shows, providing them with a far greater audience than attended most club meetings. The Marian White Arts and Crafts Club proudly noted that "our radio station" wanted programs from the club's various departments and promptly responded with short talks three times a week. In the fall of 1929 KGIR broadcast the Rotana Club's Montana products dinner from the Masonic Temple, a gala evening celebrating Montana-grown products and featuring speeches and music. The Camp Fire Girls and the Rocky Mountain Garden Club were only two of the many other female clubs who accepted Craney's invitation to initiate programs.[37]

■ ■ ■

Historians of radio have noted how directly and personally Americans responded to the new medium. Listeners welcomed broadcasters into the family circle. Through their letters to stations, they created a democratic dialogue of praise, criticism, and suggestion in which they conveyed a sense of themselves as direct participants in the broadcast experience. Stations and the networks encouraged fans to correspond with them. Before pollsters developed sophisticated canvassing techniques, audience mail was the only way that stations could know how far and how well their signal was received, who was listening, and how they responded to programming. In the early 1930s more than two-thirds of all NBC programs explicitly requested audiences to write back to them—"to keep those cards and letters coming in"—and the volume of mail was phenomenal. In 1926 NBC received 383,000 communications; in 1929, one million; and in 1931, seven million. CBS claimed it received more than twelve million pieces of mail in 1931.[38]

During the 1930s much of the mail to stations was in response to free offers of prizes in exchange for a cereal box top or some other evidence of the purchase of a sponsor's product. Pictures of

Little Orphan Annie, magnet rings, slide whistles, and Tom Mix decoder rings kept the mail bags of America full during the depression. The box-top craze so overwhelmed programs that Montana senator Burton K. Wheeler declared with disgust that the air had become a pawnshop. During the Christmas season of 1937, KGIR offered a free prize for every letter to Santa Claus it received. For a seasonal program, selected letters were read on the air, interspersed with chatter between Santa and his helpers. After two such shows, the station had received three thousand letters and exhausted its grab bag. Hoping to slow the flow, it asked that further letters include a sales receipt from a station advertiser. Three thousand more letters poured in.[39]

Broadcasters' invitations to the radio audience encouraged a letter-writing habit that ranged from participating in contests to conveying intimate thoughts and opinions to the president of the United States. Craney was no fan of Franklin Roosevelt, nonetheless, he acknowledged FDR's importance to the development of radio: "He took the front page off the newspapers and put it on radio." At times the largest volume of mail KGIR received was in response to programs sponsored by the Farmers' Union, which discussed New Deal legislation and urged people to write to President Roosevelt.[40]

KGIR's tally of mail in the mid-1930s recorded the mushrooming of listener correspondence. The station received 5,770 letters in 1934 and 23,065 in 1938. Butte women outnumbered men two to one as correspondents, paralleling national trends in which women outdistanced men who wrote radio fan mail. National studies also determined that lower-income people and those with little education wrote the most letters to radio stations, stars, and advertisers. The small number of letters to KGIR that were saved, 165 of them from 1933 and 1935, tends to support that claim. Nevertheless, Butte was a working-class community, and it is natural that the majority of letters to KGIR would have come from working-class households. Of the 15,322 men employed in Butte in 1930, 62 percent were engaged either in mining or manufacturing in contrast to the 10 percent employed as professionals or in clerical positions. Of those whose occupations could be determined, miners made up 31 percent of the adult males who wrote the letters preserved in KGIR's files. Only one of the remaining adult male writers was in management. A few women married to professionals, managers, and business owners also sent their opinions to the station. However, 80 percent of the adult women writers were either wedded to working-class men or were themselves wage-earners. KGIR's mail bags also supported a CBS study that concluded that low-income families listened more often to the radio than did middle- and upper-income families who had a higher rate of radio ownership but also had the money to spend on other forms of entertainment.[41]

National studies estimated that the majority of letter-writers responded to contests. But KGIR correspondents sent as many unsolicited letters and replies to surveys that did not promise any material reward as they did to prize offers. During nine months in 1934, the station received 2,121 survey responses compared to 2,071 responses to offers. In 1935 the number of letters seeking prizes was only seventy-six more than the 6,253 other letters received. KGIR listeners clearly liked to tell the management what was on their minds.[42]

The letters Craney preserved date from station anniversaries in 1933 and 1935 when he asked listeners to explain why they liked their favorite programs and offer suggestions for new shows and appropriate sponsors. The responses offered far more than programming suggestions. Gratuitous advice, pungent criticism, and heartfelt best wishes accompanied both thoughtful and absurd ideas. Some wrote to say that KGIR was the "only half-way decent program on the air," others to warn that it was playing too much jazz and should "crowd the trash off the air." Some fans signed off playfully, like Helen and Virginia Mae Howland, who closed with "Jello-fully yours." George Hardesty, a carpenter, eloquently conveyed the fondness that many listeners felt for their radios and KGIR. Writing in 1933, Hardesty described his radio as a powerful spur to the imagination and spoke of the relief it delivered during the psychologically bleak days of the 1930s:

> There was a time when I saw a Movie twice a week, but not in these slim times. And with my radio, I really can't say that I mind so much. Any evening there are shows come to me over KGIR, but Wednesday evening when Sherlock Holmes unravels his mysteries, I am positive I don't miss my shows. I can see the two old gentlemen, as if they were in my room, poreing over their G. Washington Coffee [the show's sponsor]. Certainly I am entirely unaware of a depression when one of these life and death mysteries is on, and honestly, anything that can make me do that is worth a lot. Thats one of the reasons I like it, perhaps the main one.[43]

All over the country, radio fans attested to the cheering effects of comedy and drama programs during the depression, and the

Butte audience was no exception. The character that elicited far and away the most responses from KGIR listeners was Ed Wynn's "Fire Chief," sponsored by Texaco. Fans wrote, "He will cure the worst case of the Blues and even make you forget the Depression," "Ed sure keeps the entire radio audience in an uproar from start to finish, which is just what is needed by all of us during these trying times," and, "It is humorous and produces a *'good laugh'* which I consider necessary to offset the serious problems of this strenuous life of ours." Wynn's show also provoked some poignant compositions. Young Harry Lonner sent in this dispatch:

> A dance orchestra is on the air. Dad is reading the newspaper. Ma is busy with some sewing or other household task. Sis and I are doing schoolwork. Suddenly, comes the shrill scream of a siren! The clang of bells! Ed Wynn is on the air! Dad lets the newspaper drop in his lap, Ma comes into the parlor and sits close to the radio; and Sis and I stop our schoolwork . . . the fun now starts. Dad, Sis and I grin and chuckle after every joke, but Ma laughs till her sides ache. This is the one big reason why I like the Texaco Program. For fifteen minutes Dad forgets about his job, Ma quits worrying about how she is going to pay the bills, and I am happy to see them happy. Old Man Depression is forgotten and Happiness is King.[44]

In fact, it seemed that the loss of a radio, more than any other deprivation, made children feel the impact of the depression. In 1938 the Princeton Radio Research Project examined data collected in 1935 on the effect of unemployment on a father's authority. Just as building a radio in the 1920s was an emblem of masculinity, so was keeping one in the 1930s. A father who had to sell the family radio lost stature in the eyes of his children and increased his own feelings of inadequacy. As one man said, "Whenever the children started crying because there was no radio in the house I felt bad as hell to think that I had to sell the one thing that was giving them so much pleasure."[45]

For the unemployed in Butte, as in other parts of the country, radio became the chief source of entertainment and a vital link to the outside world. Time and again, writers to KGIR expressed gratitude that they had been able to buy their radios during good times, because now they were their only source of pleasure and news. Using empathy and imagination, listeners transported themselves, however briefly, from their woeful surroundings. The travails of Little Orphan Annie made "our troubles so small compared to our more unfortunate fellow beings." The radio compensated those not able to travel during the vacation season—even though unemployment guaranteed that "most of us are having quite a long vacation"—by taking them to the Mountains of the Moon or the jungles of Malaysia and Africa. And the radio was egalitarian. As Ted Wilson, a clerk at Southside Hardware, remarked, "It is a A-one entertainment equally alluring for the rich or poor."[46]

Many radio fans took programs far more seriously and invested them with more importance than advertisers or writers ever imagined. They accepted radio almost uncritically, as a wise seer who provided advice, pleasure, and testimonials for reliable products. Audiences wrote amazingly innocent and intimate letters to fictional characters and national corporations. Mrs. J. W. Larson, a miner's wife, lauded a children's program sponsored by General Mills because Skippy taught

> the boys and girls a healthful, clean and honest living. . . . Personaly, Skippy's program has helped me a great deal. My little girl is four years old, she can't tell time yet, but she never lets me forget Skippy. Skippy has taught her to brush her own hair and not to forget to clean her theeth and fingernails. Before Skippy was on the air I couldn't get her to eat any cereal, but now I have no trouble. She don't get Wheaties very often now, as her father isn't working. But she eats her oatmeal every morning. She had Wheaties every morning when her Dad was working.[47]

Other listeners also commented on the positive effects they hoped that radio would have on youngsters. Ray Manning complimented Sherlock Holmes episodes for not instilling "in the youth of today any pernicious ideas." Several people praised a program on hunting and fishing sponsored by the Butte Anglers Club. Fred Dorhofer, the son of a teamster, wrote that he and his brother, aged thirteen and fifteen, always tuned in before going to their Scout meeting. Perhaps they absorbed the messages that Eva Carlson felt the program conveyed: "fair play and sportsmanship, . . . the preservation of game and fish," and "comradeship between fathers and sons."[48]

Craney's calls during the 1930s for new programs and sponsors elicited a wide variety of suggestions and documented the energy and thought that many listeners put into "their station." A high school boy, Robert Spiegel, envisioned a group of college boys from the School of Mines who would "pull jokes, sing campus songs and really make it a jolly program." Spiegel, who signed himself "a real radio fan," thought the athletic department of the Montana Hardware store would be an appropriate sponsor, and he even coined a slogan, "Let your boy be comfortable and safe in Montana Hardware equipment." Mrs. C. N. Bucher, convinced that the American people were rapidly becoming "dentally conscious," advised a weekly one-hour program that would mix musical selections, household hints, and dental topics. Mrs. Bucher was—not coincidentally—the wife of a dentist.[49]

More than one person thought a show relating tales of Butte and Montana history would be entertaining. Mrs. T. H. Wilkinson suggested having pioneers relate their experiences of settling the area or perhaps retelling some surprising tales of hunting and fishing, such as that of "the wily coyote who unable to catch a rabbit because it could run as long as he, set his mate well out on the route to help him and run it in relays." After all, she concluded, "Butte is a good old town and just full of good stories to tell." H. C. Howard proposed a different way of exploring Montana, a series of "short enthusiastic talks" recounting the "delights of motoring in Montana and describing each week some historical or scenic spot that is little known in the state and describing how it is reached, the condition of the roads to this spot and various points of interest along the route." The show could be accompanied by popular music and paid for by service stations, hotels, auto camps, or businesses patronized by tourists.[50]

Homemakers recommended programs that would interest them during the day: a morning exercise routine, advice to young housekeepers on arranging furniture, reports on new clothing styles, and a menu contest of meals "that the average housewife could afford to serve." From Adah Daugherty, wife of a salesman, came a letter that could have gotten her a job in any advertising agency. After noting that the standard radio program consisted of music with a few announcements of the show's sponsor, she stated it was

well and good . . . but, there are things dear to the heart of every woman, and dearest of these is her personal appearance. If she could go to the radio and tune in on a beauty talk that would deal with any phase of a woman's face, hair, figure, hands, and feet, I dare say that only the door bell could draw her away. These things she might be able to get in the advertisements in the current magazines, or an occasional article, but the busy woman has very little time for reading. There is a psychological difference between reading the printed word, and hearing the same spoken. The

latter catches the instant attention and is retained longer. With
this given by some firm or firms in Butte, and the talk read by a
woman, it would prove most effective.

Daugherty continued with a discussion of possible sponsors and a
reflection on the future of advertising, "Radio is the new means of
advertising, and is here to stay. More and more firms are going to
adopt clever methods of advertising, and owing to the depression,
more vigorous methods." She acknowledged that the intrinsic worth
of the product was immaterial and that by appealing to women's van-
ity a manufacturer could successfully peddle anything: "Even though
two different face creams would do the same work, yet the one that
is explained, and extolled to the woman, is the one which she will buy.
Woman is eternally looking for the fountain of youth . . . she will be
a susceptible listener to a program on beauty talks, and the firm to
which she is listening will be the one to gain." In words reminiscent
of the personal testimony advertisements popular in magazines of the
time, she concluded, "I am a woman. I know."[51]

Daugherty was unusual in analyzing the advertising industry's
relationship to radio with such perspicacity. The overwhelming
majority of listeners who wrote to the station and mentioned sponsors conveyed a naive gratitude that corporations were providing
them with so many hours of delight. Some avowed they enjoyed the
advertising as much as the programming. Mrs. Henry Webking
claimed that "the K.G.I.R. announcer tells us so much about the firm
and its products during the course of the program, and in so few
well chosen words, that we really enjoy the advertising and absorb
it as much as we do the request numbers." Fans appeared to feel
that the least they could do to demonstrate their appreciation was
to buy the sponsor's product. Margaret Carolus, who enjoyed the
Jack Benny program paid for by Jello, found the advertising so com-
pelling "that it has encouraged me to eat and like Jello—though I
had never cared for it before." Clarence Roper testified that smoking Edgeworth tobacco gave him as much of a thrill as the music
on the Edgeworth program. Ruth O'Brien begged KGIR to "keep
Orphan Annie on the radio for a little ten-year-old like me" and
promised "I'll drink lots and lots of Ovaltine."[52]

Such promises and testimonials suggest the power advertisers
exerted on the radio audience. Craney's device for generating new
ideas may have provided the kernels for only a few marketable programs, but it appeared to reap a harvest of radio fans joining in their
own seduction by consumer culture. Radio sales days and contests,

in which the prize was determined by sales receipts, linked chance and consumption to the pleasures of popular culture. In 1930 the station held a contest with the prize of a Baby Austin automobile. Every dollar a customer spent at a KGIR advertiser was matched with a coupon that was good for a ride in the chauffeur-driven car. The coupons were collected, and KGIR gave away the automobile one evening at the Winter Garden ballroom. The ballroom manager, assisted by a dancer from the floor, selected the winning ticket. Radio grafted onto Butte's already flourishing field of commercial amusements, and lotterylike games meshed with the mining town psychology of risk and profit-seeking.[53]

The lure of winning a prize coaxed listeners into experimenting with the language of sales, extolling the virtues of any and all products. The impetus of a contest may have led listeners to embellish their appreciation of certain products, but the internal structure of their letters, the way in which writers linked product use to their daily lives, and the effort with which men, women, and children sat down to write lengthy missives—often much longer than that required or desired by contest rules—suggest respondents' earnestness. Radio made "thousands of people feel free to sit down and write a friendly and personal letter to a large corporation." In effect, radio "humanized" a corporate business world that had grown increasingly impersonal and detached from daily life. In turn, corporations exploited this feeling by developing more and more personalized advertisements, eventually personifying products such as Lucky Strike cigarettes, "a better friend than others."[54]

Still, the texts of Butte's letter-writing radio fans could also demonstrate the facility with which they learned to master the manipulative language of the advertising industry. What either interpretation indicates is that they were not critical of the campaign that advertisers used to spread the ethic of mass consumerism. On the contrary, as with Adah Daugherty, even when a fan understood the mechanics of what advertisers were trying to do, her response was not outrage but suggestions for how to do it better. Quick studies, Butte listeners learned the lessons of radio and turned them to their own purposes. In 1932 WAAIME set out "Seth Parker" barrels in local stores to garner donations for needy children. In 1933 members of the Marian White Arts and Crafts Club dramatized a radio show as their Christmas program. A few years later Butte High School students staged a "clever burlesque on the currently famous Major Bowes Amateur Hour" during a school assembly and gave a repeat performance in the evening for the public.[55]

■ ■ ■

When the Lynds first observed the popularity of radio in Middletown in the early 1920s and commented upon the ingenuity it sparked in some people, they also hypothesized that radio, along with national advertising and syndicated newspapers, would standardize much of Middletown's culture. They expressed the beliefs of many contemporary observers. When they returned ten years later, they believed their hypothesis proven. The local radio station, affiliated with a national network, had bound listeners to national standards of programming. Dorothy Johnson, too, believed homogenization had occurred: Everyone "could listen to the same demagogues, howl at the same comedians, make a fad of the new slang." Radio made everyone "sophisticated, part of the great outside world." It even changed the way that people responded to their environment, "Listeners became addicts, so accustomed to having sounds of any old kind coming into the house that they were nervous when it was quiet. . . . For better or worse, the quiet, the isolation, the parochialism was gone." Yet, the Lynds also found that radio had worked as a local community-builder, forging links between the residents of an "increasingly large and diverse city."[56]

Both processes took place in Butte. KGIR brought forces of homogenization to the mining city, but throughout the 1930s the station continued to air programs that spotlighted local talent, extolled the unique virtues of the Montana landscape, and caused listeners to feel an allegiance to KGIR, not only gratitude to national sponsors. As much as fans appreciated syndicated shows, they loved listening to themselves and their neighbors more. Jim Harmon declared that "the very stuff of radio was imagination," and KGIR permitted citizens to let their imaginations run riot. Symons's amateur hour nourished the dreams of local performers; a gala broadcast of the program packed the Broadway Theater. Neighbors guessed at the hidden messages conveyed by songs on the request hour. Families gathered around the radio to hear their sons and daughters sing, play in jazz bands, and recite poetry. Members of different ethnic communities waited for special holiday programs that featured their musical heritage. Private delights, when broadcast, assumed the luster of public importance.[57]

The effect that radio had on listeners is reflected in the pleasurable memories that people associate with KGIR. Mona Daly "vividly" recalled, many years later, the afternoon in the 1930s on which her voice teacher at the Webster school chose her and a classmate to go to the KGIR studio and sing a duet of "Juanita"—"a definite thrill." Fifty years after he first heard the melodies, Jacob Jovick could name eighty-one songs that KGIR played on the request hour, and thirty-one different programs to which he listened, and still apologize because "there were others I don't recall."[58]

In 1937 Craney inaugurated a community-based program aimed at shortening Montana's divisive distances and reaching an audience greater than Butte. "Let's Get Acquainted" was a series of broadcasts from the surrounding areas that featured local bands, choruses, musicians, and storytellers. One of the first programs came from the Big Hole Basin, southwest of Butte and still accessible only by dirt roads, where a group tried to broadcast the Old Settlers' Picnic. Technical difficulties squashed their first attempt, but they finally succeeded in allowing the KGIR audience to hear an old-time fiddler, the ladies' quartet, and interviews with pioneer ranchers.[59]

Ed Craney, his small staff, and the KGIR audience composed a score that harmonized strains of local, regional, and national culture. Craney had hoped that radio would make Montanans "realize that there was more in Montana than the little town that they lived in." To gain that end, he invited Montanans' participation in his enterprise. May Gates of Opportunity was one of twenty-four would-be news editors who volunteered their services to pass on the tidings of their communities to the KGIR audience. KGIR's listeners thus had access not only to national news, New York opera, and southern string band music but also to "all the news and gossip that is told each evening at the Opportunity store"—and in stores in Butte, Melrose, Rocker, Deer Lodge, Twin Bridges, and a handful of other communities in KGIR's broadcast radius. KGIR introduced its audience to nationally standardized programs that some analysts feared—and others hoped—would erase the cultural diversity of America. The station's commitment to airing the voices of its own region, however, guaranteed a medley of cultural expression. In its first decade KGIR became a source of delight, education, and emotional relief to thousands weathering the Great Depression, and May Gates spoke for many when she exclaimed, "What a wonderful invention the radio has been."[60]

KGIR's success was due in part to the fact that, as imaginative as radio technology was, KGIR programming built upon established patterns of Butte's leisure. Radio reinforced and accelerated allegiances to commercial amusements by wedding pleasure to consumption. It accepted gendered divisions of leisure and constructed advertising as well as entertainment around the broadest cultural norms of men as breadwinners and women as housewives. Yet radio was not completely like the plethora of other commercial pastimes in Butte—movies, dance halls, speakeasies, nightclubs, and gambling arcades. Men, women, and children all enjoyed the radio, and in the comfort of their own homes or those of their neighbors. No one in the city claimed that radio threatened the moral well-being of the populace. In fact, listeners praised its wholesomeness, a quality that became a theme of recreation in the mining city in the 1930s. FDR heralded the New Deal over KGIR's airwaves. When the New Deal arrived in Butte, it brought with it jobs, loans, roads, and sidewalks. Accompanying them came a new program of public recreation and arts, the first systematic challenge to Butte's world of cheap amusements.

NOTES

1. Margaret Micky and Willie to Ed Craney, 1 February 1929, Edmund B. Craney Papers (hereafter cited as EBC Papers), box 2, file 6, MHSA.

2. Douglas, *Inventing American Broadcasting*, 305–7, 321; Frost, "Radio Dreams That Can Come True," 18.

3. Marquis discusses the periodization of the radio industry in "Written on the Wind." Cohen also discusses the decline of local control over broadcasting in "Encountering Mass Culture at the Grassroots," and *Making a New Deal*, 141–43, 327–28. McChesney analyzes the triumph of commercial radio in *Telecommunications, Mass Media, and Democracy*, as does Smulyan, in *Selling Radio*.

4. Fiftieth Anniversary Program, KGIR-KXLF, tape recordings in possession of Scott Steen. My thanks to Scott Steen for sharing tapes of KGIR programs with me.

5. Tyler, ed., *Television and Radio*, 9; Barnouw, *Tower in Babel*, 71; Lynd and Lynd, *Middletown*, 269; Michael Popovich, interview by Mary Murphy, Butte, 24 August 1988.

6. On the origins of the Radio Boys and Radio Girls' series, see Commire, *Something about the Author*, vol. 1; and Johnson, comp. and ed., *Stratemeyer Pseudonyms*. Some of the titles in the series include *The Radio Boys as Soldiers of Fortune*, *The Radio Boys with the Iceberg Patrol*, *The Radio Boys in Gold Valley*, *The Radio Girls on Station Island*, and *The Radio Girls at Forest Lodge; or, The Strange Hut in the Swamp*.

7. O'Brien, "It's Great to Be a Radio Maniac," 16; Winfred Slauson, interview by Mary Murphy, Butte, 12 August 1988; Vermilya, "QRX for a New O.W.," 31. My thanks to Dale Martin, Sr., for sending me material from his *QST* collection. Covert discusses gender attitudes toward radio technology in "'We May Hear Too Much'"; also see Douglas, *Inventing American Broadcasting*, 308.

8. On the hunger to hear distant voices, see Douglas, *Inventing American Broadcasting*, 301; Smulyan, "The Rise of the Radio Network System," 105–7; McMeans, "The Great Audience Invisible," 412, 414; and Slauson interview. Johnson, "The Small-Town World before Radio," 52; *Saturday Evening Post*, 18 December 1926, 118; Morgan, "Who Forgot Radio?" 117.

9. Richards, "History of Radio Broadcasting in Montana," 16, 24–25, 29, 40, 52–58, 66, 73, 77.

10. Barnouw, *Tower in Babel*, 128–31, 158, 238; Shaw, *The Jazz Age*, 127. Young is quoted in Marchand, *Advertising the American Dream*, 90.

11. Marchand, *Advertising the American Dream*, 107, 306, 116, 94; Barnouw, *Tower in Babel*, 239; Marquis, "Written on the Wind," 388; Schiller, *Mass Communications and American Empire*, 25.

12. *Montana Free Press*, 3 January 1929, 5; biographical sketch in description of EBC Papers, MHSA; Edmund B. Craney, telephone interview by Mary Murphy, 15 October 1988; Richards, "History of Radio Broadcasting in Montana," 87–88; Fiftieth Anniversary Program. With few exceptions, pioneer radio stations were owned by Westinghouse, newspapers, or radio manufacturers for the purpose of boosting equipment sales and generating publicity. They were not considered money-makers as such. See Barnouw, *Tower in Babel*, 114; Mitchell, *Cavalcade of Broadcasting*, 79.

13. Clipping, undated, EBC Papers, box 112, file 10, MHSA; *Montana Standard*, 5 January 1929, 1–2; Butte City Council Minutes (3 April 1929), 18:527, 553.

14. Richards, "History of Radio Broadcasting in Montana," 90; Fiftieth Anniversary Program.

15. Clipping, undated, EBC Papers, box 112, file 10, MHSA; Mr. and Mrs. Edward Flannigan to KGIR, 1 February 1929, EBC Papers, box 2, file 6, MHSA.

16. Clipping, *Montana Standard*, 3 March 1929, EBC Papers, box 112, file 10, MHSA; *Montana Standard*, 5 March 1929, 1, 9.

17. *Montana Standard*, 23 March 1929, 9, 6 March 1929, 5; U.S. Department of Commerce, Bureau of the Census, *Abstract of the Fifteenth Census*, 431–32; Research Committee on Social Trends, Inc., *Recent Social Trends*, 942; U.S. Department of Commerce, Bureau of the Census, *Fifteenth Census of the United States*, 6:80.

The average annual earnings for a fully employed metal miner in the United States in 1920 was $1,639; in 1925 it was $1,455; in 1930 it was $1,551; and in 1935 it was $1,239. In 1925 a family income of $1,500 to $1,800 was considered to provide "minimum health and decency plus modest recreation" for a family of five. An income of $2,000 to $2,400 provided an "American" standard of life. Earnings figures are in U.S. Department of Commerce, Bureau of the Census, *Historical Statistics of the United States*, 166. Standard of living is discussed in Levine, "Workers' Wives," 52.

18. Marchand, *Advertising the American Dream*, 91; *Saturday Evening Post*, 18 December 1926, 70; *McCall's*, August 1928, 45. Cohen discusses pat-

terns of installment buying among the middle and working classes in "Chicago Workers in the 1920s," 8. Olney notes that expenditures on radios and phonographs increased relative to other durable goods spending after 1921 in *Buy Now Pay Later,* 40.

19. *Presbyterian Reporter,* February 1930, 5; undated clipping, EBC Papers, box 112, file 10, MHSA.

20. At some point Craney did a special survey of what kinds of radios KGIR listeners had. The report showed an 84 percent response rate but was not dated. EBC Papers, box 121, file 3, MHSA. McMahon, ed., *Radio Collector's Guide,* 38, 53–54, 85, 133–34, 147–48, 171–72; Slauson interview. The seven companies that manufactured the majority of Butte radios were RCA, Majestic, Philco, Crosley, Victor, Temple, and Bremer Tully.

21. Craney interview; Lazarsfeld, *Radio and the Printed Page,* 103; Lynd and Lynd, *Middletown in Transition,* 265. Stern and Stern also discuss the neighborly role of local radio in "Neighboring."

22. *Montana Standard,* 11 March 1979, 17–18.

23. *Butte Daily Post,* 16 March 1929, EBC Papers, box 112, file 10, MHSA; *Montana Standard,* 10 May 1929, 1. On the Butte Male Chorus, see Edwards, "History of Musical Organizations in Butte," and script, 1932, EBC Papers, box 117, file 6, MHSA. The reference to Chinese records is in an unreferenced clipping, 1929, EBC Papers, box 112, file 10, MHSA.

24. On the amateur hour fad, see MacDonald, *Don't Touch That Dial,* 47–48; Ray Schilling, interview by Mary Murphy, Butte, 31 August 1988; and Art Chappelle, unrecorded interview by Mary Murphy, Butte, 29 July 1988. The Lynds observed that, for Middletown boys, forming a jazz band was seen as a relatively distinguished occupation and a possible avenue out of industrial work. See *Middletown,* 244.

25. *Montana Standard,* 7 April 1929; undated clippings, EBC Papers, box 112, file 10, MHSA; Irene Shimin Harkins, interviewer unidentified, tape recording, 1979, in possession of Scott Steen.

26. Mrs. Henry Webking to KGIR, n.d., EBC Papers, box 3, file 9, MHSA; George Hardesty to KGIR, 2 February 1935, EBC Papers, box 117, file 7, MHSA; Carden, "Come Wander Back with Me," 42; Nellie Thompson to KGIR, 1 February 1933, EBC Papers, box 3, file 9, MHSA.

27. E. B. Craney to Mr. McClelland (vice president, NBC), 6 April 1929, EBC Papers, box 2, file 7, MHSA; Fiftieth Anniversary Program; Archie McTaggart, text of radio address, 28 November 1931, EBC Papers, box 121, file 7, MHSA.

28. List of courtesy announcements, 1936–37, EBC Papers, box 122, file 8, MHSA; Police Chief Shay, text of radio address, 18 October 1935, EBC Papers, box 124, file 3, MHSA.

29. Listener Survey Reports, EBC Papers, box 116, file 4, box 3, file 9, and box 121, file 3, MHSA.

30. Wertheim, "Relieving Social Tensions"; MacDonald, *Don't Touch That Dial,* 27–29, 39, 42, 47, 51; Barnouw, *Tower in Babel,* 273.

31. Listener Survey Reports, EBC Papers, box 121, file 3, MHSA; Best, *Nickel and Dime Decade*, 63.

32. *Montana Standard*, 6 February 1929, 1; undated clippings, EBC Papers, box 112, file 10, MHSA; Bill McKernan, interview by Mary Murphy, 9 September 1988. By the 1930s, competition between newspapers and radio for advertising dollars had led to a national newspaper boycott of radio logs and a steady decline in coverage of radio developments. A survey of newspapers owned by the Anaconda Company corroborated Craney's claim that after 1930 coverage of KGIR dropped sharply, and the newspaper and the radio station launched no more joint ventures. On the rivalry between newspapers and radio, see MacDonald, *Don't Touch That Dial*, 282–86, and Barnouw, *Tower in Babel*, 207. Richards has surveyed the company-owned newspapers, see "History of Radio Broadcasting in Montana," 129.

33. Marchand, *Advertising the American Dream*, 93; "KGIR to Dear Listener" letter, 13 September 1927, EBC Papers, box 116, file 4, MHSA.

34. Mrs. George McCoy to KGIR, 2 February 1933, and Nellie Sacry to KGIR, 1 February 1933, EBC Papers, box 3, file 9, MHSA; Mrs. V. Marchiando to KGIR, n.d, and Helen T. Jensen to KGIR, 18 November 1937, EBC Papers, box 116, file 4, MHSA; Mrs. Fred Everinghaus to KGIR, 6 February 1933, and Mrs. George Hardesty to KGIR, n.d., EBC Papers, box 3, file 9, MHSA.

35. Harmon, *The Great Radio Heroes*, 165–76; Crosby, "Seven Deadly Sins of the Air," 76–77; MacDonald, *Don't Touch That Dial*, 248, 232–33; Meehan, "The 'Soaps' Fade," 13–16.

36. Lazarsfeld, *Radio and Printed Page*, 52–53; Virginia Anderson to KGIR, 31 January 1935, EBC Papers, box 117, file 7, MHSA; Mrs. Dan Friesz to KGIR, 30 January 1935, EBC Papers, box 117, file 9, MHSA; Mrs. Arthur Matteson to KGIR, 28 January 1935, EBC Papers, box 117, file 9, MHSA.

37. Minutes, 3 April 1930, and 17 April 1930, Marian White Arts and Crafts Club Records (hereafter cited as MWA&CC Records), BSBA; clippings, *Montana Standard*, 17 March 1929, 10 October 1929, EBC Papers, box 112, file 10, MHSA.

38. Marchand has an especially good discussion of the personal identification audiences made with the radio; see *Advertising the American Dream*, 354–58. Sussman, *Dear FDR*, 14. For another analysis of political letter writing see Hall et al., *Like a Family*, chap.6.

39. Harmon, *Great Radio Heroes*, 124–31; Barnouw, *Tower in Babel*, 243; "Santa Claus" report, EBC Papers, box 124, file 3, MHSA.

40. Sussman, *Culture as History*, 13, 16, 113; Craney interview; Richards, "History of Radio Broadcasting in Montana," 95–96.

41. KGIR Audience Mail Returns, 1933–38, EBC Papers, box 112, file 9, MHSA; Susman, *Dear FDR*, 143, 139; U.S. Department of Commerce, Bureau of the Census, *Fifteenth Census of the United States* 4:926–27. There are 165 listeners' letters in the KGIR collection from 1933 to 1935. I was

able to determine through the 1934 and 1936 Butte city directories the occupation of 111 correspondents or, in the case of married women and children, the occupations of their husbands or fathers. No directories were published in 1933 and 1935. Best, *Nickel and Dime Decade*, 63.

42. KGIR Audience Mail Returns, 1933–38, EBC Papers, box 112, file 9, MHSA. For other analyses of fan mail and the preferences of radio audiences, see Ollry and Smith, "An Index of 'Radio-Mindedness'"; Meyrowitz and Fiske, "The Relative Preference of Low Income Groups for Small Stations"; and Sayre, "Progress in Radio Fan-Mail Analysis."

43. Mrs. D. E. Strah to KGIR, 6 November 1937, EBC Papers, box 116, file 4, MHSA; B. E. Lyons to KGIR, 1 February 1933, EBC Papers, box 117, file 7, MHSA; Helen and Virginia Mae Howland to KGIR, n.d., EBC Papers, box 117, file 9, MHSA; George Hardesty to KGIR, 1933, EBC Papers, box 117, file 7, MHSA.

Hardesty's reference to the two old gentlemen poring over their G. Washington Coffee probably means that the show's sponsors employed a method of advertising called the interwoven commercial. In this format the product was introduced into the story line so that the message of the particular comestible's superiority reached listeners clearly but in a tasteful fashion. No doubt Sherlock Holmes and Doctor Watson were drinking George Washington Coffee while they pondered each week's mystery. See Marchand, *Advertising the American Dream*, 104–6.

44. MacDonald, *Don't Touch That Dial*, 113; Kathryn Combo to KGIR, n.d., Floyd Ball to KGIR, 1 February 1933, J. W. Macom to KGIR, 1 February 1933, and Harry Lonner to KGIR, n.d., all in EBC Papers, box 117, file 7, MHSA.

45. Holter, "Radio among the Unemployed."

46. Gertrude McCarthy to KGIR, n.d., EBC Papers, box 117, file 9, MHSA; Helen Anderson to KGIR, n.d., and Ted Wilson to KGIR, 1 February 1933, EBC Papers, box 117, file 7, MHSA.

47. Mrs. J. W. Larson to KGIR, 1 February 1933, EBC Papers, box 3, file 9, MHSA. Marquis in "Written on the Wind" (395) notes how difficult it was for listeners to distinguish between fact and fiction when it came to radio characters and commercials.

48. Ray Manning to KGIR, 1 February 1933, EBC Papers, box 117, file 7, MHSA; Fred E. Dorhofer to KGIR, n.d., and Eva Carlson to KGIR, 5 February 1933, EBC Papers, box 3, file 9, MHSA.

49. Robert Spiegel to KGIR, 1 February 1933, and Mrs. C. N. Bucher to KGIR, 3 February 1933, EBC Papers, box 3, file 9, MHSA.

50. Mrs. T. H. Wilkinson to KGIR, n.d., Mildred Nelson to KGIR, 2 February 1933, and H. C. Howard to KGIR, 2 February 1933, all in EBC Papers, box 3, file 9, MHSA.

51. Ada E. Green to KGIR, 1 February 1933, and Mrs. Bruce E. Dalton to KGIR, 1 February 1933, EBC Papers, box 3, file 9, MHSA; Mrs. A. R. Grenon to KGIR, 1 February 1932, EBC Papers, box 122, file 7, MHSA;

Adah Daugherty to KGIR, n.d., EBC Papers, box 3, file 9, MHSA.

52. Webking to KGIR, EBC Papers, box 3, file 9, MHSA; Margaret Carolus to KGIR, 4 February 1935, EBC Papers, box 117, file 9, MHSA; Clarence Roper to KGIR, n.d., and Ruth O'Brien to KGIR, 1 February 1933, EBC Papers, box 117, file 7, MHSA.

53. Miscellaneous memos, drafts of advertisements, EBC Papers, box 114, file 7, box 117, file 8, MHSA.

54. Marchand, *Advertising the American Dream*, 93, 356–58.

55. Minutes, 7 December 1932, Women's Auxiliary to the American Institute of Mining Engineers Records, Butte Chapter, BSBA; minutes, 21 December 1933, MWA&CC Records, BSBA; *The Mountaineer*, 1936, 96.

56. Lynd and Lynd, *Middletown*, 271; Johnson, "The Small-Town World before Radio," 53; Lynd and Lynd, *Middletown in Transition*, 263–65.

57. Harmon, *Great Radio Heroes*, 251.

58. Mona Daly to Mary Murphy, 3 August 1988, and Jacob Jovick to Mary Murphy, 7 August 1988, in possession of author.

59. Radio script, "Let's Get Acquainted," EBC Papers, box 121, file 2, MHSA.

60. Richards, "History of Radio Broadcasting in Montana," 105; announcement of program, September 1930, letters from would-be editors, and May Gates to KGIR, 10 October 1930, EBC Papers, box 114, file 8, MHSA.

7

Depression Blues and
New Deal Rhythms

*The New Deal might well include a provision that every boy
and girl has a right not only to life and liberty but to the
pursuit of wholesome leisure activities.*
—BASCOM JOHNSON AND PAUL KINSIE

We all belong to a leisure class.
—FEDERAL ART PROJECT SLOGAN

In 1938 Frank Stevens, director of the Montana Federal Art Project, invited Montana Sen. James E. Murray to an exhibition at the newly created Butte Art Center. After describing the
impressive attendance the center had enjoyed since opening,
Stevens reflected, "There has, of course, always been in Butte a deep
inherent feeling for fine things concealed beneath a vigorous exte-
rior." Indeed, Stevens had tapped widespread interest in art in the
mining city. Bodies as diverse as the Miners' Union, the Anaconda
Company, and the Junior League supported the center's work. Ex-
posure to these various patrons forged Stevens's analysis of art appreciation. Walking through the gallery one day, Stevens and his
assistant overhead a group of Junior Leaguers discussing painters
of the Italian Renaissance. Delighted to come upon such a conver-
sation, Stevens was nonetheless startled to hear one matron remark,
"I can make out some of these names, but how do you pronounce
the name of this son-of-a-bitch?" He later reflected, "You could hardly blame her; we went in and found it was Pollaiuolo."[1]

The New Deal created an opportunity for Butte to redesign the
contours of community leisure, culture, recreation, and entertainment. Economic hard times tested the city's wide-open, vice-ridden
amusements. Miners' high wages evaporated in the face of long
layoffs, forcing the curtailment of boisterous commercial entertainments. Voluntary associations faced declining memberships and

shrinking financial resources and had to cut back on programs designed to make Butte into a family town. During the New Deal, the federal government stepped into this vacuum with programs to encourage public recreation, employ artists and writers, and compile local history. Many hoped that the recreational and cultural face of Butte would be permanently changed by these projects, which some hoped would eventually be supported by local government. While the depression lingered, the New Deal approach was successful, but with the return of prosperity Butte made its choice. It did not opt for combined commercial, volunteer, and publicly funded recreation, but reverted to its past, resurrected established patterns of commercial entertainment and reliance upon voluntary associations, and abandoned nascent forms of publicly funded play.

■ ■ ■

The year 1929 was a banner one for Butte. The debut of KGIR seemed just one more indicator of expanding prosperity. Housing construction was up. The city made record improvements in street lighting and road building. Orders for new cars in January were 300 percent above those for the same period in 1928. The coffers of the Red Cross were reassuringly full. The city had a labor shortage despite the fact that the Anaconda Company's Mutual Labor Association had issued more than 3,200 new rustling cards since September 1928. Anaconda advertised for miners in the East and raised wages to lure men underground. In April 1929 the company announced another twenty-five cent raise, bringing the basic underground daily wage to $6, the highest ever paid in the Butte mines or in any other metal mine in the country. Copper output in ACM mines during the first six months of 1929 equaled the maximum for any other similar period. When the *Engineering and Mining Journal* looked back at the year, it concluded, "The mining industry of Montana in 1929 has been prosperous, labor has been satisfied with the high wages and good living conditions, and stockholders of the leading companies have received substantial dividends." The dark days of 1921, when the mines shut down for nine months, seemed long past and unlikely to return.[2]

Butte watched the stock market crash of October 1929 with the horrified fascination that gripped the rest of the country, but it had little immediate effect on the mining city. Nevertheless, shrewd observers could foretell that this crash signaled the biggest bust in Butte's long boom-and-bust history. As the depression strangled manufacturing and choked the expansion of utilities, the demand for copper—and its price—plummeted. In 1929 copper sold for eighteen cents a pound, eight cents in 1931, and five cents in 1933. Anaconda stock dropped precipitously—from a high of $175 per share on the New York Stock Exchange in 1929 to just $3 per share in 1932. Butte workers suffered tragic consequences. Employment in the mines shrank 84 percent between 1929 and 1932. In 1931 the company began to shut down entire mines. By December, wages had been reduced to their lowest level since 1921. On New Year's Eve of 1931 the Tramway Mine closed, leaving only four Anaconda mines operating. More than eight thousand men had been laid off since the depression began.[3]

As in other parts of the country, men and women delayed marriage, children, divorce, and major consumer purchases. In 1932 the Silver Bow clerk of the court issued only 390 marriage licenses, one hundred fewer than the year before and 150 fewer than in 1930. People could not afford to get married, but neither could they afford to divorce. It was not merely the legal costs that deterred couples from parting, but the facts that divorce often put women in a precarious financial situation and that men found it easier to get relief if they had a family to support. Whereas the court issued 247 divorce decrees in 1930, it recorded only 158 decrees in 1932. Another indication of reduced circumstances was the decline in the number of automobile licenses issued in the county. Even when they owned automobiles, many residents did not have the money to run them. Butte motorists purchased 12 percent fewer auto licenses in 1932 than they did in 1931.[4]

Men and women worked part-time when they could, scrounged odd jobs, and bartered goods and services to survive. Ann Pentilla's job as a bookkeeper was cut to three days a week. On the $9.50 she brought home, she supported her parents, sister, and uncle. Miners who retained jobs rotated two weeks on and two weeks off. The Anaconda Company was one of the first corporations in the country to institute rotating part-time labor for its regular employees as a way to distribute available work. Men flocked to the mines when word spread that they might be hiring. On the day the Badger State Mine reopened, three thousand men mobbed the employment office, some having arrived at 2:30 A.M. for the 8:00 A.M. call. Julia Harrington's family "were alright" during the depression because their employment was spread across the economy. Julia kept her job clerking at the hardware store, although her wages were slashed; one brother worked in the clerk of the court's office, and another worked two weeks on and two off in the mines. But her fiancé's family was hard-hit. With five miners in the family, only one had work. Mrs. McHugh "wasted" only egg shells and potato peelings because "she couldn't find any use for them."[5]

Many men reverted to earlier mining practices and headed into the surrounding mountains to look for gold. Indeed, for five years during the 1930s the School of Mines offered a well-attended course in placer mining. The depression also prompted the use of a novel reduction technique. Depression-era placer miners shoveled gravel into sluice boxes constructed with mercury-filled riffles in the box floor. As water pushed the gravel across the floor boards, the gold settled to the bottom, into the holes where it amalgamated with the mercury. Miners then cut a large baking potato in half, hollowed out the insides of both halves, put the gold-mercury combination inside, and used toothpicks to hold the potato together. Then, with the tuber placed in an oven at baking temperature, the mercury vaporized through the flesh of the potato. After a while, the potato was removed and its heart of gold reclaimed.[6]

Other unemployed people cut wood, made fence posts, or tried to raise vegetables. John Sconfienza recalled that small businesses, such as his family's bakery, were especially hard-hit. People tried baking their own bread rather than buying it. When the government began distributing flour, he started "bootlegging." Those who did not know how to bake brought him their flour allotment, and he made it into bread in exchange for some other good or service. Anita Watson had only unpleasant memories of the depression. She and her family lived near the streetcar route, and her sister-in-law would send her over to the streetcar stop to pick up cigarettes discarded by embarking passengers. "I was so embarrassed to do that. But I'd do anything for her just to keep her good-natured. One time there was a dime down there in the ice and I dug that out. . . . It was hard times for me in Butte. I never had a very good memory of it."[7]

The depression curtailed Butte's freewheeling night life. An anonymous worker on the WPA's Federal Writers' Project wrote that the dives where men once flocked to cash their paychecks, drink, and gamble were deserted except for the few who entered to "beg a drink." Vagrants took over the Silver City Club, shut down by the federal government for selling bootleg whiskey. The unemployed slept on the dance floor where not long ago "madly swirling feet played a hectic tune." Housewives who had bet on the greyhound races regretted their indulgences. Poverty short-circuited youth's frivolity. As a WPA writer put it, young men no longer "ran the gauntlet of the dance halls, drank red hot alcohol and made hopeful eyes at red lipped girls," and young girls who had "slaved all week for the pay check" no longer spent their weekends at the movies and dances. "With the advent of the depression these luxuries so seemingly a part of the young peoples life faded into obscurity." Lavina Richards recalled playing Chinese checkers with her friends night after night because no one had money for the movies.[8]

■ ■ ■

Between 1930 and 1932 Butte followed the pattern of other U.S. cities and the lead of President Herbert Hoover. The city marshaled the resources of private charity to meet the needs of the unemployed. Silver Bow County first felt the demand for extraordinary aid in the fall of 1930. Groups such as the Red Cross and the Associated Charities supplemented regular county welfare work that provided modest widows' pensions and supported the county hospital and tuberculosis sanitarium at Galen. By the fall of 1931 their resources were exhausted, however, and a new agency, the Silver Bow County Emergency Relief Association, was formed to minister to the increasing numbers of unemployed. In January the county's charitable organizations had assisted 628 people; by December 1931 the number requesting help had exploded to 5,894. That year, for the first time since its inception, the Joshers Club was unable to provide Christmas boxes to Butte's needy. In a telegram to the Anaconda Company managers, a coalition of Butte businessmen and politicians extended thanks to the company for its donations, noting that "many of our citizens including a very large number of modest means have gone to the limit of their resources to aid in . . . the relief of distress."[9]

The Emergency Relief Association coordinated a massive fundraising effort, collecting substantial pledges from mining companies and other businesses. Many of those with jobs subscribed 2 percent of their monthly salaries to the relief fund. As in the past, voluntary groups turned their best effort to community needs. In May 1932 the Elks produced a minstrel show at the Broadway Theater and handed over $1,152 to the Relief Association. No federal money appeared in the city until the fall of 1932, when the Relief Association applied for funds available under the Relief and Construction Act of 1932.[10]

The Relief Association was directed by a committee of businessmen, including an ACM lawyer. The company donated the salaries of relief directors and the clerical costs of administration. When Pierce Williams, a field representative for the Reconstruction Finance Corporation, visited Montana in early 1933 to establish a centralized auditing and disbursement system for federal money, he ran into difficulty in Butte. There "the Anaconda boys were all het up because they thought we had lost confidence in them." Williams found that the Anaconda Company was supplying nearly all the personnel for relief work in the city and "has been used to operating independently of the state except where it could drag the state along." Confronted by ACM power and organization, Williams left the Anaconda procedures intact except to insist that they comply with State Relief Commission regulations that allowed families to choose the grocery from which they would get their relief goods.[11]

The company had insisted that only certain grocers be allowed to disburse relief food, leading to charges of favoritism, discrimination, and cheating. Charles Hauswirth, who would be elected mayor of Butte in 1935, claimed in his muckracking broadside the *Eye Opener* that only two dozen of the more than three hundred groceries in Butte were distributing relief food. Hauswirth used the grocery issue to attack the company's control of relief: "What kind of a country is it," he queried, "when Uncle Sam puts out money for relief purposes and then we have a bunch of A.C.M. swivel chair artists dictate who shall get the business and who shall not." Capitalists, Hauswirth fumed, had "forced this condition upon us and now the representatives of the capitalists are taking government money and handing out beans and macaroni." And they handed them out grudgingly. Hanford Toppari's family was one of many who felt the sting of relief grocers. When Toppari's wife opened a pork roast he had been allotted, it was so rotten "it'd run you out of the house." Toppari took it back, and when he complained about its quality the grocer retorted, "Well, you people on relief are God-damned particular, aren't you?" Not until Toppari threatened to take the spoiled roast to the Health Department did the grocer give him fresh meat.[12]

As in many other communities across the country, Butte workers did not want direct aid. Appraisals of relief programs at various points during the depression revealed the strong preference for work relief over direct relief whenever possible. A leader of the Workers' Alliance in Butte wrote that "to the self-respecting working man or woman, work is not only desireable but necessary." Nonetheless, he continued, "this is not to say . . . that the people are foolish enough to believe that the dole is everything that the Reactionary Economic Royalists say it is. They realize that they have a right to adequate direct relief if no work is available." Leaders from all sectors of the Butte economy testified to the superiority of work relief. In an official appraisal report, the county commissioners argued that in Montana the pioneer heritage, which imbued Montanans with "an independent spirit," made it especially onerous to be dependent upon direct relief. Montanans, they contended, would rather have "the freedom of spending their check unmolested," a check that they had earned even if it was on a relief project. Work enabled a man—and, presumably, a woman—to feel that he was caring for his family, a feeling "entirely missing when he brings home an order for so much in groceries."[13]

Shortly after Franklin D. Roosevelt carried every western state in 1932—with the help of Montana politicians—New Deal money began flowing into the Treasure State. In May 1933 Congress authorized the Federal Emergency Relief Administration (FERA), which made grants of federal money to the states. That November the Civil Works Administration (CWA) initiated another work program to pull the country through the winter of 1933–34. Both agencies brought much needed work to Silver Bow County. The FERA and the CWA funded primarily construction projects that employed men at relatively unskilled labor. Both agencies, however, made efforts to hire women. While men dug storm and sanitary sewers, paved streets, and constructed playgrounds, women, in workshops jointly sponsored by the government and the Red Cross, stuffed mattresses and sewed clothes for people on relief.[14]

One special FERA women's program was a vocational camp located at Castle Rock, south of Butte. Unemployed women between the ages of sixteen and thirty-five were eligible for the eight-week training program. The project combined the attributes of summer camp with job training in traditional women's occupations. Ninety-five women lived in tents, cooked outside, and had lessons in archery, volleyball, star lore, and handicrafts. Instructors also taught child care, sewing, home management, home nursing, public speaking, advanced typing and shorthand, and bookbinding.[15]

The camp faced some health problems when the water supply trickled to a halt in mid-program. Upon investigation, camp administrators discovered that placer miners were diverting the camp's spring to their diggings. Only the intervention of the State Board of Health and the Forestry Department restored the camp's water. An epidemic of "septic sore throat" compelled the FERA to close the camp a week early. In the meantime, the project had suffered "a black eye" when one of the women returned from town drunk and a visitor widely reported the incident.[16]

The FERA women's vocational camp operated for only one summer. Administrators believed it was a success, however, and happily reported that at least one resident had subsequently enrolled at the School of Mines with FERA student aid. Handicrafts produced during the program were displayed in government exhibits of New Deal work and prompted Montana administrators to propose further crafts projects that would feature the work of Native Americans and be suitable for sale in national parks.[17]

However successful the FERA camp might have been, there was little public support for innovative projects for women in the New Deal. Indeed, it was difficult enough for women to get any work. Ellen Sullivan Woodward, head of women's work under the FERA and later the WPA, was never able to fund the number of jobs required for all the women who were declared eligible. New Deal programs rarely, if ever, challenged the traditional gender divisions of work, and that proved true in Butte as elsewhere.[18]

As the depression continued, the Roosevelt administration supplanted the FERA with much more extensive work relief. The Works Progress Administration (in 1939 changed to the Work Projects Administration) was created in May 1935 and lasted through the first years of World War II. Building upon the experiments of the FERA, the WPA provided work relief for unemployed men and women in a wide variety of programs but again concentrated men in construction and women in sewing and canning projects.

In March 1935 there were 6,671 workers on relief in Silver Bow County; 64 percent of them were men, 36 percent were women. According to government classification, the largest percentage of men on relief were semiskilled workers in manufacturing and other industries (49 percent). The remainder were clustered in categories of unskilled and semiskilled construction. Professionals formed the smallest category of men on relief. Women relief workers in Silver Bow County constituted 9 percent of the county's women but 25 percent of all women relief workers in the state. This reflected the urban nature of women's paid work in Montana, the high number of self-supporting widows, and perhaps the fact that rural women had come to the city seeking assistance. The greatest number were labeled "inexperienced" (49 percent). As might be expected, the second-largest category were women in domestic and personal service (23 percent), with smaller numbers of semiskilled workers, saleswomen, office personnel, and professionals rounding out the relief population.[19]

Women who came to Butte seeking work were often sorely disappointed. Rose C. Bresnahan, director of Women's and Profession-al Projects for the Montana WPA, reported to Woodward, "Butte has never been a good town for the employment of women; public and union opinion has forced them out of all jobs that can, by the wid-est stretch of imagination be called a man's job." The majority of women given relief work were assigned to sewing rooms, where they stitched garments for others on relief. Inspectors judged the Butte sewing rooms well ventilated and operating safely but plagued with inefficient administration—due largely to political appointments. Women in the Butte sewing rooms, like women in similar projects across the country, were paid less than men for comparable work. The labor movement in Butte attempted to negotiate higher wages but was not successful, and in its evaluation of New Deal work re-lief it complained strongly about discrimination against women. Bresnahan characterized the sewing rooms as "spirit killing" places where few marketable skills were taught. She worked hard to bring more white-collar projects to Montana for both women and men.[20]

Unemployed men and women categorized as professionals had difficulty finding compatible work. In March 1935 Ethel Arnett, director of FERA Professional Projects in Montana, complained that "county administrators are primarily interested in building roads rather than men." Even though the state's relief rolls listed such professionals as a bacteriologist and a pharmacist, as well as writers, doctors, mining engineers, and botanists, no work was earmarked for them. Arnett claimed that the agency evaluating eligibility was opposed to professional projects, believing that they built "an aris-tocracy of relief." She contended social workers preferred to "de-press all persons to the same standard of relief."[21]

The experience of Butte librarians highlighted the issues facing professionals during the depression. Unemployment led to a greater dependence on free leisure activities, and the Butte Free Public Library witnessed a tremendous increase in patronage. The unem-ployed crammed reading rooms from nine in the morning to nine at night. In 1931 the library lent twenty-five thousand more books than it did the previous year, and assistant librarian Ida Sternfels reported that Butte readers were borrowing more "front porch read-ing" than ever before: romances, detective stories, and adventure tales. When the city threatened to close the library in 1933 because of a lack of funds, the librarians quietly wrote to the American Fed-eration of Labor, got the seven required signatures, sent in their fee, and received a charter as Librarians' Union Number 19178 before anyone in Butte knew what they were doing. Then, with the backing of the city's other unions, they were able to compel the city council to keep the library open. Having worked for several months without pay, the librarians realized that although they might be professionals, they were in the same boat as many others. As Elizabeth McDonald, secretary of the new union, stated, "Anyone who has to be at the mercy of a paycheck at the end of the month is a laborer pure and simple . . . the United States government has a Department of Labor but no Department of Professions. Does not that show the policy of our government?" When the library was again faced with closure in 1935, the chair of the county FERA Workers Protective Union suggested that the library be made "a project," just like the rip-rapping of Silver Bow Creek. He argued that funds should be appropriated to "clean it up inside, buy reading material, keep the present personnel paid up to date and also employ a few of the young men and women of the county who are graduates of higher educational institutions. After all," he observed, "we are not all qualified to be ditch diggers, butchers and toy makers."[22]

Despite its limitations, the New Deal was good to Montanans. Between 1933 and 1939 Montana received more than $530 million in federal loans and grants, or $986 for each resident, ranking second in the nation in per capita expenditures. By 1938 men employed on projects that New Deal agencies sponsored had constructed or improved thousands of miles of roads and sewers and hundreds of public buildings, stadiums, parks, swimming pools, playgrounds, and privies. More than fifty thousand men and women, including many Butte miners, worked for the Public Works Administration on construction of the Fort Peck Dam on the Missouri River in eastern Montana. Relief workers also killed nearly twenty thousand predatory animals and planted thirteen thousand trees and five hundred vegetable gardens. Women stitched thousands of garments in WPA sewing rooms, cleaned public buildings, catalogued and repaired library books, and worked as local government clerks and stenographers. WPA nurses and housekeeping aides made more than two thousand home visits, taught adult and child hygiene classes, and vaccinated hundreds of Montanans. The WPA also had a social agenda beyond the creation of jobs. The first task of the WPA recreation and cultural divisions was to employ the unemployed, and to that end they hired writers, actors, musicians, and artists. But New Deal cultural planners also attempted to improve community recreational life and democratize culture.[23]

■ ■ ■

By 1935–36, more than 25 percent of all Butte families received some kind of public relief. A WPA survey of family income in the West Central–Rocky Mountain region revealed that more Butte families depended on wages for income than families in the six other cities studied, and hence the greatest number of people were made destitute by unemployment. Paradoxically, Butte also had the highest median income for all the cities studied. Strong craft organization persisted throughout the depression, and the Butte Miners' Union had reorganized in 1934. When people did work, they earned union wages.[24]

Butte residents welcomed the WPA, not only because it provided work and, they believed, a fairer distribution of relief but also because its projects brought the city services and amenities it sorely lacked. Frank Carden recalled that the WPA "finally got Butte out of the mud and gave us decent streets." William Burke, compiler of the Federal Writers' Project volume *Copper Camp*, noted that although vast fortunes had been made in Butte, "It finally remained for the WPA to pave hundreds of miles of streets, lay a vast network of sanitary sewers, develop parks and playgrounds and provide an Art Center for the community." Ironically, the "symphony orchestras, libraries and art galleries endowed by the copper kings are enjoyed in the cities to which the millionaires moved."[25]

One of the New Deal cultural projects that enjoyed widespread public support was the WPA Division of Recreation. Between 1936 and 1939 the WPA initiated recreation programs in every state except Maine. Like all WPA projects, the division's primary goal was to put people to work, however, administrators also had a broader social mission and the long-term goal of encouraging permanent, tax-supported state and local programs. The content of the project involved programming and training in three areas: physical recreation (sports), social recreation (card games, dancing, parades), and cultural recreation (painting, photography, crafts, drama, radio, and music). Supervisors designed special programs for children between the ages of three and six and for the disabled and institutionalized. The Montana State Department of Public Instruction sponsored the WPA recreation project, and state and local advisory councils guided its path.[26]

In Washington, D.C., a mishmash of sociological theories about the role of recreation in a democracy shaped the direction of the Recreation Division. Administrators devised a tri-level design for the program, incorporating goals for the individual, the community, and society as a whole. They sought to use physical training at the individual level to increase awareness of the body as an instrument for the "expression of total personality." They deemed recreation a complement to work and a way of filling basic human needs for "individual expression, cultural enjoyment, and self-expansion." At the community level, recreation programs were to nurture harmony and happiness by using established organizations to attract the greatest number of residents to sponsored activities. At the national level, recreation was to be the "great democratizer and unifier." WPA programs combatted "spectatoritis." People were challenged to desert the army of observers and become active participants in order to achieve personal fulfillment. One expert compared this new threshold of public recreation to the frontier. With the western frontier long closed, it was vital to keep the spiritual frontier alive by providing new experiences and adventures through recreation. In these administrators' eyes democracy was the province of the young in spirit, and recreation the means of keeping America youthful.[27]

A frequently repeated defense of the recreation program was its social usefulness in combatting juvenile delinquency. National advocates defended its costs, arguing that the country would spend far more controlling the crime and delinquency that was subverted by youths' participation in the program. In 1936 George Misevic, director of Butte's recreation division, claimed that juvenile delinquency had declined 33 percent since the project's inception. Young people, he claimed, were kept so busy at clean and healthful pursuits that they no longer had time to "loaf on the streets and in the alley."[28]

Although many of the recreation programs targeted specific age groups and genders, the overall emphasis was on family recreation, seen as an alternative to commercial recreation and a way to bind families together. As one WPA motto proclaimed, "The family that plays together, stays together." Sports projects tended to be designed for men and children, although in 1937 the WPA sponsored a Butte women's basketball league. A special facility for single men, especially older men, was established in the basement of the Arcade and opened from 11 A.M. to midnight. There, men who lived in boardinghouses and no longer had the money to patronize commercial establishments could congregate to hear radio broadcasts, read the newspaper, and play checkers and cards. But the majority of social and cultural programs cultivated families. Group singing, arts and crafts classes, dancing, and dramatics were designed for family participation. Recreation Division publications provided instructions for games to be played at home. If family recreation could be made attractive, children would prefer staying at home to visiting pool halls, and parents would cease "making endless and unsatisfying rounds of night clubs." By democratically participating in recreation, even the roles of family members could be redefined. For instance, one WPA publication contended that through the democratic, cooperative choice of family recreation, "Dad becomes a personage and a personality, rather than just the finance department," and "Mother is no longer the cook and general housekeeper submerged in the daily necessities of the children." Recreation specialists urged parents not to simply observe their children at play, but to "guide them in their interests and join in enthusiastically."[29]

On a more pragmatic level, recreation leaders hoped that pageants, parades, ball games, and boxing matches would dissipate the pent-up energy, frustration, and anger of the unemployed. In Montana the WPA established its first two recreation programs in Anaconda and Butte. The state relief commission explicitly stated that the recreation program was an experimental "antidote" to the growing dissatisfaction and unrest of Butte and Anaconda's unemployed. Some felt that it succeeded in that regard. In an application to the WPA to continue recreational projects, Mayor Hauswirth noted that the program had improved depression-eroded morale and that "many have been diverted from anti-social thinking and conduct." WPA leaders stressed recreational activities as a way of fostering cooperation, sportsmanship, and democracy, and "stabilizing" the nation.[30]

Within a few weeks of its initiation in Butte in 1935 the recreation program had hired twenty-one instructors and had more than eight thousand weekly participants. During the next four years WPA recreation became an integral part of the city's social life. The roster of local sponsors included sports clubs, educational institutions, voluntary associations, the newspapers, and the Miners' Union. Churches turned over their parish halls for story telling, handicrafts, dancing, and card playing. Instructors taught every imaginable sport, game, and craft in vacant lots and fire halls and on playgrounds throughout the city.[31]

The recreation program sparked enthusiasm in many neighborhoods. On the north side of the city WPA workers and residents transformed a debris-filled gully into a small playground and celebrated their accomplishment by recreating the site in miniature on a float in a Butte parade. At the Boulevard fire station, "community nites" every two weeks drew more than four hundred men, women, and children for group singing and other activities. Two piano players volunteered their services, workers handed out typed song sheets, and neighbors sang along. Other programs included dancing, acrobatics, and boxing.[32]

Recreation programs were not evenly distributed. The heavily immigrant East Side had fewer organizations with the resources necessary to co-sponsor projects and, because much of the area lay outside the city limits, it was dependent upon the sparser governmental resources of the county. The WPA faced the same problems that had confronted every group that tried to provide community recreation in Butte: a paucity of facilities and uneven cooperation from the city or county governments. Yet New Deal programs were perhaps most needed on the East Side. When a WPA nursery school on East Galena Street closed in 1937, school superintendent Douglas Gold reported that "many mothers, mostly foreign-speaking, came morning after morning with their children in the hope that we would be able to reopen this school." Citizens formed the East Side Progressive Club for the sole purpose of acquiring recreational facilities for the neighborhood. In 1937 they wrote to Senator Murray and expressed their hopes for a swimming pool, regulation baseball field, and a park. By 1939 they had succeeded only in winning construction of a playground.[33]

East Side neighborhood groups, first in conjunction with the FERA and then with the WPA, had converted the Arizona Street fire station into a community center with a reading and card room for unemployed men and a gymnasium for children. At one Christmas party the local sponsors presented children with roller skates and harmonicas. WPA recreation leaders taught violin and harmonica, boxing, gymnastics, and crafts. The center was one of the few places where East Side children could play indoors, and parents considered it essential for keeping them "off the street and mine dumps." It was also one of the few projects that attracted families from different ethnic groups. In 1940 the city—over the protests of neighbors, the Miners' Union, and the Union's Ladies' Auxiliary and in spite of private offers to purchase the building for up to $3,000— leased it to the Veterans of Foreign Wars for $1 a year.[34]

■ ■ ■

Administrators reported that East Side residents welcomed WPA-sponsored naturalization and Americanization classes but ignored other recreational programs. "Various reasons" were given, including the lack of facilities and a mix of nationalities that appeared reluctant to come together in the community-oriented activities WPA organizers favored.[35]

One inhibiting factor may have been the "American scene" focus of all the New Deal art and recreation programs. The initial New Deal art program, the Public Works of Art Project, limited the work it commissioned to realistic portrayals of the contemporary "American scene." Although the WPA Federal Art Project (FAP) did not require its artists to adhere to this theme, "Americanism," nonetheless, permeated the various cultural projects. Holger Cahill, an art critic and authority on American folk art, directed the FAP. His vision colored the division's work and had a profound impact upon one of the most acclaimed products of the FAP, the *Index of American Design*, a portfolio of meticulous reproductions of American decorative folk art. After some deliberation, Cahill decided that it would be limited to the folk art of Americans of European origin, work produced between the colonial period and the end of the nineteenth century. Thus, the folk art of immigrants who happened to arrive in America in the twentieth century was, for all practical purposes, defined as non-American. In the WPA Recreation Division, the same focus on "American" folk patterns was apparent. The national office directed all regional branches to draw upon the folklore materials collected by the Federal Writers' Project as fodder for their programs and "revive the honestly beautiful folklore of our country." In the West, this meant that the project celebrated Native American designs. Unfortunately, in many cases the interpretation of native folklore was distilled into trite depictions of cowboys and Indians. WPA recreation supervisors tried to lure Italian, Slavic, Lebanese, and Finnish women into programs where they would make doilies, stenciled luncheon sets, and patchwork quilts decorated with rural western and American Indian motifs. Apparently the WPA gave no consideration to the rich decorative traditions of its clients' own ethnic heritage. Thus, indifference or even resentment of "cultural nationalism," as well as a lack of facilities, may explain the failure of the Recreation Division's efforts on the East Side.[36]

Montana did not qualify for all of the New Deal cultural programs. Because the primary aim of WPA projects was to employ out-of-work artists, only states that had significant numbers of musicians, actors, writers, and visual artists on their relief rolls were eligible for cultural projects. The law required that 90 percent of the workers be drawn from relief rolls; the remaining 10 percent could be non-relief supervisory personnel. Montana did not have enough unemployed musicians or actors to warrant a Federal Music Project or Federal Theater Project, and musicians there protested the decision. They saw WPA administrators reinforcing the prejudices of easterners who thought of the intermountain West as a cultural wasteland. Bruno David Ussher, regional director of the Federal Music Project, informed the national director that Montanans did not really understand the music program. Because a report showed that several hundred Butte residents were interested in the project, he assumed that they had confused it with the recreation program, because "Montana is not exactly what might be called in general terms a music consuming state." Robert W. Stevens, a Montana pianist and conductor, disagreed. He pleaded for a music program, remonstrating that the musical activities of the Recreation Division were fine in their place, but "the *poor* people (many on relief) don't want merely to be tickled. They want their children to have *music culture* which they cannot afford." He continued, "When we see the magnificent work you do in the big centers, we cry for help in these rural borders. . . . The recreational folks are fine in helping make folks happy, but they are still longing, in this locality, for the *real bread* of music education."[37]

Although the New Deal failed to enrich Montanans' musical and theatrical repertoire, a branch of the Federal Art Project did bring the work of internationally renowned artists to the state and encouraged Montana's own visual artists. The task of getting Montana's Art Project off the ground fell to Rose C. Bresnahan, the state director of the Women's and Professional Division of the WPA. Bresnahan was the perfect choice for the job. Fifty years old at the time of her appointment to the WPA, she had a long and varied work history and a record of political involvement that prepared her to administer a controversial relief program. Bresnahan had sold insurance and real estate, been assistant circulation manager for the *Anaconda Standard,* and, when she was in her twenties, homesteaded in Grass Range in central Montana. In 1919 she had gone "slumming" with the Anaconda sheriff to ferret out bootleg joints. In 1923 a representative of the League of Women Voters described her as a young, socialistic firebrand. An activist in the Democratic party and several women's clubs, she had broad organizational and political skills. She also had a wry sense of humor that helped her weather her job.[38]

Bresnahan's position required her to solicit sponsorship of programs from groups that were frequently hostile to the WPA. Although it seemed obvious that private charity could not ease the misery of the depression, many voluntary groups resented the federal government's invasion of their turf. A tinge of bitterness seeped through the minutes of the Women's Auxiliary of the American Institute of Mining Engineers (WAAIME) when they decided to cease their support of the East Side Neighborhood House—even though it still wanted their help—because federal aid was now available. WAAIME also aborted its plans for a library in the nearby mining camp of Basin because the FERA had stepped in to establish one there. One member of the Joshers claimed that it was not the lack of donations that halted the club's annual Christmas fund-raiser, but the preemptory takeover of charity by the New Deal. The Joshers had, in fact, stopped distributing Christmas baskets before FDR became president. This member's memory said more about his attitude toward the New Deal than conditions at the time. The Montana Federation of Women's Clubs also had mixed feelings about the New Deal. Clubs grudgingly supported WPA sewing rooms and the National Youth Administration. A WPA official reported that the federation gave the Women's and Professional Division an exhibit space at their biennial meeting but would not give them any time on the program to speak.[39]

It is not difficult to understand the attitude of such groups. Most members were middle class, and although they felt the impact of the depression they did not experience the destitution of thousands of miners and their families. The need for relief programs did not have personal force. So much of these volunteers' sense of purpose and worth in the community was tied to their fund-raising and charity work that it was undoubtedly hard to see that work usurped by an impersonal bureaucracy distributing funds on a scale they could never hope to equal. Just as many of the unemployed had difficulty accepting the help the New Deal offered because it hurt their pride, many volunteers found that New Deal agencies unwittingly robbed them of the satisfaction they derived from caring for their community. Voluntary associations were in demand as sponsoring agencies for many projects. Because the bulk of money came from the government, however, and relief workers carried out the labor, sponsorship was often nominal. Middle-class caregivers could not rid themselves of the long-held conviction that poverty was an individual problem and that those on relief were getting a free ride. That attitude, combined with resentment over being displaced by government agencies, contributed to the middle class's reluctance to support WPA programs.

The Federal Art Center in Butte, one of the hundreds of WPA community art centers established throughout the country, built a bridge between middle-class groups and the WPA. Art was something that clubwomen could rally around, and the Butte Art Association and the Junior League became two of the center's major sponsors. In fact, Bresnahan notified Holger Cahill that most of the organizations that contributed to the Art Center were "of an anti-W.P.A. trend." For that very reason, she hoped that the center would be a big success. The state WPA director, Joseph E. Parker, echoed her remarks when he asked for an exemption from hiring a local relief worker as the center's director. Parker informed his superior that the sponsors wanted a "high grade" director with actual gallery experience. He believed the benefits of wooing new supporters of a WPA project warranted hiring a director from outside Montana. His supervisor concurred and transferred Frank L. Stevens of the California Art Project to Montana.[40]

With Stevens's appointment assured, Bresnahan turned to other responsibilities, advising him to "go out of your way to see that the initial showings are of the highest possible type. Remember that towns like Butte are apt to be more appreciative of the old type art, rather than the new, and will gradually need to be educated to the more startling things." The Art Center in Butte became the heart of the state's art project, dedicated to providing the people with wider opportunities to "study, appreciate, and enjoy the visual arts." Exhibits assembled in Washington, D.C., came to Butte and from there traveled to other cities around the state. Stevens heeded Bresnahan's advice, however, and the opening exhibit was a show of familiar Montana and Butte artists.[41]

Stevens found Butte "hungry for pictures" but not for modern art. Butte citizens preferred "good solid fare," representational and self-explanatory. The most popular show during the project's first year was an exhibit of works owned by the former steward of the now-bankrupt but once exclusive Silver Bow Club. Stevens described them as "musty old oils in those gingerbread, rococo gold frames so dearly loved in the mauve decade." With his next exhibit Stevens learned more about his audience. It was a show featuring works depicting impressions of circuses, carnivals, street fairs, and fiestas, "as modern" in treatment as the modern art about which viewers had previously complained. Visitors loved this show, however, and Stevens concluded that the Butte audience was "sympathetic to any sort of technique that touches on a favorite theme." In 1938 he brought to the center shows of German artist Käthe Kollwitz's prints,

Berenice Abbott's photographs of "Changing New York," and selections from the Museum of Modern Art exhibit New Horizons of American Art, which showcased the best of FAP artists' work. Abbott's photographs stirred great interest. Local photographers talked of doing a "Changing Butte" project, and the Junior League formed its own camera club.[42]

Residents embraced the art center. Teachers from Butte High and Butte Central brought their classes to view exhibits, and Central's nuns and priests frequently visited on weekends. Stevens kept the galleries open every day of the year "because in those days the miners worked in three shifts, and you couldn't tell when they could get off." Just as listeners to KGIR did not hesitate to call or write the radio station with their complaints and suggestions, art viewers freely expressed their opinions on what Stevens exhibited. The Butte carpenters hired to remodel a room in the school administration building for the center followed specifications provided by the WPA but suggested some modifications. They believed the Butte crowd would have a "hands-on" approach to art appreciation and recommended adding extra supports to the exhibit walls. The carpenters' counsel may have been only a ruse to get a little extra work, but Stevens did describe spectators "draped" over the cases. Although some aficionados may have thought this behavior lacked proper respect, it clearly revealed that Butte audiences were not intimidated by art exhibits. Their desire to touch, their willingness to comment, and their impulse to emulate should be seen as a mark of great success in popularizing art.[43]

The center not only brought the works of major European and American artists to the hinterland but it also provided a new gallery for the work of Montana artists. Stevens exhibited Blackfeet crafts and the work of William Standing, an Assiniboin from the Ft. Peck Indian reservation, who also illustrated *Land of Nakoda: The Story of the Assiniboine Indians,* a volume sponsored by the Federal Writers' Project. The gallery featured one Butte woman's embroidery, tempera paintings of Montana flora, and the paintings of Elizabeth Lochrie, who became one of the region's most famous western artists. In one attempt at experimental art, the center showed paintings produced by an art class at the state hospital for the mentally ill. Stevens distinguished the work of these students from that of a therapy group, contending that a number of the works were "deliberate abstractions." In the exhibit the paintings were accompanied by the patients' written commentaries.[44]

The Federal Art Project was widely praised throughout the nation. In 1936 Lewis Mumford published an open letter to Franklin Roosevelt in the *New Republic* and argued for the project's continuation on the grounds that it provided a home for artists and spread the seeds of fine art far beyond a "few metropolitan hothouses." Mumford recognized that the propagation of art had created hybrids rather than "a single arbitrary stereotype" of what American art should be. The cross-fertilization of nationally recognized artists with struggling local painters, sculptors, and photographers "resulted in a great diversity of efforts, vividly shot through with the colors of the local region and the local community."[45] Certainly, Butte's Art Center produced such a harvest.

■ ■ ■

While the WPA remained in force, public recreation and art flourished in Butte. Evaluations of WPA programs attested to their popularity. Stanley D. Griffiths, assistant principal of Butte High School, believed the recreation program was "essential" to the community. He lamented the past lack of city and county support and feared that Butte, without continued assistance from the federal government, would fall back into old patterns of neglecting the recreational needs of young people. Griffiths hoped that the WPA's work would lay a foundation for a permanent national program for public health and recreation. Some Silver Bow County commissioners also praised the WPA recreation and cultural programs. They believed there would be "little objection and considerable support" to continue them "if the funds were available to carry them on." Nevertheless, Griffiths's fears proved well-founded. As World War II pulled the economy out of depression and put men and women back to work, the government dismantled New Deal programs. Despite their positive evaluation, neither the city nor the county picked them up.[46]

Roosevelt ordered all WPA programs liquidated by February 15, 1943. Well before that date, extensive cuts had been made, and existing WPA projects had been turned to defense work. In March 1942 the art program had become the Graphics Section of the War Services Program. Gardening and canning projects that had fed the needy were transformed into victory gardens. Montana sewing rooms stitched garments for Italian nationals detained at Ft. Missoula. Recreation projects adopted a new motto: "America Fit Will Be America Invincible."[47]

The longest-running WPA projects in Montana were in Silver Bow County. The Butte sewing room and a Walkerville sewer project closed down in mid-February 1943, and Joseph Parker, state administrator, received permission to continue several nursery schools until April. Montana politicians and the labor movement fought to keep the Butte sewing room open. The county commissioners lobbied Senator Murray, arguing that Butte had "a large male population producing copper, zinc, manganese and other war metals. The related female population must be used here or remain idle or on direct relief." Parker, too, lent his support, reminding Washington that the women who worked in the sewing room were, for the most part, elderly widows or the wives of workers incapacitated by tuberculosis and mine accidents. They were not able to move to other locations to take up war work, and Montana had not received war contracts that could employ them. Parker and Murray did their best to get the sewing room designated as a production center for military clothing. But the army refused, stating that the equipment in the Butte facility would not provide the double-needle stitching specified for military wear, nor was it feasible to reequip the operation.[48]

What was the New Deal's legacy to Butte? According to Parker, the WPA alone spent almost $4.5 million in the city between 1935 and 1941. Building projects wrought physical changes that were striking and durable—miles of storm sewers, paved streets, and new sidewalks. Construction work, sewing, housekeeping, and small white-collar projects permitted many men and women to survive the depression with dignity. A handful of artists and writers had employment and gained recognition of their work from wider audiences. It is impossible to calculate what effect art education may have had on individuals in the community, but the dream of WPA administrators that cultural programs would become institutionalized in local communities did not materialize in the mining city.[49]

By 1943 Howard C. Beresford, regional recreation representative for the Community War Services Program, reported that Butte's community recreation efforts were "at their lowest ebb." With the mines running at full capacity, men and women returned to predepression entertainments. Dog racing, numbers games, bingo, blackjack, and other forms of gambling were "booming as never before." All-night clubs and bars prospered, and customers readily found "professional and amateur sex." Children, however, "have practically been shoved onto the dumps of the copper mines." There was no supervised playground or outdoor pool in operation; baseball and softball leagues were the only scheduled sports. Beresford believed that the lack of public recreation was "a community condition as old as Butte," and one that would not change until the

Anaconda Company, the city, the county, labor, public schools, churches, and the women's groups joined together to support recreation. That union would require surmounting decades of division and mistrust.[50]

Butte's inability to provide noncommercial recreation revealed the fissures in the community. The city, county, and public school district guarded their individual domains jealously and rarely collaborated. Voluntary groups distrusted the government and preferred to rely on their own resources, no matter how limited and scattered those might be. Rival Catholic and Protestant hierarchies were unwilling to cooperate or credit each other for community improvements. The unions sometimes worked in solidarity but more often craft loyalty divided their efforts, and workers seeking to protect jobs and high wages frequently refused to support volunteer efforts that they saw as competition. In the background loomed the Anaconda Company, its economic power mostly silent but always a potential threat to any course not directed from company headquarters.

Howard Beresford acknowledged that the divisions in Butte were deeper than in any other community in which the Community War Services Program worked. His staff was constantly courting one group or another because it could not organize a central coordinating committee. Beresford prophesied that fear of economic reprisals would preclude the formation of any such committee—even for a benign purpose like public recreation—until the company gave its approval, and the company was reluctant to do so. Anaconda appeared to resist any kind of communitywide organization that might reconcile differences that kept the various powers in the city and county at loggerheads and thus benefited company dominance.[51]

The experience of the American Social Hygiene Association (ASHA) confirmed Beresford's observations. The ASHA tried unsuccessfully to drum up support in Butte for the control of venereal disease through the elimination of prostitution. Field workers for the ASHA found individuals sympathetic to their cause but could not enlist the company, the Catholic church, or the local government in any sort of anti-vice campaign. Each had its own reasons for refusing, which substantiated Beresford's assessment of the rifts plaguing Butte society. Although the company professed a desire for a "wholesome" town, no executive would speak publicly against gambling or prostitution, nor did the company allow the newspapers it controlled to take a stand against vice. Prostitution and gambling were such integral and lucrative parts of the local economy that few businessmen opposed them. Some members of the community, whom the ASHA logically supposed would support its work, found themselves immobilized by a conflict of interest. For example, Mrs. H. G. Martinelli, vice president of the PTA Council, strongly favored the eradication of prostitution. But her husband was a bar owner, and other reformers' desires to lump together all vice and wipe out everything from prostitution and slot machines to liquor quashed her interest in working with the ASHA. The Catholic church never took an active stance against vice, either. Too many of its members and donors made livings as tavern owners, policemen, politicians, and others involved in "unwholesome" but profitable businesses. No priest with the inclination to support a reform movement dared to act without the permission of the Right Reverend Monsignor Michael M. English, head of the church in Butte. Monsignor English did not oppose the gambling interests, nor did he want Catholics helping any reform movement that might make the administration of the new Protestant and Republican mayor look good.[52]

According to Beresford, the only redeeming feature of public recreation in the early 1940s was the Butte Youth Center, a suite of redecorated rooms in the Grand Hotel. Catholics, Protestants, the PTA, and the Junior League raised funds, and the unions donated materials and labor. In 1943 the Junior League paid the director's salary, and in 1945 the AAUW raised the money. The committee that sponsored the center did not even bother to seek public funds. As Beresford observed, "Butte is so accustomed to 'passing the hat' and staging individual drives, that it has not occurred to the committee that there might be public funds available." The past reluctance of the city to earmark money for public recreation undoubtedly also influenced the committee's actions.[53]

During the New Deal years some Butte citizens had tried to break old habits. Charles A. Hauswirth, a Progressive Republican, was elected to four consecutive two-year terms as mayor between 1935 and 1941, the year he died in office. An anomaly in Butte, Hauswirth was the only mayor ever elected to more than two terms and was one of only eight Republicans elected between 1879 and 1979. He wanted to change Butte's traditional image, "to refrain absolutely from boosting Butte as a mining camp, but advertise it in every conceivable way as an up-and-coming city." Charles Hauswirth, with the help of the federal government, did make some changes in Butte, but his tenure was too brief to make much headway against decades of custom. He and New Deal work programs made permanent contributions to the infrastructural needs of "an up-and-coming city," but the cultural impact of their efforts was more transitory. As reports from the early 1940s indicate, public recreation declined abysmally. With the close of the Federal Art Center, Montana artists were once again left to their isolated pursuits. It was not until 1976 that Butte reestablished a small art museum.[54]

The rifts between power bases in the city and the refusal of the Anaconda Company to take a lead either in eliminating vice or encouraging alternative forms of recreation meant that old patterns of mining town leisure, which catered to adult men, prevailed. The responsibility for noncommercial recreation once again devolved to voluntary associations, which continued to be of enormous importance to Butte's social life but on the whole could have only limited and fractured impact.

· · ·

Ironically, perhaps the most lasting legacy of the New Deal's cultural programs in Butte was a work that perpetuated the very image of the city that Mayor Hauswirth sought to change. *Copper Camp: Stories of the World's Greatest Mining Town, Butte, Montana*, first published in 1943, went through its sixth printing in 1976. It is the best-known book on Butte, cited by just about everyone who writes anything about the city, and despite more current scholarship *Copper Camp* remains local residents' authority on Butte history. Published through the sponsorship of the Montana State Department of Agriculture, Labor and Industry, *Copper Camp* was compiled by workers of the Federal Writers' Project, in particular by William A. Burke.

William Burke was born in Butte in 1893 and started working in the mines when he was sixteen. He labored as a nipper, or errand boy, on the night shift while he went to high school, and he returned to the underground at intervals between a job as a postal clerk, a stint in the U.S. Navy, and a year "bumming" around the country. In the 1920s he worked as an advance man for stage shows, a newspaperman for the *Butte Miner* and the *Montana Free Press*, and a manager of movie theaters. Sometime during the 1930s he enrolled in the WPA and was assigned to the Writers' Project. In what remains of the Montana Writers' Project files, there are a few short stories by Burke. They reveal a broad sense of humor and an admiration for the men who worked Butte's mines. *Copper Camp* is shaped by those qualities. Others contributed to the book, but George D. Marsh, state supervisor of the FWP, acknowledged that the book was based almost entirely on Burke's observations, memories, and research.[55]

Burke's method was "anecdotal grubbing." The book is a compendium of facts and folklore that canonized Butte's boisterousness, wide-open social life and tolerance of eccentricity. The title is indicative. *Copper Camp* is a collection of stories about a mining camp, not an industrial city, a community that is playful not responsible, high-spirited and reckless not discreet or prudent. The first chapter, "Introduction to Butte the Bizarre," sets the tone. *Copper Camp* was not presented as a sociological study; it is not clear how much Burke intended it be a history rather than a story. Like many similar volumes in the American Guide series (the main product of the Federal Writers' Project), *Copper Camp* is a blend of myth, truth, and error, replete with local color, intimate detail, interesting facts, and interesting fictions. Regardless of the intent of its authors, *Copper Camp* has become Butte's accepted history. Its tales form the foundation of Butte's past, in part because *Copper Camp* is not the story of the copper kings and the Anaconda Company. Its life flows from the heartbeats and footsteps of miners, beggars, prostitutes, cooks, actresses, saloonkeepers, and newsboys.[56]

In the mid-1940s Joseph Kinsey Howard, Montana's most astute journalist, who found Butte endlessly fascinating, wrote about the mining city's appeal. It was "not mass movements which stick in one's memory as most closely associated with Butte," even though the Western Federation of Miners was born in the city and the Socialists, the Wobblies, and the Mine, Mill and Smelter Workers all waged spectacular struggles in Butte. It was rather the stories of heroes, clowns, and fools that came to mind when one thought of Butte. Frank Little, IWW martyr; Mary MacLane, outrageous writer; Augustus Heinze, charismatic copper king; and Manus Duggan, hero of the Speculator Fire, became the stuff of Butte history. Tragic, comic, powerful, sly, and valiant characters, whose stories people learned, embellished, and repeated, shaped Butte's psyche.[57]

Stories were Butte's strength and its curse. Stories allowed Butte to cloak poverty in a mantle of eccentricity, turning beggars into "characters," such as Shoestring Annie, Callahan the Bum, Nickel Annie, and Crazy Mary. Stories permitted the murder of a labor organizer, the quashing of civil liberties, and the ugliness of martial law to be sanitized into a detective story: "Who killed Frank Little?" Excesses of alcohol and violence became motifs in tales of boyish exuberance and male comradeship. Defeat and powerlessness hid behind a curtain woven of suspense, novelty, and buffoonery.

Yet, stories have also helped Butte to endure. Folktales such as "Marcus Daly Enters Heaven," in which a mucker ridicules the thinly disguised copper king Marcus Daly, who has come down in the mine to spy on his workers, reaffirmed the equality of all men who shared the dangers of the underground. The power of these stories and heroes continues. Montana writer Ron Fischer's 1988 short story "The Speculator Fire" is narrated by Manus Duggan's son, a son he never saw because Manus suffocated in the Speculator before his wife gave birth. Young Duggan pieces together the story of the mine fire from the memories of the men whose lives Manus saved, men eager to give him some sense of his father: "I guess they wanted to give Manus back to me somehow. So, they'd tell their stories. Over the years, the stories changed sometimes. Maybe they remembered wrong or maybe they were just starting to remember it right."[58]

Butte's almost perverse pride in its wide-open character was a response to people's belief in the all-encompassing power of the company. Butte's bars, gambling dens, dance halls, and brothels were among the few public institutions not owned or controlled by Anaconda. It was not only the hazards of mining and the grim environment of Butte that propelled men and women to frenzied gaiety, but also the thought that here were arenas of self-expression denied them elsewhere in a city ringed by the "copper collar," in which the company owned the mines, the newspapers, the utilities, and the parks. Joseph Kinsey Howard recognized that the insecurity of mining life underlay people's desire for "a good time," so that "a new suit, a gown, and a party are only too often preferred to a coat of paint on the house." Butte residents kept their assets movable and reluctantly invested in their city. A nationwide economic survey in 1939 revealed that they put much of their money in savings accounts and baby bonds and very little in real estate. Howard feared that Butte's tolerance, its live-and-let-live attitude, had become apathy. Resignation to the vagaries of a boom-and-bust economy and the power of Anaconda had led people to countenance corrupt politics, inadequate public services, and a lack of cultural amenities.[59]

In Butte, people invested in savings accounts, new automobiles, good clothes, and good times—experiences and memories—the possessions of a transient people. Regardless of the fact that many families remained in Butte for generations, as long as the city was tied to copper, the threat of unemployment loomed over the working class and encouraged people to acquire or improve only what they could take with them. Memories, some ripened, some bleached from the truths that spawned them, became the reward for surviving Butte.

NOTES

1. Frank L. Stevens to James E. Murray, n.d., James E. Murray Papers (hereafter cited as JM Papers), box 795, file 5, K. Ross Toole Archives, University of Montana, Missoula; Frank L. Stevens, interview by Betty Hoag, Los Angeles, 2 June 1964, 34.

2. *Montana Standard,* 1 January 1930, 1; *Montana Free Press,* 31 January 1929, 1; *Engineering and Mining Journal* (hereafter cited as *EMJ*), 19 January 1929, 138 ; *Montana Free Press,* 10 January 1929, 4; *Montana Standard,* 2 April 1929, 1; *EMJ,* 17 August 1929, 266, 28 December 1929, 1014.

3. Malone, Roeder, and Lang, *Montana: A History of Two Centuries,* 295; "Information to Accompany Application to the Governor of Montana for Relief Funds," Silver Bow County Emergency Relief Fund, 13 August 1932, 3, Montana Governors' Papers, box 54, file 5, MHSA; *EMJ,* 14 December 1931, 506; *Montana Standard,* 31 December 1931, 1, 2. Mullins notes that, contrary to many accounts, the West and particularly West Coast cities experienced the depression at the same time and to the same degree as other parts of the country. See *The Depression and the Urban West Coast,* 5.

4. Butte statistics were reported in the *Montana Standard,* 31 December 1932, 5. For national statistics on marriage, birth, and divorce rates, see Ware, *Holding Their Own,* 6–7. For a discussion of the disruptive effects of the depression on families, see Helmbold, "Beyond the Family Economy."

5. Ann Pentilla, interview by Ray Calkins and Caroline Smithson, Butte, 27 April 1979, 25; *EMJ* 133 (January 1932): 56; Hanford Toppari, interview by Ray Calkins, Butte, 1 May 1980, 10–11; McHugh, "Gulch and I," 11.

6. Montana News Association Inserts, 1938; Clarence Miller, interview by Ray Calkins, Butte, 13 June 1980, 24; *Newsletter of the Klepetko Chapter of the Society for Industrial Archaeology* 4 (December 1989): 4.

7. Anonymous, "Mr. Average Citizen Butte," 5, in "State Guide-field copy, Butte," WPA Records, MSU; John Sconfienza, interview by Ray Calkins, Butte, 27 June 1979, 8; Anita Stewart Watson and Marshall Watson, interview by Laurie Mercier, Corvallis, 21 June 1983. On the plight of some women during the depression, see Helmbold, "Downward Occupational Mobility."

8. Anonymous, "Mr. Average Citizen Butte," 5–6; *Montana Standard,* 21 January 1932, 7; Lavina Richards and Dolores Morgan LaBranche, interview by Betty Hoag, Butte, 29 November 1965, 18.

9. Civil Works Administration, Montana, *A Report of C.W.A. Activities,* 107–8; Ore, "Labor and the New Deal in Butte," 21–22; *Montana Standard,* 25 December 1931, 1.

10. Civil Works Administration, Montana, *A Report of C.W.A. Activities,* 107–8; *Montana Standard,* 4 May 1932, 2; Ore, "Labor and the New Deal in Butte," 23.

11. Ore, "Labor and the New Deal in Butte," 22; Leipheimer, *The First National Bank of Butte,* 34; Pierce Williams to Fred C. Croxton, 27 March 1933 and 15 May 1933, "Records Relating to Emergency Relief to State,

Montana Correspondence," RG 234, box 62, "Reconstruction Finance Corporation Approved State Loan Correspondence" file, NA.

12. *Eye Opener,* 1 April 1933, 1, 2; Toppari interview, 15. For further accusations regarding ACM abuse of relief distribution, see Kinney, "Montana Challenges the Tyranny of Copper."

13. Herb Wurst, "Statement of Workers Alliance Leader," 28 February 1938, and Silver Bow County Commissioners to Montana Community Improvement Appraisal Committee, 4 March 1938, Works Progress Administration Records, WPA Division of Information, Appraisal Report Files, RG 69, box 206, "County Reports, S-T" file, NA. On the range of attitudes people had about relief, see Phillips and Sternsher, "Victims of the Great Depression."

14. Lowitt, *The New Deal and the West,* 1–7; Malone, Roeder, and Lang, *Montana: A History of Two Centuries,* 303; Ore, "Labor and the New Deal in Butte," 27–29; Civil Works Administration, Montana, *A Report of C.W.A. Activities,* 37–56. Sen. Burton K. Wheeler declared for FDR in the fall of 1931. Thomas J. Walsh, the state's senior senator, was chair of the Democratic National Convention; J. Bruce Kremer of Butte was chair of the National Rules Committee; and Frank C. Walker, also of Butte, was the Democratic party's treasurer.

15. *Montana Standard,* 12 July 1934, 5.

16. Joseph E. Watson to W. O. Wheary, 17 October 1934, and Agnes Pauline to Ellen S. Woodward, 8 November 1934, RG 69, box 171, file 453.1, NA.

17. Pauline to Woodward, 27 February 1935, and 19 March 1935, RG 69, box 171, file 453.1, NA.

18. On the status of women workers in the New Deal, see Hargreaves, "Darkness before the Dawn"; Kornbluh, "The She-She-She Camps"; Rose, "Discrimination against Women"; Scharf, *To Work and to Wed;* Swain, "'The Forgotten Woman'"; Wandersee, *Women's Work and Family Values;* and Ware, "Women and the New Deal."

19. Works Progress Administration, Division of Social Research, *Workers on Relief in the United States,* 525, 565.

20. Rose C. Bresnahan to Woodward, 11 January 1937, WPA Central Files, "State: Mont. 1935–44," RG 69, box 1812, "Mont. 660 A-Z, Jan. 1939" file, NA; Bresnahan to Woodward, 27 March 1937, 12 April 1937, and 26 May 1937, Bresnahan to Mary H. Isham, 4 May 1937, RG 69, box 1813, "661 Mont., Jan-July 1937" file, NA; Julia G. Spier to Silver Bow County Board of Commissioners, 28 February 1938, Etta Bessette to Silver Bow County Board of Commissioners, Herb Wurst, "Statement of Workers Alliance Leader," and Denis McCarthy to Silver Bow County Board of Commissioners, WPA Division of Information Appraisal Report File, RG 69, box 206, "County Reports S-T" file, NA. For conditions in other New Deal sewing rooms, see Faue, *Community of Suffering and Struggle,* chap. 6, and Tidd, Jr., "Stitching and Striking."

21. Ethel Arnett to W. J. Butler, 16 March 1935, RG 69, box 170, file 450, NA.

22. Butte City Council Minutes (20 April 1932), 18:1144–45; *Montana Standard,* 16 June 1931, 1; McDonald, "The First Librarians' Union"; Emmet Carney to James E. Murray, 3 January 1935, JM Papers, box 649, file 3, UM. McDonald believed that the Butte local was the first librarians' union in the country.

23. Arrington and Reading, "New Deal Economic Programs"; Saindon and Sullivan, "Taming the Missouri and Treating the Depression"; "An Evaluation and Appraisal of the Federal Work Program in Montana," 6–11.

24. U.S. Department of Labor, Bureau of Labor Statistics, *Family Income and Expenditure,* 20, 26, 10. The figure of 25.5 percent of the city's population receiving some kind of public relief would undoubtedly have been higher had the survey included working-class neighborhoods abutting the city limits.

25. Carden, "Come Wander Back with Me," 11; Writers' Program, Work Projects Administration, *Copper Camp,* 11.

26. Creech, "The Work Project Administration Division of Recreation Projects." My thanks to Bill Creech, archivist at the National Archives, for sharing this work. WPA of Montana, Division of Education and Recreation, "Planning Our Leisure."

27. "WPA of Montana Division of Professional and Service Projects, Education-Recreation Semi-Monthly Bulletin," 12 June 1940, WPA Central Files, "State 1935–1944, Montana," RG 69, box 1806, "Mont. 651.3" file, NA; Eduard C. Lindeman, "Status of the WPA Recreation Program," box 1, "WPA Recreation Program" file, NA; G. Ott Romney, "Quotations on Recreation," 28 May 1935, box 6, "Quotations; Recreation; General" file, NA.

28. Frazier, "Why Pay the Fiddler?" Misevic is quoted in *Montana Standard,* 5 July 1936, 6. For another analysis of the relationship between delinquency and recreation during the depression, see Gelber, "'A Job You Can't Lose.'"

29. On the activities of the Butte recreation program, see *Montana Standard,* 28 June 1936, 11, 5 July 1936, 6, 18 April 1937, sec. 1, 9, 12 February 1939, 8. The Arcade lounge is described in "Semi-Annual Report, Butte Recreation Program, July 1–December 31, 1939," RG 69, box 4, "Butte, Montana" file, NA. The goals of family recreation are discussed in WPA of Montana, "Family Recreation," and WPA of Montana, "Christmas Bulletin for December 1938."

30. Montana Relief Commission, "Report on Recreation Project," 28 May 1935, RG 69, box 1811, "651.36, Mont. Jan 1937" file, NA; WPA Project Proposal from City of Butte, 23 August 1935, WPA Collection, BSBA; WPA of Montana, "Christmas Bulletin for December 1938"; WPA of Montana, "Family Recreation," 1.

31. Montana Relief Commission, "Report on Recreation Project," 28 May 1935; "Semi-Annual Report, Butte Recreation Program, 1939."

32. "Semi-Annual Report, Butte Recreation Program, 1939"; W. Fred Edwards, "Community Nite Programs and Their Development in Butte," in "WPA of Montana Division of Professional and Service Projects, Education-Recreation Semi-Monthly Bulletin," 28 February 1940, RG 69, box 1807, "Mont. 651.314, Jan 1941–Feb 15, 1942" file, NA.

33. Douglas Gold to Silver Bow County Board of Commissioners, 4 March 1938, WPA Division of Information, Appraisal Report File, RG 69, box 206, "County Reports, S-T" file, NA; John J. Brennan to Murray, 13 August 1937, JM Papers, box 795, file 5, UM; "Semi-Annual Report, Butte Recreation Program, 1939."

34. "Semi-Annual Report, Butte Recreation Program, 1939"; Butte City Council Minutes (21 August 1940), 20:669, (4 September 1940), 20:682, (6 November 1940), 20:723–24, 726.

35. WPA of Montana, Division of Professional and Education Service Projects, "Semi-Monthly News Bulletin, 16 August 1939," RG 69, box 1806, "Mont. 651.31, Jan 1941" file, NA; "Semi-Annual Report, Butte Recreation Program, 1939."

36. "Semi-Annual Report, Butte Recreation Program, 1939"; memo to regional recreation directors from Irma Ring, WPA Division of Recreation, RG 69, box 1, "Regional Agencies" file, NA; and WPA, Montana, "Arts and Crafts" (mimeo booklet), 1939, WPA Division of Recreation, RG 69, box 15, "Montana" file, NA. The literature on the New Deal Federal One projects is vast. Some works that discuss the "cultural nationalism" of the New Deal art programs include Aaron and Bendiner, eds., *The Strenuous Decade;* Contreras, *Tradition and Innovation;* McKinzie, *The New Deal for Artists;* Melosh, *Engendering Culture;* O'Connor, *Federal Support for the Visual Arts;* O'Sullivan, "Joint Venture or Testy Alliance?"; and Stott, *Documentary Expression and Thirties America.*

37. Hallie Flanagan to Mrs. S. J. Vas Binder, 10 August 1936, WPA Central Files, "State, 1935–44, Montana," RG 69, box 1806, "651.312, 1935–38" file, NA; Ray Hart to Jacob Baker, 24 December 1935, and Ray Hart to Harry L. Hopkins, 4 January 1936, box 1806, "Mont. 651.3" file, NA; Bruno David Ussher to Lawrence Westbrook, 4 January 1936, and Robert W. Stevens to Ussher, 17 December 1936, box 1806, "651.311, Mont. 1935–Jan 1941" file, NA.

38. For biographical information, see Bresnahan's "Application for Position, Department of Labor," RG 69, box 1789, "Mont, 630, A-D" file, NA. Bresnahan received broad-based support for her appointment to the WPA from Democrats, women's groups, and the labor movement. See correspondence to Sen. James Murray in JM Papers, box 14, file 11, UM.

39. "Annual Report," 1932, Minutes, 4 May 1932, "Annual Report," 1933, Women's Auxiliary to the American Institute of Mining Engineers Records, Butte chapter, BSBA; Finlen, *Meet Some Folks,* 115. On the attitude

of the Montana Federation of Women's Clubs toward the New Deal, see *The Montana Woman* (February 1937): 14–15, and Agnes Pauline to Ellen S. Woodward, 22 August 1936, RG 69, box 1813, file "661 Mont., May-Aug 1936," NA.

40. Rose C. Bresnahan to Holger Cahill, 30 November 1937, and Joseph E. Parker to Ellen S. Woodward, 14 December 1937, RG 69, box 1807, "651.315, Mont." file, NA.

41. Bresnahan to Cahill, 30 November 1937; *Montana Standard,* 8 April 1938, 1.

42. Frank L. Stevens to Cahill, 16 January 1939, and 9 February 1939, RG 69, box 1807, "651.315, Mont. 1937–Aug 1939" file, NA; Stevens to Cahill, 28 December 1938, box 1808, "Mont. 651.3152, Jan 1939–Jan 1941" file, NA; Stevens to Cahill, 31 January 1939, box 1807, file 651.315, NA; *Montana Standard,* 6 November 1938, 7.

43. Stevens interview, 39; Bresnahan to Cahill, 18 January 1938, RG 69, box 1807, file 651.315, NA; Stevens to Cahill, 16 January 1939. On the FAP's community art centers, see Harris, "Nationalizing Art." On comparable projects in other western states, see Dieterich, "The New Deal Cultural Projects in Wyoming," and South, "The Federal Art Project in Utah."

44. *Montana Standard,* 13 August 1938, 5; Stevens to Walter M. Kiplinger, 30 March 1942, RG 69, box 1806, "651.3115/3118, Mont." file, NA. For more about Standing's career, see Ewers, "William Standing," and Kennedy, ed., *The Assiniboines. The Assiniboines* is a reprint of *Land of Nakoda* with additional introductory material about the original volume's creators.

45. Mumford, "A Letter to the President."

46. Stanley D. Griffiths to Mayor of Butte and Board of County Commissioners, 28 February 1938, and Silver Bow Board of County Commissioners to Montana Community Improvement Appraisal Committee, 4 March 1938, WPA Division of Information, Appraisal Report File, RG 69, box 206, "County Files, S-T" file, NA. Many other positive reports from representatives of labor, business, and local government are in this file.

47. *Final Report on the WPA Program, 1935–43;* Community Service Programs Division, "Montana WPA."

48. Joseph E. Parker to J. B. Convery, 17 December 1942, Silver Bow Board of County Commissioners to JM, 28 May 1942, Parker to James E. Rowe, 5 January 1943, Butte Miners' Union No. 1 to JM, 15 January 1943, Parker to JM, 25 February 1943, JM to Lewis R. Knox, 26 February 1943, and unreferenced clipping, 26 February 1943, all in JM Papers, box 796, file 2, UM.

49. *Montana Standard,* 23 March 1941, 1.

50. Howard C. Beresford to Mark A. McCloskey, 9 August 1943; Beresford to Sherwood Gates, 27 November 1943, Records of the Office of Community War Services, RG 215, box 147, "Butte, Mont. 800" file, NA.

51. Beresford to Gates, 3 February 1944, Beresford to Gates, 13 April

1945, and Beresford to Gates, 20 October 1944, RG 215, box 147, "Butte, Mont, 800" file, NA.

52. "Field Report of Dr. Walter Clarke on Butte, Montana," 4–5 February 1949, and "Field Report of Patrick Kelley," 4 April 1949, 5 April 1949, 12–14 June 1949, 15 June 1949, 6–9 September 1949, 12–13 October 1949, American Social Hygiene Association Records, box 108, file 5, SWHA.

53. Beresford to Gates, 3 February 1944, 27 November 1943.

54. *Montana Standard,* 12 April 1941, 1; Howard, *Montana,* 95.

55. Writers' Program, Work Projects Administration, *Copper Camp,* v. For biographical information on William Burke, see the "Men at Work" file in the WPA materials collection at MSU. In "The Copper Pen," Roeder refers to *Copper Camp* as the codification and embellishment of Butte lore. See note 2. Only a few files from the Montana Writers' Project not related to livestock history seem to have survived, and those are at MSU.

56. Writers' Program, Work Projects Administration, *Copper Camp,* v-vi; Stott, *Documentary Expression,* 115.

57. Howard, *Montana,* 99. For background on Howard, see Roeder, "Joseph Kinsey Howard."

58. Green, "Marcus Daly Enters Heaven"; Green, "At the Hall"; Green, *Wobblies, Pile Butts, and Other Heroes,* 177–205; Fischer, "Diamond Dust," 59.

59. Howard, "Butte," 300–301; Renne, *A Preliminary Report,* 64, 77–90.

Conclusion

Butte, Montana, was first and foremost a mining city, a metropolis built upon fabulous wealth and fabulous stories. For miners and their families Butte promised a hardscrabble living. Sometimes—when the price of copper was high—miners were richly rewarded, but their work was always heavily taxed. The threats of silicosis, tuberculosis, fire, or a maiming fall of rock jeopardized their lives and the livelihoods of their families. Although the families of middle-class merchants and professionals did not share the same trials as the working class, their fate, too, depended on the mines, whose headframes punctuated the skyline of the Hill, stark reminders of the reason all had come to that high, cold valley.

The nature of work in Butte molded the nature of play. Hard work and hard play were partners. Miners risked their lives daily, and a sense of living on the edge spilled over into leisure time. Recklessness characterized many of Butte's amusements. Condemned vices in other American cities were tolerated pastimes in Butte, a city designed for adult men. A friend warned writer J. K. Hutchens that "Butte is a place that no one should visit until he has reached a certain age." He meant that not only did one need skill to survive Butte's mines, but also that one needed skill to survive its amusements. Butte provided pleasures for people who paid their own way and who could presumably take care of themselves while they were playing. In the twentieth century that group included increasing numbers of women. Those who sought to provide recreation for children and young adults were constantly frustrated by the lack of interest and support.

The maintenance of urban pleasures was primarily a commercial proposition. Faced with the choice of supporting public recreation or spending money in private amusements, Butte residents chose to invest in the private sector. Both the city government and the Anaconda Company assisted in this enterprise; neither encouraged public recreation or restrained wide-open Butte. This attitude was most clearly demonstrated during Prohibition and the depression. Neither the local government nor the Anaconda Company lent moral or physical weight to the enforcement of the Volstead Act or to the continuation of New Deal recreation programs. Maintaining a wide-open town was presumably a cheap way of keeping workers happy. Before World War II, Butte citizens who wanted a park system, recreation programs, or restrictions on vice never garnered enough strength to make any lasting impact on the city or the company. In a community dominated by a single industry, the wise did not oppose company policy, whether it was stated explicitly or implied by silence.

Most of Butte's middle class limited its cultural and civic activities to projects sponsored by voluntary groups or to typically unsuccessful alliances with crusading state officials. Working-class residents' commitment to community improvement was restricted by their dependence on Anaconda jobs and by the unpredictability of employment in a boom-and-bust economy. The patterns of amusement set in Butte's early years as a mining camp persisted well into the twentieth century. Men who had no guarantee of long-term work preferred to pay for immediate pleasures rather than invest in long-range community endeavors.

The most effective challenges to the nature of leisure in Butte came from women seeking to share the commercial pleasures enjoyed by men. Women "pioneers" had made inroads before World War I, but when it came to the public amusements of respectable women, Butte was a conservative town. "Public" women were prostitutes. The city did not have a large work force of "women adrift" who created a vibrant street life in America's larger cities. The majority of young single women in Butte lived at home with their families and were subject to the rules of conduct of family and neighborhood. It was a major adjustment to accept the advent of respectable women at play in amusement halls and on the street. Not until the late 1910s and early 1920s did Butte's working women challenge men's proprietary claim to the city's public amusements. The nationwide spread of commercial culture, advertising, movies, and radio helped Butte women join their sisters elsewhere who were changing their deportment as well as their styles of dress. During Prohibition women drank in public in new speakeasies and nightclubs. They gambled in keno parlors designed for women and at the gaming tables of gambling halls. They cheered at prizefights and danced at roadhouses. Although not everyone approved of their behavior, they were not automatically labeled "bad," "loose," or "fallen" as they would have been a decade earlier. The recreation of Butte in the 1920s and 1930s involved a tug-of-war between men, seeking to preserve the sanctity of traditional male venues of commercial amusement, and women, seeking greater access to them. The result was not a straightforward integration of male domains but the creation of new social institutions, such as speakeasies, nightclubs, and dance halls, which welcomed women and their money and fashioned a more heterosocial commercial culture.

Butte residents did what they could to balance the precariousness of life in a mining town and their need to feel a sense of community. Divisions of class and ethnicity and a lack of strong leadership on the part of city officials precluded the development of any kind of citywide network of shared interests. But in their own neighborhoods and small communities, based on ethnicity or occupation or love of literature and art, citizens worked to make Butte a more humane environment and enjoy the pleasures the city offered. Living with the mining industry engendered a particular psychology. Residents depended on boom times but girded themselves for busts. It was not something people thought about every day, but it subtly affected their behavior and shaped their institutions. Butte was a mining city dependent on and proud of its industry, reveling in its wide-open reputation and living for the moment.

Bibliography

Abbreviations

AAA   Archives of American Art, Washington, D.C.
BSBA   Butte–Silver Bow Public Archives, Butte
LC   Library of Congress, Washington, D.C.
MHSA   Montana Historical Society Archives, Helena
MHSL   Montana Historical Society Library, Helena
MSU   Merrill G. Burlingame Special Collections, Montana State
        University Libraries, Bozeman
NA   National Archives, Washington, D.C.
SWHA   Social Welfare History Archives, Walter Library, University of
        Minnesota, Minneapolis
UM   K. Ross Toole Archives, University of Montana, Missoula
WMM   World Museum of Mining, Butte

Interviews and Reminiscences

When transcripts of interviews are available, it is noted. Otherwise all interviews and reminiscences are on cassette tapes.

Beamish, Lillian. Interview by Laurie Mercier, 29 July 1982. Interview 319. MHSA.
Blakeley, James. Interview by Ray Calkins, 15 November 1979. Transcript. BSBA.
Bontempo, Dominick. Interview by Judy Cusick, 26 November 1982. Interview 550. MHSA.
Canavan, Marian. Interview by Mary Murphy, 20 May 1987. Transcript. BSBA.
Carlisle, Herbert. Interview by Laurie Mercier, 26 February 1982. Interview 240. MHSA.
Casey, Josephine Weiss. Interview by Alice Finnegan, 18 May 1989. Transcript. In possession of A. Finnegan.

Cavanaugh, John. Interview by Ray Calkins, May-June 1980. Transcript. BSBA.

Chappelle, Art. Unrecorded interview by author, 29 July 1988.

Connors, John. Interview by Laurie Mercier, 8 December 1982. Interview 418. MHSA.

Copenhaver, Blanche. Interview by Mary Murphy, 21 February 1980. BSBA.

Craney, Edmund B. Telephone interview by Mary Murphy, 15 October 1988.

Fiftieth Anniversary Program, KGIR-KXLF, 3 reels. In possession of Scott Steen, Butte.

George, Charles A. ["Sonny O'Day"]. Interview by Sam Gilluly, 18 June 1972. Interview 44. MHSA.

Goldberg, Aili. Interview by Mary Murphy, 29 February 1980. Transcript. BSBA.

Grover, Archie. Interview by Julie Foster, 20 August 1982. Interview 338. MHSA.

Harkins, Irene Shimin. Interviewer unidentified, 1979. In possession of Scott Steen, Butte.

Hawke, Bill. Interview by Sarah DeMoney, 1976. BSBA.

Hileman, Alma E. Interview by Ray Calkins, 27 June 1980. Transcript. BSBA.

Holloway, Hedley. Interview by Laurie Mercier, 9 March 1982. Interview 242. MHSA.

Horst, Betty. Unrecorded interview by author, 23 May 1988.

Hoy, Catherine. Interview by Ray Calkins and Caroline Smithson, 11 May 1979. Transcript. BSBA.

Jordan, Jean. Personal reminiscence, 1976. BSBA.

Jursnick, Frank. Interview by Ray Calkins, 6 June 1979. Transcript. BSBA.

Knierim, Bernice. Interview by Diane Sands, 3 August 1987. Interview 1028. MHSA.

Koski, Gus. Interview by Kathy Tureck, 23 September 1982. Interview 490. MHSA.

Loughran, James M. Interview by Ray Calkins, 2 July 1980. Transcript. BSBA.

MacDonell, Katherine G. Interview by Diane Sands, 8 June 1987. Interview 1012. MHSA.

Maffei, Camille. Interview by Russ Magnaghi, 4 May 1983. Interview 583. MHSA.

Martin, Dorothy A. Interview by Mary Murphy, 23 May 1988. Transcript. BSBA.

McKernan, Bill. Interview by Mary Murphy, 9 September 1988. BSBA.

McNelis, Mike. Interview by Alice Finnegan, 18 October 1985. Transcript. In possession of A. Finnegan.

Merzlak, June. Interview by Ray Calkins, 16 June 1980. Transcript. BSBA.

Miller, Clarence. Interview by Ray Calkins, 13 June 1980. Transcript. BSBA.

Mucahy, Mae. Interview by Gary Stanton, 28 August 1979. AFS 20,441. American Folklife Center, LC.

Mulhern, Bessie Towey. Interview by Laurie Mercier, 23 November 1981. Interview 213. MHSA.

Myllymaki, Saima. Interview by Laurie Mercier, 19 March 1982. Interview 251. MHSA.

O'Leary, Pat. Interview by Ray Calkins, 22 July 1980. Transcript. BSBA.

Onkalo, John. Interview by Ray Calkins, February 1980. Transcript. BSBA.

Panisko, Frank. Interview by Ray Calkins, 6 May 1980. Transcript. BSBA.

Pasini, Luigi and Norma Pasini. Interview by Russ Magnaghi, 4 May 1983. Interview 582. MHSA.

Pentilla, Ann. Interview by Ray Calkins and Caroline Smithson, 27 April 1979. Transcript. BSBA.

Petroni, Angelo. Interview by Russ Magnaghi, 4 May 1983. Interview 581. MHSA.

Popovich, Michael. Interview by Mary Murphy, 24 August 1988. BSBA.

Quinn, Frank. Personal reminiscence, 1976. BSBA.

Ramsey, Preston K. Interview by Ray Calkins, 26 March 1979. Transcript. BSBA.

Raymond, Helen Shute. Interview by Laurie Mercier, 9 October 1981. Interview 196. MHSA.

Roberts, Murel L. Interview by Ray Calkins, 8 August 1980. Transcript. BSBA.

Scanland, Lisle. Interview by Laurie Mercier, 22 June 1983. Interview 653. MHSA.

Schilling, Ray. Interview by Mary Murphy, 31 August 1988. BSBA.

Sconfienza, John. Interview by Ray Calkins, 27 June 1979. Transcript. BSBA.

Segna, Victor Giuseppe and Louise Zanchi. Interview by Russ Magnaghi, 3 May 1983. Interview 580. MHSA.

Shifty, Inez. Interview by Mary Murphy, 14 October 1987. BSBA.

Simonich, Joe. Personal reminiscence, 1976. BSBA.

Slauson, Lena Brown. Interview by Mary Murphy, 2 December 1987. BSBA.

Slauson, Winfred. Interview by Mary Murphy, 12 August 1988. BSBA.

Sloan, Anne. Interview by Laurie Mercier, 28 July 1982. Interview 317. MHSA.

Sontum, Olga. Interview by Ray Calkins, February 1980. Transcript. BSBA.

Stevens, Frank L. Interview by Betty Hoag, Los Angeles, 2 June 1964. Transcript. AAA.

Sullivan, Edward. Interview by Laurie Mercier, 25 February and 10 March 1982. Interview 243. MHSA.

Toppari, Hanford. Interview by Ray Calkins, 1 May 1980. Transcript. BSBA.

Trbovich, Mary. Interview by Mary Murphy, 4 November 1987. BSBA.

Tweet, Nellie. Interview by Claudia Claque Tweet, 24 July 1982. Interview 555. MHSA.

Watson, Anita Stewart and Marshall Watson. Interview by Laurie Mercier, 21 June 1983. Interview 548. MHSA.

Webster, Val. Interview by Mary Murphy, 24 February 1980. Transcript. BSBA.

Manuscript Sources

American Social Hygiene Association Records, SWHA.

Anaconda Copper Mining Company Records, 1876–1974, MHSA.

Associated Charities of Butte, Montana, Biennial Reports, 1900–1904, MHSL.

Association against the Prohibition Amendment and the Women's Organization for National Prohibition Reform Papers, Eleutherian Mills Historical Library, Wilmington, Delaware.

E. W. and G. D. Beattie Records, 1872–1935, MHSA.

Board of World's Fair Managers of the State of Montana Records, 1891–94, MHSA.

Beatrice Bray Papers, WMM.

Children's Bureau Records, NA.

Edmund B. Craney Papers, MHSA.

Daughters of Norway, Solheim Lodge No. 20 Records, BSBA.

Andrew "Shorty" Felt Diary, 1919, BSBA.

Homer Club Records, MHSA.

Joseph Kinsey Howard Papers, 1927–54, MHSA.

Leggat Collection, MSU.

Marian White Arts and Crafts Club Records, BSBA.

Montana Attorney General Records, 1893–1969, MHSA.

Montana Council of Defense Records, MHSA.

Montana Federation of Colored Women Records, 1921–78, MHSA.

Montana Governors' Papers, 1893–1962, MHSA.

Montana Relief Commission Records, 1934–36, MHSA.

James E. Murray Papers, UM.

National American Woman Suffrage Association (Montana) Records, 1913–19 and undated, MHSA.

National League of Women Voters Papers, LC.

National Recreation Association Records, SWHA.

New Deal Collection, BSBA.

Jeannette Rankin Papers, 1917–63, MHSA.

Reconstruction Finance Corporation Records, NA.

Margaret Sanger Papers, LC.

Teddy Traparish Papers, BSBA.

Woman's Club of Butte, Montana, Yearbooks, 1901–23, MHSA.

Women's Auxiliary to the American Institute of Mining Engineers Records, Butte chapter, BSBA.

Works Progress Administration Records, MSU.

Works Progress Administration Records, NA.

Pamphlets

Alderson, Mary Long. *Thirty-Four Years in the Montana Woman's Christian Temperance Union, 1896–1930.* Helena: by the author, ca. 1932.

American Legion, Silver Bow Post No. 1. *Silver Bow County in the World War.* n.d. BSBA.

Butte Business Men's Association. *Butte, Montana.* Butte: McKee Printing Co., n.d.

Club Histories District II: Montana Federation of Women's Clubs. 1964.

Kelly, John Bailey. *Children of Copperland.* New York: Board of Home Missions of the Presbyterian Church in the U.S.A., 1923.

Meaderville Volunteer Fire Department, Our Golden Anniversary Year, 1910–1960, Fifty Years of Community Service, 1960. MHSL.

"Observing Thirty Years with the Present Butte Country Club House." 18 August 1945. BSBA.

Price, Esther G. *Fighting Tuberculosis in the Rockies: A History of the Montana Tuberculosis Association.* Helena: Montana Tuberculosis Association, 1943.

Proceedings of the First Session of the Montana State Federation of Negro Women's Clubs. Butte: Oates and Roberts, 1921.

"Report of the Synodical Executive." *Minutes of the Synod of Montana,* 1928, 1932.

"Silver Anniversary of the Circle of Serbian Sisters, 1934–1959, Holy Trinity Orthodox Church." 1959. BSBA.

Government Documents

FEDERAL

Final Report on the WPA Program, 1935–43. Washington, D.C.: GPO, 1946.

Official Records of the National Commission on Law Observance and Enforcement. *Enforcement of Prohibition Laws.* Volume 4. *Prohibition Surveys of the States.* 71st Cong., 3d sess., S. Doc. 307. Washington, D.C.: GPO, 1931.

Thirteenth Census, 1910, Montana, volume 16: *Silver Bow* (microfilm of manuscript).

U.S. Department of Commerce. Bureau of the Census. *Historical Statistics of the United States, Colonial Times to 1970.* Part 1. Washington, D.C.: GPO, 1975.

———. *Thirteenth Census of the United States Taken in the Year 1910,* volume 2: *Population, 1910. Reports by States, Alabama-Montana.* Washington, D.C.: GPO, 1913.

———. *Thirteenth Census of the United States Taken in the Year 1910,* volume 4: *Population, 1910, Occupation Statistics.* Washington, D.C.: GPO, 1914.

———. *Abstract of the Fourteenth Census of the United States 1920.* Washington, D.C.: GPO, 1923.

———. *Fourteenth Census of the United States Taken in the Year 1920,* volume

3: *Composition and Characteristics of the Population by States.* Washington, D.C.: GPO, 1923.

―――. *Fourteenth Census of the United States Taken in the Year 1920,* volume 4: *Population, 1920, Occupations.* Washington, D.C.: GPO, 1923.

―――. *Fifteenth Census of the United States: 1930. Population,* volume 3, part 2: *Reports by States: Montana-Wyoming.* Washington, D.C.: GPO, 1932.

―――. *Abstract of the Fifteenth Census of the United States, 1930.* Washington, D.C.: GPO, 1933.

―――. *Fifteenth Census of the United States: 1930. Population,* volume 4: *Occupations, by States.* Washington, D.C.: GPO, 1933.

―――. *Fifteenth Census of the United States: 1930. Population,* volume 6: *Families.* Washington, D.C.: GPO, 1933.

U.S. Department of Commerce. Bureau of Mines. *Review of Safety and Health in the Mines at Butte,* by G. S. Rice and R. R. Sayers. Bulletin 257. Washington, D.C.: GPO, 1925.

U.S. Department of the Interior. Bureau of Mines. *Lessons from the Granite Mountain Shaft Fire, Butte,* by Daniel Harrington. Bulletin 188. Washington, D.C.: GPO, 1922.

―――. *Major Disasters at Metal and Nonmetal Mines and Quarries in the United States (Excluding Coal Mines),* by John Hyvarinen, Leland H. Johnson, and D. O. Kennedy. Information Circular. Washington, D.C.: GPO, April, 1949.

U.S. Department of the Interior. Census Office. *Abstract of the Twelfth Census of the United States 1900.* Washington, D.C.: GPO, 1902.

U.S. Department of Labor. Bureau of Labor Statistics. *Family Income and Expenditure in Selected Urban Communities of the West Central-Rocky Mountain Region, 1935–36,* volume 1, by A. D. H. Kaplan, Faith M. Williams, and Mildred Parten. Bulletin 646. Washington, D.C.: GPO, 1939.

―――. *Family Income and Expenditure in Selected Urban Communities of the West Central-Rocky Mountain Region, 1935–36,* volume 2, by A. D. H. Kaplan and Faith M. Williams. Bulletin 646. Washington, D.C.: GPO, 1940.

U.S. Department of Labor. Children's Bureau. *Public Dance Halls: Their Regulation and Place in the Recreation of Adolescents,* by Ella Gardner. Publication 189. Washington, D.C.: GPO, 1929.

U.S. District Court, Montana, District of Montana Criminal Register and Dockets. RG 21, NA, Pacific Northwest Region, Seattle.

U.S. Military Intelligence Reports: Surveillance of the Radicals in the United States, 1917–41. Microfilm: University Publications of America.

U.S. Treasury Department, Bureau of Prohibition. *Annual Reports of the Commissioner of Prohibition.* Washington, D.C.: GPO, 1927, 1928, 1929, 1930.

WPA Division of Social Research. *Workers on Relief in the United States in March 1935,* volume 1: *A Census of Usual Occupations.* Washington, D.C.: GPO, 1938.

STATE AND LOCAL

An Evaluation and Appraisal of the Federal Work Program in Montana, Report of the Montana State Appraisal Committee Under the Plan of the United States Community Improvement Appraisal, 1938. MHSL.

Annual Reports of the City Officers, City of Butte for the Fiscal Years Ending April 30, 1908–09. No publication information.

Annual Reports of the City Officers, City of Butte for the Fiscal Years Ending April 30, 1910–11. Butte: McKee Printing, n.d.

Annual Reports of the City Officers of the City of Butte, Montana, Fiscal Year Ending April 30, 1912. Butte: Butte Miner Company, Printers, n.d.

Butte City Council Minutes, 1917–41. BSBA.

Butte City Health Department. "Report of the Health Officer, May 1914." Typescript. BSBA.

Carroll, William E., comp. *The Revised Ordinances of the City of Butte, 1914.* City Council of the City of Butte, [1914].

City of Butte Police Blotters, 1919, 1920, 1921. BSBA.

Civil Works Administration, Montana. *A Report of C. W. A. Activities in Montana, November 15, 1933 to March 29, 1934.* MHSL.

Department of Agriculture, Labor and Industry. *Montana Resources and Opportunities Edition* 3 (August 1928).

Laws, Resolutions and Memorials of the State of Montana Passed at the Tenth Regular Session of the Legislative Assembly. Helena: State Publishing Co., 1907.

Montana State Board of Health. *1954 Annual Statistical Supplement.*

"Petition of Centennial Brewing Company, Re Revocation of Liquor License at 27½ West Granite St." 17 January 1912. City Council Petitions. BSBA.

Renne, R. R. *A Preliminary Report of the Butte Economic Survey.* Butte: City of Butte, with the assistance of Work Projects Administration, 1939.

"Report of Committee Appointed by the Sixteenth Legislative Assembly to Investigate the High Cost of Living." 1919. Bound typescript. MHSL.

Silver Bow County Board of Health. "Report on Sanitary Conditions in the Mines and Community, Silver Bow County, December, 1908–April, 1912." Typescript. MHSA.

Silver Bow County Board of Health. "Report Showing Results of Inspection of Dwellings, Hotels, Rooming Houses, and Boarding Houses and Their Surroundings." 1912. Typescript. MHSA.

Works Progress Administration of Montana, Community Service Programs Division. "Montana WPA." n.d. Typescript. MSU.

Works Progress Administration of Montana, Division of Education and Recreation. "Christmas Bulletin for December 1938." WPA Collection, BSBA.

———. "Planning Our Leisure." n.d. WPA Collection, BSBA.

Works Progress Administration of Montana, Education and Recreation

Section, Professional and Service Division. "Family Recreation." n.d. WPA Collection, BSBA.

Newspapers and Periodicals

Anaconda Standard
Anode
Butte Bulletin
Butte Daily Post
Butte Evening News
Butte Miner
Engineering and Mining Journal
Eye Opener
Helena Catholic Monthly
Montana Free Press
Montana Standard
Mountaineer
Presbyterian Reporter
Woman's Voice

Dissertations, Theses, and Unpublished Papers

Alderson, Mrs. Matt W. "A Half Century of Progress for Montana Women." 1934. Typescript. MSU.

Appelman, Anna Nason. "Montana, I Return to You." n.d. Bound typescript. MHSL.

Axline, Jonathan Alan. "'This is a Case for the Police!': The Butte Police Department, 1914–1920." M.A. thesis, Montana State University, 1985.

Bahin, Louis J. "The Campaign for Prohibition in Montana: Agrarian Radicalism and Liquor Reform, 1883–1926." M.A. thesis, University of Montana, 1984.

Carden, Frank. "Come Wander Back with Me to Butte, Montana in the Year of 1923." 1988. Typescript. BSBA.

———. "A Ride on an Open Trolley Street Car from South Gaylord Street to the Columbia Gardens in the early 1920's." [ca. 1987]. Typescript. BSBA.

———. "A Walk from 228 S. Gaylord Street to Park and Main Streets and Beyond in Butte, Montana in the 1920's and 1930's." [ca. 1987]. Typescript. BSBA.

Creech, William Robin. "The Work Project Administration Division of Recreation Projects, 1936–1939." 1984. In possession of author.

Davitt, Kimberly J. "Female Visions and Verse: Turn-of-the-Century Women Artists and Writers in the Montana Landscape." M.A. thesis, University of Montana, 1993.

Edwards, W. Fred. "History of Musical Organizations in Butte." In "Butte

Past and Present." 1936. Mimeo. Vertical file, Butte–Silver Bow Free Public Library.

Ellis, Leonard Harry. "Men Among Men: An Exploration of All-Male Relationships in Victorian America." Ph.D. diss.: Columbia University, 1982.

Fischer, Ronald Glenn. "Diamond Dust." M.F.A. thesis, University of Montana, 1988.

Frisch, Paul Andrew. "The 'Gibraltar of Unionism': The Working Class at Butte, Montana, 1878–1906." Ph.D. diss., University of California, Los Angeles, 1992.

Hopwood, Jon. "History of the Silver Bow Club." 1980. Unpublished paper. MSU.

Kemper, W. A. "Butte: Past, Present and Future." [ca. 1916]. Typescript. MHSL vertical file "Butte, Mont—History, 1."

King-Powers, Stacy. "Caught in the Crossfire: Violence Against Women, Butte, Montana, 1895–1920." M.A. thesis, Montana State University, 1985.

Martin, Dale, and Brian Shovers. "Butte, Montana: An Architectural and Historical Inventory of the National Landmark District." Report prepared for the Butte Historical Society, 1986.

McHugh, Julia. "The Gulch and I." [ca. 1986]. Typescript. BSBA.

McNay, John Thomas, Jr. "Breaking the Copper Collar: The Sale of the Anaconda Newspapers and the Professionalization of Journalism in Montana." M.A. thesis, University of Montana, 1991.

Minton, Daniel. "Population Control: Butte, Silver Bow County Board of Health and Spanish Influenza of 1918." 1991. Unpublished paper. BSBA.

Murphy, Mary. "Report on a Survey of Historic Architecture on Butte's West Side." Report prepared for the Butte Historical Society, 1981.

———. "Women on the Line: Prostitution in Butte, Montana, 1878–1917." M.A. thesis, University of North Carolina, Chapel Hill, 1983.

"Narrative History of Homer Club—Butte, Montana, 1891–1941." n.d. Typescript. BSBA.

Nasstrom, Kathryn L. "'More Was Expected of Us': The North Carolina League of Women Voters and the Feminist Movement in the 1920s." M.A. thesis, University of North Carolina, 1988.

Ore, Janet. "Labor and the New Deal in Butte, Montana: The International Union of Mine, Mill and Smelter Workers' Strike of 1934." M.A. thesis, Washington State University, 1987.

———. "Suburban Schools in Butte, Montana." National Register of Historic Places Inventory Nomination Form, 1987.

Ostberg, Jacob H. "Sketches of Old Butte." 1972. Typescript. Butte–Silver Bow Free Public Library.

Parpart, Jane L. "The Household and the Mine Shaft: Gender and Class Struggles on the Zambian Copperbelt, 1924–66." Paper for discussion at the Postgraduate Seminar on Women in Africa, University of London,

Institute of Commonwealth Studies, Centre for African Studies, SOAS, 1985.

Perry, Elizabeth Israels. "Youth, Community Morality, and Censorship in the 1920s: Regulating the Dance Halls." Paper presented at the annual meeting of the Organization of American Historians, 1988.

Putnam, Edison K. "The Prohibition Movement in Idaho, 1863–1934." Ph.D. diss., University of Idaho, 1979.

Richards, Ron P. "The History of Radio Broadcasting in Montana." M.A. thesis, Montana State University, 1963.

Roeder, Richard Brown. "Montana in the Early Years of the Progressive Period." Ph.D. diss., University of Pennsylvania, 1971.

Satterthwaite, Thomas Charles. "Cornelius Francis Kelley: The Rise of an Industrial Statesman." M.A. thesis, Montana State University, 1971.

Shovers, Brian Lee. "Miners, Managers, and Machines: Industrial Accidents and Occupational Disease in the Butte Underground, 1880–1920." M.A. thesis, Montana State University, 1987.

Shutey, Rudolph J. "The Butte Labor Strike of 1920." Honors thesis, Carroll College, 1961.

Treloar, Sam. "Reminiscences of the Butte Mines Band." n.d. Bound typescript. MHSL.

Ward, Doris Buck. "The Winning of Woman Suffrage in Montana." M.A. thesis, Montana State University, 1974.

Books

Aaron, Daniel, and Robert Bendiner, eds. *The Strenuous Decade: A Social and Intellectual Record of the 1930s.* Garden City: Doubleday, 1970.

Allen, Frederick Lewis. *Only Yesterday: An Informal History of the 1920s.* New York: Harper and Bros., 1931.

Allingham, Margery. *Traitor's Purse.* New York: Doubleday, Doran, 1941.

Amott Teresa L., and Julia A. Matthaei. *Race, Gender, and Work: A Multicultural Economic History of Women in the United States.* Boston: South End Press, 1991.

Atherton, Gertrude. *Adventures of a Novelist.* New York: Liveright, 1932.

———. *Perch of the Devil.* New York: Frederick A. Stokes, 1914.

Bailey, Beth L. *From Front Porch to Back Seat: Courtship in Twentieth-Century America.* Baltimore: Johns Hopkins University Press, 1988.

Balch, Emily Greene. *Our Slavic Fellow Citizens.* New York: Charities Publication Committee, 1910.

Banner, Lois W. *American Beauty.* Chicago: University of Chicago Press, 1983.

Barnouw, Erik. *A Tower in Babel: A History of Broadcasting in the United States.* Volume 1, *to 1933.* New York: Oxford University Press, 1966.

Barth, Gunther. *Instant Cities: Urbanization and the Rise of San Francisco and Denver.* Revised edition. Albuquerque: University of New Mexico Press, 1988.

Bell, Frank. *Gladiators of the Glittering Gulches*. Helena: Western Horizons Books, 1985.

Benson, Susan Porter. *Counter Cultures: Saleswomen, Managers, and Customers in American Department Stores, 1890–1940*. Urbana: University of Illinois Press, 1986.

Best, Gary Dean. *The Nickel and Dime Decade: American Popular Culture during the 1930s*. Westport: Praeger Publishers, 1993.

Bigart, Robert. *Montana: An Assessment for the Future*. Missoula: University of Montana Publications in History, 1978.

Black, Naomi. *Social Feminism*. Ithaca: Cornell University Press, 1989.

Blair, Karen J. *The Clubwoman as Feminist: True Womanhood Redefined, 1868–1914*. New York: Holmes and Meier, 1980.

———. *The Torchbearers: Woman and Their Amateur Arts Associations in America, 1890–1930*. Bloomington: Indiana University Press, 1994.

Bodnar, John E. *The Transplanted: A History of Immigrants in Urban America*. Bloomington: Indiana University Press, 1985.

Braley, Berton. *Songs of the Workaday World*. New York: George H. Doran Co., 1915.

Brandes, Stuart D. *American Welfare Capitalism, 1880–1940*. Chicago: University of Chicago Press, 1976.

Brennan, Thomas. *Public Drinking and Popular Culture in Eighteenth-Century Paris*. Princeton: Princeton University Press, 1988.

Brinig, Myron. *Singermann*. New York: Farrar and Rinehart, 1929.

———. *Wide Open Town*. New York: Farrar and Rinehart, 1931.

Brown, Dorothy M. *Mabel Walker Willebrandt: A Study of Power, Loyalty, and Law*. Knoxville: University of Tennessee Press, 1984.

———. *Setting a Course: American Women in the 1920s*. Boston: Twayne Publishers, 1987.

Brown, Ronald C. *Hard-Rock Miners: The Intermountain West, 1860–1920*. College Station: Texas A&M University Press, 1979.

Burke, Bill. *Rhymes of the Mines*. Vancouver: by the author, 1964.

Burnham, John C. *Bad Habits: Drinking, Smoking, Taking Drugs, Gambling, Sexual Misbehavior, and Swearing in American History*. New York: New York University Press, 1993.

Butler, Anne M. *Daughters of Joy, Sisters of Misery: Prostitutes in the American West, 1865–90*. Urbana: University of Illinois Press, 1985.

Butte City Directory. Helena: R. L. Polk, 1889–1940.

Calkins, Ray, comp. *Looking Back from the Hill: Recollections of Butte People*. Butte: Butte Historical Society, 1982.

Calvert, Jerry W. *The Gibraltar: Socialism and Labor in Butte, Montana, 1895–1920*. Helena: Montana Historical Society Press, 1988.

Carnes, Mark C. *Secret Ritual and Manhood in Victorian America*. New Haven: Yale University Press, 1989.

Carson, Mina. *Settlement Folk: Social Thought and the American Settlement Movement, 1885–1930*. Chicago: University of Chicago Press, 1990.

Celebration of the Gift of Faith, 1884–1984: Western Montana Catholic Directory. Helena: Diocese of Helena, 1984.

Chaplin, Charles. *My Autobiography.* New York: Simon and Schuster, 1964.

Clark, Dennis. *The Irish Relations: Trials of an Immigrant Tradition.* East Brunswick: Associated University Presses, 1982.

Clark, Norman H. *Deliver Us from Evil: An Interpretation of American Prohibition.* New York: W. W. Norton, 1976.

————. *The Dry Years: Prohibition and Social Change in Washington.* 2d ed. Seattle: University of Washington Press, 1988.

Clawson, Mary Ann. *Constructing Brotherhood: Class, Gender, and Fraternalism.* Princeton: Princeton University Press, 1989.

Cobble, Dorothy Sue. *Dishing It Out: Waitresses and Their Unions in the Twentieth Century.* Urbana: University of Illinois Press, 1991.

Cohen, Lizabeth. *Making a New Deal: Industrial Workers in Chicago, 1919–1939.* Cambridge: Cambridge University Press, 1990.

Commire, Anne. *Something about the Author.* Volume 1. Detroit: Gale Research Book Tower, 1971.

Contreras, Belisario R. *Tradition and Innovation in New Deal Art.* Lewisburg: Bucknell University Press, 1983.

Cott, Nancy F. *The Grounding of Modern Feminism.* New Haven: Yale University Press, 1987.

Couvares, Francis G. *The Remaking of Pittsburgh: Class and Culture in an Industrializing City, 1877–1919.* Albany: State University of New York Press, 1984.

Cressey, Paul G. *The Taxi-Dance Hall: A Sociological Study in Commercialized Recreation and City Life.* Chicago: University of Chicago Press, 1932.

Cunningham, Mary S. *The Woman's Club of El Paso: Its First Thirty Years.* El Paso: Texas Western Press, 1978.

Dallas, Sandra. *Buster Midnight's Cafe.* New York: Random House, 1990.

Daniels, John. *America via the Neighborhood.* New York: Harper and Brothers, 1920.

D'Emilio, John, and Estelle B. Freedman. *Intimate Matters: A History of Sexuality in America.* New York: Harper and Row, 1988.

Derickson, Alan. *Workers' Health, Workers' Democracy: The Western Miners' Struggle, 1891–1925.* Ithaca: Cornell University Press, 1988.

Douglas, Susan J. *Inventing American Broadcasting, 1899–1922.* Baltimore: Johns Hopkins University Press, 1987.

Doyle, Don Harrison. *The Social Order of a Frontier Community: Jacksonville, Illinois, 1825–70.* Urbana: University of Illinois Press, 1978.

Drury, Clifford Merrill. *Presbyterian Panorama: One Hundred and Fifty Years of National Missions History.* Philadelphia: Presbyterian Church in the United States of America, 1952.

Duffy, Joe H. *Butte Was Like That.* Butte: Tom Greenfield, 1941.

Duis, Perry R. *The Saloon: Public Drinking in Chicago and Boston, 1880–1920.* Urbana: University of Illinois Press, 1983.

Emmons, David M. *The Butte Irish: Class and Ethnicity in an American Mining Town, 1875–1925*. Urbana: University of Illinois Press, 1989.

Erenberg, Lewis A. *Steppin' Out: New York Nightlife and the Transformation of American Culture, 1890–1930*. Chicago: University of Chicago Press, 1981.

Ewen, Elizabeth. *Immigrant Women in the Land of Dollars: Life and Culture on the Lower East Side, 1890–1925*. New York: Monthly Review Press, 1985.

Fahey, Edmund. *Rum Road to Spokane: A Story of Prohibition*. Missoula: University of Montana Publications in History, 1972.

Fass, Paula S. *The Damned and the Beautiful: American Youth in the 1920's*. New York: Oxford University Press, 1977.

Faue, Elizabeth. *Community of Suffering and Struggle: Women, Men, and the Labor Movement in Minneapolis, 1915–1945*. Chapel Hill: University of North Carolina Press, 1991.

Federal Writers' Project of the Work Projects Administration. *Montana: A State Guide Book*. New York: Hastings House, 1939.

Ferguson, Charles W. *Fifty Million Brothers: A Panorama of American Lodges and Clubs*. New York: Farrar and Rinehart, 1937.

Filene, Peter G. *Him/Her/Self: Sex Roles in Modern America*. 2d ed. Baltimore: Johns Hopkins University Press, 1986.

Finlen, James T. *Meet Some Folks*. New York: Carlton Press, 1983.

Flaherty, Cornelia M. *Go with Haste into the Mountains: A History of the Diocese of Helena*. Helena: Catholic Diocese, 1984.

Foy, Eddie, and Alvin F. Harlow. *Clowning Through Life*. New York: E. P. Dutton, 1928.

Frank, Dana. *Purchasing Power: Consumer Organizing, Gender, and the Seattle Labor Movement, 1919–1929*. Cambridge: Cambridge University Press, 1994.

Freeman, Harry C. *A Brief History of Butte, Montana*. Chicago: Henry O. Shepard, 1900.

Garber, Marjorie. *Vested Interests: Cross-Dressing and Cultural Anxiety*. New York: Routledge, Chapman and Hall, 1992.

Geologic Atlas of the Rocky Mountain Region, United States of America. Denver: Rocky Mountain Association of Geologists, 1972.

Gilkeson, John S., Jr. *Middle-Class Providence, 1820–1940*. Princeton: Princeton University Press, 1986.

Gitelman, H. M. *Legacy of the Ludlow Massacre: A Chapter in American Industrial Relations*. Philadelphia: University of Pennsylvania Press, 1988.

Glasscock, C. B. *The War of the Copper Kings: Builders of Butte and Wolves of Wall Street*. New York: Grosset and Dunlap, 1935.

Goldman, Marion S. *Gold Diggers and Silver Miners: Prostitution and Social Life on the Comstock Lode*. Ann Arbor: University of Michigan Press, 1981.

Gordon, Elizabeth Putnam. *Woman Torch-Bearers: The Story of the Woman's Christian Temperance Union*. 2d ed. Evanston: National WCTU Publishing House, 1924.

Gorn, Elliott J. *The Manly Art: Bare-Knuckle Prize Fighting in America.* Ithaca: Cornell University Press, 1986.

Green, Archie. *Wobblies, Pile Butts, and Other Heroes: Laborlore Explorations.* Urbana: University of Illinois Press, 1993.

Griswold, Robert L. *Fatherhood in America: A History.* New York: Basic Books, 1993.

Gutfeld, Arnon. *Montana's Agony: Years of War and Hysteria, 1917–1921.* Gainesville: University Presses of Florida, 1979.

Guttmann, Allen. *Sports Spectators.* New York: Columbia University Press, 1986.

Hall, Jacquelyn Dowd. *Revolt against Chivalry: Jessie Daniel Ames and the Women's Campaign against Lynching.* New York: Columbia University Press, 1979.

Hall, Jacquelyn Dowd, James Leloudis, Robert Korstad, Mary Murphy, Lu Ann Jones, and Christopher B. Daly. *Like a Family: The Making of a Southern Cotton Mill World.* Chapel Hill: University of North Carolina Press, 1987.

Harmon, Jim. *The Great Radio Heroes.* New York: Ace Books, 1967.

Hewitt, Nancy A. *Women's Activism and Social Change: Rochester, New York, 1822–1872.* Ithaca: Cornell University Press, 1984.

Horowitz, Daniel. *The Morality of Spending: Attitudes toward the Consumer Society in America, 1875–1940.* Baltimore: Johns Hopkins University Press, 1985.

Howard, Joseph Kinsey. *Montana: High, Wide, and Handsome.* New Haven: Yale University Press, 1943.

Hutchens, John K. *One Man's Montana: An Informal Portrait of a State.* Philadelphia: J. B. Lippincott, 1964.

James, R. Francis. *High, Low and Wide Open.* New York: Macaulay, 1935.

Johnson, Deidre, compiler and editor. *Stratemeyer Pseudonyms and Series Books: An Annotated Checklist of Stratemeyer and Stratemeyer Syndicate Publications.* Westport: Greenwood Press, 1982.

Josephson, Hannah. *Jeannette Rankin, First Lady in Congress: A Biography.* Indianapolis: Bobbs-Merrill, 1974.

Kasson, John F. *Rudeness and Civility: Manners in Nineteenth-Century Urban America.* New York: Hill and Wang, 1990.

Katz, Jack. *Seductions of Crime: Moral and Sensual Attractions in Doing Evil.* New York: Basic Books, 1988.

Kennedy, Michael Stephen, ed. *The Assiniboines.* Norman: University of Oklahoma Press, 1961.

Kerr, K. Austin. *Organized for Prohibition: A New History of the Anti-Saloon League.* New Haven: Yale University Press, 1985.

Kessler-Harris, Alice. *Out to Work: A History of Wage-Earning Women in the United States.* New York: Oxford University Press, 1982.

Kitchen Secrets of the Daughters of Norway. Portland: Nu-Way Printing and Envelope Company, 1956.

Kleinberg, S. J. *The Shadow of the Mills: Working-Class Families in Pittsburgh, 1870–1907.* Pittsburgh: University of Pittsburgh Press, 1989.

Kobler, John. *Ardent Spirits: The Rise and Fall of Prohibition.* New York: G. P. Putnam's Sons, 1973.

Kyvig, David E. *Repealing National Prohibition.* Chicago: University of Chicago Press, 1979.

Lankton, Larry. *Cradle to Grave: Life, Work, and Death at the Lake Superior Copper Mines.* New York: Oxford University Press, 1991.

Lazarsfeld, Paul F. *Radio and the Printed Page.* New York: Duell, Sloan and Pearce, 1940.

Lee, Rose Hum. *The Chinese in the United States of America.* Hong Kong: Hong Kong University Press, 1960.

Leipheimer, E. G. *The First National Bank of Butte.* St. Paul: Brown and Bigelow, 1952.

Lemons, J. Stanley. *The Woman Citizen: Social Feminism in the 1920s.* Urbana: University of Illinois Press, 1973.

Lender, Mark Edward, and James Kirby Martin. *Drinking in America: A History.* New York: The Free Press, 1982.

Lowery, Geraldine. *The American Legion in Montana, 1919–1963.* American Legion, Department of Montana, 1965.

Lowitt, Richard. *The New Deal and the West.* Bloomington: Indiana University Press, 1984.

Lynd, Robert S., and Helen Merrell Lynd. *Middletown: A Study in American Culture.* New York: Harcourt, Brace, 1929.

———. *Middletown in Transition: A Study in Cultural Conflicts.* New York: Harcourt, Brace, 1937.

MacDonald, J. Fred. *Don't Touch That Dial: Radio Programming in American Life, 1920–1960.* Chicago: Nelson-Hall, 1979.

MacLane, Mary. *I, Mary MacLane.* New York: Frederick A. Stokes, 1917.

———. *The Story of Mary MacLane.* Chicago: Herbert S. Stone, 1902.

Macleod, David I. *Building Character in the American Boy: The Boy Scouts, YMCA, and Their Forerunners, 1870–1920.* Madison: University of Wisconsin Press, 1983.

Madeleine: An Autobiography. New York: Harper and Brothers, 1919.

Malone, Michael P. *The Battle for Butte: Mining and Politics on the Northern Frontier, 1864–1906.* Seattle: University of Washington Press, 1981.

Malone, Michael P., Richard B. Roeder, and William L. Lang. *Montana: A History of Two Centuries.* Revised edition. Seattle: University of Washington Press, 1991.

Marchand, Roland. *Advertising the American Dream: Making Way for Modernity, 1920–1940.* Berkeley: University of California Press, 1985.

Marcosson, Isaac F. *Anaconda.* New York: Dodd, Mead, 1957.

Martin, Theodora Penny. *The Sound of Our Own Voices: Women's Study Clubs, 1860–1910.* Boston: Beacon Press, 1987.

McCarthy, Kathleen D., ed. *Lady Bountiful Revisited: Women, Philanthropy, and Power.* New Brunswick: Rutgers University Press, 1990.

McChesney, Robert W. *Telecommunications, Mass Media, and Democracy: The*

Battle for the Control of U.S. Broadcasting, 1928–1935. New York: Oxford University Press, 1993.

McKinzie, Richard D. *The New Deal for Artists*. Princeton: Princeton University Press, 1973.

McMahon, Morgan E., ed. *Radio Collector's Guide, 1921–1932*. Palos Verdes, Calif.: Vintage Radio, 1973.

McNamee, Graham. *You're on the Air*. New York: Harper and Bros., 1926.

McNelis, Sarah. *Copper King at War: The Biography of F. Augustus Heinze*. Missoula: University of Montana Press, 1968.

Melman, Billie. *Women and the Popular Imagination in the Twenties: Flappers and Nymphs*. New York: St. Martin's Press, 1988.

Melosh, Barbara. *Engendering Culture: Manhood and Womanhood in New Deal Public Art and Theater*. Washington, D.C.: Smithsonian Institution Press, 1991.

Meyerowitz, Joanne J. *Women Adrift: Independent Wage Earners in Chicago, 1880–1930*. Chicago: University of Chicago Press, 1988.

Miller, Robert E. *The Hands of the Workmen: A History of the First Hundred Years of the Grand Lodge of Montana, Ancient, Free and Accepted Masons*. Helena: Centennial Committee, 1966.

Minutes of the Synod of Montana of the Presbyterian Church U.S.A., 1926, 1928, 1932.

Mitchell, Curtis. *Cavalcade of Broadcasting*. Chicago: Follett Publishing, 1970.

Mormino, Gary Ross. *Immigrants on the Hill: Italian-Americans in St. Louis, 1882–1982*. Urbana: University of Illinois Press, 1986.

Mowry, George E., and Blaine A. Brownell. *The Urban Nation, 1920–1980*. Revised edition. New York: Hill and Wang, 1981.

Mullins, William H. *The Depression and the Urban West Coast, 1929–1933: Los Angeles, San Francisco, Seattle and Portland*. Bloomington: Indiana University Press, 1991.

Muncy, Robyn. *Creating a Female Dominion in American Reform, 1890–1935*. New York: Oxford University Press, 1991.

Nasaw, David. *Children of the City: At Work and at Play*. Garden City: Doubleday, 1985.

———. *Going Out: The Rise and Fall of Public Amusements*. New York: Basic Books, 1993.

Neverdon-Morton, Cynthia. *Afro-American Women of the South and the Advancement of the Race, 1895–1925*. Knoxville: University of Tennessee Press, 1989.

Noel, Thomas J. *The City and the Saloon: Denver, 1858–1916*. Lincoln: University of Nebraska Press, 1982.

Norwood, Stephen H. *Labor's Flaming Youth: Telephone Operators and Worker Militancy, 1878–1923*. Urbana: University of Illinois Press, 1990.

O'Connor, Francis V. *Federal Support for the Visual Arts: The New Deal and Now*. Greenwich: New York Graphic Society, 1969.

Odem, Mary. *Delinquent Daughters: Protecting and Policing Adolescent Female*

Sexuality in the United States, 1885–1920. Chapel Hill: University of North Carolina Press, 1995.

Olney, Martha L. *Buy Now Pay Later: Advertising, Credit, and Consumer Durables in the 1920s.* Chapel Hill: University of North Carolina Press, 1991.

O'Reilly, John Boyle. *The Butte Blue Book: A Social and Family Directory 1901.* Butte, 1901.

Ostrander, Gilman M. *The Prohibition Movement in California, 1848–1933.* Berkeley: University of California Press, 1957.

Ostrander, Susan A. *Women of the Upper Class.* Philadelphia: Temple University Press, 1984.

Pascoe, Peggy. *Relations of Rescue: The Search for Female Moral Authority in the American West, 1874–1939.* New York: Oxford University Press, 1990.

Paul, Rodman W., ed. *A Victorian Gentlewoman in the Far West: The Reminiscences of Mary Hallock Foote.* San Marino: Huntington Library, 1972.

Peiss, Kathy. *Cheap Amusements: Working Women and Leisure in Turn-of-the-Century New York.* Philadelphia: Temple University Press, 1986.

Petrik, Paula. *No Step Backward: Women and Family on the Rocky Mountain Mining Frontier, Helena, Montana, 1865–1900.* Helena: Montana Historical Society Press, 1987.

Piatt, Guy X., ed. *The Story of Butte.* Butte: Standard Manufacturing and Printing, 1897.

Pleck, Joseph H., and Elizabeth H. Pleck, eds. *The American Man.* Englewood Cliffs: Prentice-Hall, 1980.

Pruitt, Elisabeth, ed. *Tender Darkness: A Mary MacLane Anthology.* Belmont: Abernathy and Brown, 1993.

Quinn, Larry D. *Politicians in Business: A History of the Liquor Control System in Montana.* Missoula: University of Montana Press, 1970.

Research Committee on Social Trends. *Recent Social Trends in the United States: Report of the President's Research Committee on Social Trends.* New York: McGraw-Hill, 1933.

Reynolds, Francis J., ed. *The New World Atlas and Gazetteer, 1924.* New York: P. F. Collier and Son, 1924.

Root, Grace C. *Women and Repeal: The Story of the Women's Organization for National Prohibition Reform.* New York: Harper and Brothers Publishers, 1934.

Rosenzweig, Roy. *Eight Hours for What We Will: Workers and Leisure in an Industrial City, 1870–1920.* Cambridge: Cambridge University Press, 1983.

Rosner, David, and Gerald Markowitz. *Deadly Dust: Silicosis and the Politics of Occupational Disease in Twentieth-Century America.* Princeton: Princeton University Press, 1991.

Rothman, Ellen K. *Hands and Hearts: A History of Courtship in America.* New York: Basic Books, 1984.

Rotundo, E. Anthony. *American Manhood: Transformations in Masculinity from the Revolution to the Modern Era.* New York: Basic Books, 1993.

Sammons, Jeffrey T. *Beyond the Ring: The Role of Boxing in American Society.* Urbana: University of Illinois Press, 1988.

Scharf, Lois. *To Work and to Wed: Female Employment, Feminism, and the Great Depression.* Westport: Greenwood Press, 1980.

Schiller, Herbert I. *Mass Communications and American Empire.* New York: Augustus M. Kelley, 1969.

Scott, Anne Firor. *Making the Invisible Woman Visible.* Urbana: University of Illinois Press, 1984.

———. *Natural Allies: Women's Associations in American History.* Urbana: University of Illinois Press, 1993.

Shaw, Arnold. *The Jazz Age: Popular Music in the 1920's.* New York: Oxford University Press, 1987.

Shore, Chester K., comp. *Montana in the Wars.* Miles City: American Legion of Montana, 1977.

Sims, Anastatia. *Feminism and Feminity in the New South: White Women's Organizations in North Carolina, 1883–1930.* Columbia: University of South Carolina Press, in press.

Skeels, Lydia Lowndes Maury, ed. *One American Family: Some Maury Memories, Legends, and Records.* Storrs: Parousia Press, Volume 1, 1981, Volume 2, 1987.

Smulyan, Susan. *Selling Radio: The Commercialization of American Broadcasting, 1920–1934.* Washington: Smithsonian Institution Press, 1994.

Sochen, June. *The New Woman: Feminism in Greenwich Village, 1910–1920.* New York: Quadrangle, 1972.

Spence, Clark C. *Mining Engineers and the American West: The Lace-Boot Brigade, 1849–1933.* New Haven: Yale University Press, 1970.

Stansell, Christine. *City of Women: Sex and Class in New York, 1789–1860.* Urbana: University of Illinois Press, 1986.

Stearns, Marshall W. *The Story of Jazz.* New York: Oxford University Press, 1956.

Stegner, Wallace. *Angle of Repose.* Garden City: Doubleday, 1971.

Stivers, Richard. *A Hair of the Dog: Irish Drinking and American Stereotype.* University Park: Pennsylvania State University Press, 1976.

Stott, William. *Documentary Expression and Thirties America.* New York: Oxford University Press, 1973.

Susman, Warren I. *Culture as History: The Transformation of American Society in the Twentieth Century.* New York: Pantheon Books, 1973.

Sussmann, Leila A. *Dear FDR: A Study of Political Letter-Writing.* Totowa: Bedminster Press, 1963.

Swett, Ira L. *Montana's Trolleys-II: Butte; Anaconda; Butte, Anaconda and Pacific.* South Gate, Calif.: Interurbans Magazine, 1970.

Timberlake, James H. *Prohibition and the Progressive Movement, 1900–1920.* Cambridge: Harvard University Press, 1963.

Tyler, Poyntz, ed. *Television and Radio.* New York: H. W. Wilson, 1961.

Waldron, Ellis, and Paul B. Wilson. *Atlas of Montana Elections, 1889–1976.* Missoula: University of Montana Publications in History, 1978.

Wandersee, Winifred D. *Women's Work and Family Values, 1920–1940.* Cambridge: Harvard University Press, 1981.

Ware, Susan. *Holding Their Own: American Women in the 1930s.* Boston: Twayne Publishers, 1982.

West, Elliott. *The Saloon on the Rocky Mountain Mining Frontier.* Lincoln: University of Nebraska Press, 1979.

Wheeler, Burton K., with Paul F. Healy. *Yankee from the West.* Garden City: Doubleday, 1962.

White, Kevin. *The First Sexual Revolution: The Emergence of Male Heterosexuality in Modern America.* New York: New York University Press, 1993.

Wilson, Gary A. *Honky-Tonk Town: Havre's Bootlegging Days.* Helena: Montana Magazine, 1985.

Wilson, Margaret Gibbons. *The American Woman in Transition: The Urban Influence, 1870–1920.* Westport: Greenwood Press, 1979.

Winick, Charles, and Paul M. Kinsie. *The Lively Commerce: Prostitution in the United States.* Chicago: Quadrangle Books, 1971.

Writers' Program, Work Projects Administration. *Copper Camp: Stories of the World's Greatest Mining Town, Butte, Montana.* New York: Hastings House, 1943.

Wyman, Mark. *Hard Rock Epic: Western Miners and the Industrial Revolution, 1860–1910.* Berkeley: University of California Press, 1979.

Young, Louise M. *In the Public Interest: The League of Women Voters, 1920–1970.* New York: Greenwood Press, 1989.

Young, Otis E., Jr. *Black Powder and Hand Steel: Miners and Machines on the Old Western Frontier.* Norman: University of Oklahoma Press, 1976.

Articles

Anderson, Lauri. "Butte's Trolleys." *Montana Historian* 5 (Autumn 1974): 10–11.

Anderson, Walter. "Speakeasy as a National Institution." In *Selected Articles on the Problem of Liquor Control.* Compiled by Julia E. Johnsen. New York: H. W. Wilson, 1934.

Arrington, Leonard J., and Don C. Reading. "New Deal Economic Programs in the Northern Tier States, 1933–1939." In *Centennial West: Essays on the Northern Tier States,* edited by William L. Lang, 227–43. Seattle: University of Washington Press, 1991.

Babor, Thomas F., and Barbara G. Rosenkrantz. "Public Health, Public Morals, and Public Order: Social Science and Liquor Control in Massachusetts, 1880–1916." In *Drinking: Behavior and Belief in Modern History,* edited by Susanna Barrows and Robin Room, 265–86. Berkeley: University of California Press, 1991.

Bailey, Jody, and Robert S. McPherson. "'Practically Free from the Taint of the Bootlegger': A Closer Look at Prohibition in Southeastern Utah." *Utah Historical Quarterly* 57 (Spring 1989): 150–64.

Bales, Robert F. "Attitudes toward Drinking in the Irish Culture." In *Society, Culture, and Drinking Patterns,* edited by David J. Pittman and Charles R. Snyder, 157–87. New York: John Wiley and Sons, 1962.

Bancroft, Caroline. "Folklore of the Central City District, Colorado." *California Folklore Quarterly* 4 (October 1945): 315–42.

Banning, Margaret Culkin. "On the Wagon." *Harper's Monthly Magazine* 163 (June 1931): 11–21.

Baritz, Loren. "The Culture of the Twenties." In *The Development of an American Culture.* Second edition, edited by Stanley Coben and Lorman Ratner, 181–214. New York: St. Martin's Press, 1983.

Barrett, James R. "Why Paddy Drank: The Social Importance of Whiskey in Pre-Famine Ireland." *Journal of Popular Culture* 11 (Summer 1977): 155/17–166/28.

Bedinger, Margery. "The Irrepressible Butte, Citadel of Copper." *Baltimore Sun,* magazine section, 15 November 1931, 12.

———. "Last Stand of the Wild West." *Billings Gazette,* 15 November 1931, 7, 15.

Binford, Jessie F. "Taxi-Dance Halls." *Journal of Social Hygiene* 19 (December 1933): 502–9.

Bowden, A. O. "The Women's Club Movement: An Appraisal and Prophecy." *Journal of Education* 111 (3 March 1930): 257–60.

Boylan, Anne M. "Timid Girls, Venerable Widows and Dignified Matrons: Life Cycle Patterns among Organized Women in New York and Boston, 1797–1840." *American Quarterly* 38 (Winter 1986): 779–97.

Brady, Marilyn Dell. "Kansas Federation of Colored Women's Clubs, 1900–1930." *Kansas History* 9 (Spring 1986): 19–30.

Brinig, Myron. "The Synagogue: A Story of Two Generations of American Judaism." *Munsey's Magazine* 81 (March 1924): 259–69.

Brissenden, Paul F. "The Butte Miners and the Rustling Card." *American Economic Review* 10 (December 1920): 755–75.

Brod, Harry. "The Case for Men's Studies." In *The Making of Masculinities: The New Men's Studies,* edited by Harry Brod, 39–62. Boston: Allen and Unwin, 1987.

Brundage, David. "The Producing Classes and the Saloon: Denver in the 1880s." *Labor History* 26 (Winter 1985): 29–52.

Burk, Ann. "The Mining Camp Saloon as a Social Center." *Red River Valley Historical Review* 2 (Fall 1975): 381–92.

Burnham, J. C. "New Perspectives on the Prohibition 'Experiment' of the 1920's." *Journal of Social History* 2 (Fall 1968): 51–68.

Butler, George. "Impressions of a Hobo." *Pacific Review* 11 (September 1921): 197–210.

Chadwick, Robert A. "Montana's Silver Mining Era: Great Boom and Great Bust." *Montana Magazine of Western History* 32 (Spring 1982): 16–31.

Christie, Mrs. W. J. "The Women's Clubs of Montana." *Rocky Mountain Magazine* 2 (March 1901): 579–91.

Clapp, Mary Brennan. "Highlights and Sidelights on the Cosmopolis of the Rockies." *Anaconda Standard,* 4 February 1923.

Clawson, Mary Ann. "Nineteenth-Century Women's Auxiliaries and Fraternal Orders." *Signs* 12 (Autumn 1986): 40–61.

Cohen, Lizabeth A. "Embellishing a Life of Labor: An Interpretation of the Material Culture of American Working-Class Homes, 1885–1915." *Journal of American Culture* 3 (Winter 1980): 752–75.

———. "Encountering Mass Culture at the Grassroots: The Experience of Chicago Workers in the 1920s." *American Quarterly* 41 (March 1989): 6–33.

———. "On Their Own Terms: Mass Culture and the Working-Class World." *Chicago History* 18 (Summer 1989): 22–39.

Conway, Jill. "Women Reformers and American Culture, 1870–1930." In *Our American Sisters: Women in American Life and Thought,* edited by Jean E. Friedman and William G. Shade, 301–12. Boston: Allyn and Bacon, 1973.

Cooney, Bryon E. "The Saloons of Yester-Year." *Montana American,* 18 July 1919, 64.

Couvares, Francis G. "The Triumph of Commerce: Class Culture and Mass Culture in Pittsburgh." In *Working-Class America: Essays on Labor, Community, and American Society,* edited by Michael H. Frisch and Daniel J. Walkowitz, 123–52. Urbana: University of Illinois Press, 1983.

Covert, Catherine L. "'We May Hear Too Much': American Sensibility and the Response to Radio, 1919–1924." In *Mass Media between the Wars: Perceptions of Cultural Tension, 1918–1941,* edited by Catherine L. Covert and John D. Stevens, 199–220. Syracuse: Syracuse University Press, 1984.

Cranz, Galen. "Women in Urban Parks." *Signs* 5 (Spring 1980): S79–S95.

Crosby, John. "Seven Deadly Sins of the Air." In *Television and Radio in American Life,* edited by Herbert L. Marx, Jr., 74–83. New York: H. W. Wilson, 1953.

Critoph, Gerald E. "The Flapper and Her Critics." In *"Remember the Ladies": New Perspectives on Women in American History, Essays in Honor of Nelson Manfred Blake,* edited by Carol V. R. George, 145–60. Syracuse: Syracuse University Press, 1975.

Davenport, Walter. "The Richest Hill on Earth." *Collier's,* 6 February 1937, 9–11, 53.

Davidoff, Leonore. "The Separation of Home and Work?: Landladies and Lodgers in Nineteenth- and Twentieth-Century England." In *Fit Work for Women,* edited by Sandra Burman, 64–97. Canberra: Australian National University Press, 1979.

Derickson, Alan. "Industrial Refugees: The Migration of Silicotics from the Mines of North America and South Africa in the Early Twentieth Century." *Labor History* 29 (Winter 1988): 66–89.

Dickson, Lynda F. "Toward a Broader Angle of Vision in Uncovering Women's History: Black Women's Clubs Revisited." *Frontiers* 9, no. 2 (1987): 62–68.

Dieterich, Herbert R. "The New Deal Cultural Projects in Wyoming: A Survey and Appraisal." *Annals of Wyoming* 52 (Fall 1980): 30–44.

Donovan, Ruth Godfrey. "The Nebraska League of Women Voters." *Nebraska History* 52 (Fall 1971): 311–28.

Dubbert, Joe L. "Progressivism and the Masculinity Crisis." In *The American Man*, edited by Joseph H. Pleck and Elizabeth H. Pleck, 303–20. Englewood Cliffs: Prentice-Hall, 1980.

Erenberg, Lewis A. "From New York to Middletown: Repeal and the Legitimization of Nightlife in the Great Depression." *American Quarterly* 38 (Winter 1986): 761–78.

Ewen, Elizabeth. "City Lights: Immigrant Women and the Rise of the Movies." *Signs* 5 (Spring 1980): S45–S65.

Ewers, John C. "William Standing (1904–1951): Versatile Assiniboin Artist." *American Indian Art Magazine* 8 (1983): 54–63.

"The Experience and Observations of a New York Saloon-Keeper." *McClure's Magazine* 32 (January 1909): 301–12.

Filene, Peter. "The Secrets of Men's History." In *The Making of Masculinities: The New Men's Studies*, edited by Harry Brod, 103–19. Boston: Allen and Unwin, 1987.

Fine, Lisa M. "Between Two Worlds: Business Women in a Chicago Boarding House, 1900–1930." *Journal of Social History* 19 (Spring 1986): 511–19.

Fishbein, Leslie. "'Dancing Mothers' (1926): Flappers, Mothers, Freud, and Freedom." *Women's Studies* 12 (March 1986): 241–50.

———. "The Demise of the Cult of True Womanhood in Early American Film, 1900–1930." *Journal of Popular Film and Television* 12 (Summer 1984): 66–72.

Fisher, Arthur. "Montana: Land of the Copper Collar." *The Nation*, 19 September 1923, 290–92.

Frank, Dana. "'Food Wins All Struggles': Seattle Labor and the Politicization of Consumption." *Radical History Review* 51 (Fall 1991): 65–89.

Frazier, Corinne Reid. "Why Pay the Fiddler?" *Parent's Magazine* 12 (February 1937): 20–21, 71–74.

Freedman, Estelle B. "The New Woman: Changing Views of Women in the 1920s." *Journal of American History* 61 (September 1974): 372–93.

———. "Separatism as Strategy: Female Institution Building and American Feminism, 1870–1930." *Feminist Studies* 5 (Fall 1979): 512–29.

Freeman, Ruth, and Patricia Klaus. "Blessed or Not?: The New Spinster in England and the United States in the Late Nineteenth and Early Twentieth Centuries." *Journal of Family History* 9 (Winter 1984): 394–414.

Frost, Stanley. "Radio Dreams That Can Come True." *Collier's*, 10 June 1922, 9, 18.

Gelber, Steven M. "'A Job You Can't Lose': Work and Hobbies in the Great Depression." *Journal of Social History* 24 (Summer 1991): 741–66.

———. "Working at Playing: The Culture of the Workplace and the Rise of Baseball." *Journal of Social History* 16 (Summer 1983): 3–22.

Gilbert, Sandra M. "Soldier's Heart: Literary Men, Literary Women, and the Great War." In *Behind the Lines: Gender and the Two World Wars*, edited by Margaret Randolph Higonnet, Jane Jenson, Sonya Michel, and Margaret Collins Weitz, 197–226. New Haven: Yale University Press, 1987.

Gittell, Marilyn, and Teresa Shtob. "Changing Women's Roles in Political Voluntarism and Reform of the City." *Signs* 5 (Spring 1980): S67–S78.

Gordon, Jean, and Jan McArthur. "American Women and Domestic Consumption, 1800–1920: Four Interpretive Themes." *Journal of American Culture* 8 (Fall 1985): 35–46.

Gray, W. Russel. "For Whom the Bell Tolled: The Decline of British Prize Fighting in the Victorian Era." *Journal of Popular Culture* 21 (Fall 1987): 53–64.

Green, Archie. "At the Hall, in the Stope: Who Treasures Tales of Work?" *Western Folklore* 46 (July 1987): 153–70.

———. "Marcus Daly Enters Heaven." *Speculator* 1 (Winter 1984): 26–32.

Greenfield, Elizabeth. "Shakespearean 'Culture' in Montana, 1902." *Montana Magazine of Western History* 22 (Spring 1972): 48–55.

Gullett, Gayle. "City Mothers, City Daughters, and the Dance Hall Girls: The Limits of Female Political Power in San Francisco, 1913." In *Women and the Structure of Society: Selected Research from the Fifth Berkshire Conference on the History of Women*, edited by Barbara J. Harris and JoAnn K. McNamara, 149–59. Durham: Duke University Press, 1984.

Gusfield, Joseph R. "Status Conflicts and the Changing Ideologies of the American Temperance Movement." In *Society, Culture, and Drinking Patterns*, edited by David J. Pittman and Charles R. Snyder, 101–20. New York: John Wiley and Sons, 1962.

Gutfeld, Arnon. "The Murder of Frank Little: Radical Labor Agitation in Butte, Montana, 1917." *Labor History* 10 (Spring 1969): 177–92.

———. "The Speculator Disaster in 1917: Labor Resurgence at Butte, Montana." *Arizona and the West* 11 (Spring 1969): 27–38.

Hacker, Louis M. "Rise and Fall of Prohibition." In *Selected Articles on the Problem of Liquor Control*. Compiled by Julia E. Johnsen. New York: H. W. Wilson, 1934.

Hall, Jacquelyn Dowd. "Disorderly Women: Gender and Labor Militancy in the Appalachian South." *Journal of American History* 73 (September 1986): 354–82.

Haller, Mark H. "Philadelphia Bootlegging and the Report of the Special August Grand Jury." *Pennsylvania Magazine of History and Biography* 109 (April 1985): 215–33.

Hand, Wayland D. "The Folklore, Customs, and Traditions of the Butte Miner." *California Folklore Quarterly* 5 (January 1946): 1–25, and 5 (April 1946): 153–78.

Hansen, Karen V. "'Helped Put in a Quilt': Men's Work and Male Intimacy in Nineteenth-Century New England." *Gender and Society* 3 (September 1989): 334–54.

Hantover, Jeffrey P. "The Boy Scouts and the Validation of Masculinity." In *The American Man*, edited by Joseph H. Pleck and Elizabeth H. Pleck, 285–301. Englewood Cliffs: Prentice-Hall, 1980.

Hapgood, Hutchins. "McSorley's Saloon." *Harper's Weekly*, 25 October 1913, 15.

Hargreaves, Mary W. M. "Darkness Before the Dawn: The Status of Working Women in the Depression Years." In *Clio Was a Woman: Studies in the History of American Women,* edited by Mabel E. Deutrich and Virginia C. Purdy, 177–88. Washington, D.C.: Howard University Press, 1980.

Harris, Jonathan. "Nationalizing Art: The Community Art Centre Programme of the Federal Art Project, 1935–1943." *Art History* 14 (June 1991): 250–69.

Harvie, Robert A., and Larry V. Bishop. "Police Reform in Montana, 1890–1918." *Montana Magazine of Western History* 33 (Spring 1983): 46–59.

Haywood, Robert. "George Bellows's Stag at Sharkey's: Boxing, Violence, and Male Identity." *Smithsonian Studies in American Art* 2 (1988): 3–15.

Helmbold, Lois Rita. "Beyond the Family Economy: Black and White Working-class Women during the Great Depression." *Feminist Studies* 13 (Fall 1987): 629–55.

———. "Downward Occupational Mobility during the Great Depression: Urban Black and White Working-Class Women." *Labor History* 29 (Spring 1988): 135–72.

Hewitt, John D. "Patterns of Female Criminality in Middletown, 1900 to 1920." *Indiana Social Studies Quarterly* 38 (Autumn 1986): 49–59.

High, Stanley. "A Dry Warns the Drys." *Harper's Magazine* 165 (June 1932): 1–10.

Hilder, John Chapman. "New York Speakeasy: A Study of a Social Institution." *Harper's Magazine* 164 (April 1932): 591–601.

Hoke, Travis. "Corner Saloon." *American Mercury* 22 (March 1931): 311–22.

Holter, Frances. "Radio among the Unemployed." *Journal of Applied Psychology* 23 (February 1939): 163–69.

Howard, Joseph Kinsey. "Boisterous Butte." *Survey Graphic* 28 (May 1939): 316–20, 348–51.

———. "Butte: City with a 'Kick' in It." In *Our Fair City,* edited by Robert S. Allen, 297–323. New York: Vanguard Press, 1947.

Jackson, Hugh. "The History of Volunteering in Wyoming." *Annals of Wyoming* 59 (Spring 1987): 38–47.

Johnson, Bascom, and Paul M. Kinsie. "Prostitution in the United States." *Journal of Social Hygiene* 19 (December 1933): 467–91.

Johnson, Charles S. "The Montana Council of Defense." *Montana Journalism Review* 16 (1973): 2–16.

Johnson, Dorothy M. "The Small-Town World before Radio." *Montana Magazine of Western History* 24 (Spring 1974): 44–53.

Johnson, Judith R. "Kansas in the 'Grippe': The Spanish Influenza Epidemic of 1918." *Kansas History* 15 (Spring 1992): 44–55.

Jones, Walter R. "Casper's Prohibition Years." *Annals of Wyoming* 48 (Fall 1976): 264–73.

Kasson, John F. "Civility and Rudeness: Urban Etiquette and the Bourgeois

Social Order in Nineteenth-Century America." *Prospects: The Annual of American Cultural Studies* 9 (1984): 143–67.

Kennedy, Albert J. "The Saloon in Retrospect and Prospect." *Survey Graphic* 22 (April 1933): 203–6, 234, 237, 239–40.

Kingsdale, Jon M. "The 'Poor Man's Club': Social Functions of the Urban Working-Class Saloon." In *The American Man*, edited by Joseph H. Pleck and Elizabeth H. Pleck, 255–83. Englewood Cliffs: Prentice-Hall, 1980.

Kinney, Ward. "Montana Challenges the Tyranny of Copper." *The Nation*, 25 July 1934, 98–99.

Kleinberg, S. J. "Success and the Working Class." *Journal of American Culture* 2 (Spring 1979): 123–38.

Knox, Jessie C. "The Redemption of 'Barren Butte' by Flowers and a Woman's Faith." *Garden Magazine and Home Builder* 41 (May 1925): 256–57.

Kornbluh, Joyce L. "The She-She-She Camps: An Experiment in Living and Learning, 1934–1937." In *Sisterhood and Solidarity: Workers' Education for Women, 1914–1984*, edited by Joyce L. Kornbluh and Mary Frederickson, 253–83. Philadelphia: Temple University Press, 1984.

Kosso, Lenore M. "Yugoslavs in Nevada, Part I." *Nevada Historical Society Quarterly* 28 (Summer 1985): 69–89.

Kusmer, Kenneth L. "The Functions of Organized Charity in the Progressive Era: Chicago as a Case Study." *Journal of American History* 60 (December 1973): 657–78.

Kwitny, Jonathan. "The Great Transportation Conspiracy." *Harper's* 262 (February 1981): 14–21.

Kyvig, David E. "Sober Thoughts: Myths and Realities of National Prohibition after Fifty Years." In *Law, Alcohol, and Order: Perspectives on National Prohibition*, edited by David E. Kyvig, 3–20. Westport: Greenwood Press, 1985.

———. "Thirsting after Righteousness: The Opposition to National Prohibition." Introduction to the microfilm guide for the Papers of the Association against the Prohibition Amendment and the Women's Organization for National Prohibition Reform. Eleutherian Mills Historical Library, Wilmington, Delaware.

———. "Women against Prohibition." *American Quarterly* 28 (Fall 1976): 465–82.

Larsen, T. A. "Montana Women and the Battle for the Ballot." *Montana Magazine of Western History* 23 (Winter 1973): 24–41.

Lears, T. J. Jackson. "Some Versions of Fantasy: Toward a Cultural History of American Advertising, 1880–1930." *Prospects* 9 (1984): 349–405.

Lee, Rose Hum. "Social Institutions of a Rocky Mountain Chinatown." *Social Forces* 27 (October 1948): 1–11.

Lerner, Gerda. "Early Community Work of Black Club Women." *Journal of Negro History* 59 (April 1974): 158–67.

Levine, Lawrence W. "American Culture and the Great Depression." *Yale Review* 74 (Winter 1985): 196–223.

Levine, Susan. "Workers' Wives: Gender, Class and Consumerism in the 1920s United States." *Gender and History* 3 (Spring 1991): 45–64.

Locke, Mary Lou. "Out of the Shadows and into the Western Sun: Working Women of the Late Nineteenth-Century Urban Far West." *Journal of Urban History* 16 (February 1990): 175–204.

Lunbeck, Elizabeth. "'A New Generation of Women': Progressive Psychiatrists and the Hypersexual Female." *Feminist Studies* 13 (Fall 1987): 513–43.

Marquis, Alice Goldfarb. "Written on the Wind: The Impact of Radio during the 1930s." *Journal of Contemporary History* 19 (July 1984): 385–415.

Marsh, Margaret. "Suburban Men and Masculine Domesticity, 1870–1915." *American Quarterly* 40 (June 1988): 165–86.

Martin, Dale. "School for Struggle: The Butte Newsboys Strikes of 1914 and 1919." *Speculator* 2 (Summer 1985): 9–11.

Mason, Gregory. "Satan in the Dance-Hall." *American Mercury* 2 (June 1924): 175–82.

Mattern, Carolyn J. "Mary MacLane: A Feminist Opinion." *Montana Magazine of Western History* 27 (Autumn 1977): 54–63.

Maury, Reuben. "Home." *Scribner's Magazine* 79 (June 1926): 639–47.

Maynard, Steven. "Rough Work and Rugged Men: The Social Construction of Masculinity in Working-Class History." *Labour/Le Travail* 23 (Spring 1989): 159–69.

McClernan, Henry. "Sixty Million Years of History: The Formation of Butte Copper." *Speculator* 1 (Summer 1984): 16–19.

McClymer, John F. "Gender and the 'American Way of Life': Women in the Americanization Movement." *Journal of American Ethnic History* 10 (Spring 1991): 3–20.

McCullough, David J. "Bone Dry?: Prohibition New Mexico Style, 1918–1933." *New Mexico Historical Review* 63 (January 1988): 25–42.

McDannell, Colleen. "'True Men as We Need Them': Catholicism and the Irish-American Male." *American Studies* 27 (Fall 1986): 19–36.

McDonald, Elizabeth. "The First Librarians' Union." *Wilson Bulletin for Librarians* 10 (June 1936): 675–76.

McGovern, James R. "The American Woman's Pre-World War I Freedom in Manners and Morals." *Journal of American History* 55 (September 1968): 315–33.

McMeans, Orange Edward. "The Great Audience Invisible." *Scribner's Magazine* 73 (April 1923): 410–16.

Meehan, Thomas. "The 'Soaps' Fade but Do Not Die." In *Television and Radio,* edited by Poyntz Tyler, 13–18. New York: H. W. Wilson, 1961.

Melendy, Royal L. "The Saloon in Chicago—I." *American Journal of Sociology* 6 (November 1900): 289–306.

Mercier, Laurie K. "'We Are Women Irish': Gender, Class, Religious, and Ethnic Identity in Anaconda, Montana." *Montana Magazine of Western History* 44 (Winter 1994): 28–41.

Merz, Charles. "The Issue in Butte." *New Republic,* 22 September 1917, 215–17.

Meyer, B. H. "Fraternal Beneficiary Societies in the United States." *American Journal of Sociology* 6 (January 1901): 646–61.

Meyerowitz, Joanne. "Sexual Geography and Gender Economy: The Furnished Room Districts of Chicago, 1890–1930." *Gender and History* 2 (Autumn 1990): 274–96.

Meyrowitz, Alvin, and Marjorie Fiske. "The Relative Preference of Low Income Groups for Small Stations." *Journal of Applied Psychology* 23 (February 1939): 158–62.

Miller, Barbara. "'Hot as Live Embers, Cold as Hail': The Restless Soul of Butte's Mary MacLane." *Montana Magazine* (September-October 1982): 50–52.

Modell, John. "Dating Becomes the Way of American Youth." In *Essays on the Family and Historical Change,* edited by Leslie Page Moch and Gary D. Stark, 91–126. College Station: Texas A&M University Press, 1983.

Montgomery, David. "Class, Capitalism, and Contentment." *Labor History* 30 (Winter 1989): 125–37.

———. "Thinking about American Workers in the 1920s." *International Labor and Working-Class History* 32 (Fall 1987): 4–24.

Morgan, David. "Masculinity, Autobiography and History." *Gender and History* 2 (Spring 1990): 34–39.

Morgan, Edward P. "Who Forgot Radio?" In *Problems and Controversies in Television and Radio,* edited by Harry J. Skornia and Jack William Kitson, 117–27. Palo Alto: Pacific Books, 1968.

Mullen, Pierce C., and Michael L. Nelson. "Montanans and 'the Most Peculiar Disease': The Influenza Epidemic and Public Health, 1918–1919." *Montana Magazine of Western History* 37 (Spring 1987): 50–61.

Mumford, Lewis. "A Letter to the President." *New Republic,* 30 December 1936, 263–65.

Murphy, Mary. "Women's Work in a Man's World." *Speculator* 1 (Winter 1984): 18–25.

Murphy, Miriam B. "'If Only I Shall Have the Right Stuff': Utah Women in World War I." *Utah Historical Quarterly* 58 (Fall 1990): 334–50.

Myers, Rex. "The Butte Rail Connection: Mining and Transportation, 1880–1980." *Speculator* 1 (Summer 1984): 30–37.

Nye, Russel B. "Saturday Night at the Paradise Ballroom; or, Dance Halls in the Twenties." *Journal of Popular Culture* 7 (Summer 1973): 14–22.

O'Brien, Patrick G. "Prohibition and the Kansas Progressive Example." *Great Plains Quarterly* 7 (Fall 1987): 219–31.

O'Brien, Howard Vincent. "It's Great to Be a Radio Maniac." *Collier's,* 13 September 1924, 15–16.

O'Dane, Arthur [Reuben Maury]. "Hymn to an Oasis." *American Mercury* 6 (October 1925): 190–96.

Ollry, Francis, and Elias Smith. "An Index of 'Radio-Mindedness' and Some Applications." *Journal of Applied Psychology* 23 (February 1939): 8–18.

O'Sullivan, Thomas. "Joint Venture or Testy Alliance? The Public Works of Art Project in Minnesota, 1933–34." *Great Plains Quarterly* 9 (Spring 1989): 89–99.

Page, Ada. "Mary Goes Back to Sand and Barrenness." *Overland Monthly* 87 (November 1929): 345, 368.

Papanikolas, Helen Z. "Bootlegging in Zion: Making and Selling the 'Good Stuff.'" *Utah Historical Quarterly* 53 (Summer 1985): 268–91.

Peiss, Kathy. "Commercial Leisure and the 'Woman Question.'" In *For Fun and Profit: The Transformation of Leisure into Consumption,* edited by Richard Butsch, 105–17. Philadelphia: Temple University Press, 1990.

———. "Making Faces: The Cosmetics Industry and the Cultural Construction of Gender, 1890–1930." *Genders* 7 (Spring 1990): 143–69.

Perry, Elisabeth I. "'The General Motherhood of the Commonwealth': Dance Hall Reform in the Progressive Era." *American Quarterly* 37 (Winter 1985): 719–33.

Phelan, John J. "Our Dancing Cities." *The Survey,* 29 January 1921, 631–32.

Phillips, William R., and Bernard Sternsher. "Victims of the Great Depression: The Question of Blame and First-Person History." In *Hitting Home: The Great Depression in Town and Country,* revised edition, edited by Bernard Sternsher, 267–84. Chicago: Ivan R. Dee, 1989.

Powers, Madelon. "Decay from Within: The Inevitable Doom of the American Saloon." In *Drinking: Behavior and Belief in Modern History,* edited by Susanna Barrows and Robin Room, 112–31. Berkeley: University of California Press, 1991.

Pumphrey, Martin. "The Flapper, the Housewife and the Making of Modernity." *Cultural Studies* 1 (May 1987): 179–94.

Putnam, Edison K. "Travail at the Turn of the Century: Efforts at Liquor Control in Idaho." *Idaho Yesterdays* 33 (Spring 1989): 13–19, 22–24.

Rapp, Rayna, and Ellen Ross. "The 1920s: Feminism, Consumerism, and Political Backlash in the United States." In *Women in Culture and Politics: A Century of Change,* edited by Judith Friedlander, Blanche Wiesen Cook, Alice Kessler-Harris, and Carroll Smith-Rosenberg, 52–61. Bloomington: Indiana University Press, 1986.

"Report of the Thirty-fourth Annual Meeting of the Montana WCTU." *Woman's Voice* (October 1917): 1–24.

"Report of the Thirty-fifth Annual Meeting of the Montana WCTU." *Woman's Voice* (October 1918): 1–24.

Richardson, Anna Steese. "Is the Women's Club Dying?" *Harper's Magazine* 159 (October 1929): 605–12.

Richie, Atha Albert. "The Real Facts about Those Famous Old Hand-Drilling Contests." *Engineering and Mining Journal* 152 (November 1951): 84–85.

Roberts, Elizabeth A. M. "Women's Strategies, 1890–1940." In *Labour and Love: Women's Experience of Home and Family, 1850–1940,* edited by Jane Lewis, 222–47. New York: Basil Blackwell, 1986.

Roeder, Richard B. "The Copper Pen: Butte in Fiction." In *Montana and the West: Essays in Honor of K. Ross Toole,* edited by Rex C. Myers and Harry W. Fritz, 144–66. Boulder: Pruett Publishing, 1984.

———. "Joseph Kinsey Howard: His Vision of the West." *Montana Magazine of Western History* 30 (Winter 1980): 2–11.

Rose, Kenneth. "Booze and News in 1924: Prohibition in Seattle." *Portage* 5 (Winter 1984): 16–22.

———. "'Dry' Los Angeles and Its Liquor Problems in 1924." *Southern California Quarterly* 69 (Spring 1987): 51–74.

———. "The Labbe Affair and Prohibition Enforcement in Portland." *Pacific Northwest Quarterly* 77 (April 1986): 42–51.

———. "Wettest in the West: San Francisco and Prohibition in 1924." *California History* 65 (December 1986): 284–95, 314–15.

Rose, Nancy E. "Discrimination against Women in New Deal Work Programs." *Affilia* 5 (Summer 1990): 25–45.

Rosemont, Penelope. "Marvelous Mary MacLane." In *Free Spirits: Annals of the Insurgent Imagination,* edited by Paul Buhle, Jayne Cortez, Philip Lamantia, Nancy Joyce Peters, Franklin Rosemont, and Penelope Rosemont, 31–38. San Francisco: City Lights Books, 1982.

Rotundo, E. Anthony. "Body and Soul: Changing Ideals of American Middle-Class Manhood, 1770–1920." *Journal of Social History* 16 (Summer 1983): 23–38.

———. "Learning about Manhood: Gender Ideals and the Middle-class Family in Nineteenth-Century America." In *Manliness and Morality: Middle-class Masculinity in Britain and American, 1800–1940,* edited by J. A. Mangan and James Walvin, 35–51. New York: St. Martin's Press, 1987.

———. "Romantic Friendship: Male Intimacy and Middle-Class Youth in the Northern United States, 1800–1900." *Journal of Social History* 23 (Fall 1989): 1–25.

Ruckman, Jo Ann. "'Knit, Knit, and Then Knit': The Women of Pocatello and the War Effort of 1917–1918." *Idaho Yesterdays* 26 (Spring 1982): 26–36.

Ruiz, Vicki L. "'Star Struck': Acculturation, Adolescence and Mexican American Women, 1920–1950." In *Small Worlds: Children and Adolescents in America, 1850–1950,* edited by Elliott West and Paula Petrik, 61–80. Lawrence: University Press of Kansas, 1992.

Ryan, Mary P. "The Projection of a New Womanhood: The Movie Moderns in the 1920's." In *Our American Sisters: Women in American Life and Thought,* edited by Jean E. Friedman and William G. Shade, 366–84. Boston: Allyn and Bacon, 1973.

Rydell, Robert W. "The Culture of Imperial Abundance: World's Fairs in the Making of American Culture." In *Consuming Visions: Accumulation and Display of Goods in America, 1880–1920,* edited by Simon J. Bronner, 191–216. New York: W. W. Norton, 1989.

Saindon, Bob, and Bunky Sullivan. "Taming the Missouri and Treating the

Depression: Fort Peck Dam." *Montana Magazine of Western History* 27 (Summer 1977): 34–57.

Sands, Diane. "Using Oral History to Chart the Course of Illegal Abortions in Montana." *Frontiers* 7, no. 1 (1983): 32–37.

Sayre, Jeanette. "Progress in Radio Fan-Mail Analysis." *Public Opinion Quarterly* 3 (April 1939): 272–78.

Schudson, Michael. "Women, Cigarettes, and Advertising in the 1920s: A Study in the Sociology of Consumption." In *Mass Media between the Wars: Perspectives of Cultural Tension, 1918–1941,* edited by Catherine L. Covert and John D. Stevens, 71–83. Syracuse: Syracuse University Press, 1984.

Sheehan, Nancy M. "'Women Helping Women': The WCTU and the Foreign Population in the West, 1905–1930." *International Journal of Women's Studies* 6 (November-December 1983): 395–411.

Shepherd, William G. "Sin in the Desert." *Collier's,* 23 August 1930, 10–11, 42.

Shi, David E. "Advertising and the Literary Imagination during the Jazz Age." *Journal of American Culture* 2 (Summer 1979): 167–75.

Simmons, Christina. "Modern Sexuality and the Myth of Victorian Repression." In *Gender and American History since 1890,* edited by Barbara Melosh, 17–42. New York: Routledge, 1993.

Sims, Anastatia. "'The Sword of the Spirit': The WCTU and Moral Reform in North Carolina, 1883–1933." *North Carolina Historical Review* 64 (October 1987): 394–415.

Slatta, Richard W. "Comparative Frontier Social Life: Western Saloons and Argentine Pulperias." *Great Plains Quarterly* 7 (Summer 1987): 155–65.

Smith, Michael D. "What Is Sports Violence?: A Sociolegal Perspective." In *Sports Violence,* edited by Jeffrey H. Goldstein, 33–45. New York: Springer-Verlag, 1983.

Smith-Rosenberg, Carroll. "The New Woman as Androgyne: Social Disorder and Gender Crisis, 1870–1936." In *Disorderly Conduct: Visions of Gender in Victorian America.* New York: Alfred A. Knopf, 1985.

Smulyan, Susan. "The Rise of the Radio Network System: Technological and Cultural Influences on the Structure of American Broadcasting." *Prospects* 11 (1987): 105–17.

Somers, Dale A. "The Leisure Revolution: Recreation in the American City, 1820–1920." *Journal of Popular Culture* 5 (Summer 1971): 125–47.

South, Will. "The Federal Art Project in Utah: Out of Oblivion or More of the Same?" *Utah Historical Quarterly* 58 (Summer 1990): 277–95.

Stearns, Peter N. "Men, Boys and Anger in American Society, 1860–1940." In *Manliness and Morality: Middle-class Masculinity in Britain and American, 1800–1940,* edited by J. A. Mangan and James Walvin, 75–91. New York: St. Martin's Press, 1987.

Stern, Jane, and Michael Stern. "Neighboring." *The New Yorker,* 15 April 1991, 78–93.

Stevenson, Robert Alston. "Saloons." *Scribner's Magazine* 29 (May 1901): 571–79.

Stringer, Arthur. "The Weaker Sex." *Saturday Evening Post,* December 18, 1926, 10–11, 51, 53–54.

Susman, Warren I. "Culture and Civilization: The Nineteen-Twenties." In *Culture as History: The Transformation of American Society in the Twentieth Century,* edited by Warren I. Susman. New York: Pantheon Books, 1973.

Swain, Martha H. "'The Forgotten Woman': Ellen S. Woodward and Women's Relief in the New Deal." *Prologue* 15 (Winter 1983): 201–13.

Swenson, Mary E. "To Uplift a State and Nation: The Formative Years of the Alabama League of Women Voters, 1920–1921." *Alabama Historical Quarterly* 37 (Spring 1975): 115–35.

Tandberg, Gerilyn G. "Sinning for Silk: Dress-for-Success Fashions of the New Orleans Storyville Prostitute." *Women's Studies International Forum* 13, no. 3 (1990): 229–48.

Tarbell, Ida M. "Ladies at the Bar." *Liberty,* 26 July 1930, 6–10.

Taylor, Paul S. "Mexican Women in Los Angeles Industry in 1928." *Aztlán* 11 (Spring 1980): 99–131.

Terris, Virginia. "Mary MacLane—Realist." *Speculator* 2 (Winter 1985): 42–49.

Tidd, James Francis, Jr. "Stitching and Striking: WPA Sewing Rooms and the 1937 Relief Strike in Hillsborough County." *Tampa Bay History* 11 (Spring-Summer 1989): 5–21.

"The Top 100 Industrials." *Forbes,* 15 September 1967, 56, 64.

Tubbs, Stephenie Ambrose. "Montana Women's Clubs at the Turn of the Century." *Montana Magazine of Western History* 36 (Winter 1986): 26–35.

Vandenberg-Daves, Jodi. "The Manly Pursuit of a Partnership between the Sexes: The Debate over YMCA Programs for Women and Girls, 1914–1933." *Journal of American History* 78 (March 1992): 1324–46.

Vázsonyi, Andrew. "The *Cicisbeo* and the Magnificent Cuckold: Boarding-house Life and Lore in Immigrant Communities." *Journal of American Folklore* 91 (April-June 1978): 641–56.

Vermilya, Irving. "QRX for a New O.W." *OST,* July 1921, 29–31.

Walsh, Francis. "Lace Curtain Literature: Changing Perceptions of Irish American Success." *Journal of American Culture* 2 (Spring 1979): 139–46.

Walter, Dave. "Montana's Silver Lady." *Montana Magazine* 76 (March-April 1986): 68–73.

———. "Who Murdered Tom Manning? In a Company Town, Company Justice." *Montana Magazine* (September-October 1989): 54–59.

Ware, Susan. "Women and the New Deal." In *Fifty Years Later: The New Deal Evaluated,* edited by Harvard Sitkoff, 113–32. New York: Alfred A. Knopf, 1985.

Wertheim, Arthur Frank. "Relieving Social Tensions: Radio Comedy and the Great Depression." *Journal of Popular Culture* 10 (Winter 1976): 501–19.

Wheeler, Leslie. "Montana's Shocking 'Lit'ry Lady'." *Montana Magazine of Western History* 27 (Summer 1977): 20–33.

"When Drilling Contests Saw Titans as Rivals on Rock." *Butte Miner,* 19 November 1922, mag. sec., 3.

White, Martha E. D. "The Work of the Woman's Club." *Atlantic Monthly* 93 (May 1904): 614–23.

Wild, Paul. "Recreation in Rochdale, 1900–40." In *Working-Class Culture: Studies in History and Theory,* edited by J. Clarke, C. Critcher and R. Johnson, 140–60. New York: St. Martin's Press, 1980.

Winkler, Allan M. "Drinking on the American Frontier." *Quarterly Journal of Studies on Alcohol* 29 (June 1968): 413–45.

Winsberg, Morton D. "European Immigration to the Mountain States, 1850–1980—Changing Patterns." *Journal of the West* 25 (January 1986): 103–6.

Yellis, Kenneth A. "Prosperity's Child: Some Thoughts on the Flapper." *American Quarterly* 21 (Spring 1969): 44–64.

Zellick, Anna. "Fire in the Hole: Slovenians, Croatians, and Coal Mining on the Musselshell." *Montana Magazine of Western History* 40 (Spring 1990): 16–31.

Index

Mary Murphy, associate professor of history at Montana State University, Bozeman, is coauthor of *Like a Family: The Making of a Southern Cotton Mill World.* She holds a Ph.D. and a master of arts degree from the University of North Carolina at Chapel Hill and a bachelor of arts degree from the University of Massachusetts at Boston.

Books in the Series WOMEN IN AMERICAN HISTORY

U.S. Women in Struggle: A *Feminist Studies* Anthology
Edited by Claire Goldberg Moses and Heidi Hartmann

In a Generous Spirit: A First-Person Biography of Myra Page
Christina Looper Baker

Mining Cultures: Men, Women, and Leisure in Butte, 1914-41
Mary Murphy